MW00622447

To Barry

In Liberty & Aloha

Fred & Miki Booth

Memoirs
of a Community Organizer
from Hawaii

MIKI BOOTH

NEW PATRIOT PUBLISHING

NEW PATRIOT PUBLISHING

www.newpatriotpublishing.com

Hardcover Edition
ISBN – 0-9828885-6-2
ISBN – 978-0-9828885-6-8

Electronic Editions (Ebook)
ISBN – 0-9828885-9-7
ISBN – 978-0-9828885-9-9

Printed in the United States of America

Dedicated
to
Lt. Col. Terry Lakin

Because the truth matters, the Constitution matters.

Table of Contents

Foreword vii

Introduction...ix

Sheila and the Angry Congressman 1

Mecca's *That* Way! 4

An Inside Job? 7

Tea or Kool-Aid?..13

FairTax..32

Upside Down and Inside Out 38

Capt. Tom Snyder 41

Tripler Army Medical Center...46

Who Is Barak Obama? The Great Cover Up.........................48

A "Non-Negotiable Commitment to Africa".........................58

The Trampling 68

Rest Camp 71

Harleys, FairTax and Joe the Plumber 85

GOOOH Get Out Of Our House 89

A Weird Little Man in African Garb...................................103

"I'll Hunt You Down and Cut Your Heart Out!" 108

Samuel Adams, Thomas Jefferson & Thomas Paine 114

Running the Good Race 125

Black Robes and Firing Back...139

The Palintologists 142

Obaachan's House 151

Kaluakauka — The Doctor's Pit 168

Hunting Vermin 173

Photos 183

Sooner Bags Seat at National Tea Party 215

"This Piece of Junk" 221

The Hotel Executive 231

The Wahiawa House 235

Mokuleia Ranch 244

Aloha, Hawai'i 259

A Blessing in Disguise 274

Code Red Rally 284

Dr. Manning's CIA-Columbia Sedition Treason Trial 292

Prisoner No. 89996 306

Is the GOP a Party of Morons? 312

Hawai'i Department of Health On the Ropes 333

Wise Up O'Reilly 349

Death Threats 351

Dr. David A. Sinclair 355

Felony Forgery 363

Finding Kaluakauka 372

Crimes Have Been Committed 376

Come Talk Story 390

Epilogue 402

Foreword

by Neil Turner

One Sunday afternoon in May, 2010, I arrived at La Guardia airport in NYC with two octogenarians in tow — to attend the first Citizens Court Trial in over a hundred years. (More about that later.)

As we retrieved our bags, we started looking about for our Hawaiian "community organizer", Oklahoma congressional candidate, sharpshooter and animal-lover, Ms. Miki Booth. Miki was flying in to be an expert witness at that trial, and she had agreed to organize our transportation to the hotel where we were all staying for the next four days.

We old codgers (I'm just 75, one of the younger fellas) found Miki to be all that we had heard and more: fun-loving, intelligent, dedicated, and thoroughly organized and efficient. The trial we were attending was the CIA Columbia Obama Sedition & Treason Trial being held by Dr. James David Manning. Miki, whose husband and son were both born in Hawaii (1949 & 1981), was scheduled to testify concerning what real "certified" Hawaiian birth certificates look like, as opposed to the fraudulent and forged certification of live birth that had been posted as authentic by Obama's press secretary, Robert Gibbs, on various websites.

[NOTE: Recently, a document expert, Douglas B. Vogt, issued a 13 page affidavit regarding the purported "long form" version of Obama's Hawaiian birth certificate, which had been posted on the White House website. Vogt's affidavit is crystal clear in depicting the document as fraudulent, both through Vogt's experience and expertise in documents, imaging and scanning, and with what can be described as 'truly common sense' when you witness the fraud yourself by reviewing the images of the document. We come to the conclusion that since it was released by Obama (the Obama administration) that Obama now "owns" it and can therefore be charged with the crimes of Mispersonization of Identity as well as forgery in the first degree, both high crimes rendering Obama unfit for the office of president and unfit to have access to America's top security secret as commander in chief. Every day that he continues to hold that office is a major security breach, endangering the lives of Americans everywhere.]

Miki's testimony was included in the deliberations by the jury as they reached their verdicts of GUILTY on all counts. You can look at those testimonies and verdicts at www.CRS-Reports.org to see the argument that Obama never attended Columbia University, and that his degree in political science is therefore a worthless piece of paper as is his Hawaiian certification of live birth.

Like me, Miki was never involved in or concerned with politics — until we were awakened in 2008 by the sudden appearance of a virtual "ghost" running for president of our beloved country on the Democrat ticket — Barack Hussein Obama. It has changed our lives and our knowledge of and dedication to the Constitution like nothing we could have ever imagined.

Miki's book, *Memoirs of a Community Organizer from Hawaii*, will make you laugh while it makes you cry — sometimes with sadness and sometimes with joy over her love of life, her family, her animals, her friends, and her country. You'll be lazily reading along about life on the farm, then turn the page for a stunning revelation about her family history, or her friends and acquaintants, or the politics of Hawaii, or the real story about some of our prominent figures in government office today. You'll find yourself unable to put it down, anxiously anticipating the next "shocker" ahead.

Jerome Corsi's best-seller *Where's The Birth Certificate?* deals in documented facts about the greatest fraud ever perpetrated upon America since its founding over 230 years ago. Miki Booth's *Memoirs of a Community Organizer from Hawaii*, deals with all the nitty-gritty of patriotic citizens rising up to support, protect, and defend their beloved Constitution, while giving you some exciting insight into how this Hawaii-raised daughter of a Japanese mother and a Massachusetts Marine father, grew up to be a thoroughly organized nemesis to one of America's most infamous community organizers, Mr. Barry Soetoro, aka Barack Hussein Obama.

———— ✺ ————

Former U.S. Army helicopter pilot Captain Neil Turner was born and raised in Rhode Island and was living in California for the last 25 years, when, as a CA elector for the Constitution Party in 2008, he learned that he was doubly disenfranchised when his vote as a citizen and his vote as an elector were both compromised by having a constitutionally-ineligible non-natural born citizen on the ballot. He soon became an Article II Constitutionalist and has been fighting alongside Miki Booth ever since to try to restore our nation to the Constitutional Republic that it once was.

Introduction

Once upon a time in paradise lived a little girl who loved horses. She loved them so much, she prayed at bedtime and wished on the first star she saw every evening for a horse of her own. There were places to ride on rented horses at various stables and ranches across her island home, and she knew exactly where each one of them was located. Not a day went by that she didn't plead with her mother or father for a horse of her own or to take her to a riding stable where she could pay by the hour to ride a rental horse.

Her favorite place to go were the stables at Kaneohe Marine Corps Air Station (KMCAS) on the windward side of O'ahu where her daddy worked and mama shopped the commissary. Sister to five siblings and second oldest, she knew money was always tight and horses were an extravagant plaything for a little girl. She never relented, though, and believed that one day her wishing and praying would someday earn her a dream come true.

Eventually her wish was realized. By the time her fifty-eighth birthday rolled around, she was finally living her dream. Settled onto a small acreage in Oklahoma with four beautiful horses, a loving husband, and grown son who was always a "good" boy, she couldn't have asked for more.

After retiring three years earlier, she now lived a life of sleeping late, playing with the dogs and horses, chickens, ducks, geese, and cat. The occasional ride along the trails in the woods next to her house with the dogs following was truly idyllic. Cheyenne, a large chestnut quarter horse with a long white blaze down her face, had proven herself trustworthy enough to be ridden anywhere.

Life was good. She was happy. Then Barack Hussein Obama arrived on the scene.

Chapter 1

Sheila and the Angry Congressman

Around four o'clock in the morning my husband and I awoke to the sound of Ping Yei, our cat, meowing at the window. Her yowls accompanied the familiar sound of her claws grabbing and releasing the window screen as she hung sideways for maximum attention.

I felt Fred getting up to let her in, so I stayed in bed. Within a few seconds I heard Ping crunching her dry food from a bowl on my dresser, placed out of reach of Brandi, a rescued puppy, who grew up to be a Great Dane.

I had hardly fallen back to sleep when Brandi and Sheila, another rescue pup, hopped off their places on the bed and shook and stretched their bodies, signaling that it was their time to go outside. Again it was Fred who rose to the occasion. It usually was.

"You've got to come see this," he called to me from the doorway. "Snowflakes as big as cornflakes!"

We were expecting a lot of snow. I got up and turned on a light to find my slippers and something warm to put on to take a look. About that time Brandi came into the lighted closet, and I saw her back covered with huge snowflakes. I burst out laughing. She couldn't have been outside more than two seconds. The stark white of the snow against black Brandi was striking. I could have seen it even in the dark. Worried that she would shake them off and create wet spots all over everything, I grabbed Fred's fresh towel, which was the closest thing I could find, and wiped the snow off her back and tail.

Fred came in and we laughed.

"Are you going to try to make it to Grove?" he asked. Grove, 25 miles away, was a pick up location for the Banner, northeastern Oklahoma's only conservative newspaper. The free newspaper is printed on Wednesdays, and I volunteer to distribute the paper every Thursday.

However, this Thursday morning we already had about five inches of snow, and it was still falling. Fred told me he would call me from work and let me know the road conditions. It already didn't look good to me. I could see enough of the state highway that runs past our place, and there were hardly any cars or trucks going by on an otherwise busy workday morning.

I held the storm door open while Fred gave me a kiss and walked out with his container of coffee. He pointed toward the fenced yard to the north and assured me that the chickens, ducks, Lucy the goose, and Cinnamon Turkey had been taken care of, their food put inside the chicken house, sheltered from the falling snow. He also turned off the heater in their house and left the door open for any of them wanting to venture outdoors. I didn't see anyone yet, but it was still early.

Still holding the door open, Sheila and I watched Fred back his car and turn to go up the driveway with the sound of snow crunching under his tires. Before I shut the door I looked down to make sure Sheila's head wasn't in the way. It was. I slowly closed it on her face, forcing her to back up.

As part of our everyday ritual, Fred always prepares a cup of instant coffee for me so that all I have to do is add hot water. Then I can sit down to FOX News, which he leaves on for me. Since we have a DVR, I can rewind the broadcast and catch up on the news Fred has already watched, fast-forwarding through commercials and any footage of Obama. We would later talk about what was happening in the world, but more importantly, what was happening in U.S. politics.

This morning, as she does every morning, Sheila was curled up next to me on the couch, so insecure to ever leave my side, her head and paws draped over the side of the couch. U.S. Representative Steve Cohen of Tennessee, a Democrat, was likening Republican critics of Obamacare to the Nazis and their propaganda minister Joseph Goebbels. "You repeat the lie, you repeat the lie, you repeat the lie . . ." His angry voice in cadence with his banging fist shocked Sheila out of her sleep. She stared at Cohen and growled viciously. Cohen's demeanor and angry voice posed a threat to our quiet household, and she reacted instinctively.

I burst out laughing, the kind of laugh that if I had coffee in my mouth it would have come out my nose.

Mom laughed. Everything is okay. Sheila went back to sleep.

Fred called me an hour later, "I'm here at work. I made it. I did slip and slide sideways through the intersection, though. It was pretty snow-packed at the intersections, but otherwise I was driving 50 miles per hour."

We agreed I should not try to drive to Grove. Having lived in Hawai'i most of our lives, neither of us had had much experience driving in snow and ice.

I told Fred about Sheila growling at the "demented congressman." I couldn't remember his name. Fred knew who I was talking about, though. Everyone was talking about him.

Fred laughed and said Sheila was a smart girl. Indeed, the Blue Heeler pup abandoned on the highway nearly four years ago was very smart.

It was eight o'clock in the morning and like clockwork Poppy, our fourteen year old Miniature Pinscher, was popping up and down on the floor in front of me — her signal it was time to eat.

This signaled, too, time for me to turn off the television and start my chores before I sat down at the computer.

Chapter 2

Mecca's *That* Way!

I've heard many people say they would or should write a book but never did. A friend I've known since "hanabata (snotty nose) days," as we say in Hawai'i, told me several years ago that she was going to write a book about the eight years she spent in Sudan married to a Muslim. Some of the tales she told me after she escaped from him and returned to Hawai'i disturbed my sensibilities, but I agreed that her experiences were fascinating, and she should write that book.

I asked her several months later how her book was coming, and she said she had only been entertaining the idea. "That's a pipe dream," she said. "It's impossible to get published, especially when no one's ever heard of you."

Made sense. Made a lot of sense coming from my childhood friend, whom I always considered the smartest person I knew. However, I did question her lack of good sense to marry the Muslim she met at the University of Hawai'i and then questioned her sanity when she moved with him to Sudan.

We'd lost touch and for the eight years she spent in Africa, immersed in Islamic culture and subject to her husband's increasing brutality, I spent on the mainland married to an alcoholic and subject to brutality as well.

Coincidentally, we both ended up back home in Hawai'i around the same time. My friend hid out. But while her rich Sudanese husband had unlimited resources to hunt for her, I didn't have to worry. I was free.

At thirty years old, divorced, and back in home territory, I was starting life all over again. My now ex-husband agreed to give me a divorce as long as I didn't try to take anything with me.

"I'll hunt you down and cut your heart out," he told me. I didn't doubt him. He'd made good on other threats to beat or punish me and did so with impunity. That's my fault. I had never told anyone.

But I was free. I was happy. My intelligent friend, Karen (not her real name), and I "talked story" well into the night at my little pie-shaped studio apartment in Honolulu. We talked about our awful experiences and shared hopes for the future.

After months passed, it appeared Karen's husband had stopped looking for her, and she moved back in with her parents at their waterfront estate on Kaneohe Bay.

Karen's parents passed away, and she was left living alone in the million-dollar house with her dog. Her brother wanted her out so he could put the home on the market, but she wanted to stay. While the battle of the attorneys raged, Karen stayed in the house, and her brother rented the rooms to several Muslim University of Hawai'i students.

Insulted and injured, my friend was understandably bitter. She had grown to hate the Muslim "call to prayer" five times a day in Sudan, and now she detested the young men who spoke in Arabic and kneeled on their prayer mats praising Allah in her home in Kaneohe.

On one of my visits, we were headed to Karen's room, the master bedroom on the second floor, passing the rooms rented by the students. One door was open, and I glanced at the young man kneeling on a prayer mat facing the window overlooking Kaneohe Bay.

Karen stopped and I almost ran into her. She backed up, gestured with her right arm, and spoke to him in Arabic.

"What did you say?" I asked her. She told me he was looking north over the bay and said to him, "Hey asshole! Mecca's that way!"

I burst out laughing. I didn't like Muslims. Their values and their system of law and order frightened me.

Karen had enlightened me about a number of sharia mandates, such as female circumcision and the mandate that husbands are duty bound to have sex with their wives every night to produce sons. I wondered if she might have thought that was a good thing in the beginning, but I know she didn't in the end. She told me that when he held a gun to her head so she would endure his "duty," her plan to escape began formulating. According to her husband, she was a failure anyway — the eight-year marriage produced no offspring, male or female. She had no friends in Sudan other than the few she regularly saw at the American Club, where Europeans hung out as well. The tension wasn't limited to Sudan; once on a trip into Saudi Arabia, officials kept her passport until she left, making sure she was gone. They didn't like Western influence on the women in their country.

My friend, Karen, occasionally entertained the idea of writing about her experiences, but if she ever did, I wouldn't know; we're no longer friends. She voted for Obama, and we haven't spoken since.

Chapter 3

An Inside Job?

When I woke up on November 5, I knew the nightmare was real. When I went to sleep the night before, I still had hopes that McCain might pull off the election, and we would avoid a catastrophic mistake, a horrible anti-American wind that would become a hellish cyclone.

I had said things, I had written things, I had warned people: "Please, please do not vote for this man. He's hiding so much. He's got people lying for him, doing illegal things. He's lying. There's cheating going on in his campaign. He's hiding foreign donations! He has ties to radicals and terrorists. He's not a Christian even though he claims he is." If people had listened to Hillary Clinton, they would know this, but then she made a deal with the powers that be and clammed up about Obama.

Many people believed I was right, but they warned me. "Be careful," they said. "You're challenging some very powerful people."

I was once a quiet, subdued woman, the kind who would take abuse and say nothing. But now, something in me stirred. With this election, I felt moved to make a stand, and for the first time, I felt I had a voice.

During the campaign that year, I sent out political e-mails. One that I sent to classmates I went to high school with in Hawai'i went as follows: "You guys have to believe me. Obama is a fraud. He wants globalization, a one-world order, one-world currency, and will tear down our country's representative government to do it. The rich of the world will have us at their mercy. Islam and the Arab ruling rich will want the best places for their second home, like Hawai'i. If that happens, you will all become their servants. Sharia law will become the law of the land, and if you don't like it, they will round you 'infidels' up and execute you. If this all happens, I will be the first to get my head cut off for saying what I'm saying."

I got answers from my classmates: "Remove me from your list." "STOP SENDING ME E-MAILS." "ENOUGH ALREADY! I'm voting for him anyway." "And you want Sarah Palin? That stupid woman?!" "I would never vote for a Republican — They're MURDERERS!" "John McCain will get us into another war."

I wasn't expecting such a backlash. Surely, I thought, they will come around when they connect all the dots as I had. But that wasn't to be. I started getting pro-Obama, "Vote for Obama" e-mails from them. I blocked them all and deleted them from my address book. I was sad. It had been less than a year before that I had reconnected with many of those classmates at our fortieth class reunion in Hawai'i.

Only one classmate remained on my side. He was someone who knew what I was saying was real. He knew a lot of the intricacies of the workings of government, he knew human nature, he knew what went on in foreign governments, and he had seen and experienced enough military involvement to assure me I was on the right track. Before he retired to live a quiet existence on the Big Island of Hawai'i, he was a Navy SEAL.

The best assurance I got from my retired SEAL friend was that I wasn't alone. But that wasn't enough to bring out the bravery in me to stay on a mission to alert and inform.

On November 5 I realized that's it. It's over. Nothing more can be done. Obama pulled off the biggest hoax imaginable. He had a lot of help. His connection to Bill Ayers and their connection to Annenberg and the Woods Foundation, and their connection to CAIR and their connection to Rashid Khalidi and their collective connections to radicals known and unknown, seen and unseen, along with the connections to big labor unions, ACORN, Chicago's corrupt politicians and businessmen, and to anti-American religious leaders all coalesced into one entity — the Democratic Socialist Party.

The Democrat Congress for the previous two years under Nancy Pelosi and Harry Reid had been spending so recklessly and proposing and passing bills that were so outrageously unconstitutional it was breathtaking. Americans had to start waking up!

Concern mounted across the country when people recognized that a far-left president teaming up with tried and true socialist legislators in government would ruin our already fragile economy and ruin our country. We were on the brink. We saw what was coming and tried to warn everyone we knew. The response we got from everywhere was disheartening when we realized that so many people blamed George W. Bush for every ill facing us. We tried to inform them that most of the damage of late had been caused by the Democratic Congress. They refused to listen. It was all George Bush's fault. Many of us spent countless hours trying to reason with these people. Surely they would accept logic and reason; these are our friends, our neighbors, our families. But to no avail. Some people, like me, knew from experience that you cannot argue with those whose minds are shut, and so we walked away rejected and dejected.

There was the economic bailout. When John McCain put his campaign on hold and rushed back to Washington to make the vote, I didn't know if that was a good thing or a bad thing for him to do, but polls reflected that the American people overwhelmingly did not want Congress bailing out Wall Street. Regardless, representatives and senators, including super-conservative Senator Tom "Dr. No" Coburn, who later said he was convinced that had they not passed the first "bailout" ATMs would go empty, voted for the bill.

The Emergency Economic Stabilization Act of 2008 proposed by Secretary of the Treasury Henry Paulson and signed into law by President George W. Bush did not do what it was supposed to do, and a second round of bailouts quickly followed under Obama's treasury secretary Timothy Geithner. It was sickeningly reminiscent of Keystone Kops running around mindlessly throwing ideas and money against a wall and hoping something would stick. The predictable reaction to the crises and what would become the Obama administration's mode of operation to any challenge is poorly thought out, extremely wasteful, corrupt, and wholly unconstitutional.

After the election, our critics were telling us to, "Get over it!" And many people stopped complaining and went back to life as usual. "You can't fight city hall, and you can't stop progress" was the mentality of many, and they acceded to giving the new president a chance.

An intangible feeling of fear of this man kept me awake many nights. My thoughts were logical and coherent, connecting the dots of what I knew and what I learned every day that went by. The dots always added up to a sinister plot, a possible coup d'état. Indeed, the Democrats had been shredding the Constitution, the supreme law of the land, and manipulating the Declaration of Independence. It was an inside job putting the most liberal, unqualified, unknown, un-American candidate into the highest office in the land and thus making him the most powerful man on earth.

I knew my phone had been tapped. During my furious e-mailing campaign leading up to the election, there were times I picked up my phone to make a call and heard tones of someone else on the line dialing. I'd had the same land line number since 1999 and never, never had that happened before, but Fred tried to reassure me that it was just my imagination.

On the morning after the election, I woke up to Brandi and Sheila jumping on my bed and licking my face as they do every morning. It was just another day for them. That morning I tried to go about my usual morning rituals. After I got my glasses and a warm housecoat on, I made my way to the den where Fred was watching Gretchen, Steve and Brian on FOX News. I sang to him, "Good Morning, good morning, good morning, good morning . . ." while I posted up and down on an imaginary horse. Fred sang the same in reply — just another of our fun rituals we'd been doing for almost thirty years of marriage.

As I listened to the television, I realized that nothing more was being said about Obama's questionable campaign dealings, the forged ballots, his socialist tendencies, his radical ideology and connections, and on and on. All the newscasters were addressing him as "President Obama." Even FOX News had succumbed to the power of the New World Order.

November 5, 2008 — It was all over. Everyone, it seemed, accepted their fate.

I was scared about the e-mails I had written. I was reduced to a meek, introverted woman, much the way I'd been before Obama arrived on the scene. Fred and I made it a point to ignore the inauguration festivities but otherwise kept up on the news. Fred noticed how subdued I was and tried to lift my spirits. He got me to agree that, yes, let's give it a chance, maybe it won't be so bad, but already Obama was out with his pens, making good his promise of closing Gitmo, oblivious to the hue and cry of the American public.

As much as I tried to be hopeful, or at least pragmatic, Obama soon proved that he was not the moderate person he had advertised himself to be. People started to comment, "Whoa, I didn't sign up for this," but still willing to give him a chance, they looked for any reason to cut him some slack.

I couldn't do that. Too many things niggled at the back of my mind. Subprime mortgages were emerging as the culprit of the financial meltdown. Fannie Mae and Freddie Mac employed a lobbying strategy to get lawmakers on their side. They strategically directed campaign contributions to lawmakers controlling Congress and sitting on committees that regulate their industry. In the 2008 cycle, then—Senator Obama received the third-largest amount of $105,849 from Fannie and Freddie. Chris Dodd received the most at $133,900 and second-highest was John Kerry's $111,000. Hillary Clinton's take was $75,550.

There's nothing illegal about this; it's done all the time, we're told. But this is what's wrong with government. It's the cronyism, the "you scratch my back and I'll scratch yours." If it's not corrupt, it's certainly immoral as hell.

I remembered something else. Obama was a lawyer representing ACORN in a lawsuit against the state of Illinois. Along with a team of Chicago lawyers, Obama won the 1995 suit forcing the state of Illinois to implement the "Motor Voter" bill, a law designed to make it easier for people to vote by allowing them to register at the same time they apply for a driver's license. Millions of people register this way, but only a small percentage of them usually bother to vote, leaving a considerable pool of names available to those intent on participating in election fraud. The capacity for runaway fraud in just such a law is not lost on the Association of Community Organizers from Reform Now (ACORN), nor was it lost on Obama and his conspiracy to steal the 2008 presidential election.

Obama also instructed new community organizers in his leadership role with ACORN. He taught them the tactics of leftist icon/guru Saul Alinsky's Rules for Radicals and directed them to the targets: the banks that weren't enthusiastic about making home loans to people with no money down, who couldn't afford them and had no means of repaying them.

"Pressure them! Stir up dissatisfaction and discontent! Agitate! Agitate! Your job is getting people to move, to act, agitate to the point of conflict!" instructed the Rules for Radicals. And under the guidance of Barack Hussein Obama, ACORN did just that. Showing up in hoards with picket signs and bullhorns, they shouted and chanted and demanded the banks give loans to anyone and everyone because everybody has a right to home ownership.

It was clear to me as it was to others that Obama had a hand in the financial collapse of 2008. There is no doubt in my mind: HE DID THIS, and now he owns the means by which to repay those who helped him do it.

For most of 2008 and the first two months of 2009, my memories are just kind of a blur. There's nothing on my calendar pages to remind me of what was going on then. What notable information had been written on the dates that are now covered up by white-out tape? One thing is for sure, my own future felt quite uncertain.

Chapter 4

Tea or Kool-Aid?

The days and the weeks passed, and I tried to focus on my life on what I call the "funny farm," taking care of the animals. Keeping up sixteen acres of pasture and grounds and feeding and caring for four horses and more than two dozen chickens, geese, ducks, Cinnamon, my pet turkey, and Ping, the cat, is a full time job. I stayed busy and for the first time since I began my campaign against Obama's bid for the presidency, I saddled up Cheyenne and took a ride in the surrounding woods with Brandi, Sheila and little Poppy following behind. I used my camera phone to take a picture from atop Cheyenne and text-messaged it to Fred.

"Wow!" he messaged back. "It's about time you got back to doing what you love best."

But my idyllic days of doing what I love were short-lived. In February 2009, I watched a news feature on FOX News about a group staging a reenactment of the Boston Tea Party.

That's what we need, I thought, a rebellion to tell Obama's tyrannical government that we have had it, and we're not going to take it anymore.

Bob Basso, a motivational speaker, longtime Hawai'i resident and radio/TV personality, had created a series of YouTube videos in the character of Thomas Paine calling for a "Second American Revolution." The videos circulated on the Internet, and people everywhere were standing up and saying, "I've had enough, and I'm not going to take it anymore!"

I answered the call. I was ready for action. I was chomping at the bit to tell our elected officials that they worked for us. I wanted to tell them to "STOP THE SPENDING!" and "STOP TRAMPLING ON THE CONSTITUTION!" "LET'S GET BACK TO THE IDEALS ESTABLISHED BY OUR FOUNDERS!" "NO MORE BAILOUTS!" "WE WANT LIMITED

GOVERNMENT!" "FREE MARKET PRINCIPLES!" "OUR RIGHT TO BEAR ARMS SHALL NOT BE INFRINGED!" "WHAT PART OF 'SHALL NOT BE INFRINGED' DO YOU NOT UNDERSTAND?"

I had a lot to say, and it seemed as though there were others out there who were already out there saying it. I had no idea what to do, but I was ready for action. I was angry, and I wasn't going to let the "Axis of Evil" (Obama, Pelosi, and Reid) dismantle our constitutional republic if I had anything to do with it. I now knew there were others just like me, and if enough of us banded together to fight for a cause as noble as rescuing the very heart and soul of our beloved nation, I believed we could do it.

The next call to action came from CNBC's Rick Santelli, on the floor of the Chicago Mercantile Exchange calling for a "Tea Party" during a rant protesting government overreach into the financial sector and the takeover of car companies and other businesses. His message became an instant classic. He captured the mood of the country. Soon, there were Tea Parties springing up in towns and cities from coast to coast. It was exciting. It was something we could do in our own communities to make our voices heard. With tax day only two months away, word spread calling for a national day of protest on Wednesday, April 15.

I was a member of the Patriotic Resistance, known at that time as resistnet.com, an offshoot of Grassfire.com, a leader in the conservative movement online. I checked the website for listings of any upcoming events in Oklahoma. The closest Tea Party I could find was in Tulsa, an hour and a half away. I began calling people I knew to see if they wanted to go, but it was a working day and the few people I knew had to work.

Then it hit me: I didn't need to drive all the way to Tulsa. I could plan a Tea Party rally right in my own town. The date was already set; all I had to do was select a location and time, let people know, and they would show up with signs and American flags, and we'd all be part of a modern-day revolution. I called the city parks and recreation office to find out if I needed a permit for using Riverview Park. I didn't. The pavilions in the park were on a first-come, first-served basis, so I just needed to make sure someone got there early enough to hold our spot. The covered area of the pavilion was somewhat small, but we could use the picnic tables provided for our sign-up sheets, petitions, and stacks of flyers and literature.

Then, I received an e-mail from AFA (American Family Association) announcing their T.E.A. (Taxed Enough Already) website for information and assistance for planning Tea Parties, as well as a registration database to list scheduled events with links to websites and e-mail. "This is so great," I remember thinking. There were already hundreds of Tea Parties listed. I checked Oklahoma and found several locations throughout the state, but nothing yet was planned for Miami, so I registered my event and called it the Route 66 Tea Party. I hoped the name would draw people from Kansas and Missouri, since we're so close to both states and the iconic highway ties us together.

I was so overwhelmed with excitement, and I felt empowered for the first time in a long time. But then I got nervous. What if I held a revolution and nobody came? I felt obligated to put together a program and find a speaker or speakers. But what about music and a sound system? Would we need it? How much would that cost? What if it rains? The pavilion wouldn't be big enough for more than twenty people or so because of the picnic tables. How much would it cost to put a notice in the paper? Can I really pull this off?

All of a sudden, I lost my nerve. This was all waaaay outside my "comfort zone" and I wilted like a four-leaf clover in the hot sun. "I don't need to do this," I thought. "I don't even know anybody in Miami. Surely one of the leaders in the business community will answer the call. I'll go to the Tulsa rally." I knew a few people in Tulsa. Alan, my son, lives there. I knew he'd go with me unless he couldn't get away from work. The rally would be at lunchtime, so he could at least meet me and stay for a little while. After all, it's the least he could do for his mom.

I had caved. Gone was the determined patriot willing to step into an uncomfortable situation to fight for her country and lead others to take up signs and raise their voices to pledge their allegiance to the flag that represents our nation, a country of freedom and liberty bought and paid for by the blood of our founding fathers.

I would still do my part; I just didn't want to do the planning, organizing, and shelling out the money it would take to put on an event. But I couldn't stop imagining my own rally. It would be pretty cool. And after all, I'd had enough experience as an event planner over the course of my career in the hospitality industry. It wasn't as if I didn't know what to do. I was just tired of dealing with people. I didn't even like getting on the phone when I had to call in a problem with my phone company.

No, I didn't want to do it. It was just too much work, and even though I didn't currently have a job, I was needed at home. The funny farm was my responsibility; the animals needed me, and I was comfortable in my element. They were my family, and I was happy alone with them in the day and happy at night with Fred. Why would I want to leave my comfort zone if I didn't have to?

Then something happened. Pancho, a local businessman and heavy-equipment operator, came to our house to give an estimate on some bulldozing work we needed done. Pancho and Fred were talking, and I heard Pancho make a disparaging remark about government regulations. I'd never spoken to him directly before, but I interjected a question, "Pancho, what did you think of the election?"

"What a disaster that was." He answered. "We've got a socialist politician with no qualifications or experience running our country. That can't be anything but bad." He continued, "John McCain was no prize either. How about that Sarah Palin, though, don't you love her?"

I assured him I did and Fred, too.

Had I not heard Pancho's remark about government, I would have gone on thinking he was a typical Democrat, a local good ole' boy like most of the residents of Ottawa County where we've lived since 1999. I was so encouraged to learn that he was a fellow patriotic resistor that I told him I was starting a revolution. "Dang," he said. "I was gonna do that."

I was committed. I had a partner. All the ideas I had floating around in my head for the Tea Party started swirling again.

"Hey, Pancho, can we use one of your flatbed trailers for a stage?" I asked.

He replied, "Hon, you can have anything you want."

Later that day, I received a phone call from Ray Wilson, who had seen my Miami listing on the AFA website. He'd been thinking of putting together a rally and had revisited the site to post his information when he saw my listing. We discussed each other's ideas. Ray wanted to go with my plan. He runs a busy air conditioning and heating business and didn't have the luxury of time the way I did. We exchanged e-mails and promised each other we'd stay in touch.

Others also saw the listing on the AFA website and either called or left a message on the site, which the website then forwarded to me. The new contacts expanded my address book. Most of the phone calls I received were from people who wanted to attend and asked for specifics on location and time.

The next person to step up to help was Shelly Picher (not her real name), an experienced activist who'd had many dealings with the proverbial city hall. She was petite but would back down to no one. Shelly knew Miami and the surrounding areas like the back of her hand. She immediately went to work looking for an alternate location in case we had bad weather. She also would check with people she knew for a sound system, and she stayed in touch with me daily. "What a dynamo!" I thought. "I'll bet city officials don't enjoy seeing her come through the door, especially if they know she's there to ask some very pointed questions."

Within a week of meeting Ray and Shelly, I scheduled a meeting in Grove, Oklahoma, to plan our April 15 rally. Fred and I had a few friends and acquaintances there who I knew would come. I rented a small conference room in the community center and put a notice in the local paper. Shelly, always on the ball, called the local radio station with the details, and they announced the meeting in their community events time slots, and then I e-mailed a press release to area media.

About a dozen people showed up. I halfway expected at least one reporter to attend. None did but I still managed to look at the meeting as a success. Charlie Miller, a longtime friend who'd moved recently to Grove from California, was there. Charlie Woltz, a retired Tulsa fireman, and his wife Nelda wanted to help. So did Barry Helin, a retired Marine, and Channa Morton, a healthcare professional from Miami. Others who came signed the attendance sheet and said they would see us on tax day at the park in Miami. Charlie, Nelda, Barry, and Channa all agreed to come to my house on April 8 for a planning meeting for the April 15 event.

The thirty-minute ride home on the dark, twisty highway around Grand Lake was a lonely one. If I had known then that I would spend thousands of miles and countless lonely hours of driving in my Dodge minivan traveling to and returning from Tea Parties and related events like this one, would I have continued on as I did? I don't know. At the time I couldn't see beyond the April 15 protest rally in the coming weeks, and all I could think about then was my successful meeting and finding people who love our country and would fight fiercely to protect our God-given right to "life, liberty, and the pursuit of happiness."

On Wednesday, April 8 at six o'clock in the evening a week before the rally, expecting volunteers to arrive anytime, I put out some pupus (the Hawai'ian term for appetizers or snacks) I'd made earlier. Fred had insisted I have pupus for our guests, like cone sushi, teriyaki meatballs, and tiny Spam musubi (rice cake) wrapped in nori (seaweed). I told him I didn't think it was necessary, since haoles (Caucasians) on the mainland don't really do that; no one would expect more than just some chips and dip. He persisted: we were an Island home. There was even a sign on the front door that said "Hawai'i Style — Please remove your shoes. Mahalo!" But Fred wanted pupus, so pupus we would have.

Charlie and Nelda arrived. Channa brought her husband, Scott, with her. Shelly arrived with her sister, and Barry Helin came. When Ray Wilson joined us, we got started. The first order of business was to circulate a sign-up sheet with e-mail addresses and phone numbers, which everyone would get a copy of before they left. I divvied up and handed out a small stack of the 500 flyers for the rally that I had designed and printed in color from my computer. Shelly had several great ideas and volunteered to visit the local radio stations with a copy of the press release and announcement.

Channa and Scott had a lot of experience providing refreshments and organizing the sporting groups their two boys participated in, so they volunteered to provide iced tea, lemonade, and cups.

Soon, it seemed everyone knew of some way to help. Someone knew how to get hold of a sound system through a guy who deejayed parties and events with karaoke. Someone else mentioned a YouTube video where Tea Party participants signed their names on a roll of brown butcher paper. The roll, they said, was something like fifty feet long. Everyone liked that idea. Someone volunteered to bring the paper, and said they would bring pens and markers as well. I volunteered to contact the DJ, and then I told everyone about Pancho providing a flatbed for our stage.

We went over some materials printed off the Internet. One item was a proposed bill introduced in the House, the Enumerated Powers Act, H.R. 450, which requires that "Each act of Congress shall contain a concise and definite statement of the constitutional authority relied upon for the enactment of each portion of that Act." The two-sided flyer I held in my hand contained instructions on what to do to compel our representatives to either co-sponsor the bill or publicly explain why they wouldn't. It went on to explain why, even if the bill had 435 co-sponsors, the chairman of the Rules Committee and the Judiciary Committee could simply refuse to move the bill from the committee to the floor for a vote. Since Democrats chaired both the House Rules Committee and the House Judiciary Committee, instructions on the flyer recommended bombarding them both with phone calls and e-mails demanding that H.R.450 be brought to the House floor for a recorded vote. (Fast-forward: the 112th Congress has announced that it will have an enumerated powers requirement, and with Republicans now chairing those two committees, the chances are excellent for passage of this bill.)

We decided on a few more flyers that we would print up and set on the tables for take-aways, such as information from the conservative organizations Americans for Tax Reform, Numbers USA, and Americans for Prosperity, which would later play a large role in the "Kill the Bill" and "Hands Off My Health Care" campaigns to stop Obamacare. We would also have flyers for H.R. 1207, Ron Paul's audit of the Federal Reserve. There would be four further items that would require signatures: two petitions — the "Re-Ratification of the Constitution of the United States by the People of the Route 66 Miami, OK, Tea Party, 4/15/2009" and the "Petition for Redress of Grievances," in addition to a sign-up sheet, and the attendance scroll.

When we wrapped up our meeting, everyone had a least one assignment. We snacked on the pupus and had some drinks and everyone started to leave. I held out my hand for handshakes as my guests departed, but got hugs instead.

Plans were shaping up. I finally reached the DJ, and he agreed to provide the sound system with a couple of stand-up mics. He had a large selection of patriotic music he would play before and after the program. I booked him for his $200 fee; I had the money saved up from my biweekly allowance of $160 and always kept a few weeks of cash saved up.

On the Internet and through e-mails, I found some great ideas for signs and even some templates I printed out and took to a printer to reproduce. I spent another hundred dollars or so on an assortment of 12 x 18 card stock signs. One of my favorites that I taped to the back window of my van read, "I'm a Right Wing Extremist . . . I Own a Gun!" I made signboards of other quotes by Thomas Jefferson, George Washington, and the very popular black and tan sign of the segmented snake and the nine principles and twelve values. Popular among the young kids who came were the slogans, "Stay Out of My Piggy-Bank," and one with an image of a Kool-Aid pitcher next to a pot of tea asking, "Which One Are You Drinking?"

I depleted my allowance stash and started cutting into our household money for reams of paper and ink. The ink was very expensive, and I was constantly running out of yellow and dark magenta, so I started printing everything in black. When my printer began leaving a wide streak of black and gray on the pages and I was told the turn-around time for repair would be two weeks, I bought a new printer and paid for it with household money. I couldn't wait.

"Wouldn't it be great," I thought, "if we could have a costumed founding father speak to the crowd?" I didn't even answer myself. I reached for the phone book and looked up Roy's Costume Shop in Joplin, a professional costumer I'd used before in my position as director of sales and marketing at the Holiday Inn and Convention Center years earlier. They answered my phone call, and I was glad to hear they were still in business and open for several more hours, so I jumped in my car and headed for Joplin, another thirty-minute drive.

The costumes for George Washington and Thomas Paine were both really cool, but I was slanted toward Thomas Paine because I wanted him to read the speech, "The Second American Revolution," written and performed by Bob Basso on the YouTube video, which as of summer of 2011 was viewed by 3.5 million people. I called Charlie Woltz knowing he would be game to dress up to play the role of Thomas Paine and read the script. He was happy to do it as long as he could read from something and not have to speak off-the-cuff. I rented the costume and advised Charlie he would need to go to Roy's to be fitted for the costume and shoes.

I kept flipping the pages of the catalog in the costume shop to look at the General George Washington image. His military coat looked resplendent in dark blue with a red collar and lapels, shiny gold buttons, and gold epaulettes. A pea green vest came with it, as well as a white long-sleeved shirt to be worn under the vest and a white puffy scarf at the neckline. But it was the "really cool" tri-cornered hat that convinced me we just had to have a George Washington. I knew the other Charlie (Miller) was coming to the rally and would also be willing to play a role; he agreed to be our George. "What do you want me to do?" he asked, and I answered, "Just walk around shaking hands with everyone and let them take photos with you."

An idea came into my head immediately. We would take photos of rally attendees with George Washington and Thomas Paine and post them on the Route 66 Tea Party website. Jared Johnson, a clever and innovative website designer and network administrator in Joplin, had volunteered to design and maintain the website and to set up e-mail accounts. We made sure that our flyers carried the information so we could be found on the Internet.

I made the arrangements for Charlie Miller to be fitted with all the parts of the General George Washington costume, which, of course, included breeches, leggings, and buckled shoes, and bought a second wig for him.

With only a precious few days before the rally, I couldn't find anyone who wanted to be the MC. I realized the inevitable: it would default to me. I suffered anxiety and sleeplessness. I thought back to my days in Hawai'i, working in the hotel industry, and that seemed like a lifetime ago. I had been chairman of the advisory board for Joplin's Convention and Visitor's Bureau as well as vice president of Soroptimist International of Joplin so public speaking was second nature to me, but that was years ago before the breakdown. No, I wasn't looking forward to standing before a crowd and re-entering the public arena. Right up until April 15, I thought of excuses to bail out at the last minute if I needed to.

We got word that Republican Senator Tom Coburn had scheduled a series of town hall meetings on April 15. His second stop of the day would be at the Miami Civic Center, located a few blocks from Riverview Park where the rally was to be held.

April 15 arrived all too soon. Tens of thousands of people across the nation were going to come together and tell the government we are TAXED ENOUGH ALREADY. I got to the park at nine o'clock in the morning. Pancho arrived shortly afterward, backing his flatbed into position. Several more people arrived early and offered to help. They pitched in and began unloading boxes of printed material and supplies from my van and carried them to the tables in the pavilion. It was a beautiful day, and people were already arriving and setting up their lawn chairs and displaying their signs.

A woman and her sister offered to help, and I asked them to distribute signs to those who didn't bring any. They asked me how much they should charge, and I said, "No charge, just give them away."

"What?" They couldn't believe it. "People will pay for these. They're great signs."

I said, "Okay, how about three dollars apiece?" I hadn't thought about selling them; I was going to be busy enough without worrying about collecting money. Those two dear ladies, Cheryl and her sister Jan, pitched right in when I told them I wanted to get away and go to Coburn's town hall for a little while. They asked what needed to be done and then got right to work enlisting others. The Tea Party was in good hands. I drove to the civic center.

I walked in while Coburn was in the middle of answering someone's question. He finished his answer and looked around the room for another raised arm to call on. At the back of the room stood several people, men and women in suits. A couple of reporters were taking notes, and I walked toward them. I planned to stand at the back of the room and look around to see if I knew anyone. One of the reporters looked down at my T-shirt, looked back up at me, and scowled. I realized he didn't like the message he saw on my shirt: an image of Uncle Sam pointing his finger and saying, "I Want YOU to Speak English!"

I looked around for someone, anyone I knew. No one looked familiar. Definitely NOT a patriotic crowd. No red, white, and blue to be seen anywhere, and not one single sign. The sixty or so people sitting in the folding chairs were all dressed in office attire. They were business owners, managers, and city employees and a retired blue-haired couple holding hands.

I saw two young boys with their parents about five rows from the back. The mother turned. It was Channa. She smiled at me, and my instinct to "get outta Dodge" dissipated. I sat down in the nearest empty seat and focused on Senator Coburn.

None of the questions being asked were of interest to me. The city workers and local businesspeople wanted to know what the federal government was going to do for them. I wanted to know what was being done in the Senate to curtail spending and stop borrowing. I wanted him to address the national debt and deficits. There seemed to be no concern about government overreach into our lives and the threat of losing our right to bear arms through treaties with the United Nations bent on banning our guns, courtesy of Hillary Clinton and Barack Obama. Nobody mentioned the Constitution — the law of the land. Questions were formulating in my head. "If no one else is going to bring up these hard questions," I thought, "I will. If not me, who? If not now, when?"

I raised my hand. I was going to ask him about H.R. 450, hoping he would tell everyone about it. I held my hand high when Coburn asked for more questions. Other hands went up. One after the next, the senator chose others, some even getting in two questions, and yet I was ignored.

Okay, I got it. It was personal. It was me. I got up to leave and turned to the back of the room. To my surprise, there stood my two Charlies, resplendent in their Colonial attire, Thomas Paine peering at me through his wire-rimmed spectacles.

They had seen I was being ignored. The two Charlies made me stand between them, and we all raised our hands. Coburn called on us and remarked about some "special visitors," and many people turned their heads. There was some murmuring, and then everybody turned their heads to look at us.

"Do you think H.R. 450 has a chance of making it out of committee?" I asked.

"I don't know bills by their numbers; we have too many of them to remember." He sounded perturbed. "What is it about?"

"Enumer . . . " I began.

"Enumerated Powers Act," Coburn completed. "That's a bill I support and took part in drafting." He said he was glad the question was asked and went on to explain and elaborate, and he did so very well. I was pleased.

The two Charlies stayed for the rest of the meeting, and I returned to the park. Cars were lined up on both sides of the road and stretching further and further away from the pavilion and stage, but people were making the long walk with their flags, signs, and lawn chairs. A line had formed, and volunteers made sure everyone registered their attendance, autographed the scroll, and signed both petitions. I had nothing to do, at least for the moment. But soon, I was being introduced all around, and more people wanted to help and were directed to me. Slowly, I felt the confidence swelling within me as I thrilled with every exchange.

Finally, the DJ and his sound equipment were set up on the flatbed, two standing microphones to mark the stage and a couple of speakers on the ground, playing an anthem to the growing crowd. Channa, Scott, and their two sons set up the lemonade and tea station.

Paper cups donated by Charlie's Chicken and Ribs were stacked conveniently next to the self-serve coolers, the familiar logo of a boxing chicken decorated the cups.

A young lady with an impressive still camera introduced herself as a student of nearby Pittsburg State University, located not far past the Kansas state line. She asked for permission to take pictures and video for a public relations project she was working on. I asked if she would be our official photographer to document our event, and she was pleased to accept. Her finished project was later featured on our website. She did an incredible job.

I got up on the stage and the DJ did a sound check. I saw that there were still people arriving, but I wanted to start the program on time so I introduced myself and welcomed everyone. I kept my voice steady though my heart was racing. Then, Scott Morton gave the invocation. There were several people with flags, and we invited them to come up on the stage for The Pledge of Allegiance. Several ladies lined up with their flags, and George Washington led us in the Pledge. I followed next with the speech I'd written, denouncing ever-increasing government overreach and outrageous crammed-down legislation. I don't remember exactly how my speech went, but I remember at several points everyone applauded.

I had spent several days crafting my speech, just spending a few minutes every day adding things as I thought them up.

Days earlier, I had played the Bob Basso YouTube, "The Second American Revolution" while I transcribed the words on a steno pad. My shorthand is non-existent, so I painstakingly wrote the lines in long hand, making it necessary to back the video up and start again, over and over. When I went to type up the speech, I couldn't read my own writing, so had to go back to the video several more times to get it right. It was worth it.

After I finished my own speech, it was Charlie's turn to step up to the microphone, and I thought, "How fine he looks in his costume" as he began reading.

What would have happened in 1789, 1942, or 9/11 if a top government official stepped in front of the people and publicly proclaimed America was a nation of cowards? He would have been run out of the country on a rail, packaged, and tarred and feathered at least.

But that's what happened in 2009, and you did nothing.

Have you become a nation of cowards, America? With the greatest show of arrogance and disdain any Congress ever showed any citizenry, your un-functionally elite, self-interested, non-representing "representatives" passed the largest spending bill in history without reading it, and you did nothing.

You want them to obey your constitutional mandate and secure your borders, and they ignore you. You ask them to enforce your immigration laws, and they ignore you. You say, "Stop the madness of handing 300 billion dollars of a bankrupt treasury to illegal alien welfare, rewarding them for making a mockery of your laws," and they ignore you.

And now, in open defiance of the overwhelming will of the people, are preparing more amnesty programs. You say, "Stop exploiting my nation's vital industries to foreign shores," and they ignore you.

You say "no" to using your money to bail out failed, corrupt, and greedy businesses, and they ignore you. You say, "Implement the e-verify system so American jobs can go to American workers," and they ignore you.

If your self-serving Congress were a business, they'd all be in jail now. The biggest traitors among you hold elected office. Only when they feel the wrath of "We the People" marching in the streets from California to New York shouting "We're mad as hell and we want our country back!" will they get the message.

They work for you!

Wake up, America! While you were playing with the toys of your consumer wealth, you lost much more than your bloated economy of living beyond your means. You lost your representative democracy. Your servants have become your masters. Taxation without representation is tyranny. Still you look to government to solve problems they created in the first place. You're sucking at the hind teat of a dead cow.

Why isn't there a three-million-people march on Washington, a nationwide taxpayer revolt, thousands of cars and trucks surrounding your nation's capital, bringing your failed government to a standstill? Democracy doesn't repress power, it unleashes it to "We the People." Take it now. They dictated an economic solution to you. Now it's time to stick it to them — with the "We the People" stimulus package.

Start by first removing the elite privileges that place your non-representing "representative" above you, not with you. Require all laws that apply to the rest of the country to equally apply to Congress. Repeal

Congress's right to vote for their own raises. Balance the federal budget. Force your legislators to now do what you have to do: live within your means. If you don't, you're committing national suicide. Make Congress pay into the Social Security system. They make laws for it; now they might be interested in thinking twice before they allow twenty million illegal aliens to reap the benefits of a retirement program that legal citizens paid into all of their lives. Long-term power corrupts. Limit Congressmen from serving more than two terms. That's all you give your president. Let them search for their own 401(k) instead of the gross unfairness of awarding them their full salary for the rest of their lives after only serving one term. Stop paying for lawmakers' insurance premiums. After all, they're only part-time employees. They might pass some laws on insurance companies if they had to find one themselves.

Throw out of office every congressman and woman who didn't bother reading the biggest spending bill in history before they voted for it. With the money you save from all of the above, put it into increased benefits for the men and women of the armed forces. They never fail you. Start with no war unless you intend to win it. Make English the official language of America. You talk of "united we stand" but do nothing to make it happen. Give every legal alien a chance to succeed. Not one cent of taxpayer money for illegal immigrants. We are a nation of laws and do not reward lawbreakers.

Wake up, America. You've allowed yourselves to become little more than cowering spectators watching the nation your grandparents built — the richest, most powerful self-sufficient republic in history, with the highest standard of living any nation ever achieved.

Now, in the middle of the greatest unprecedented decline in modern history, the world's only superpower can't defend its borders, balance its budget, win its wars, manufacture its own products, or protect its own currency. Your total government debt obligation in the next several years is approaching the gross domestic product of the entire world. You've diminished the future of your children, grandchildren, and ten more generations of Americans.

On September 11, 2001, 300 million Americans put aside what divided them and rallied around what united them. You proudly flew your flags. You wore T-shirts that said "These colors don't run." Then your leadership told you to do nothing; let your professional army do the fighting. Perhaps you learned to do nothing too well. Two hundred thirty-three years ago, the silent majority in Boston got fed up with taxation without representation and held a little Tea Party to prove the anger of "We the People" is on the march. It started the first American Revolution. Now it's time to start the second American Revolution. Take an envelope, put a tea bag inside. Simple. Seal it. Send it to your non-representing "representative" in Congress. They'll get the idea: We're mad as hell, and we want our country back. Look in the mirror. There is your leader. Phone your talk radio host. Call for a tax protest. Set your Internet communities on fire with the idea. If you decide to do nothing again, then buy a gun. You'll need it.

My name is Thomas Paine. Don't give up hope, America. Your country needs a new greatest generation to answer the call. Get into the fight. It's a good time to be a patriot. The second American Revolution has just begun.

We had a small stack of printed copies of the speech on a table free to all. Under the last line of the speech was the note: "Send a tea bag to your employees in the government."

The copies disappeared fast and someone said, "We could have sold those. Let's remember that next time." And I followed up with, "We'll print them on parchment paper and make them really nice."

Everything was going well, just as I had imagined. There were several more speakers, all who engaged the crowd, and I returned to the stage to thank the crowd and remind everyone to sign the petition, the scroll, and the sign-in sheet.

Cheryl and Jan counted up the money they received for the signs. It was over $300. I almost fell over. There was the money to pay the DJ, and the remaining hundred nearly covered the cost of the signs. I hugged Cheryl and Jan, and they hugged me back. We were now fast friends.

People stayed to visit, chat, exchange information, ask questions, and generally just enjoy being among people who comforted each other in the knowledge that we were not alone. So many came to thank me before leaving, and I would see many of these new friends on and off and here and there over the next couple of years. In parting, we would say, "See you on the battlefield." We were indeed in a battle to save our country.

Two men approached me to thank me and give me words of encouragement. Then they asked what I thought about FairTax. I told them I had heard of it but didn't know enough to form my own opinion. Wrong answer, apparently, because one of the men seemed irritated and said, "Well, there's not much to learn. It's the simplest thing in the world," and then they both walked away. When I got home, I researched FairTax and by nightfall I was a dyed-in-the-wool advocate for H.R. 25/S. 296, The FairTax Act. (I later became an official volunteer community coordinator for my congressional district.)

I'd been told there would be a reporter from the local paper, Miami News Record, but none had shown. I wasn't expecting a reporter from across the state line in Joplin, Missouri, but the largest paper in the area, the Joplin Globe, did send a reporter and included the Route 66 Tea Party in an article featuring a Tea Party held in Joplin, where 500 people attended. The Globe estimated that 250 showed up for the Route 66 Tea Party in Miami. Not too shabby for a little town that's still struggling to survive after "Black Friday," August 23, 1985, when the town's largest employer, tire company BF Goodrich, closed its sprawling factory. When the severance pay ran out, the county went from having one of the highest per capita incomes in the state to among its lowest.

Shelly Schultz, Managing Director of the Miami News-Record called for an interview, and our story appeared on the front page of the Sunday paper:

AREA RESIDENTS SPEAK OUT ABOUT GOVERNMENT SPENDING, NATIONAL DEBT
Sunday, April 19, 2009
By Shelly Schultz

About 250 residents gathered at Riverview Park Wednesday in protest of the "abandonment of the Constitution and ideals on which it was founded."

Miami's tax day "Tea Party" supporters were among tens of thousands who gathered nation-wide to say, "We're not going to take it anymore."

"It was an opportunity for people to get together and voice their opinion," said Miki Booth, one of the Tea Party organizers. "People don't have to just sit in front of their TV and scream at it anymore."

Prior to the organized gathering, U.S. Sen. Tom Coburn M.D., held a "town hall" meeting in Miami to address the issues of Oklahoma and the nation.

Coburn expressed the lack of leadership in our country.

"With times being tough for everyone in the nation, it's time that people get involved in their community and make a change," said Coburn. "We need to change Congress."

"We have a totally inefficient government and the American people are finally stepping up and holding the U.S. accountable, and this is how we get our country back," said Coburn. "The goal is to live free, and we all have to sacrifice, and the only way to sacrifice is to hold us accountable."

Tea Party supporters held signs expressing their dissatisfaction with "ridiculous spending without representation" and confirming that "the Constitution is not for sale."

"We love our country," said Booth. "But we are here to tell the government they work for us. We're mad as hell, and we're not going to take it anymore."

Organizers of the Route 66 Tea Party rally are keeping up the momentum. One day after a highly successful protest against big government and out of control spending, the next event on the planning calendar was already scheduled.

Supporters will rally again from 2:00 to 4:00 p.m., Saturday , April 25 in Grove.

On July 4th the group will be focusing on the issue of taxes.

"The July 4th focus of the fair tax is to educate and explore and understand how it compares to the current tax code," said Booth. "Americans are weary of a tax system that burdens average Americans and allows lawyers and legislators to continue 'gaming' the system."

The FairTax Rally begins at 2:00 p.m. at Riverview Park, following a picnic style event with patriotic music and entertainment.

When the story of our Tea Party rally appeared on the front page of the Sunday edition, residents found it truly remarkable — not only for being on the front page of the most highly read edition, but also because it addressed an issue that many people of the area regarded with scorn, suspicion, and downright contempt.

County and city government had already chosen or defaulted to the Obama-Pelosi-Reid agenda. "Tea Party" people, according to our own City Council members, were nothing but a bunch of racists and nazis who hated the idea of a black president. They swallowed the liberal media swill and eagerly drank regularly from the new regime's Kool-Aid pitcher of propaganda.

Immediately, the newspaper received an angry call. Shelly shared the fallout with me, but she also told me about the many positive calls she received from people wanting to know when the next event would be. Many were disappointed that they didn't know about the rally. Support for the conservative movement overwhelmingly outnumbered the occasional complaint.

It was about that time when Cheryl told me that there were two women who had tried to make a scene at the rally before it began. They circulated among the gathering group and made disparaging and provocative comments before leaving in a huff. Channa was aware of them as well and said she had seen one of the women before but couldn't place where. Eventually, we found out the woman worked for a community assistance program under the umbrella of ACORN. Well, that explained it all. Enlightened conservatives were well aware of the rampant voter fraud and illegal activities of ACORN and other union entities that swept Obama into power. The complaints made to the newspaper office were coming from one or two women, and they both worked for ACORN.

This is not to say that the local populace was on our side. Registered Democrats far outnumbered Republicans, and most people were blissfully ignorant of politics and allowed decades of nepotism, cronyism, and, yes, corruption to flourish in a closed society of city and county government. But conservatives were finding their voice

More and more, people penned their opinions. For the first time it seemed maybe something might come of complaining about city hall or bringing attention to situations they had kept their mouths shut about because it just hadn't seemed worth it. Our local Tea Party activities continued to get into the Miami News-Record, sometimes a free announcement, but other times I paid for ads. But the next big event we staged landed us back on the front page of the News-Record.

On July 4, 2009, our Route 66 Tea Party staged a FairTax rally that drew a hundred people. Not bad for a holiday usually spent with family or out of town. Although the focus was on FairTax, we also joined Americans for Prosperity in protesting Obama's healthcare scam. The organization had sent 100 bright yellow signs that read "NO OBAMACARE! CALL CONGRESS" and listed the phone number to the congressional switchboard. Fred was the photographer at this event, and he took three shots so he could make a panorama of everyone holding up the signs. The picture of 100 people in a sea of yellow signs graced the front page of the News-Record the following day.

It prompted a complaint to Shelly, "If I read one more thing about that Miki Booth, I'm canceling my subscription!"

The exposure we enjoyed through the News-Record was as short-lived as Shelly's tenure as managing editor. One of the largest and most valuable accounts, an Indian tribe, canceled all of their advertising. Apparently they were not happy with the anti-liberal tone of some of the letters to the editor. Losing such an important account was devastating to the future of the newspaper and to Shelly's career. Staunch Democrats and born-into-a-culture-of-government-dependency Indian tribes almost exclusively share the tenets of socialism. The leadership of this particular tribe attended Obama's inauguration and traveled to Washington on other invitations from the Obama White House. This particular tribe owns the Downstream Casino, Oklahoma's state-of-the-art and newest Indian gaming facility complete with hotel and conference center. This particular tribe also employs my husband, Fred, as director of security at one of their casinos.

Shelly's days were numbered, and after much political jockeying at the newspaper, she was demoted and eventually left. I was beyond disappointed. I was outraged at what amounted to an attack on free speech and the strong-arm deliberate flexing of Democrat muscle. After Shelly left, I never saw or spoke to her again.

As for Fred's career, only time will tell if he retires for a second time on the date planned or does so earlier or even later. But in the meantime, he keeps his head down while mine is always popping up like a "whack-a-mole." But when all's said and done, each and every day we end up with our heads together safe in our secluded acreage with the dogs, chickens, ducks, Lucy, the goose, Cinnamon Turkey, and Ping, the cat.

Chapter 5

FairTax

On April 16, 2009, I had one Tea Party under my belt and was ready to move on to another project. The two men who had questioned me about FairTax the day before motivated me to find out what it was about. It didn't take long for me to jump in with both feet because it dawned on me that this might be the thing that saves our country from bankruptcy and could save We the People from the chains of taxation bondage. It was the most exciting thing that everyone, I mean everyone, could get behind. Nobody likes the IRS. Nobody likes the over-60,000-page tax code. Nobody likes April 15. Nobody likes to get audited. I used to think that only rich people trying to get away from paying their share of taxes were audited. Boy, was I wrong! Fred and I were audited in 2004, so when I decided to promote FairTax and abolish the IRS, it became a full-time job.

I met Carol Chouinard, district director of fairtax.org, when I visited the website to volunteer my services. Carol called me, and we became good friends. Before long, I would sign on to be a community organizer for District 2 Oklahoma, reporting directly to Carol. With the momentum following the successful Tax Day Tea Party little more than a week earlier, I had scheduled another gathering featuring FairTax on April 25, which was also Australia and New Zealand's ANZAC Day, their national holiday similar to our Memorial Day commemorating the April 25th landing of the ANZAC troops on the Gallipoli Peninsula in Turkey during World War I. By that time, we had an impressive e-mail list of close to 100 members who had signed up on the fifteenth. We notified everyone through route66teaparty@yahoo.com and placed one small ad in the local paper and ran a couple of free event announcements. Only about twenty-five people showed up to hear our FairTax speaker, Dr. Jeff McIlroy, from Tulsa and to enjoy the short program paying tribute to our active-duty troops and veterans and acknowledging the sacrifices of the Australia and New Zealand Army Corps ANZAC.

Also included in our program was a feature of interest to local Miami and Ottawa County residents presented by an area veteran. Newcomers like me were fascinated by the information we heard. I'd often wondered what GAR stood for on the sign at the huge cemetery north of town. I learned it stood for "Grand Army of the Republic." The veterans' cemetery is also the burial place of fifteen British cadets who died while training at the Spartan School of Aeronautics in Miami between 1941 and 1945. The cadets' graves are side by side, and at the end of the row is the grave of Frantie Hill.

Frantie began taking care of the burial plots after noticing that some of them were neglected. She spend the remaining forty years of her life attending to the fallen cadets' graves as well as maintaining an attachment to their families by exchanging letters and photos. Frantie Hill walked three miles from her home to the cemetery to pull weeds and take care of the burial plots. She planted roses and irises. Initially the graves were marked with wooden crosses, and the British government later replaced them with granite markers. Frantie Hill died June 4, 1982, at age 91. After the rally, several of us drove out to GAR Cemetery to visit the memorials of the fallen British cadets and Frantie Hill. The experience reminded me that sometimes even the small gestures can make a big difference and bring comfort to many people.

Dr. McIlroy held a FairTax question-and-answer session at the end of his presentation. Although I had a general understanding of how FairTax worked, getting into the nuts and bolts of the legislation really prepared me to answer questions I myself would be asked at future events and by my friends on the Internet.

I would have that opportunity countless times over the next year and a half. At the beginning of my presentations I would read, "The FairTax proposal is a comprehensive plan to replace federal income and payroll taxes, including personal, gift, estate, capital gains, alternative minimum, Social Security/Medicare, self-employment, and corporate taxes. The FairTax proposal integrates such features as a progressive national retail sales tax, dollar-for-dollar revenue replacement, and a rebate to ensure that no American pays such federal taxes up to the poverty level. Included in the FairTax Plan is the repeal of the Sixteenth Amendment to the Constitution. The FairTax allows Americans to keep 100 percent of their paychecks (minus any state income taxes), ends corporate taxes and compliance costs hidden in the retail cost of goods and services, and fully funds the federal government while fulfilling the promise of Social Security and Medicare."

Many people immediately shrank at the idea of a 23 percent sales tax until they understood that there is already 20 percent or more of federal taxes imbedded into every product bought in America. Someone will always argue with me that the price of new items will never go down, that the new federal tax will just be added on top of what they already pay. And there are those who cannot believe that the IRS will ever go away and who will argue up and down that lawyers and crooks (to be redundant) will always find ways to scam the new system and make matters worse. I don't see how that can be when 60,000+ pages of tax code would be replaced with a 200-page book.

One of the most effective points I've learned to make, and what is readily understood by canny Tea Party members, is that when all punitive taxes are eliminated, the thirteen to fourteen trillion dollars in offshore investments and accounts (nearly matching our national debt) would probably be brought back home by companies/corporations with no reason not to do so. This would be an instant shot in the arm to our economy.

You would think no one would object to receiving a prepaid rebate (prebate) check to every registered household, so no American would pay tax on necessities up to the federal poverty level. This, and many other features, is how the FairTax completely untaxes the poor and lowers the tax burden on most, while making the overall rate progressive. The FairTax is progressive based on lifestyle and spending choices, rather than simply punishing those taxpayers who are successful. You'd think people would see how much freer life would be with the FairTax instead of the federal income tax. Unfortunately, some people cannot see beyond the prebate being an opportunity for thievery. The saying that comes to mind very frequently these days is strain at a gnat and swallow a camel.

With the FairTax, you pay no tax on used goods. The amount you pay to fund the government is completely visible. You are taxed once on any good or service. If you choose to buy used goods, be it a car, a home, or an appliance, you do not pay the FairTax. If, as a business owner or farmer, you buy something for strictly business purposes (not for personal consumption), you pay no FairTax, which is also called a consumption tax. Simply put, there is no business-to-business tax. The

FairTax is charged just as state sales taxes are charged today. When you decide what to buy and how much to spend, you see exactly how much you are contributing to the government with each purchase.

With the FairTax, retail prices would no longer hide corporate taxes or their compliance costs, which drive up costs for those who can least afford to pay — 20 percent or more of all retail prices. According to Dr. Dale Jorgenson, well-known economist of Harvard University, hidden taxes are passed on to the consumer in the form of higher prices for everything we buy. If competition does not allow prices to rise, corporations lower labor costs, again hurting those who can least afford to lose their jobs. Finally, if prices are as high as competition allows and labor costs are as low as practicable, profits and dividends to shareholders are driven down, thereby hurting retirement savings for mom and pops and pension funds invested in corporate America. But with the FairTax, the sham of corporate taxation ends, competition drives prices down, more people in America have jobs, and retirement and pension funds see improved performance.

You would think a plan supported and endorsed by eighty independent economists and called "the most thoroughly researched piece of legislation to ever go before Congress" would garner more support from the public. However, there are still many skeptics, and worse, opponents of the FairTax mislead and keep the general public in the dark. Those are the entities that thrive on the current system and will do everything in their power to keep FairTax from becoming a viable solution.

Democrat talking points vilify Republicans for not wanting to raise taxes on anyone during a down economy, especially the so-called rich, who are actually the job creators. With FairTax, each time they purchase a new mansion, new yacht, new limo, new clothes and jewelry, anything new, they will pay to fund the government. So, too, will the criminal underground that pays nothing into our federal coffers but cost American tax payers billions and billions to maintain their criminal lifestyle. With FairTax, each time they buy something new, they will pay federal taxes. When I see criminals wearing their bling and driving Cadillac Escalades, I get angered and want to kick some congressional ass for not endorsing FairTax. Twenty-three percent of the price they paid for their expensive trappings could have gone to fund the government.

And then there is the myth that the FairTax is just another flat tax. Nothing could be further from the truth. A flat tax is still a tax on income. With the Republican takeover of Congress in 2010, Rep. Rob Woodall immediately took the torch and led the FairTax movement to the astonishing accomplishment of filing the legislation with more sponsors than ever on the opening day of the legislative session. Forty-seven representatives signed up on day one.

Sen. Saxby Chambliss, also of Georgia, introduced S. 13 with five Senate co-sponsors on January 25, 2011: Richard Burr, NC; Tom Coburn, OK; Jim DeMint, SC; Johnny Isakson, GA; and Jerry Moran, KS.

In the last Congress, the 111th Congress, Carol and I attended a Chamber of Commerce meeting in a suburb of Tulsa where Dan Boren, our District 2 U.S. Congressman, was the guest speaker. Nine of us showed up in FairTax gear — hats, T-shirts, jackets, and vests — to "ask" Boren to sign up to support the FairTax. Over the years, he had teasingly told Carol that he would consider it; it sounded as if he thought it was good legislation, but still he hadn't supported it.

Boren had a reputation of saying what he thought his constituents wanted to hear but in reality, and up until the Obamacare fiasco, voted 98 percent of the time with Nancy Pelosi and his party — a typical politician.

While we were in line to get some lunch, Carol spotted Boren in line at the back of the room, so we made a beeline to talk to him. Carol had a lot of history with Boren and reminded him of the many times he'd said he would consider FairTax and told him in so many words that it was time for him to put his money where his mouth was. I stood by for my chance to pounce, and when Carol finished her piece I jumped in and spoke as a representative of the Tea Party movement, explaining how FairTax is what We the People want instead of a repressive tax system. FairTax is about freedom and jobs. It's about smaller government and returning power to the people.

Carol got his commitment, and he announced it when he took the podium. What a coup for us! We got the first and only Democrat to co-sponsor FairTax in the 111th Congress.

At that time, Dan Boren didn't know who I was. There were several questions I had for him that stemmed from serious concerns voiced at every rally and discussed among my friends and neighbors. Thinking ahead, I had worn a jacket over my FairTax T-shirt because what I had to say was coming from a concerned constituent and not necessarily opinions shared by the FairTax supporters in the room.

Boren made his opening speech and asked for questions. My hand shot up. "What party do you belong to?" I asked. "Is it the party of out-of-control spending, bailouts, corporate takeovers, cram-down legislation, the party of Nancy Pelosi . . . ." I had more to say, but I was cut off.

"What's your question?" a man shouted.

"Yeah, what's your question?" another yelled.

I finished my question: "Mr. Boren, is that your party?"

I sat down stunned. I honestly thought everyone was concerned about the frightening overreach of the new administration. Of course, this was before I understood that there are Republicans, there are Constitutional Conservatives, and then there are Democrats and Socialists. At the time, I knew little about politics; I just knew that I was afraid for our country. I was glad I wore a jacket over the FairTax logo. I didn't know whether others were embarrassed by the smackdown for me or not, but my face burned. Boren's reply and the next question taught me all I needed to know.

Boren answered that he was "not in lockstep with Nancy Pelosi or the president," that he listens to his constituents and makes decisions based on what he hears from them. He lied again when he said he frequently disagrees on the issues. Then he asked for more questions and a man raised his hand and said, "Tell us about your new baby."

Chapter 6

Upside Down and Inside Out

On January 8, 2011, we heard the news that Arizona U.S. Representative Gabrielle Giffords of Arizona had been shot in the head during a political gathering. The morning after the shooting my husband said, "Anyone who makes more of this than a crazy person acting out is adding to the fear and confusion of an already horrific situation." He told me he had to shut off FOX News that night while I was asleep on the couch because he couldn't stand the "talking heads" of the "so-called" fair and balanced cable news station discussing the possible influence of the Tea Party movement. I told him he should have awakened me so I could hear what they were saying. After all, I'm a Tea Party leader and they were talking about me. It didn't matter, though, because by the time bits and pieces of information came in on the shooter, Jared Loughner, a different picture emerged and had nothing to do with Tea Parties.

I didn't hear any talk about Tea Party involvement, except a public statement made by a Tea Party leader offering sympathy and repudiation of a senseless act of violence and terror. Instead, Congresswoman Maxine Waters, a Democrat from California, was making statements about her fear of being shot not just in her district but while walking to and from the Capitol building. Her normally hysterical voice was raised several octaves higher as she demanded that security for public servants be stepped up. This was a typical knee-jerk reaction coming from the far-left faction of Congress and especially so with Waters, a registered member of the Democratic Socialist Party. Overreaction is what we've come to expect from the Obama administration and the socialist/communist/Marxist tenets of his appointed czars, cabinet and supporters.

Within hours of the shootings in Arizona, the anti-gun voices came in from all directions. There were accusations that conservatives,

Sarah Palin, and even Rush Limbaugh were responsible for the massacre. The law enforcement official responsible for responding to and overseeing the crime scene in Pima County, Sheriff Clarence Dupnik, made inflammatory accusations of anger, hatred, and bigotry before gathering facts and establishing order and calm. The nation turned their attention on Dupnik, appalled at seeing a man of law and order transform himself into a political pundit guilty of the very rhetoric he accused others of using.

Listening to the news coverage of the tragedy, Fred and I could only look at each other and shake our heads. We were as shocked and saddened as anyone. But the reactions coming from Democrats were so absurd they would ordinarily be laughable, but we learned that their intent was no laughing matter.

Fred and I discussed the horror of the unfolding events. We tried to make sense of things and asked ourselves how something like this could be prevented. We agreed it's nearly impossible to stop a madman from acting on his sick impulses, but there are lines of defense that if known by the general public could deter such actions from taking place. We knew gun-control laws would be reevaluated amid this hysteria. It is my firm belief that conceal-carry laws have prevented crimes when potential perpetrators think twice that maybe some bystander is armed.

Fred is a retired police officer with twenty-five years of service in the Hawai'i state system, fifteen years in the Honolulu Police Department, and ten years in the Hawai'i County Police Department. He's well aware of the federal law which permits him to carry a firearm in every one of the fifty states and the District of Columbia, Puerto Rico, and U.S. possessions such as the U.S. Virgin Islands.

However, when we discuss travel plans and road trips, we question what would happen if we got stopped in a township like Madisonville, Monroe County, Tennessee, with a firearm. Law-abiding citizens have been arrested for far less by law enforcement officials due to ignorance and sometimes in willful violations of law and even making up laws to suit their purpose. We love to take road trips and follow those roads less traveled, the little highways and byways of rural America, but the possibility of getting stopped and thrown into jail with the key thrown away is a risk we're not willing to take, so road trips will have to stay on the back burner like everything else in life until we know what the future has in store. Right now it's looking pretty damn bleak.

The Obama years have been an emotional roller coaster for me, and I'm sure for many other Americans. For the past two years, we've witnessed the methodical destruction of our once proud republic. Everything is upside down and inside out, and no one in government, the military, or the Supreme Court will take anything we have to say seriously.

It took a long time for the Tea Parties to get serious consideration in the national debate. A tsunami of citizen patriots affected the outcome of the historic 2010 midterm elections, and we did it without the support of television and the print media. We flat out didn't have the money to compete with normal channels of promotion. Instead, we were a true organic movement coalesced by one true thing: to restore and uphold the Constitution of the United States of America. Very few outside the grass roots groups really understand what we're all about. We continue to be mischaracterized by outsiders, and much of it is intentional. Everyone wants a piece of us and for sure we've witnessed a culling of patriots from our ranks. However many of us remain true to the cause for smaller, fiscally responsible government with solutions based on free market principles. We weren't Democrats. We weren't even Republicans. We'd had it with both parties. We were betrayed time and again by the Republican Party, betrayed even by Sarah Palin and her loyalty to party. Had she not meddled in certain races, we would have elected Constitutional Conservatives instead of RINOS (Republicans in name only) who do not look to the Constitution as the law of our land. But be that as it may, Sarah Palin loves this country, and I do believe she does what she thinks is right. She's a powerhouse to counter the progressive agenda from railroading our great nation into oblivion.

Chapter 7

Capt. Tom Snyder

"Enough, you uma kichingai, horse-crazy girl, go outside play."

I knew to behave when the Japanese came out, or Mama might tell Daddy how bad I was, and then I would really get in trouble. All Kazuko's kids knew that. Playing outside with the others wasn't so bad. In fact, I rarely spent much time indoors. "Outside" was the Paradise within paradise for me. There were dirt piles where ranches could be built using my imagination, and little sections of plastic fencing or broken chopsticks could form the corrals to hold the plastic horses and cows. I would rip up handfuls of lush Bermuda grass for the horses' bedding and feed for the cows.

Outside, there were a million things to do, most of it fun and exhilarating, except for the chores. There was always work to do, such as feeding the chickens, hanging the wash, sweeping the lanai, and cleaning the yard, and the never-ending job of picking up coconuts and fallen debris from the lush plants that grew everywhere without much encouragement from anyone.

Childhood for me, my brothers, and sisters, six in all, was a wonderful time filled with adventure, good fun, and occasional mischief. No matter how naughty we were talking back to Mama or ignoring her order to finish homework or do a chore, if we brought home crabs or fish we'd caught in the bay, we would be praised for supplying dinner, and any transgressions would be forgiven.

Kaneohe Bay was our backyard. Our father, Tom Snyder, raised us kids to appreciate and experience marine life from the shallowest tide pools to the deepest depths of the Pacific Ocean. Dad was a Marine in every sense of the word. As crazy as I, his eldest daughter, was about horses, he was about the sea.

Captain Tom, as he was known most of his life, would tell us kids about his dreams of one day "sailing the seven seas." Before he died in

1987 he had fulfilled some of that dream by sailing his cutter, "Shoestring," around Hawai'ian waters and visiting South Pacific islands like Palmyra, due south of Hawai'i, and the Marshall Islands in the Federated States of Micronesia.

When we were little, I remember Dad staying up late at night, and we would peek out from our room to see him bent over a lighted worktable, delicately weaving fine black thread through a "deadeye," which would become a turnbuckle on a model of the Cutty Sark, the world's last tea clipper. Daddy loved everything about sailing ships, and he could tell you the name of every single part of a boat. Just point at it, and he'd tell you what it was. Point out a ship in the harbor or a picture book, and he could tell you whether it was a ketch, a schooner, sloop, brig, clipper, barquentine, or brigantine.

There were model ships made of balsa all around our house in various stages of completion. To Mom's consternation, they took up valuable space needed to conduct household business, be it a desk to pay bills or a counter to fold clothes. Regular cleaning was sometimes a disaster because even the finest feather duster could bring down the rigging, so delicate were the thread ropes and the thinner-than-paper cloth fashioned into sails.

I remember one such accident when mom was working around a particular ship and bumped the mast, causing it to fall, bringing down the rigging and sails in a domino effect. It was a terrible disaster and awful news to break to Dad when he got home. Mom, my brother, and I who had witnessed the "wreck of the Hesperus" banded tightly together as my dad entered through the door to the kitchen. "Dad," I blurted out, "there was an awful storm and your ship got wrecked!" He took the news surprisingly well. I heard my parents joking about it later. My dad wondered if "Hurricane Kazuko" did it out of spite, or if she really did it by accident.

Dad was born and reared in Worcester, Massachusetts, and was of French, Dutch, German, and even a little Mohawk Indian stock. Looking at photos of him when he was sixteen years old, cigarette in hand, he looked every bit the restless teenager itching to break free of small-town America and join the Navy to see the world. My brother, Tame´, (sounds like Tommy) was a year older than I and very smart. He told me to keep a secret that he learned about our father — that he lied about his age to get into the Navy, but they found out and kicked him out. When he turned legal age, he joined the Marines, who were happy to have him.

We knew less about Mom's family. We grew up wondering why she wouldn't eat chicken or birds of any kind, although she would cook them for us. Mom descended from the privileged class of Samurai, but the family fell on hard times as a result of the government restructuring. Her father was never the same after the government took everything away. As a result, the chickens that were once beloved family pets were slaughtered by her father for food. She was so traumatized she could never eat chicken again.

My grandfather, Kyukichi Konno, was the superintendent of a high school in Sapporo, the largest city on the northern island of Hokkaido. His father and all the Konnos before him, and for 600 years prior, were Samurai and worked for the government. Mom's grandfather was a highly paid 2-sword-ranked Samurai.

I was little when somebody knocked on the door, and my mother went to answer it. She came back in the room, and I asked her, "Who was it?" She looked scared, white as a sheet. She said, "It's my father. He's dead." When I was much older, I figured that it had been someone who had come to inform her of his passing, and so I asked her again about the visit. She said plainly, it was her father himself. He came to say goodbye to her and then disappeared.

Years later, on the one-year anniversary of my own father's death, I was visited by my dad's ghost, too. My son Alan was five years old, and we were living in our Hilo house on the Big Island. I was at home alone. I walked into the kitchen and smelled the fragrance of Old Spice, my dad's favorite after-shave. It was unmistakable. I walked in and out of the kitchen several times sniffing the air, and it was distinctly only in the kitchen. I checked the cupboards and everywhere to see where the smell was coming from but to no avail. Then I remembered grandfather Konno's visit to mom, and it hit me. It was Daddy. I sat down at the kitchen table and sensed that Daddy had sat down too. I spoke to him. He listened. I asked him if everything was going to be okay with him. He said, "Yes." I heard him. The fragrance of Old Spice might have been imagined, but hearing his voice was unmistakable, and then he was gone as mysteriously as he had appeared.

At the time my dad died, he held a captain's license to pilot the largest ships sailing the oceans of the world. A year and a half earlier my dad took his sister to the airport to return home to Massachusetts.

After seeing her off and while walking to his car, he suffered a heart attack. It wasn't the first one. He'd had heart trouble for a few years, but the latest attack was pretty bad. He would need bypass surgery and was admitted to Tripler Army Medical Center, commonly referred to as "Crippler" by the locals. We were about to find out why.

Fred and I were living on the Big Island. We moved there from O'ahu when Alan was just a year old. I was waiting for a call from my younger sister to hear how Daddy's operation went. When she called me, her voice was full of worry. "The doctor said the operation went fine," she said, "But I'm worried. Daddy still isn't out from under the anesthesia. He's still not awake, but the doctor said some people just take longer to recover."

I told my sister to call me with any developments, but there were no developments, not that day, not any day for the next week. Daddy was in some kind of coma, and doctors were now saying they didn't know what was wrong. My sisters wanted me to come to Oahu. They didn't know what to do. The doctors wanted to meet with the family, and my sisters wanted me there. They didn't want Mom there, and Mom didn't want to be at that meeting. She wanted to hear whatever news there was, good or bad, from us.

At the meeting, we learned from the surgeon and another doctor that Daddy had suffered anoxia to his brain stem. They didn't know how that happened, but now they were conceding that, "What you see is what you get." The doctor, a captain in his military uniform, actually said that. Our dad wasn't coming out of the coma or whatever it was. My sisters had known from the outset that something was horribly wrong. Our father's eyes were open and staring blankly while his body writhed in a repetitive motion, his arms moving only as far as the leather restraints would allow. They watched this peculiar movement for more than a week and couldn't describe it. Now I was seeing it for myself, and I knew he was horribly brain damaged. He couldn't possibly recover from this.

A more pressing issue was that he had gas gangrene in his right arm that would require a procedure called "debride," where the infected flesh would be surgically removed. Also, it was possible Daddy's entire arm might have to come off. Amazingly, where one doctor told us, "What you see is what you get." Another told us they'd never seen a case like this, but that it was possible our dad could recover some level of consciousness. He kept saying, "He could still come out of it."

We took that one slim little glimmer of hope and gave it to Mom. We'll have to see what happens, we told her. In the meantime, they had Daddy in the intensive care ward, and even if he lost his arm, well, he'd make a great one-armed sailor or pirate. That's what we told her.

Mom smiled.

I stayed for a week and my father's condition remained the same. They didn't remove his arm, but his other arm developed gas gangrene too, and now both arms were bandaged.

I wanted to stay on O'ahu and go with my mother and sisters every day to see Dad, but work was pressing. I had used all my vacation time, and contract negotiations were piling up. Fred and Alan had been without me for a week and were ready for me to come home, too.

I heard from my sister every day. Eventually, Daddy stopped moving and his eyes, which had been permanently open and covered with a thick ointment, were closed.

The next development sent my sister straight to a phone to call me, she had pulled the sheets at the bottom of the bed up and over Dad's feet, they were black with gangrene.

The dreaded middle of the night call came at four o'clock in the morning. It was my youngest sister's husband. "It's over," he said.

Chapter 8

Tripler Army Medical Center

I'd been to Tripler Army Medical Center before. My older brother, Tame´, was in a horrible motorcycle wreck at age 16 and in a body cast for what seemed like forever. His legs were broken, his hip and lower back shattered. I visited him at Tripler when his legs were in traction. I could see pins through his flesh attached to wires keeping his legs elevated. He shared a ward with many other young men, but they were there because of injuries they sustained in Vietnam.

Tame´ got to know some of his ward mates and heard their accounts of war, of their battles and injuries, of others dying. Whenever I visited him, he was usually upbeat and joking, as was his nature. He got very solemn when he talked about some of the others in the ward, like those he knew weren't going to make it and others in such excruciating pain they made it difficult for him to sleep at night, hearing them cry out in pain, weep, or beg for drugs. I almost quit going. I was witness one day to a soldier screaming and crying for pain-killers. He was in horrible pain and was being ignored. My brother was really upset. He told me he didn't understand why they wouldn't just give him the morphine he was screaming for.

I was really affected by these soldiers. My heart went out to all of them. Some were only a few years older than me. I told my brother I wasn't going to come back. I felt so sorry for them and totally helpless. My brother understood, but then he got comments from a couple of the guys that my visits helped them because no one came to visit them. They had no relatives or friends in Hawai'i and liked seeing me come to the ward. So my visits resumed, and I always brought stuff with me. My brother would call and give me a shopping list of what some of the guys needed, and when I got to the ward my brother would tell me who got what, and I would deliver the items and get the nicest and most sincere thanks from those recipients. Unfortunately there weren't all that many requesting items; too many were too sick and injured to even know I was there.

My brother recovered and was eventually drafted into the Army even though he should have had a medical deferment. About two years after he was drafted, he was kicked out along with others for possession of marijuana.

The next and last time I ever went to Tripler was to answer a call for blood donors. It was summer and I had just graduated from high school two months earlier. It was all over the news: The aircraft carrier USS Forrestal was limping into Pearl Harbor with 161 injured men on board. They would need blood. Donors were requested to go to Tripler Army Medical Center in advance of the Forrestal's arrival. There had been a tragic disaster. A fire and chain-reaction explosions had killed 134 sailors and injured many more.

I drove to the hospital and filled out the paperwork, and a lady looked it over and said, "We can't take you. You have to be eighteen." I told her I'd be eighteen in five months, and she looked like she might consider that but when she saw that I weighed ninety-nine pounds she turned me away. I didn't even weigh a hundred pounds and the minimum was a hundred twenty.

I'd nearly forgotten about the incident back on July 29, 1967, but was reminded during the 2008 presidential election. John McCain had been on the Forrestal when the tragic event happened. There were even suspicions and accusations that he was a "hot-dog" pilot and was responsible for the horrific incident. A report explaining that McCain "wet-started" his A-4E Skyhawk to shake up the guy in the F-4 Phantom behind his jet is quite plausible. That he was the only Forrestal crewman to be immediately transferred makes his role in the disaster not only plausible but probable. His father could no doubt have influenced any decision with regard to his son. John S. McCain Sr. was soon to become commander of all U.S. forces in the Vietnam theater as Commander in Chief, Pacific Command (CINCPAC).

Chapter 9

Who Is Barak Obama? The Great Cover Up

Saturday, February 5, 2011, dawned at my house with another two inches of snow on top of the nearly two feet dumped on us four days before. At the moment, most of my political involvement included forwarding political e-mails I received and touching base by phone with other patriots in the Tea Party movement, just to keep the spirit alive and stay on my toes with the current events.

On the news that morning Fred and I were watching the latest events in Egypt. The crowd was peaceful, but they were dug in and would not leave until Mubarak left. But that didn't look as if it was going to happen anytime soon. Dictators will not go easily; drunk with power and riches, they have no empathy for the people outside their elitist circle. I told Fred we are seeing our future with Obama: he will not go easily either. Even now he is demonstrating his contempt for Americans and the rule of law by ignoring, no, snubbing Rep. Darrell Issa on his first major document deadline as new chair of the House Oversight and Government Reform Committee investigating the "Fast and Furious" gun walking scandal. The Obama administration sent a short letter promising to comply in response to a major information request of Homeland Security. Two "request" deadlines have now come and gone. Will DHS and top government officials respond to Issa's subpoenas? "Not bloody likely," I told Fred. "Look at his actions so far." An Internet posting from the Daily Caller notes that on or about January 20, 2011, DHS's Office of General Counsel instructed career staff in the Privacy Office not to search for documents responsive to Issa's request.

We learned from FOX News today that the radical Muslim cleric who called for the death of a Danish cartoonist and was kicked out of and banned from France and Canada showed up in the trunk of a BMW being smuggled into California.

Fred asked me what Janet Napolitano, secretary of Homeland Security, had to say about the cleric's capture. His question was rhetorical, of course. We were still reeling from the absurdity of her telling the Israeli government, on her visit there, how to secure their borders. It is clear to us now that Homeland Security put off releasing details of the capture on the border, much like Robert Gibbs, White House press secretary, did when he was asked about the assassination attempt on Egypt's vice president. He paused like a deer in the headlights before saying, "I'm not going to . . . get into that question." Like Napolitano, Gibbs had not been told how they should report those incidents, what spin to put on them. It was easy for me to imagine what might be going on in the White House over these issues: Obama was too bored and too deeply in over his head to participate and contribute intelligently to solving the problems of international affairs or protecting our borders. Valerie Jarrett was now in charge of the entire administration. What comes out of Obama's mouth are Valerie Jarrett's words. The only thing that excites Obama anymore is getting out and campaigning, receiving adulation from his throngs of admirers, and Valerie Jarrett will make that happen for him.

When my morning chores were finished, I checked my e-mails. I was getting close to 200 a day, so I had recently changed my habit of trying to read and forward as many as possible to scanning the subject manner and choosing those I thought were most important. An e-mail entitled "Obama Is Clueless — Absolutely Clueless," caught my attention. It was exactly my own viewpoint.

According to a posting by political blogger "Ulsterman" his White House "insider" reported that Obama was clueless and unprepared for the events unfolding in Egypt and was becoming increasingly fearful of his chances of re-election in 2012.

Valerie Jarrett, Obama's chief advisor and confidante, was running everything, and Obama's role was just to "look good." If something went well, he was happy and outgoing, but if something made him look bad he would lash out and pout.

They strategized to keep Obamacare protected so as not to be a "liability" in 2012 while spending significant time and resources preparing legal arguments for the coming Supreme Court case. If Obamacare was their first focus, then concern for the birth certificate or "birther" related issues ran a close second.

The political blogger wrote, "Most recently, Jarrett expressed concern over newly-passed requirements on eligibility to run for office in states. If only one or two states clarified eligibility, the White House would simply use those states as examples of 'anti-Obama racism.' They likely would not win the electoral votes in those states but could use the scenario to gain sympathy and support over the challenge from other states."

According to Ulsterman's insider, Obama would sit silently and motionlessly as discussions over eligibility took place.

"That strikes me as pretty damn odd, don't you think?" the insider reported. "People are discussing whether or not you are actually eligible to run for re-election in 2012, and you don't say a word on the subject? He just sat there with that weird little smile."

I was familiar with Ulsterman. I'd read his exposés of White House accounts from his anonymous D.C. "insider." The information was exceptionally astute, convincing and oftentimes bore out as accurate. The left closely monitors negative reporting of Obama's goings-on and jump to discredit the reports and smear the reporters. They are schooled in the Alinksy method of shutting down any dialogue harmful to their agenda, and they go out in force against Ulsterman. I've found the more they attack someone or something, the more truthful it must be and, therefore, imperative for them to destroy. Today's posting lifted my spirits. They are scared of us "birthers," we're getting to them and they don't like it one bit. They can use the "anti-Obama racism" card against the one or two states that pass eligibility requirements. Heck, they've sure been successful neutralizing those demanding to see his birth certificate.

But they're really not going to like the fact that as of June 2011, eleven states already proposed bills requiring proof of eligibility. Just yesterday, Dr. Orly Taitz, well-known dentist and lawyer in California who emigrated from communist Russia by way of Israel, called me. We had a long conversation regarding state legislatures moving ahead on this issue. Oklahoma State Rep. Mike Ritz and State Sen. Anthony Sykes have just authored such a bill. While on the phone, Fred asked who I was talking to. I told him "Orly Taitz." His eyes got big. "The Orly Taitz?" he asked incredulously. That was pretty exciting news for both of us, actually. She's a heroine to many Americans, a leader in the legal fight to compel Obama to release his records, and she's done so at great expense to her career, her family, and her very self.

I've had a couple of occasions to speak with Orly by phone, but mostly we've communicated through e-mail and her blog. She's been targeted time and again by liberal extremists hacking her website and issuing death threats and hate mail, given the moniker "Queen of the Birthers," and excoriated by Obama's enablers. But she perseveres and does so with exceptional wisdom and grace. After our long conversation yesterday, Fred asked me what she's like. I told him she's very dedicated to keeping our country from falling into communism. She's been there and lived it, and it's something she came to the United States to be free of. There was no way she could stay silent when Obama arrived on the scene promising "change." "So she's like you," he said, and I answered, "Kinda."

But in reality, I'm hardly in the same league as Orly. We both passionately speak out against Obama and his criminal enterprise, but Orly speaks from places few of us have ever been, and from those places she is driven.

Orly lives in California with her husband, Latvian-born Yosef Taitz, and their three boys. She was born to Jewish parents, both science teachers, in Chişinău, Moldavian SSR in the Soviet Union, the area now known as Moldavia. Orly immigrated to Israel in 1981 where she obtained a degree in dentistry at Hebrew University. It was there she met Yosef in 1987, and he proposed four months later. Orly immigrated to the United States in May that year, and she and Yosef were married in Las Vegas, Nevada. In 1992 Orly became a naturalized United States citizen. She received her law degree from Taft Law School and was admitted to practice law in California in December 2002.

She holds a second degree black belt in Taekwondo, and speaks five languages: English, Hebrew, Romanian, Russian, and Spanish.

Sometimes our conversations provided moral support for each other, but mostly we exchanged information vital to advancing legal efforts to hold Obama accountable for his numerous violations to the rule of law. I was one of Orly's contacts during Oklahoma's effort to pass eligibility legislation, Senate Bill 91, which passed the Republican-controlled House by a vote of 77-13 and cleared all the committees. The bill would have stopped Obama from being placed on the 2012 ballot since he could not produce a valid long-form birth certificate. All indications were that Governor Mary Fallin would sign the bill into law following a final vote, but that final vote didn't happen. The bill stalled with Speaker of the House Kris Steel.

Oklahomans like myself were scratching our collective heads, the same heads that were banging against Kris Steel's door pleading with him to place the bill up for vote. But we couldn't get him to listen to us, though Lord knows we tried.

Orly worked tirelessly to encourage all patriots in Oklahoma and around the country to call Speaker Steel and House Majority Leader Dan Sullivan and demand immediate scheduling of the eligibility bill. As we made our calls and voiced our demands we began to focus more closely on Dan Sullivan. Orly spoke to members of the Oklahoma House and learned that Steel was greatly influenced by Sullivan, who is a lawyer, and advises Steel.

Rumors of alleged insurance fraud and forgery by Sullivan had been swirling for some time, and it was reported that Sullivan's ex-wife forwarded a large file of documents to the authorities pointing to the fraud. At the time this was all going on, Orly advised us that there was no prosecution of Sullivan in the works. Whether he was being investigated at all was anyone's guess.

Like the other eleven or so states with eligibility bills in the pipeline, the effort to advance OK SB91 cooled when Obama finally released a long-form birth certificate, albeit a fraudulent document.

February 6, 2011, while Fred watched the Super Bowl, I worked on my memoirs, guided by the entries and notes in the 2009 calendar. Much of my activities centered around H.R. 25/S. 296, the FairTax bill. Every once in a while as I was typing my FairTax recollections, I would check e-mails to see if anything important came up and oh, boy, something did!

Dr. Lyle Rapacki sent me the PDF file of the report, "Findings of the Senate Select Committee on Homeland Security RE: Ft. Hood, Texas Shooting."

Lyle and I had stayed in close communication since serving together on the CIA-Columbia Trial Transcript Committee meeting, where we reviewed the 400 or so pages of transcription of the May, 2010 trial, along with Dr. James David Manning, Pastor of ATLAH Church in Harlem, and several other members from across the country.

"Thanks, Lyle!" I said, and went to work forwarding it to everyone on my lists, but not before I added a couple of notes.

First I highlighted a paragraph on page 8 of the report that pretty much summed up the B.S. that goes with political correctness.

Evidence of [Hasan's] radicalization to violent Islamist extremism was on full display to his superiors and colleagues during his military medical training. An instructor and a colleague each referred to Hasan as a "ticking time bomb." Not only was no action taken to discipline or discharge him, but also his Officer Evaluation Reports sanitized his obsession with violent Islamist extremism into praiseworthy research on counterterrorism.

Hasan's peers cite political correctness as the reason no one would take action against him, yet his "superiors" would deny that political correctness played a part:

Several of Hasan's superiors were simply not concerned with his views. One superior concluded that he was devoutly religious but not an extremist, adding that he was not alarmed by [Hasan's] religious expressions because similar expressions of other religions would be accepted. Another superior thought that his religion was part of his identity, and that Hasan's inner conflict concerning military operations in Muslim countries was an understandable internal reaction by a service member to combat against that service member's co-religionists.

Major Nidal Hasan's public displays of radicalization toward violent Islamist extremism during his medical residency and post-residency fellowship were clear and led two officers to describe him as a "ticking time bomb."

Born in Arlington, Virginia, in 1970, he graduated from Virginia Tech with an engineering degree in 1992 and began active duty with the U.S. Army in 1995. In 1997, he entered medical school at the Uniformed Services University of the Health Sciences (USUHS), the Military Services' leading educational institution for medical professionals, and graduated in 2003. From 2003 to 2007, Hasan was a resident in the psychiatric program at Walter Reed Army Medical Center, and from 2007 to 2009 he was a fellow in a post-residency graduate program at USUHS. During his medical residency and post-residency fellowship, his views were no secret to his superiors and colleagues, and he showed clear evidence of escalating radicalization to violent Islamist extremism. Witnesses reported that Hasan expressed support in open class presentations for many of the principles of violent Islamist extremism, and this support is reflected in written academic papers Hasan prepared during this time frame.

The next two years were the final year of Hasan's Walter Reed residency and the first year of his USUHS fellowship (2006-2008), and it was then that his radicalization to violent Islamist extremism came into plain view.

I highlighted the time frame of 2008 to bring attention to something else that Nidal Hasan was doing between April 2008 to January 2009 that is not included in the Fort Hood Report. Nidal Hasan was a Task Force Event Participant of the Homeland Security Policy Institute's Presidential Transition Task Force "Thinking Anew — Security Priorities for the Next Administration" and listed on page 29 of the report. Nidal Hasan, Uniformed Services University School of Medicine, shares the panel with another Muslim, Waleed Alshahari, political officer from the Embassy of Yemen.

"Whose bright idea was it to enlist wolves to design the sheep's pen?" I asked myself. It's obviously the logic used in this situation, judging by the recommendations in the HSPI report that the president should "employ a strategy that amplifies voices within the Muslim world that seek to counter radicalization and recruitment, and that exercises care regarding the use of lexicon" and to "foster respect for and adherence to international law."

I've come to believe that the radicalization and recruitment they're trying to stop is us — the Tea Party movement — because they sure as heck are not trying to stop radical Islam. And there it is: be careful not to use any politically incorrect words. So, we can't say any words that might hurt their feelings, but they can kill us just because we don't share their ideology?

Another interesting tidbit I got from the HSPI report is the identity of who dictated the closure of Guantanamo; it was P.J. Crowley of the Center for American Progress, and HSPI Director Frank Cilluffo suggested abandoning the term "War on terror," to which Crowley agreed and suggested using "struggle against violent extremism." Stephen Flynn of the Council on Foreign Relations called for an open society that engages the world — George Soros' agenda.

Speaking of Guantanamo, I knew from the very beginning that Obama's intent was to shut down the entire base and give the land back to Castro. Obama's and Democrats' close relationship with Cuba has always been very unsettling to me, especially the Congressional

Black Caucus members' personal friendships with the communist regime.

Janet Napolitano was later confirmed as Secretary of Homeland Security and became the front person to step up to the microphones, but she never talks about securing our borders saying instead that the border is as secure as it's ever been. Why does she go against any attempt to fix the mayhem on the border? Maybe it's because in the entire HSPI manual there's absolutely no mention of securing our borders.

The FBI report on Nidal Hasan, ticking time bomb, doesn't give us the names of those superiors who weren't concerned with his views and just thought he was devoutly religious. Who are these people? Why won't they name names? They're obviously still protecting those protecting Obama. Obama was sure quick to tell us not to jump to conclusions. What other conclusion would we draw when Hasan yells, "Allahu Akbar!" while he unloads on unsuspecting and unarmed military and civilian personnel. Could one of these superiors be Dr. Van Coots, commander of Walter Reed Army Medical Center, who issued a memo to all hospital staff wishing them a Muslim Muharram greeting. He responded to criticism by saying he would also send a Christmas greeting to the staff, but his rebuttal included a pouty little sentence that the memo wasn't intended to be shared outside of the hospital staff.

What was Van Coots' role in progressing Hasan through the ranks? In the last month of Hasan's residency, he chose to fulfill a requirement to make a scholarly presentation on psychiatric issues by giving an off-topic lecture on violent Islamist extremism. Hasan's draft also presented extremist interpretations of the Koran as supporting grave physical harm and killing of non-Muslims. He even suggested that revenge might be a defense for the terrorist attacks of September 11, 2001.

Around the same time, in the last month of Hasan's residency, the psychiatric residency program director questioned whether Hasan was fit to graduate. He thought Hasan was "very lazy" and "a religious fanatic," but graduate he did.

The 91-page special report by Joseph I. Lieberman, chairman, and Susan M. Collins, ranking member of the U.S. Senate Committee on Homeland Security and Governmental Affairs found failures in the FBI, failures in the Department of Defense, failures to work together and failures even to agree who does what, but nowhere in the report do they use the words "Muslim terrorist."

Much of the report reflects on what a great job the FBI does and showers kudos on Director Mueller whose term was fast approaching its end. But Obama stepped in and requested an unheard of two-year extension citing the importance of continuity at a time of major changes in leadership and was confirmed by all 100 senators. Obama's socialist agenda needs Mueller to maintain the status quo — that is — keeping at bay any investigations into Obama's personal history.

Gen. Petraeus would take Leon Panetta's position at the CIA so Panetta could move to Secretary of Defense. Not one member of the Senate had reservations about Panetta, giving final approval by a unanimous 100-0 vote on June 21, 2011, to Obama's nomination for defense secretary. No matter, Panetta has a deep and dark history of personal relationships with members of the Communist Party, most notably Mr. and Mrs. Hugh DeLacy, who are known to have met with communist espionage agents. But worse, according to Accuracy in Media, Panetta was never vetted by the FBI. During his tenure as U.S. Representative he sought to undermine President Reagan's pro-defense policies at every turn.

What I find even more distressing is the continual bent toward the socialization of our country, especially under Obama. One must remember that the radical left wing movement in America has rebranded itself the "Progressive movement," and these Progressives are operating at the highest levels in our government advancing their socialist ideology, while shielding themselves from the nasty labels of "communism" and "socialism." In a PEW Research Center survey 68 percent of Americans reacted positively to the word "progressive" while only 23 percent had a negative reaction. Conversely 59 percent of Americans had a negative reaction to the word "socialism" while only 29 percent had a positive reaction to the word.

The Progressives' intent is to weaken our military presence in the world which makes perfect sense from the perspective of the larger goal of installing a global socialist regime to manage the affairs of the world. For that to happen the American military must be subjugated to the demands of the "common global good." With Leon Panetta taking his role as defense secretary on June 30, 2011, the regime again performed a successful coup, and the senate conservatives who proudly call themselves "Reagan Republicans" are none the wiser. They've given away their military policy of Reagan's "peace through strength" to a closet communist.

As for Panetta's background getting totally glossed-over, disgraced Congressman Anthony Weiner explains in sour grapes fashion how that happened as quoted on the conservative website Right Wing News:

"[We] find no evidence that the Panetta-DeLacy relationship was ever examined by the FBI or the Senate when Panetta was being considered and confirmed for the post of CIA director. The major media have been even more derelict, content to cover the Panetta hearings for secretary of defense in a cursory manner and then turn their attention back to something that is easier and more fun to cover which is sure to attract interest."

Like so many leaders who have the power to find out the truth behind Obama's hidden past, FBI Chief Robert Mueller chose not to do so and, in fact, ignored countless requests to investigate, along with a 3,000-signature appeal spearheaded and submitted by Arnie Rosner of California who has been at the forefront of seeking the truth behind Obama's meteoric rise to power through the corrupt cesspool of Chicago politics. Mueller has never acknowledged a single request for an investigation. Is he not up to the task, or is he part of the cover-up?

Chapter 10

A "Non-Negotiable Commitment to Africa"

On September 26, 2010, Fred and I returned home from a weeklong cruise sponsored by WorldNetDaily and hosted by owner Joseph Farah and his wife, Elizabeth. It was a wonderful and informative experience with many highlights. We listened to extraordinary speakers like Dr. Judith Reisman, distinguished senior fellow in the study of social trends, human rights and media forensics, famous for going after the left-wing Kinsey Institute, exposing perverted sex studies of children, and working to dismantle the institution. There were several literary giants such as David Kupelian, author of The Marketing of Evil: How Radicals, Elitists, and Pseudo-Experts Sell Us Corruption Disguised as Freedom. Aaron Klein, author of The Late Great State of Israel: How Enemies Within and Without Threaten the Jewish Nation's Survival and Schmoozing with Terrorists, gave several fascinating talks drawn from his experiences as a journalist based in Israel. Jerome R. Corsi, Ph.D., author of The Obama Nation, was present at all the planned functions and conferences and was readily accessible for questions and answers.

When I met Dr. Corsi, I handed him my binder containing copies of every Hawai'i birth certificate owned by members of the Booth family and research we'd done. We were thrilled to learn that he would have a new book out in early 2011 titled Where's the Birth Certificate? The title supports WorldNetDaily's billboard campaign asking what millions of Americans want to know. Fred told Dr. Corsi to keep the binder and use anything he wanted from it.

On the cruise, Fred and I were invited to dine at the head table with the Farahs, and we were honored to share the table with Floyd and Mary Brown, Western Center for Journalism and Floyd Reports; Dr. Alan Keyes, former Ambassador to the United Nations; David Kupelian, The Marketing of Evil; and Jeremiah and Mary Denton.

Jeremiah Denton wrote When Hell Was in Session, detailing his amazing story of nearly eight years of abuse, neglect, and torture as an American POW at the Hanoi Hilton. In 1966, he appeared on a television interview from prison and blinked the word "torture" in Morse code, confirming for the world that atrocities were taking place in the prison. In his book, Denton describes his shock to learn, upon his return, of the moral decline in America, as well as his efforts to restore traditional values to American society. Fred and I became an unofficial part of the WorldNetDaily "Tea Party at Sea" as well as the Conference in Miami, where Joseph Farah invited me to read LTC Terry Lakin's thank you letter to his supporters.

LTC Terry Lakin disappeared three days before Christmas after his court martial. He had made headlines when he challenged Obama's eligibility by asking for proof in the form of an official birth certificate, a long-form document proving hospital, attending physician, and the circumstances surrounding Obama's birth. For nearly a week, no one knew where Terry was. Was he still at Fort Mead? Was he in Leavenworth? We were worried. There were thousands of us who watched in terror as time and again Terry was vilified by the military court martial system. The judge, Army Col. Denise R. Lind, said she would not allow her court to be used to "embarrass" Obama. Military police laughed at a comment to "taser him and throw him in the van." We were distraught as things went from bad to worse. But we all got the message — don't question the "powers that be," or you will be silenced.

I later spoke to Marco Ciavolino, trustee of the Terry Lakin Action Fund, and then to Terry himself and learned that after he was sentenced, he had ten minutes to change into civilian clothes. He was then handcuffed, shackled, and taken to a cell located on a floor beneath the courtroom, where he spent two uncomfortable nights.

"They were the two most miserable nights of my life," recalled Terry. "It appeared that the cell hadn't been used in some time."

Terry suffered through the first night in the coldness of an unheated cell. Eventually, he was given a blanket.

After two nights, he was transferred to Leavenworth prison. The hardest part for him, he told us later, was not being able to communicate with anyone on the outside. And, of course, we had no way of finding out where Terry was or what was happening inside the federal penal system. We fretted and some of us cried.

"This is so WRONG!" I screamed inside my head.

A few days before the start of the new year, we finally heard from Terry. Supporters around the country sighed a collective breath of relief. January 1, 2011, had been designated "Terry Lakin Day," and at least now we knew he was okay.

Marco Ciavolino proved himself to be a marketing genius. The Terry Lakin Action Fund website attracted thousands, and the list of donors grew. Soon, Marco was hosting a weekly radio show and shared information from his phone calls with Terry with listeners. Terry kept a journal of his jail experiences, observations, and his thoughts in general. Marco posted Terry's writings, and they became a column on the website: Prison Diaries. It was a way to stay close to Terry, and as soon as we received instructions on how to write to him, we did so right away.

Mainstream media, including FOX News, washed their hands of Terry Lakin. It was up to us to keep Terry's story alive, and I read his thank you letter to Tea Party groups, conservative meetings, and on the WorldNetDaily cruise:

I cannot begin to express thanks adequately to all who support raising the valid question of the constitutional eligibility of Barack Obama. This issue should have been resolved long ago, but the media and others refused to look at the controversy objectively.

More than anyone, I wish this issue could be investigated and solved, and we as a nation could go on tackling other pressing issues. I would be on a flight tomorrow to deploy anywhere, doing my duty (caring for our wonderful troops), rather than faced with the issue of defending our Constitution on the home front.

All soldiers, when we train, and especially those on patrol in combat areas, question themselves: Will I be able to think and act quickly enough to respond correctly? Will I be able to pull the trigger fast enough and accurately to respond to the threat? Will I be able to run from cover quickly enough to protect a fallen fellow soldier? I made the decision to put myself in harm's way in a different manner — risking a jail sentence.

The military, and our country, has an urgent constitutional question that needs to be answered. We will not "get over it" as some suggest because so many patriots made the ultimate sacrifice to protect that document and all it stands for. I pursued trying to get an adequate answer to the eligibility question two years ago and came up empty-handed. This path is hard, but not like the danger of risking physical harm in combat zones. My punishment would be small compared to hazards deploying soldiers face every day. But I believe remaining true to my oath of office and to the Constitution is one all soldiers understand — as it is our solemn duty.

May God Bless our country and defend our liberties!

LTC Terry Lakin

In total, Terry was sentenced to six months in prison, his pay was forfeited, and he would be dishonorably discharged from the army. He spent Christmas in Fort Leavenworth federal prison away from his wife and three children and saw the new year come in from the inside of a prison cell.

His hasty confinement and loss of rights had been engineered by high-ranking military officials with a common thread running through the lineup; they were all Democrats. Even worse, they were all in the same command, the same building, even the same series of offices. They conspired to silence Terry in a way that was swift and thorough. No longer could he voice his concerns and ask the question of whether the orders he received to deploy to Afghanistan were legal, because if Obama was not the legitimate commander in chief, every order, every single one, was illegal.

One of the first executive orders Obama signed upon taking office was to seal all his records. To date, the public has not been allowed to see the Kapi'olani Hospital long-form birth certificate, which doesn't exist according to Hawai'i Governor Neil Abercrombie, who claimed he could not find the certificate but afterward refused further comment on his investigation, and Tim Adams, former Hawai'i elections clerk, who swears through an affidavit that his superiors told him that Obama did not have a birth certificate on file. (On April 27, 2011 Obama held a press conference and posted an electronic PDF file of an alleged long-form birth certificate on the White House website).

Citizens taking up the responsibility of asking those in positions of authority to explain why the American public is being denied access to Obama's records are being either ignored or vilified for asking.

When Fred and I returned from the WorldNetDaily cruise, I was able to check my e-mail for the first time in nearly a week. Before I left, I had received word from Dr. James Manning of ATLAH Ministries that there would be a committee meeting scheduled for some time in the future to discuss the release of court transcripts of the CIA Columbia trial that was held four months earlier in May. I was asked to serve on this new committee, and I was eager to do so. Checking my e-mail, I saw that I would only be home for a few days before having to leave for New York City for the committee meeting, so I made immediate arrangements for my trip.

When I arrived at La Guardia Airport in New York City, I called the cell phone number I was given, and a driver said he would pick me up outside the baggage claim within a few minutes and gave me a description of his car. I collected my one piece of checked luggage and went out to the curb to watch for the car.

I had met the driver, one of Pastor Manning's assistants, when I testified at the trial in May, but I had met so many people and didn't know whether I would recognize the driver sent for me. Before long I spotted an SUV parked way down the street. I walked up to the car and recognized the driver as he stood on the sidewalk outside the car. He was surprised to see me and said that Hallelujah was looking for me at the baggage claim and wondered how I'd gotten past her. We laughed. I gave him my bags and went back to the baggage claim area to look for Hallelujah. I found her right away. While she was still looking around for me, I walked right up to her and gave her a hug. Months earlier Hallelujah and I and members of the ATLAH Church, and trial supporters had walked hand in hand, two by two, black and white, fifty to a hundred patriots and faithful. We were led seven times around Columbia University by Pastor James David Manning.

I wasn't there for the final day of marching, but the walls of Columbia, like the walls of Jericho, fell and revealed the lies that Obama and the crafters of his deceptions tried to protect.

Obama never attended Columbia University, and he was found guilty on multiple counts of sedition, conspiracy, fraud and obstruction of justice. Verdicts were handed to the judiciary of the U.S. Senate, the U.S. Congress, the joint chiefs of staff, and the U.S. attorney general as well as Michael Sovern, president of Columbia University at the time Obama was purported to be there. Letters demanding Columbia's license to operate an educational institution be revoked were sent to the New York State Bar, the New York State Attorney General, New York State Regents, and the Mid-Atlantic Schools Accreditation Board.

No acknowledgment was forthcoming from any of the entities served. Private citizens followed up by sending their own letters and inquiries asking when the issue of Obama's ineligibility would be investigated. Silence or name-calling was the only response anyone received.

I was back in New York City, and my friends from ATLAH Church would safely deliver me to where I would stay for two of the three nights I would be in Harlem for committee meetings. They brought me to the apartment of Mother Keturah, who I had met at the church during the CIA Columbia trial. I was welcomed with a huge bear hug, and we bounced up and down with joy, happy to see one another again.

Now we had the actual transcripts from the trial. At the first meeting on the day after I arrived, I glanced at the finished work and estimated about 400 pages of jury selection, testimony, summation, and verdicts. All the members had received the files earlier by e-mail, but I had had time to read only a portion of the transcripts.

We reached a decision to release the transcripts but to keep the names of jury members and committee members confidential. On Tuesday, October 5, 2010, the first round of CIA Columbia trial transcripts were distributed to a broad range of media, government, and private e-mail contacts. Very shortly after, James Clapper, director of National Intelligence, was summoned to the White House. The following day, October 6, Clapper was interviewed about his hasty visit to the White House and meeting with Obama. The Washington Times ran a story titled "U.S. rethinks intelligence sharing after leaks anger Obama," citing WikiLeaks as the subject of his anger. WikiLeaks, however, had not been at the forefront of Obama's consternations since the July leak of military and diplomatic files pertaining to the war on Afghanistan, and the next dumping of 400 documents would not be apparent for at least two more weeks. Although Clapper touted WikiLeaks as the subject of Obama's ire, his comments led me to believe he was actually talking about personal concerns of Obama.

According to the Washington Times article, Clapper said the leaks were upsetting Obama. "I was at a meeting yesterday with the president," he said. "I was ashamed to have to sit there and listen to the president express his great angst about the leaking that is going on here in this town."

The intelligence chief continued, chastising "anonymous senior intelligence officials who, for whatever reason, get their jollies from blabbing to the media."

Clapper added that, "The president remarked, 'The irony here is people engaged in intelligence can turn around and talk about it publicly.' "

This doesn't sound to me like concern over WikiLeaks but more about who's covering Obama's ass. This is damage control. This is "birther" control. The timing coming on the heels of releasing the CIA Columbia trial transcripts was not lost on us. James Clapper is just another "clown" appointed by Obama and sworn to secrecy to gather and analyze potential threats to Obama's carefully concealed secrets. It became abundantly clear in December, when Clapper didn't have a clue about the biggest terror bust that went down in the UK, that maybe his focus wasn't on national intelligence but rather on looking out exclusively for Obama's interests by investigating and shutting down people like Pastor Manning and me.

If anyone still had their qualms about Clapper's effectiveness in his presumed role of protecting our nation, his astonishing remarks about the Muslim Brotherhood gave everyone pause.

The members of Obama's inner circle loosely speak of their real intentions and thoughts among themselves behind closed doors and know what they can and can't say to the public. Apparently, Clapper didn't get the memo.

Rev. Dr. James David Manning had been a vocal critic of Obama for years. He tried to alert everyone about the secrets Obama harbored and the danger he posed to our American way of life. In YouTube videos, Rev. Manning in his "boom-shaka-laka voice" warned about the "long-legged mack daddy" head pimp! Yes, Obama is nothing more than a product of affirmative action working his magic in the Chicago slums preaching "hope" and "change" and promising free stuff to every-one while cavorting with anti-American activists and subversives. Rev. Manning's videos went viral. Those of us who knew about Obama's sordid past recognized the truth in what Dr. Manning was saying.

The head pimp was groomed and shaped for a leadership role in a plan that would fundamentally change the United States of America. Some of us could see from the moment Obama arrived on the scene that he was a lie. He was not who he said he was. We believed he was lying all during his campaign, and when we tried to make public what we knew, we were shut down at every turn.

After the transcript committee meeting, I returned home with much new knowledge and insight gained from the other members and from the transcripts. We were twelve, give or take per day of conference, from all over the United States, from different professions and social statuses. We were well aware of what we were up against. Our only avenue of distributing information was by e-mail and conservative websites. Rev. Manning did his untiring best to keep his radio show broadcasts on the air and post his videos on YouTube. During the transcript meetings, guests filled in for Rev. Manning on his daily radio show. Immediately after the transcripts were released, the ATLAH.org website repeatedly was hacked, attacked, and vilified by enemies known and unknown. Mischief-makers tied his website to crude, obscene, homosexual, and other perverted sex sites. The damage was swift and lasting.

"Who does this?" we asked ourselves. Indeed, who has the power to hide Obama's records and create a phony certification of live birth and sell it to the public? Where does the power come from to give Obama the cover to support his narrative as laid out in his autobiographies? The most disturbing thing was how Americans could have voted for a man who is not a "natural-born citizen," according to Article II, Section 1, clause 5 of the Constitution of the United States when the candidate is clearly a British/Kenyan subject, where citizenship passed from his father, and clearly the candidate has "a nonnegotiable commitment to Africa" according to the mandate of Trinity United church where Obama listened to the anti-American rantings of Jeremiah Wright, Jr., for twenty years.

"How does that work?" I wondered. But I knew the truth all along and penned it in an opinion piece for the Post & Email that was also carried by conservative sites and newspapers:

OBAMA CAN DO ANYTHING HE WANTS BECAUSE THE CIA HAS HIS BACK
Did This Well-known Socialist Help to Create a History for Obama?
by Miki Booth

(October 26, 2010) — The evidence is all there for anyone to see if they take the time to look. Zbigniew Brzezinski has "spoon-fed" Obama ever since he took him under his wing from Occidental College in 1980, apprenticed him through his first job in Pakistan and Afghanistan to his second job at Business International Corporation and ultimately, by manufacturing a background, faking his academic credentials and résumé, to the top job in America.

Brzezinsky was national security advisor to Jimmy Carter from 1977-1981 and a professor at Columbia University 1960-1989, where he taught at the Institute of Communist Affairs. He's a member of the Council on Foreign Relations, trustee of the Trilateral Commission, and has attended Bilderberg meetings. He's still a prominent presence in Obama's "inner sanctum" and conveniently located near the White House at the Johns Hopkins School of Advanced International Studies, where he's professor of American foreign policy.

Obama cannot be questioned about any of this because "it's a matter of national security." No one will talk about the fake birth certificate because "it's a matter of national security." There is no attempt to investigate his stolen Social Security number, originally issued in Connecticut, because "it's a matter of national security."

Word is, the White House Press Corps members will have their credentials yanked if they were to ask Obama about his Oxy or Columbia days, his work at BIC, a well-known CIA front, or his trips to Pakistan. Also on the list of banned questions is the birth certificate, his name Barry Soetero, and his Indonesian passport of that name.

All the FOX News folks have gotten the word as to what's off limits, too. Beck can go as far as linking all the players destroying our country but can't mention the birth certificate. He "busted" Obama's mother for her involvement with Shore Bank but doesn't talk about her working for Asia Development Bank in Karachi, Pakistan, while living in a five-star hotel for years laundering money to aid Mujahadeen and Taliban. Oops, that's CIA and Pakistan; can't go there. If you do, the FCC will shut you down so fast your head will spin.

Every once in a while, though, Obama really blows it and states a falsehood that sends the CIA into a panicked frenzy to cover his misstatement. As we all know, mistakes are made when you hurriedly try to fix an error. Obama's error was saying that he signed up for selective service when he graduated from high school. That would be 1979, when there was no draft, and registration was not mandatory. The selective service "draft" was re instituted in 1980, but Obama was not an American citizen and was working for Brzezinski so perhaps not aware until he ran for president, and the problem surfaced, so a record for Obama had to be created. Unfortunately for Obama's "fixers," creating a record after the fact is a difficult thing to do, and faced with time constraints, they were forced to settle on a flawed document and probably unwittingly linked that document to another fraud, his Social Security number.

Brzezinski has been there for Obama all along, and their secrets have to stay hidden because of national security measures. It's really sad that America has been hijacked by wicked people such as Brzezinski, Soros, Kissinger, the Clintons, Obama, and all the godless members of their One World team.

If our country is to survive, we only need one brave patriot to break through the CIA's code of silence into the mainstream and let the treasonous pieces fall where they may.

Intelligence specialist Lyle J. Rapacki, PhD sent me a kind letter applauding my article and posted an assessment on PA Pundits International, "The relentless pursuit of common sense" — A Variety of Opinion From Various Writers

I beamed. I was international.

Chapter 11

The Trampling

I got caught up in a riot in high school. It was more like a stampede that left me dazed and injured and kept me away from large crowds thereafter.

The day started out innocently enough at James B. Castle High School in Kaneohe. I had just begun eighth grade there, and the students were notified that there would be an all-school assembly in the auditorium. I got there early with another classmate and sat down near the double doors to the main entry. We got out our notebooks to study while we waited for the doors to open.

Before long, a crowd had gathered, and those of us sitting on the concrete sidewalk stood up to maintain our place in line. As more students arrived, the line disappeared and soon it was just a mass of bodies waiting outside the double doors.

Some troublemakers started pushing people, and those people shoved back. Students were complaining and saying, "Knock it off." The bullies pushed harder, and when the doors opened, they shoved their way into the crowd to be the first in the doors. The big main doors to the auditorium opened into the crowd and into me. I had nowhere to go to get out of the way of the opening door.

The bullies continued to push. Others pulled on the doors, and I tripped over someone on the ground and went down. Others fell and girls were crying. Students were yelling and bullies now were kicking. I was being deliberately kicked. Someone stepped on my hair, and as I struggled to get up, I felt my hair being yanked from my scalp. I felt a hard blow to my back. It wasn't a kick; it was a boy falling on top of me. I was scared, I was hurt. I curled up with my knees to my chest and covered my head with my arms and waited for the madness to stop.

And then it was over. Teachers were there. They started helping those of us on the ground to stand up. I was asked if I was hurt, and I said that I was okay. One girl was badly injured; I watched a teacher pick her up and carry her towards the office where the nurses' station was located.

My books and notebook folder were scattered on the ground, and I gathered them up. One of the barrettes I had in my hair was laying on the sidewalk, a huge hank of long brown hair attached to it. I touched my head where the barrette should have been and felt a painful lump and burning abrasion where my hair had been ripped out. Then I saw that my blouse was ripped, so I held my books up against me to hide my torn clothing and went into the auditorium for assembly. Students were still filing in, most totally unaware of the chaos that went on minutes before.

When my circle of acquaintances heard about what happened and that I was one of the students who got trampled, they enjoyed telling me that I was a "riot."

"It looks like a mob ran over you," they joked, and we all laughed.

I stayed away from large crowds the rest of my life, rarely attending concerts and avoiding opening night at movies. At least that held true until September 12, 2009.

I was among of group of an estimated one to two million people, and even though at times I was squeezed closely together with others I never felt so safe in all my life. That was when we answered the call to march on Washington in protest of a tyrannical government totally tone-deaf to the wishes of the American people. YouTube Thomas Paine's call for millions of people to come together and protest was reinforced with Glenn Beck's call to rally in support of the "9" principles and "12" values of the 9.12 movement. Beck asked his listeners to think back to the day after the attack on the World Trade Center.

"Remember how you felt that day?" he asked. "We were all Americans." There were no Democrats or Republicans, no white or black, just Americans, rich and poor alike, who love this country and showed their pride and solidarity by driving with their headlights on, waving flags, and singing patriotic songs.

Indeed, we could all remember how we felt the day after we were attacked. We held our families close, and reached out to neighbors, and made friends with strangers who shared our motto: We will never forget.

However, eight years later, we were again a divided country, and it seemed that people did forget. So when Glenn Beck told us to come, I knew this would be a historic event, one that I couldn't miss. I had to answer the call to duty for my country. Glenn Beck told us that we were not alone, and indeed we weren't. I was there in Washington, D.C., lined up with fellow patriotic Americans on Pennsylvania Avenue for as far as our eyes could see while we waited for the march to begin. People kept coming and coming from the direction of the White House and Washington Monument to assemble at Freedom Plaza, the designated starting point for the march to the Capitol.

The march even had to start early in order to keep traffic from backing up due to the enormous number of people lining up not only on Pennsylvania Avenue but also Independence Avenue and every side street leading to the Capitol. Actual attendance numbers have been skewed by the liberal media as much lower than what they were, but those of us who were there know. People kept coming as news of the overwhelming number of marchers were spread via text message and cell phone, and I was among them. I realized I was no longer that girl who would cower and be trampled, and if I did, at least now it would be for a cause that was worth the risk.

I believe Glenn Beck is responsible for driving the massive numbers of patriots standing up against big government and standing for the "9" principles and the "12" values that make Americans exceptional. I believe a lot of people were like me and remembered the feeling we had the day after we were attacked by Muslim extremists. We weren't going to take it lying down. We fought back because our country was worth fighting for, even if people still refused to acknowledge our efforts. Now we were faced with runaway debt, irresponsible borrowing and spending policies, and heading toward economic and moral collapse. We were fighting back because the United States of America is worth fighting and dying for.

Chapter 12

Rest Camp

In the summer of 1964, my ninth-grade year at Castle High School completed, we moved from Kaneohe to Waianae on the western side of O'ahu, where we would be closer to Daddy's work. Housing was cheaper, and we'd be close to the ocean — real pluses for a sea-loving family. The house we moved into was just outside the Waianae Army Recreation Center (since renamed Pililaau Army Recreation Center), known by all the locals as "Rest Camp."

Leaving Kaneohe on the windward side of Oahu and moving to Waianae on the western shore was a culture shock. After living in Waianae for a little while, I decided Kaneohe had been a kinder and gentler place to live. The difference was that Kaneohe at the time was predominately Japanese, who are just kinder, gentler people — humble, quiet, considerate, and kind. If they didn't hold good thoughts for someone, they generally kept that fact to themselves, my people. That's how we lived under Mom's roof. Nobody in our family was allowed to be belligerent or obnoxious, as I found many households could be. "Dysfunctional families" is what I learned later they were called.

The Waianae side was pretty rough and still is. Rental car companies used to prohibit people from going there. They said insurance would not cover them if anything happened. I don't know if that's still true, but I do know the car rental companies discourage people from going there.

A few times, Mom wanted to leave and move back to the windward side. Mom left a lot of her Japanese friends in Kaneohe, but eventually she made new friends, and so did my sisters and brothers. Everybody adjusted, that is, everybody but me.

Tamé and I enrolled at the Waianae High School, he in eleventh grade and me in tenth. For the first couple of days, my mom took us to school; after that, we had to take the bus since my younger brothers' and sisters' school was in the opposite direction of the high school. Tamé already found some friends and rode with them to school, so I was alone on my first bus trip to Waianae High. There were some raucous kids in a small group talking loud and laughing, so I kept my head down and found a seat. I knew better than to draw attention to myself; they sounded like troublemakers. I didn't make myself small enough. All of a sudden I became an object of interest and was surrounded by the loud students.

"You new, eh?" someone asked.

I looked up and saw the strangest-looking person I'd ever seen. It was a boy, I thought, but his hair was poofed up bouffant style and heavily shellacked with hair spray. He had spit curls for sideburns, dark blue eye shadow, eyeliner, and mascara, and if that didn't intimidate me enough, his fat fingers with long polished nails held a cigarette, and it was precariously close to my arm.

"I transferred from Castle," I said.

"Oh, she wen' transfah from Castle," someone mocked me. I could see where this was going, so I lowered my head and decided to keep my mouth shut.

Someone "flicked" at my hair, and a tough-looking girl with ehu (reddish) hair and lots of makeup put her face close to mine and said, "You think you pretty, eh?"

I shook my head. I honestly didn't think I was pretty.

The torment went on. "Yeah, you t'ink you pretty, and you goin' try take my boyfriend. I t'ink I goin' kick yo' ass."

I shrank into the seat and into myself while the bullies hovered over me. The burning tip of the cigarette, held by those obscenely long nails, inched closer. I didn't know what to do. Surely they would not actually hurt me, I thought. I was wrong. All of a sudden the cigarette burned into my flesh. I jumped up and ran toward the front of the bus. I heard laughing as I demanded the driver stop the bus and let me off.

I walked home along the sandy edge of the dirty highway littered with glass, gravel, and debris. I didn't have my books or my purse; they were still on the bus. I told Mom what had happened and described the boy made up to look like a woman. Mom knew about homosexuals and transvestites. She called the boy a mahu. I'd never seen a mahu or ever heard the words homosexual or transvestite before. My introduction to the first mahu, first homosexual, I ever saw was traumatic and something no fourteen-year-old girl should ever have to be confronted with. I would meet many more during my life in Hawai'i, and a few I even called friends.

That was years ago, before progressivism allowed the sexual aberration to be shoved in our faces and forced us to accept men marrying men and women marrying women, and a perverted government using propaganda to tell little children that this is normal, and the younger they are made to get used to it the better. It's sick, it's wrong, and I've no more tolerance for political correctness and letting them hijack the word "gay." The world was a better place when homosexuals stayed in the closet.

Dad took me to school the following day, and we sat down with the principal and a counselor. Both had heard a little of what had happened from the bus driver when he turned in my books and purse. I wasn't much help; I didn't know the names of those responsible or anything else about them, but when I described the mahu, they knew who I was talking about. And they knew who the girl with the ehu hair was, as well as two more girls; they were seniors who all hung out together. The principal would call them in to get their story and mete out punishment. It was a good meeting. It was settled, or so I thought.

By the end of the first week, I hadn't made any friends, although there were some friendly girls in my classes, but they had their own friends and cliques, and I had become a loner. Maybe I would find another loner to be friends with, I thought, and soon a friendly girl came up to me and started talking. She looked kind of rough around the edges, a tita, a tough girl one wouldn't want to mess with, but she was nice enough. We walked together talking, and she said she needed to go to the girls lavatory, so I went along. I waited outside the door, and in an instant I was grabbed by the mahu and several others. They grabbed me by the hair and by my arms and clothing and half-dragged, half-carried me into the girls' room. I got pummeled with fists, kicked, and felt my hair getting pulled out by the roots.

"You wanna tell on us? You t'ink you can tell on us and get away wit dat? You fakah!" they screamed over and over.

"Fight! Fight!" I could hear voices coming from outside the lavatory alerting others to the fight going on, the fight I never had a chance of winning but hadn't lost yet — I was still on my feet. While I was being held, someone sprayed hairspray into my face. They unloaded the can while I choked, unable to breathe, then they let go and ran, and I slumped to the concrete floor, gasping for air.

I was helped to the office and the school nurse did what she could to repair the visible damage. There were no bones broken, but I was bruised from head to toe, with lumps on my head and a split lip. I was pretty tough. Being a tomboy and around horses all my life, I could have held my own with the mahu and maybe one other, but not four.

The next day, Dad and I were back in the principal's office. The girls had been suspended for the time being. There was a discussion of whether to involve the police and file charges, but the principal and my dad knew we had to live there and that might just make matters worse. Probably between all four girls and the mahu, they were related to half the people in Waianae.

Teachers were scared of some of the students. For sure, teachers throughout Hawai'i had been threatened and intimidated by students who learned teachers would back down on punishment or turning them in if you threatened to burn their house down. We had one such student at my elementary school back in Kaneohe who terrorized all the kids in seventh grade. He grabbed me by my hair while I was sitting at my desk one day and yanked me backward to the floor. Everyone saw but quickly looked away as if they didn't see anything, for fear of being the next target. We knew how bullies could be, so it was decided I would go to a different school for one year and return the next since the girls, all seniors, would be gone from Waianae High.

I transferred to Nanaikapono School in Nanakuli for my sophomore year. Although it was considered a tough school in a poor neighborhood, Nanaikapono only went up to the tenth grade at that time, so I would enjoy being an upperclassman. I did like being at Nanaikapono. It was sure different from any Kaneohe school, though. There was a large community of Samoans, and it wasn't unusual to see fathers wearing lava-lava, colorful sarongs wrapped around the waist and flip-flops on their feet, holding their children's hands while walking them to and from school. I even made a friend right away. She was new to the school, too, and like me, an upperclassman in a school with grades all the way down to kindergarten. We were the big kids, and we all looked out for the little ones. My new friend had recently moved to Hawai'i from American Samoa. Her English was a little broken, but I understood her fine. Her name was Pipeline (Pi-pa-lee-nay), but I called her "pipeline," like the surfing beach.

Since moving to the west shore, I had no opportunity to be around horses, but I had little time to miss my old hobbies and friends because I had discovered a new love: surfing.

The following year, I returned to Waianae High, and after a year of surfing every day at Rest Camp, I was unmistakably a hard-core surfer with calcium-buildup surf knots on the tops of my feet and on my knees. My dark brown hair had blonde streaks bleached by the sun and salt and I sported a deep and even tan, except for a raw pink patch on top of my nose, which was in a constant cycle of burn and peel. I wouldn't use zinc oxide to protect my nose like those haole California surfers did. That would be kind of "pantie," a sissy, and I liked being thought of as tough but not in a mean way.

I enjoyed the reputation of being a dare devil early in life. Tamé would tell his friends not to "dare" his sister to do something because she would do it. He once bet a friend that I would put a live spider in my mouth if he dared me. His friend was freaked out when I gently collected a black and yellow garden spider off its web and popped it into my mouth, acted as if I swallowed it in a gulp, then opened my mouth and let the spider crawl out. I'd been doing that for years, but Tame´ always got a kick out of seeing the reaction on unsuspecting faces. Sometimes it would be a spider, sometimes baby frogs, and my favorite was holding a gecko or anole in my lips with their back legs and tail hanging out. My mother hated it, but to us kids it was hysterical, especially when Mom tried to whack me with whatever was handy, like a dishcloth or broom. I was always too quick for her.

I was flat-out quick in many ways, but most especially running. In seventh grade at Heeia Elementary in Kaneohe, I won the 880-yard run during the President Kennedy Physical Fitness Program in which all public schools participated. I was awarded a trophy and the title "fastest girl in school" along with a nickname: Speedy Gonzales.

My fame as a track star in intermediate school didn't follow me to Waianae, but once I became a good surfer, everyone was friendly to me. I had a lot of friends during my junior year at Waianae. Future world champion surfer, Rell Sunn, had graduated from high school and was well on her way to becoming the most famous woman surfer in the world, taking title after title, and went on for years relatively unchallenged until breast cancer cut her down in her prime. Rell and her family lived very close to Makaha Beach, and the Sunn girls were all good surfers. Rell's sister, Kula, was a year younger than I, and she would occasionally come to Rest Camp and surf. At the time, there were few female surfers, a sport dominated by men then. Kula was fun to be with, and I only saw her occasionally at school between classes. She called me "Mix." I was known at the time by my real name, Miyuki, which she had a hard time pronouncing. I was also known as "Miki," meaning eager and quick in Hawai'ian. I eventually dropped "Miyuki" altogether because it rhymed with "pukey," and I already had enough reasons for kids to tease me.

Other surfers called me a "goofy-footer," meaning I surfed with my right foot forward and my back to the wave on a left-to-right break. There were far fewer goofy-footers than left-footers. If someone was talking about me but didn't know my name, they could describe me as the hapa-haole goofy-footer at Rest Camp, and the other surfers would know who that was. Hapa haole meant half-Caucasian. It was evident in my looks that I was half-haole and half-Japanese. Local people could pretty much tell the difference between Asian mixtures or would ask me, "What nationality are you?" and I would answer, "Japanese haole." Eventually someone said that I was Eurasian, and I liked that so much better. The description was romantic and full of mystique.

I enjoyed my junior year at Waianae, and I never got beat up again in school, but there were still some pretty dangerous people around. One day, a huge explosion rocked the buildings at school and we were shocked, not knowing whether to dive under our desks or evacuate our school room. It turned out that some jilted boyfriend had thrown a hand grenade at the building where his former girlfriend was studying. At least that was the reason the kids were talking about, but officially the police never knew who did it.

One of my favorite classes was speech. The students were mixed class levels, with juniors, sophomores, and freshmen all together. For our first official speech to give in front of the class, I chose a lesson in surfing and brought my board to school. Everyone liked my demonstrations, descriptions, terms, and explanations of the sport or art of surfing. Much to my chagrin, a freshman student took an interest in me and started bugging me to go out with him. He loved hapa-haole girls, he would say to anyone who would listen. He said I was the most beautiful girl he'd ever seen. As nice as could be, I lied and told him that I didn't date. He started showing up at Rest Camp, but since he didn't have a surfboard, I could avoid him by staying out in the water.

He was as persistent as I was resistant. I hated it when boys glommed on to me.

On day he showed up in a car driven by a friend. They stopped in front of my house and started calling me out to go "car surfing" with them. I watched from inside the house with my sisters as this pesky suitor got on top of the roof of the car. The driver started driving up and down the street with him standing on top. The car picked up speed and the driver suddenly slammed on the brakes, sending my classmate tumbling off the roof and onto the pavement, hitting it hard and rolling. It happened right in front of our house. He didn't move right away, and though I was horrified, I didn't go outside to help. These people had to be hopped up on drugs — normal people don't do this, I thought. Eventually, my classmate began to move, and the driver of the car helped him up and back into the front seat, and they drove away.

That was the last time I saw him. He never returned to class, or if he did, I didn't see him, and he stopped bothering me. Almost four years later, shortly after I was married to my first husband and living in Kailua on the windward side of O'ahu, there was a girl murdered in Waianae, her body found buried in the sand near Makaha. The name of the murderer was familiar.

"Holy crap," I told my then husband. "This guy was my classmate at Waianae High. He was crazy and hounded me for the longest time to go out with him."

"Lucky you didn't," he said. We looked at the murdered hapa-haole girl's face on the front page of the paper. "She looks just like you."

The beach at Rest Camp had a swimming area in part of Pokai Bay, and then a rock wall jutted out from the beach, a demarcation point separating the swimming beach from the surfing one. A few hundred yards out from the surfing beach, a steel rod stuck up, marking the edge of the reef. You could always count on Rest Camp having surfable waves when the ocean hit that reef, even though they might be only a foot high. Normally during the winter months, the waves there would be two to four feet, but when the surf was up everywhere, Rest Camp would have big waves too, and six-to-eight footers weren't unusual.

When I first started surfing, my friend Mavis and I would borrow a couple of boards and paddle out to the edge of the reef and just sit straddling the boards with our legs dangling in the water. We'd practice standing up and tried to keep our balance, which wasn't easy to do. Then we'd try to step over and change boards, but we always ended up in the water. Eventually, I got my own surfboard, a nine foot, eight inch Dewey Weber, and spent every minute I could catching waves. I always kept a big glob of paraffin in my mouth, chewing it like gum; I never knew when I might have a slick spot on the surface of my board until I slipped and almost wiped out, so I always kept some handy — and in my mouth was pretty handy. It wasn't unusual for someone to ask, "Eh, you got wax?" and I'd toss them the wad I'd been chewing, which they would use and throw back unless I told them to keep it.

"Keep um. I going home," I would say, and they would pop it in their mouth and chew.

Sometimes there would be a lull in sets, and we would just talk story until we heard someone shout the word that would set us in motion: "Outside!"

The waves were building and would break further out than where we were sitting, so we would paddle vigorously to get "outside."

Mavis soon moved away, and I was a loner again. Every day after school, I'd still go to Rest Camp, where I was usually the only girl surfing and sometimes the only surfer period. But as long as there were waves to catch, I'd be catching them.

On weekends and holidays, Rest Camp would fill up with active and retired military and their families. They would rent cabins for the weekend, and the lifeguard station rented them beach toys and surfboards. But the huge surfboards they rented were difficult to surf on unless you had a little experience. The heavy rental boards we called "planks" were easily identified by their mustard yellow color with red stripes and lettering. Novices would always fall off many times until they got the hang of it, and it was kind of hazardous to be in the water when there were a lot of learners. Since I lived there and could surf anytime, I would often stay on the beach out of harm's way and watch people have fun mastering the thrilling sport.

I pretty much knew all the lifeguards and the local boys who hung out at the beach. The regular surfers looked out for me as if I was a younger sister, and it was a real thrill when famous surfers came to the beach and we got to hang out with them. Jeff Hakman of Quiksilver surf clothing fame came to Rest Camp. I was a huge fan, but he was always surrounded by groupies, and I was too timid to cut through his adoring crowd so I never even got to meet him. Buffalo Keaulana and Rabbit Kekai, legends from world-famous Makaha Beach, visited sometimes, too.

Buffalo taught me to tandem surf. First we practiced on the sand. He would lift me up and turn me so I was up on his shoulder or straight over his head doing my best to look like a graceful ballet dancer or gymnast, arms stretched out as if I was flying and my legs straight back, stiff, with toes pointed. We practiced other poses: sitting on his shoulder with my arms out and my legs crossed, toes pointed down, and standing on his knee leaning forward like a hood ornament, safely held by Buffalo's strong arms. He did all the work; all I had to do was look graceful. Not easy for a girl with two left feet and no sense of rhythm. My sisters were the graceful ones in our family having taken hula lessons as children but I had mastered dork.

After I got the hang of being swung up onto Buffalo's shoulders on dry land, we did it for real. We paddled out to where the waves were building. "This one," he said, and we both went prone on the board. He paddled a couple of times, and I felt the momentum of the wave propelling the board forward, and we both stood up. Buffalo reached around me, his right arm around my left side and his left on my right, and lifted and spun me around at the same time. I was flying, looking straight ahead and seeing all the people on the beach who were watching the spectacle of a famous surfer and a spindly little ballerina. I did my best to look good for Buffalo.

"Just pretend you're flying," he said, but I didn't have to pretend. It was as close to flying as letting go of the reins on a galloping horse and feeling the wind blow through my hair.

We went back again and again, and I got to do all the poses we had rehearsed. Every ride was perfect. Buffalo never wavered or misstepped. If anyone wanted to see us end up in the water from a wipeout, they were disappointed. Back on the beach, I felt like a celebrity. People asked how long I'd been surfing tandem. When I told them it was the first time, they didn't believe me but others talked about me being a really good surfer, which explained my ease and confidence on the water. I told them Buffalo did everything, I just went along for the ride, and Buffalo said it was easy because I was "as light as a piece of cardboard."

One day, probably a Saturday or Sunday because the beach was crowded, there were several of us local surfers sitting on our boards and talking story. There was little wave action, and we were hoping the surf would pick up. All of a sudden, there was a great commotion on the beach; people were jumping up and running to the edge of the water. They were shouting and gesturing to us, but I didn't understand what they were saying. I looked around. Another surfer looked at me and shrugged. He didn't know what they were saying either, but it became clear they were calling us into the beach. I got on my knees and started paddling in to shore, and then I heard what they were saying: "Sharks! Sharks!" and "Come In! Hurry!"

We were used to seeing an occasional shark come into Pokai Bay, and I'd encountered them diving all my life. I wouldn't panic at seeing a shark but always respected the potential for danger and so exercised caution. It was prudent to leave the water, and I calmly paddled to shore. Then I noticed the other surfers had paddled over the reef and were heading toward the shallow water, while I was paddling by myself in deep water but a straight shot to the beach. People were still yelling, and the military police, the MPs, ran to the water's edge. That's when I saw sharks swimming directly beneath me, dozens of them, and at the time, it seemed as if it were hundreds of them. It was like a solid mass of sharks and they were directly beneath me. I had a horrible thought: What if they come up from under and capsize me?

I paddled harder, trying not to look at the sharks zipping by underneath, but this was some kind of phenomenon. You see small hammerheads swimming in large schools in Hawai'i, but these sharks were about four feet long. They were not in a feeding frenzy, just moving in a very large school, but I still didn't want to fall into the water in case they might decide to start feeding. I saw black tips on their dorsals — they were Reef Black Tips, not known to be maneaters, but seeing so many of them just a few inches below me was very unnerving. I was a few feet from shore when the MPs jumped in and grabbed me out of the water, saving me from what they imagined would have been a horrible death. It would be a great story to take back to the mainland, the hero MPs who saved the surfer's life. It was a great story for me too, and I've repeated it many times over my lifetime.

My life as a blissful, carefree surfer changed when my grandmother from Japan, my Obaachan, got sick with cancer. She came to live with us, and I was needed at home to help my mother. I still got to surf every day but had to go home early to help prepare dinner or whatever Mom needed us kids to do. She would send my younger brother, Tad, to call me in when it was time for me to go home. He would stand on the beach waving his arms trying to get my attention, but I would pretend not to see him, thinking, "One more, one more wave and I'll surf it to shore." If the wind was right, I could hear him saying, "Mom says NOW!" but I was never in a hurry to go in. Then something happened that cured me of dragging my feet, literally. My brother went to the lifeguard and asked him to call me on the loudspeaker and he did. "Miyuki, come out of the water! Your mother wants you to go home, cook rice!"

Oh, my gosh. How humiliating. But it worked. "Go home, cook rice!" became a popular saying. The lifeguards teased me with it, and then it spread to the surfers, who would playfully tell others to "beat it — go home, cook rice."

Surfing etiquette dictates that you don't "grab" a wave from someone else. As the swell approaches, you look to see if someone is moving into position to take the wave, and you let them have it provided that it's not so crowded where it becomes a free-for-all, and you gotta take whatever you can get. There weren't many regular surfers at Rest Camp, and we would defer to the best surfers to get the third (last and biggest) wave of the set. So you let others go, and like a machine another would come that you could have to yourself. When several would catch the same wave we would sing, "Hey! You! Get off of my wave. Don't hang around 'cause two's a crowd on my wave!"

One day a really good haole showed up with his small and nimble hot dogging board, the kind that was gaining popularity at the time. The trend began in California but hadn't yet spread throughout Hawai'i. This blond surfer was good, and with his fast hot-dog style was "shredding" the waves with his radical maneuvers. He was so good that back then I might have said he was "bitchin." He wasn't friendly, though; he didn't smile or acknowledge the other surfers. In fact, we had never seen a more arrogant self-centered haole on our beach before. He gave no courtesy to others and grabbed whatever wave he wanted. He "kicked out" — quit the wave early to return to catch waves as they broke, the "sweet spot" of surfing.

I was in awe of his skill. It was as if the surfboard was an extension of his feet, which he hardly moved; whereas, we had to walk back and forth on our long boards to create forward momentum or step back to slow down and "stall" the board to turn and to stop.

This surfer didn't like me, maybe it was just because I was a girl. He made an effort to get on my waves and cut in front of me so I would back off. But when he cut in front of me, grabbed the nose of my board and actually pushed me off the swell and swore at me, there was no mistaking: this was on purpose. He was deliberately being a bully. I was intimated and wanted to go in, so I picked up a small wave to ride in on when he came shooting toward me with the intention of psyching me out by cutting away at the last second. But he lost control and his board hit mine.

"You fucking cunt!" he screamed at me. His board wasn't even damaged, but mine had a ding that broke through the outer fiberglass layers and into the foam, which would require repair before I could use it again. The exposed foam would suck up water like a sponge if it didn't get fixed.

Others saw what had happened, and they also witnessed the bullying that had been going on. The surfer was told to leave if he knew what was good for him. He left the camp. He wasn't military, so he didn't even belong on base. He had come from Kailua on the windward side and normally surfed near his home or the Honolulu spots such as Black Point off of Diamond Head or wherever the surf was up. I later asked my brother and his friends how they found out "his story" and they told me that he was real talkative while he was getting the shit beat out of him.

My brothers never got into surfing, but they were frequently out on the ocean fishing or diving. My dad built his own sampan, and every weekend and day off, he and my brothers and sometimes even my sisters would go fishing and bring home something exciting. The CB radio would crackle at our house, and Dad or a brother would announce their catch and give an estimated time of arrival to be met at the pier. As the boat came in, we could see the flags flying that represented the catch on board: blue for marlin, yellow for mahimahi, orange for ono (wahoo), green for aku (bluefin tuna), white for ahi (yellowfin tuna). Shark is a red flag but not considered one of the five big-game fish. Once my dad came into the harbor with an upside-down broom flying, signaling he had gotten a "clean sweep" — at least one of each of the five big-game varieties. They laid the fish on the pier. The largest was an ahi, yellowfin tuna, the prime sashimi fish that would fetch a lot of money if sold; it was approximately fifty pounds. There was one male and one female mahi-mahi. The males are very identifiable by the large forehead. Then there were a couple of large ono and several bluefin tuna or aku, and one striped marlin, making up the five big-game species. Clean sweeps are not common, and my dad's fishing prowess was legendary. My big brother, Tamé, would become a popular big-game fisherman on the Big Island of Hawai'i, catching over 500 marlins in his charter fishing career.

I was into diving but not so much fishing because I got extremely seasick, something I would eventually get over with the help of a transdermal patch behind my ear. But before that, the times I went fishing or went along to help on the charter boats would inevitably include a bout of hanging over the side "losing my cookies" or "going to Eurrrrrope" in a "Buuuuick" visiting "Raaaaalph" and "traveling by rail" and, of course, "chumming." Once, I heaved and heaved until bright yellow egg yolk-looking stuff came out and scared the heck out of me. My brother told me it was bile from my liver and that shocked me even more. He asked if I'd ever heard of throwing up your socks. I hadn't, so he told me it was a sailors' expression, that they wore yellow socks hidden by the trousers of their stark white uniforms. I don't know if that's true, but it sure seemed a good description of what I was going through. My brother said I would get used to it if I went out more frequently, but I still got sick. The droning of the engine and smell of diesel along with the motion of the boat rocking up, down, and over the swells would get me every time. Since I'm an expert on seasickness, I have a little advice for anyone who gets sick on a fishing boat: DO NOT — I repeat, DO NOT — go below to the head to throw up. A droning engine, the smell of diesel fuel, and the rocking, cramped quarters and smell of a chemical toilet will make your vomiting adventure that much worse.

Hooking up a fish makes it all worthwhile, however. I always found it thrilling to see a marlin following the lure or live bait. I would scamper up the rungs of the tuna tower and watch from high above. My brother would rig the line to an outrigger pole that held the line high out of the way of other lines in the water. He would gather up the slack from the tip of the outrigger and pull it up close to the pole, fastening it with a rubber band. As the marlin followed the live tuna, you could see the rubber band pulling as the bait panicked to get away. When the marlin took the bait, the rubber band would snap, and the line would feed out as the marlin worked the fish or lure down into its throat. My brother would count off the seconds, giving the marlin time to swallow the bait, and then yell, "Hit it," gunning the throttle to set the hook and allow the fight to begin.

My brother called it "Chinese fire drill." He was the king of multitasking. He ordered the designated fisherman to sit in the fight chair and then carried the rod and reel with marlin attached to the chair and set the butt of the rod into a swivel cup that gave the rod up-and-down stability. A special seat belt was attached to the chair and clipped to each side of the giant reel so the angler could use his back muscles to pull up on the rod. All the remaining poles with lines in the water would be "cleared" and nothing was left on the back deck except a fight between a man or woman and a very large fish.

"Pull up and crank down, pull up and crank down," my brother would instruct. A large marlin would have tremendous pull on the line, and water weighting the long lengths of suji (fishing line) put even more pressure on the pull of the fish. Marlin are the biggest and arguably the most exciting to catch. Whether you're holding the pole or someone else is, it's a thrill to see a marlin jump out of the water. Most times when you hook up you don't know what you have on the other end, so when the fish jumps and shows itself is the first indication of how large your fish is, what it is, and how much of a battle it might be to reel in. The largest marlin ever caught with a rod and reel was off the coast of Hawai'i, weighing in excess of 1,800 pounds.

Hawai'i has several big fishing tournaments each year, and some are combined with fish management and conservation projects. Marlin are caught, data is recorded, and the fish are then tagged and released.

Chapter 13

Harleys, FairTax and Joe the Plumber

By early May 2009 I was really immersing myself in the role of FairTax supporter and community organizer. I attended meetings throughout Oklahoma's District 2 and across the state lines into Missouri and Arkansas, sometimes as a speaker and sometimes to learn about issues and get familiar with the organizations and groups trying to bring sanity back to government, both local and national.

Americans for Prosperity (AFP) is a Washington, D.C.—based political advocacy group promoting economic policy that supports business and restrains governmental regulation along with promoting conservative values. Whenever their "Hands Off My Healthcare" caravans were in my area (Kansas, Missouri, and Oklahoma) I made it a point to be there to support them.

American Majority (http://americanmajority.org) is a nonprofit organization that provides training to people who desire to become effective community activists or candidates for local office. I attended an activists training meeting in Tulsa, and there was a standing-room-only crowd. I was able to put many faces to names and e-mail addresses that I had compiled since becoming a community organizer and political activist. I was thrilled to find a group of patriots from my neighboring town of Grove. They had formed a group called Get America Back (www.getamericaback.com), or GAB. I knew there was an active group of patriots in Grove, but until the meet up in Tulsa I didn't know who they were or how to reach them. I became a regular member after being a guest speaker representing FairTax and reporting updates on other issues I was involved with. The group met biweekly and drove positive conservative change in a town and a county with a long history of Democrat-run cronyism politics.

On July 13, 2009, Fred and I donned our FairTax T-shirts and rode "Ikaika" (Hawai'ian for powerful), Fred's 2003 100th-year anniversary

Harley to Springfield, Missouri. There we met Carol and Mike McLean, founders of Grass Roots Freedom Riders for FairTax. Mike had driven his FairTax Harley, and Carol followed in their support vehicle all the way from their home in North Carolina. We were headed to Columbia, Missouri, for what would be the largest FairTax rally west of the Mississippi.

Carol's car was packed full of FairTax promotional material, portable booth and tent materials, folding chairs — everything needed to support many days on the road and for the big event at the fairgrounds in Columbia. She moved stuff out of the front passenger seat so I could ride with her and we could talk story and get to know each other. Mike zip-tied FairTax flags to Ikaika, and then we started our long trek to Columbia, Fred and Mike riding side by side, police bike style, as we followed.

I was familiar with the route, having traveled to Missouri's capital, Jefferson City, numerous times in my capacity as director of sales and marketing for a hotel in Joplin. There's beautiful countryside along the secondary highways, and our route would take us through spectacular scenery of Lake of the Ozarks, one of Missouri's abundant recreational lakes. The little towns along the way were pretty unremarkable, and we drove through relatively unnoticed. But one town, Camdenton, stood out. While we were stopped at a red light, Mike got some thumbs-up signs and shout-outs for his FairTax bike. Of course, that made us all feel good to know there were supporters and people who actually knew about the legislation or plan.

I would remember I liked Camdenton when, three months later, I attended their September 17th Tea Party rally on invitation to present Get Out of Our House (GOOOH), the plan to replace all 435 members of Congress with representatives chosen by their peers and not be beholden to the money powers and lobbyists. I handed out GOOOH flyers to approximately 200 people at the rally and was interviewed by a local conservative radio show. I also made some good and lasting friendships with the Camdenton Tea Party leadership, although there are those who believe Obama was born in Hawai'i and closed their mind to any discussion to the contrary.

We arrived at the Boone County fairgrounds while the event was still being set up. Mike and Carol unloaded their car and began putting up the Grassroots Riders for FairTax booth just outside the main convention hall. I went into the building to volunteer my services and was assigned a post at one of the admission gates at the parking lot. My duty was to check for attendees without pre-registered badges and direct them to one of the volunteers with a computer to get them registered. It was remarkable to me that the number of pre-registers far outnumbered the walk-ins.

Fred stayed with me and ran errands for those of us working a stationary position. We missed some of the beginning part of the program but did listen to some of the speakers — Herman Cain who gave the keynote speech, Congressman Linder, and Neal Boortz. When Linder and Boortz went to their booth to sell FairTax books, I got my copy out of Ikaika's saddlebag, and both Linder and Boortz autographed it for me. I later raffled the book off at a Route 66 Tea Party along with a T-shirt signed by Joe the Plumber, who became a conservative icon when he confronted Obama on his socialist agenda during the 2008 presidential campaign.

An estimated 7,000 showed up for the event, perhaps more since people were coming and going for the all-day event. Fred and I hung out with Mike and Carol at their booth, where we met fellow biker Jerry Nielson of the Wisconsin chapter of Grassroots Freedom Riders. Carol Chouinard from Tulsa introduced me to another area FairTaxer, Calvin Wilkins from Vinita, Oklahoma, and we became fast friends and allies, promoting both FairTax and GOOOH. Calvin would accompany me to many political events and would eventually become one of the best supporters of the Miki Booth for Congress campaign.

At the close of the Midwest rally, Fred and I helped the McLeans break down their booth and load the remaining supplies into the car, and we headed for our hotel. We checked in, then walked across the parking lot to a restaurant to eat and have some beers. We all hit it off very well. Harleys and FairTax were the common interests that bound us together as good friends, which we are still.

We were returning from dinner and noticed Joe "the Plumber" Wurzelbacher at the porte cochere of our hotel, so we went over to meet him. He recognized Carol as the FairTax "biker chick" with the "great arms" and joked and visited with us all. I whined that I didn't get a chance to have him autograph the souvenir T-shirt I'd gotten at the rally, so he whipped out a felt marker and wrote on a back shoulder of the FairTax shirt I was wearing. He was so friendly and approachable. It was nice to know he had not let his rise to fame for exposing Obama's socialist agenda change him from being regular middle-class folk like us. He wanted to check out Mike's FairTax bike, so he got on and we gathered around for photos. Fred snapped a picture of Joe and I making the Hawaiian shaka "hang loose" sign. Joe really liked Hawai'i, and Fred got to talk about his work as a "solo-bike" officer in Honolulu escorting dignitaries like President George H. W. Bush, Prince Charles, Ferdinand and Imelda Marcos, Japanese royalty, and others. As we took the elevator to our floor, we commented on how cool Joe was and how lucky we were to run into him.

The following day we headed home; Jerry Nielsen went in one direction, back to Wisconsin, and Fred, I, and the McLeans headed in the opposite direction. At Jefferson City, Mike and Carol peeled off onto a connecting highway, and Fred and I stopped to take pictures of the Missouri Capitol.

Chapter 14

GOOOH Get Out Of Our House

July 2009 was filled with activity stemming from the Fourth of July Route 66 Tea Party on the first Saturday of the month. Only half the number of people who attended the April 15th rally attended. Approximately 100 people came and enjoyed the music and program. There was a speaker for FairTax, and local medical professionals spoke out against Obamacare and about the resulting hardships placed on doctors, hospitals, and all medical professionals. I spoke on behalf of GOOOH, which I'd only recently learned about. The plan is truly genius. Designed by Tim Cox, it's a system to revolutionize the way we select our U.S. representatives. Tim's bio is very impressive. He had worked almost twenty-five years developing complex computer systems. He created software for a spy satellite, designed software for credit card readers in gas pumps, and created innovative systems for Dell, one of the world's largest computer companies.

Fed up with the politicians who have taken over government, Tim created a system designed to bypass the two parties, sever all ties with special-interest money, replace career politicians, and hold elected officials accountable. GOOOH (pronounced "go") is a nonpartisan system that will allow you and your neighbors to choose the person who can best represent your district. It allows We the People to select true representatives, not be forced to choose between a Democrat and a Republican. GOOOH is a way to select representatives the way our founding fathers intended. It allows you to define your platform, discuss topics of importance with your peers, and if selected, to truly represent your district — not lobbyists, special interest groups, or a political party.

The GOOOH process allows Americans of every political leaning to participate in the selection of their district's representative while being considered themselves. Through GOOOH's Candidate Selection

Sessions you and your peers will select the candidate in your district who best represents your district's views. Even if you don't want to become your district's representative, you can participate in the process and have a direct say in who is chosen to represent your district. GOOOH will fund a single national campaign to promote the 435 candidates (one from each district) who are selected to run against the party politicians. Because GOOOH is a process for selecting represent-tatives (not an agenda-based party platform), it would be expected that a person left of center would be selected in San Francisco and one right of center in Colorado Springs — but it will be up to the GOOOH members in each district to decide.

For GOOOH to succeed, 500,000 participants are needed. A base of supporters will continually build until the critical mass is met, at which time the effort to have the GOOOH party added to the ballot in all fifty states and selection of the 435 nominees will begin. There are many variables involved in reaching the level of support needed, but we believe it is only a matter of time. The 2012 elections may be that time.

Abraham Lincoln said, "We the People are the rightful masters of both Congress and the courts, not to overthrow the Constitution but to overthrow the men who pervert the Constitution." I took these words to heart. Tea Party members were fed up with both parties, fed up with career politicians, and fed up with corruption and cronyism. The Constitution was being shredded. Our founding fathers were turning over in their graves. GOOOH and FairTax were an excellent fit, and I represented both when speaking at Tea Parties and other patriotic events. I believed these two organizations would save our country, and as with my commitment to FairTax, I e-mailed Tim Cox and asked, "What can I do?" He responded immediately, and within a few days I had a supply of brochures and books to take to meetings and rallies. Three weeks later, Tim called to say he was coming to Stillwater, Okla-homa, for his son's baseball tournament. We arranged a meeting place and sent out e-mail messages to others in the area interested in GOOOH. I called Billy Harrington, Oklahoma State Director of FairTax, and he was eager to meet Tim and learn more about the plan. Tim was familiar with FairTax and, in fact, included it in the candidate questionnaire.

Not long after I met Tim, he called to tell me about someone who had just learned of GOOOH and wanted to get more involved. Coincidentally, this new supporter lived only minutes away from Tim, and they got together for a meeting that night. The new contact was Dan Byfield of American Stewards of Liberty and the American Land Foundation. These freedom organizations under Dan Byfield's watch were instrumental in getting the Trans-Texas Corridor (TTC) shut down. This superhighway proposed from Mexico to Canada included the stealing of private land by the government through eminent domain.

Dan was going to the Tenth Annual Freedom 21 National Conference in Midwest City, Oklahoma, the following day and Tim asked if I would be able to meet him there to bring a case of GOOOH books and flyers so he wouldn't have to carry them on his flight. I told him "no problem" and arranged to pick Dan up at the Oklahoma City airport and get him to the conference to speak. Dan did not want me going out of my way to pick him up and insisted he could take a cab or a shuttle from the airport to Midwest City, but I said I was going that way anyway. As we drove to the conference, Dan asked how far out of my way I went to pick him up. I told the truth: "three and a half hours."

"What!" he was incredulous. I laughed.

"Tim asked me to meet you at the conference, and I said I would. Since I was coming to town anyway, I'd just swing by the airport for you." We had a laugh and hit it off really well. Besides having so much in common, freedom fighting and GOOOH, I found out that Dan and his wife also raise chickens for fresh eggs and so discussed some of the challenges faced with raising fowl.

Dan got me registered at the conference, and we found his designated table and chairs from where we could watch the program, "The Growing American Tyranny and How to Stop It." It was the last day of the conference, but some of the best speakers were scheduled, including Dan, who would talk about "coordination," networking with local government and private landowners to protect people against the TTC.

Randy Brogdon, one of our Oklahoma State senators, presented "America, we have a problem: How to Restore America to Constitutional Principles." After his speech, I approached Randy and his wife and gave them a GOOOH book. I was supporting him for governor in the mid-term election and had not met him in person, so I introduced myself and we would run into one another at rallies and Tea Party events many times over the next eleven months leading up to the Republican primary. Each time I saw him, he would give me a firm handshake, acknowledging my efforts promoting FairTax, GOOOH, and eventually my decision to run for Congress. He was pleased to learn that I was challenging Democrat Dan Boren for the U.S. House seat, and I thought for sure Randy would be our next governor because of the huge Tea Party support for him in our state. Before the Republican primary, I bowed out of the congressional race to support another candidate, and Randy would lose the primary to Rep. Mary Fallin — a RINO (Republican in name only) in the eyes of the Oklahoma Tea Party movement.

Another conservative star in our state house of representatives, Charles Key, spoke about the State Sovereignty Movement and taking back the constitutional powers of the states. Rep. Key was always in great demand to address Tea Party groups, and although I didn't get to meet him at the Freedom 21 Conference, Dan was able to get Tim's book to him before he was hustled off to an "Oklahomans-only meeting." I would have occasion to talk to Rep. Key at other patriotic venues, one being the Camdenton, Missouri Tea Party rally where I presented him with Tim Cox's GOOOH book. I knew he had been given one by Dan, but he looked at the copy I gave him and said he didn't recognize it. When I asked him several months later for feedback, he told me he hadn't read it yet and gave me the bum's rush.

Dan gave his presentation emphasizing the success of "coordination," and used the last fifteen to twenty minutes telling everyone about GOOOH. Dan had presumed I would do the presentation since I'd been doing it for the past several months by then, but I begged off. Dan was a far better speaker, and I was very intimidated to share a platform with such notable conservative leaders as Larry Pratt, executive director of Gun Owners of America; Chuck Baldwin, Constitution Party 2008 presidential candidate; Tom DeWeese, president of the American Policy Center and one of the nation's leading advocates of individual liberty, free enterprise, and property rights; and, of course, Dan.

He asked me to stand and be recognized so everyone would know to come see me for more information on the plan or to buy books. Dan did an awesome job of presenting GOOOH after just an evening of talking with Tim. When he concluded, it was time for a break, and we were swamped with people wanting to know more about GOOOH. We sold out of books, depleted our brochure supply and had only some business cards left over. I left a short time later for the three-and-a-half-hour drive home. When Dan called me the following day to say he was safely back home, he told me that many of the people who talked to him after I'd left said they felt there was some hope, that through GOOOH we had a chance of saving our country.

Three days later, on August 18, Rep. Dan Boren held a town hall meeting in Pryor, Oklahoma, which I attended. It was the third and last one for the day. There looked to be 350 to 400 people at the meeting, and I learned later that the earlier two were well attended also, anywhere from 300 to 500 of Boren's constituents. Days of e-mailing and phone trees to get people to call Boren's office to say, "Kill the Obamacare bill" paid off, and Boren announced he would vote against the bill. He had voted against the "cap and tax" bill earlier, but getting him to do it had been like pulling teeth. In the first many calls I had made, Boren's aide told me he would vote for it. But after an avalanche of phone calls organized by the many Tea Party groups, the aide's stance changed to, "He's leaning toward not voting for it."

"Wrong answer!" I hollered into the phone. "When I call you tomorrow I want the right answer, and that is he will vote NO on cap and tax!" I wasn't being any harsher than he had been arrogant and cocky in earlier phone calls I had made to the D.C. office. It was a common complaint among conservative constituents of Oklahoma's District 2. Boren didn't respond to letters and inquiries in a timely manner or would send a form letter rarely addressing the topic in question, but we were no longer going to sit down and be quiet. We made our voice heard. It worked. The Tea Party movement had crippled the phone lines at the Capitol switchboard. The people had spoken, and cap and tax went down in flames.

After Boren announced he would not vote for Obamacare, he scheduled the town hall meetings, and we speculated that he thought he would get a warm reception for siding with We the People. That was not to be, however. The majority of the people there were part of the "sleeping giant" that had been awakened and wanted answers to what in the world was going on in Washington. We wanted to hold our representatives accountable. Dan Boren had voted 98 percent of the time with Nancy Pelosi and his party. Boren introduced his staff and guests and made opening remarks as people lined up at both microphones on either side of the large room. I wanted to speak too, but didn't know how it worked until I saw long lines at the mics and hurried to get in line. Boren announced that he would stay for the full two hours so as many people as possible would get to ask questions. He specifically stated that he would not leave until 5:00 p.m. The questioning began. It was a referendum on Nancy Pelosi, Harry Reid, and Obama, the out-of-control spending that Boren had historically voted for, the czars, the debt, the deficit, taking over car companies, ACORN, and on and on. Much emphasis was put on Obamacare regardless of the fact that Boren said he wouldn't vote for it; he hadn't said a word against the legislation — he hadn't represented us at all. Someone asked him if he had voted for Nancy Pelosi, and he answered "yes." (He had voted for her twice.) When asked why, he said, "Because she was the only Democrat running." Well, at least he was truthful, but you could have heard the proverbial pin drop.

I finally got to the mic. I didn't have a question; I just wanted to make a point. Remembering how I got slammed in the earlier town hall meeting for not asking a question, I tried to stay within the two-minute time limit and get my point across before I was shouted down with, "What's your question?!"

Boren: *"Yes, ma'am?"*
Me: *"My name is Miki Booth and I'm from Wyandotte, Oklahoma. I'm from Hawai'i and I'm a community organizer."* (raucus laughter and "Go, Miki!")
Boren: *"Are you running for president?"* (laughter)
Me: *"No, actually I'm running against you, but I'll tell you about that later."* (laughter)
Boren: *"Okay."*
Me: *"I brought a visual aid."* (holding up a Hawai'ian phone book)
Boren: *"Okay."*
Me: *"It's a Hawai'ian Yellow Pages book. If it were bigger, it might represent the thousands of pages of the healthcare bill. In Hawai'i there are more lawyers than any other profession. This largest color-coded section represents attorneys and this next-largest section is restaurants. The third section is dentists and the smallest section, this slimmest section, is doctors. I think this is a good representation of the reason we left Hawai'i, our family left Hawai'i and moved here. We really love living in Oklahoma because we enjoy a lot more freedoms here that we didn't have in Hawai'i. Like, one thing I really like is shooting a gun, and the cops don't show up. (laughter) Hawai'i is such a liberal state, a very blue state — you would like it there. (laughter) I know you said you are voting*

against the healthcare bill, and I'm gonna ask you to take my message back to Washington to kill the bill and start over with tort reform: one issue, one bill. (applause) And then work on fixing Medicare, again one issue, one bill. (applause) And work on fixing Medicaid. One issue, one bill. (applause) I'd like to take this opportunity to let everyone know that since they are so ticked off with Nancy Pelosi, they have a way of telling her to 'get out of our House' by going to GOOOH.com and entering the system, and they can also run against Dan and if selected they can go on the ballot as the GOOOH candidate. Thank you."

Boren: *"Thank you."*

There is a video of this exchange on YouTube and a link on mikibooth.com. At the end of the video are these wise words in a letter sent from George Washington to Edward Carrington on May 1, 1796: "It is on great occasions only, and after time has been given for cool and deliberate reflection, that the real voice of the people can be known."

Toward the close of the meeting, there were still many people lined up at the microphones, and we were dismayed to hear that Boren had to leave early because of babysitter issues at home. We were all taken aback, especially because he had specifically stated that he would stay for the entire two hours. I looked around to see raised eyebrows and hear murmurs of "typical" and "Why am I not surprised?"

As hundreds of people filed out of the convention center, I handed out GOOOH brochures, and they were readily taken. Charlie Woltz, my Tea Party compadre who had played Thomas Paine at our first Route 66 Tea Party, got a stack from me and covered the other door. Most everyone seemed pleased to receive a brochure, but it's always the few who are hateful, rude, or have bad vibes who stick in my memory. I distinctly remember one here, a man who glared at me and, when I tried to hand him a brochure, said, "Not in that shirt!"

I looked down. I was wearing a red T-shirt that read:

PALINTOLOGIST
Pronunciation: "pA-lin-'ta-la-jist"
Sarah Palin voter who shares her Conservative values,
Maverick attitude and American style

A television reporter asked me for an interview, and I gave Charlie my stack of GOOOH brochures and went back inside the building to talk to a Channel 2 Tulsa reporter. The interview aired that evening, and others said they saw it, and it was a good interview, but I never got to see it. Government regulations dictate that my local news come from across state lines. As a subscriber to DISH satellite I called to ask them why this is especially since I pay extra for local channels. I was told that Congress is the culprit that passed legislation controlling satellite viewing areas so I'm stuck watching Missouri news and politics instead of my state of residence, Oklahoma.

In August of 2009 during the recess of the legislative session, town hall meetings were being held across the country. Also known as "recess rallies," members of Congress and the senate were being grilled by Tea Partiers. Unlike past town hall meetings that would number from a few to a few dozen, the 2009 meetings were attended by hundreds of people demanding answers — what on earth was going on in Washington DC? Video clips of some of these rallies were airing on national TV. Besides just Tea Partiers, perhaps "Constitutional Conservatives" would better describe the majority of people showing up at town halls to question their representatives. We were angry.

"You've awakened a sleeping giant," said Katy Abram to Sen. Arlen Specter, (D), PA. Katy is one of many brave women to capture the hearts of Americans upholding and defending the Constitution of the United States — the rule of law. She is now an iconic figure leading the grassroots movement completely removed from any political party. It was happening everywhere. Our voices were finally being heard, but we were being attacked at every turn. The pro-Obama and progressive forces were an ever-growing army of opposition to the conservative voices coming from the grassroots. Even the Republican establishment didn't know what to make of us and watched us cautiously.

I get very angry at Karl Rove, Republican pundit and former political advisor to George W. Bush. Before the presidential election, I agreed with him on many issues but when he went after Christine O'Donnell, Tea Party-backed winner of the Delaware Republican primary for the U.S. Senate, he destroyed our chance to elect a Constitutional Conservative and lost all credibility with the Tea Party movement. Rove joined the left in a vicious smear campaign against O'Donnell as did the Republican establishment resulting in losing to Democrat Chris Coons, socialist, backer of Obamacare and LGBT (lesbian, gay, bisexual and transgender) activist. Rove appears frequently on FOX News as a political hack as far as many of us Tea Party people are concerned. Not only does he not have a clue about what we are really about, he's drawn a line in the sand between the GOP establishment and the grassroots conservative movement.

Rove is not alone. Few commentators on FOX News understand what is really going on, and they invite people like Dick Armey of FreedomWorks to speak on behalf of the Tea Party movement, but Armey does not represent the majority of the grassroots. His true nature was revealed when his organization did not acknowledge or promote Independents or Constitutional Party candidates.

FreedomWorks is no different from any of the other Republican "umbrella" organizations co-opting the grassroots. When FreedomWorks published its list of preferred Tea Party candidates to support, Marco Rubio was on the list and easily won the Florida U.S. Senate seat and continues his meteoric rise within the establishment. He's now being touted as a potential vice president while the GOP and his handlers completely ignore the fact that Marco's parents were not American citizens when he was born. In fact, his father never sought American citizenship until Marco was four years old. All due respect, Marco may be a "native-born citizen" but he is not a "natural-born citizen" and, therefore, is not eligible for the office of vice president because the powers and duties devolve to the vice president in the event the president is unable to discharge his duties. The meaning of "natural-born citizen" is not defined in the Constitution, but it's clear the founders' intent was to prevent anyone with possible allegiance to another country from being admitted into America's government, especially the highest office in the land as commander of American military forces. In a letter dated July 25, 1787, while presiding over the writing of the Constitution, General George Washington received a letter from John Jay, founding father and the first chief justice of the United States. His letter states: "Permit me to hint, whether it would not be wise and seasonable to provide a strong check to the admission of foreigners into the administration of our national government, and to declare expressly that the command in chief of the American army shall not be given to, nor devolved on, any but a natural-born citizen."

Marco Rubio's generally accepted narrative of being born to Cuban refugees (Reference: Wikipedia, "Born to a family of Cuban exiles") is a nice story and conjures up visions of a family fleeing communist Cuba and Fidel Castro's iron hand. But Mario, Marco's father, was admitted to the United States as a legal alien on May 27, 1956, three years before Castro became dictator of Cuba. It took Mario eighteen years to apply for naturalization, and on November 5, 1975, he was granted American citizenship.

The Republican Party and Rubio's political handlers know very well that Marco is not eligible to run for president or vice president but continue a campaign of misinformation, as do supporters of Piyush "Bobby" Jindal, born on American soil to Indian nationals. The notion that anyone born on American soil is eligible to be president of the United States is spitting in the face of the founding fathers and every soldier who fought and died to uphold the Constitution of the United States of America.

The Republican Party is complicit and dangerously so. By continuing to promote Rubio and Jindal as presidential possibles, they aid and abet every socialist, communist, and Marxist destroying our constitutional republic with misinformation. It's called propaganda, and Republican politicians are guilty of it.

The Republican Party has co-opted Tea Parties from Tea Party Patriots to Tea Party Express; the bigger they get, the more politically correct they become. No one will talk about the real issues that We the People want to know about. When they have the opportunity to sit in front of a camera on major news channels and reach potentially millions of people, they will not broach the subject of Obama's illegitimacy. They will not bring up Terry Lakin. They will not ask any of the hard questions that We the People deserve answers to. Whether or not they are being warned not to bring these subjects up on national television, they do not allow them on their stage appearances and that is our voice denied.

What we're seeing with the large Tea Party organizations discrediting themselves by suing one another or jealously engaging in competition goes on at other levels as well within cities, as I've witnessed right here at home in Tulsa and throughout the state. If you show up at one Tea Party, you might not be welcome at another. Petty jealousies abound among the leadership. I've found myself caught in the middle on several occasions and even ostracized at times for a viewpoint not in keeping with the ideals or the thought processes of a leadership team. Of course, maybe they just don't like me. There's some of that too.

I was invited to speak at the recess rally on behalf of GOOOH in Muskogee at Rep. Boren's office. We met outside on the sidewalk. About thirty people came with letters to Boren that we would tape to his window. We had been encouraged to write him a letter and bring it to the rally. John McAlister, a FairTax supporter, and his wife lived in Muskogee and gave me a big welcome. I had met John at our Fourth of July rally in Miami. He had been standing by himself with a large Gadsden flag (the famous "Don't Tread on Me" flag of Revolutionary War times) and I was struck by the fact that he appeared very frail. He was obviously elderly, but there was something else. I went to speak with him and he confessed to me immediately that he was almost blind and very hard of hearing. His wife drove all the way from Muskogee so they could attend our rally. I told him about the petitions we had, and he wanted me to place his hand at the line to sign. I filled out his contact information for him as he told me his e-mail address, phone number, and such. I would learn that John is a driving force for freedom and liberty. The e-mails I received from him were of astonishing value; his typed opinions, albeit with missed keystrokes, were extremely astute and I looked forward to his e-mails every day. The next time I saw John was at the Chamber of Commerce meeting where I kinda-sorta represented FairTax, as did he.

He said he couldn't hear a lot of what was said, so I filled him in that Boren announced he would co-sponsor the bill, which made him very happy. He was pleased, too, that I remembered to make business cards for him like those I had made for myself, with contact information for Tea Party and FairTax. He held a card up close to his eyes for inspection, and what he could see of it tickled him.

I was always happy to see John. He is such an inspiration to me, and when I decided to throw my hat in the political ring John insisted we get a huge campaign sign and put it on his corner lot in Muskogee.

At the recess rally in front of Boren's office I stacked GOOOH books and flyers on a tabletop that Jim Conroy graciously offered to share with his FairTax material. Jim is another dedicated patriot I would see often at Tea Parties and conservative events around the state promoting FairTax, and soon he was promoting GOOOH as well. Many who recognized that the two programs complemented each other became proponents of both, and the number of supporters continues to grow in spite of limited funds and overwhelming opposition. Just like the Tea Party movement, GOOOH and FairTax are driven by volunteerism and word of mouth — the kind of support money can't buy.

It was at this rally that I met Daniel Edmonds, who was running for Dan Boren's seat in Congress. Although he appeared to be a Constitutional Conservative he was all in with the Republican Party. Eventually I would enter the race to do my best to circumvent Edmonds winning the District 2 U.S. House seat.

After the Pledge of Allegiance and a prayer offered by a Native American, I was introduced by the coordinator and Tea Party leader from Poteau, Elizabeth Jones, an active member of Smart Girl Politics (smartgirlpolitics.ning.com), an organization for engaging, educating, and empowering conservative women. It was the first time I'd met Elizabeth, her husband, and her precious little daughter, Chloe, although we'd spoken on the phone many times. (We would meet up again many more times for "adventures in politics," the greatest of which was meeting Sarah Palin at her book signing in Fayetteville, Arkansas.)

My presentation of GOOOH created much interest and buzz. I not only sold many of Tim's books, but I was interviewed by the local newspaper, the Muskogee Phoenix. They did a highly complimentary story on GOOOH at the rally, which surprised many due to the usually liberal tone of the publication, the "Big D" demographic, and the fact that Muskogee is the home of Dan Boren.

Mark Hughes approached me after the interview. A former Marine and radio host of Eye on Muskogee political talk radio, Mark invited me to appear on his weekly show. He would become a close friend and supporter of my bid for the U.S. House. Mark was very impressed with GOOOH. He bought several books, and I would be on his radio show many times including doing a report from the D.C. Capitol the morning after the 9.12 march. Mark was also a public relations professional skilled in marketing and graphic arts and a great mentor to this fledgling politician.

When Dan Edmonds was introduced to take the podium, there were shouts of "Will you support FairTax?" and "Will you vote for term limits?"

Edmonds looked like a deer caught in the headlights. Obviously he didn't know anything about FairTax, but said he would probably support it. His response to term limits took many of us by surprise and especially had a lasting impression on me. He didn't believe in term limits. I cannot remember exactly his argument, but basically he felt that the longer you worked in the position, the more experience you would gain and, therefore, be a better legislator. To Edmond's credit he never wavered on this position and consistently presented his argument at every debate. He would lose the Republican Primary to Tea Party favorite, Charles Thompson, but he ran a very close second, as one might expect of a candidate setting his sights on a career in politics.

I was troubled that the two-party system would continue to churn out career politicians instead of citizen representatives the way our founding fathers envisioned. Two years would be the term for a session of Congress. Article I. Section. 2: "The House of Representatives shall be composed of Members chosen every second Year by the People of the several States."

Why only two years? The answer is clear; the founders never intended for anyone to make a career of the position. At the time, the framers were hard pressed to get the working people, the shopkeepers, the farmers and producers of goods to travel long distances to serve for two long years away from family and their livelihoods to represent their peers. Their peers — not their peers' superiors, who would move to the capital and make the position their career. It was a part-time responsibility to go to the capital and vote on issues. They were to serve out their term and then return home to their regular jobs. The Senate was different. Functioning as an assembly of citizens at the highest levels of deliberation and legislation in government called for the experienced; the political leaders, diplomats, and lawyers.

The Get America Back group in nearby Grove met every other Thursday. The first meeting had about twenty people, and it grew steadily in membership. When I met the founding members at the American Majority Activist Training meeting in Tulsa, May 14, 2009, I began attending the GAB meetings and giving updates on FairTax. I usually brought copies of something informative regarding current affairs and issues to distribute. I was proud to be a contributing member. However, that all changed when I began promoting GOOOH. Long story short, the plan called for bypassing the two parties and severing all ties with special-interest money. Success of the plan threatened the Republican Party, and the GAB group leadership was decidedly Republican. It would take several subtle snubs before I caught on that I wasn't wanted, but I finally figured it out and quit attending. I did not abandon the group, however. Many members weren't aware of the rift between GAB's leadership and me. E-mail bulletins and FairTax information continued to flow between GAB members and myself. The peril of our country was too important to let pettiness stand in the way of important information exchanges. I attended one final meeting. It was the one after I returned from the march on Washington September 12, 2009. Many members knew I had gone, and I'd even called a couple of them from the Capitol.

A member was introduced to tell the group about his experiences at the rally. Apparently he was the only member fortunate enough to be able to make the trip, as the person introducing him pointed out. Someone spoke up, "Miki was there." Another spoke up, "Yeah, Miki was there." But no acknowledgment came from the group leadership. When the speaker finished, someone again encouraged the chair to "let Miki talk," but that, too, was ignored. The meeting progressed. I was burning with humiliation. I was a pariah. I had to sit there and pretend it didn't bother me, because walking out would show everyone I couldn't handle the insult. After the meeting I picked up my FairTax and GOOOH material and went home.

Chapter 15

A Weird Little Man in African Garb

Early in March of 2011, Daniel Akaka, career politician from Hawai'i, announced that he would not run for reelection in 2012. The third-oldest member of the Senate became the fifth Democrat to tell Obama of a plan to retire. Hawai'i's other senator, Daniel Inouye, became the oldest living and longest serving senator when Robert C. Byrd, Democrat from West Virginia, passed away on June 28, 2010. Sen. Inouye would not be able to help Daniel Akaka in 2012 with financial support, as he provided in 2006 to the tune of $300,000, prompting Akaka to announce his retirement.

The two long serving Hawai'i senators brought home billions of dollars in earmarks to the island state of 1.4 million people. Sen. Daniel Inouye's reputation took a hit when it became known that Central Pacific Bank, of which he was a founder and in which he had personal assets of as much as $700,000, received $135 million of federal bailout money. The FDIC had already said the bank did not meet criteria to receive funds, but a phone call from Inouye's office to the FDIC prompted approval of TARP funds for Inouye's hometown bank. There is no law against the obvious conflict of interest, because congressional rules leave that discretion to the members themselves, a policy that most definitely needs to change.

Most of the pork projects that earned Hawai'i second place in government earmarks were brought home by Inouye, self-proclaimed "number one earmarks guy in the U.S. Congress."

Recent talk of a ban on earmarks in the newly elected Republican House will severely curtail or eliminated Inouye's ability to bring home the bacon. Financial aid for native Hawai'ians for health, education, and cultural programs will be on the chopping block as well as funds long enjoyed by the Hawai'i Chamber of Commerce and the University of Hawai'i through which our tax dollars bought and paid for the new

Marxist, socialist, communist governor, and former towel attendant at the congressional fitness center in Washington, D.C., Neal Abercrombie.

Since 2006, Abercrombie voted against issues important to the security of our nation, the safety of our military troops and of Israel, our staunch ally. His pro-Islam stance should have been vetted during his run for governor of Hawai'i. It should come as no surprise that he mirrors Obama's policies.

Shortly after Abercrombie was elected, I was "chomping at the bit" to tell what I knew about him from personal experience and to tell what I knew about Hawai'i politics, a "pay to play" state. I wrote an opinion piece for the Post & Email and didn't hold back.

DOES THE NEW GOVERNOR OF HAWAII KNOW OBAMA'S TRUE PAST?

And Will He Continue the Aloha State's Cover for Him?
By Miki Booth

(December 8, 2010) — Neil Abercrombie, socialist, dope-smoking, ex-hippie, and agitator was sworn in Monday as Hawaii's governor, courtesy of Obama, organized crime and union thugs. It doesn't hurt that the majority of Hawaii's populace is composed of mindless Democrat morons who vote as they are told. I saw this train wreck coming but was powerless to slow it down or stop it. When Abercrombie gave up his U.S. House of Representatives seat to return to Hawaii to campaign for governor, I knew Obama would do whatever it took for Abercrombie to win. When Charles Djou was elected to serve out the remainder of the term, I know they were as shocked as anyone and the doubling-down began.

Neil Abercrombie came out early in support of Obama. He claims he had a personal relationship with Obama Sr., at the University of Hawaii, and he's the only person who puts Sr. together with Stanley Ann Dunham. I think this is manufactured nonsense, and the reason I say so is that I know who Abercrombie is and who he is not. He's a dyed-in-the-wool socialist even though he made a big deal of denying any such thing and has been instrumental in Obama's rise to the top. Just like the CIA covering up and/or manufacturing Obama's historic documents, Abercrombie has provided a narrative for Obama's parentage and early history. You will remember he tried to sneak language into a resolution celebrating the anniversary of Hawaii's statehood affirming Hawaii as Obama's birthplace. Representative Michelle Bachman tried to block the measure on the floor of the House due to lack of a quorum, but it was later approved. With Abercrombie as governor, it will be assured that Obama's made-up Hawai'i birth story will be documented as fact and anything contrary to their narrative for him will be gone forever.

Underneath the beauty that is Hawaii runs a frightening thread of political corruption, organized crime, union thuggery, terroristic threatening, and murder tied neatly with a bow called the Democratic party. Colleen Hanabusa wasn't just waiting in the wings to take Abercrombie's seat away from Dijou; she was groomed for the win and had the nod from Larry Mehau, protective services boss, frequently referred to as the godfather of organized crime in Hawai'i.

I remember in the 1980's on the Big Island Hawaii's Kona Coast, Abercrombie hung out with the doper misfits commiserating about the social injustice of the "haves" over the "have-nots." I used to wonder what became of the antiwar, free-love hippies of the 70's until I moved to the Big Island from Oahu and discovered they were growing their pakalolo (marijuana) and living in communes on the southern slopes of Mauna Loa. Abercrombie and the free-love set would organize and protest the new resorts and hotels by picketing and being nuisances. The handful of protesters were a source of embarrassment to working people like me. When agriculture died in Hawaii and tourism became the largest industry, most people went to work at visitor-related businesses and services. Every imaginable union, including SEIU, has a presence in Hawaii. Flash forward 30 years, and Abercrombie gets elected by the very workers of the businesses he was protesting in his dope-smoking, staph-infected, hippie days.

The Post & Email.

When our son Alan was two years old, we left O'ahu and moved to the Big Island, Hawai'i. We spent the years 1983 to 1995 living first in Kailua-Kona, then moving to Hilo and Kamuela (Waimea) with a two-year stint in Wahiawa, O'ahu, in between to take care of Fred's ailing mother before leaving the islands in May 1995. Although the police retirement system is statewide, the police departments are not, and Fred had to quit the Honolulu Police Department (HPD) to go to work for the Hawai'i County Police Department (HCPD). He had been accepted to HCPD before quitting HPD, and his state retirement and healthcare followed. The Big Island was like the Wild West compared to O'ahu, and for the police there were fewer restrictions as to the type of vehicle you could own personally and be subsidized for its use. Fred's car was a gray Pontiac Firebird with a huge red phoenix on the hood. Off-duty we cruised in a really "cool" car. On-duty, with the blue light strapped to the roof, it was his official police car, and there were many occasions where traffic violators would refuse to pull over for Fred in his flashy Pontiac Firebird with an equally flashy blue light.

These violators were, of course, visitors to the Islands and never in their wildest dreams thought this could be the police! Fred, being the laid-back Big Island cop that he was, would often give the visitor a break when they finally pulled over, and then he'd let them off with a verbal warning, or more accurately, an education. Tourists would sometimes go home with a photo souvenir of Fred in his Firebird with the blue "gumdrop" on top. Drunk drivers, though, would never catch a break from Fred. The three years he spent as a motorcycle "solo-bike" cop on O'ahu earned him admiration and status for his high volume of drunk-driving arrests. I remember stories other cops told about Fred sitting stationary on his HPD Harley shooting radar when he smelled booze coming from a passing car and gave chase, ending in a drunk-driving arrest. Fred, who rarely drank and a non-smoker, could detect the slightest odor of alcohol and marijuana. He could follow his nose and make an arrest.

During the years we lived in Kona I worked as sales manager for the Kona Hilton, and being the only sales person on the property, I handled all group markets and contract sales. My executive position required attendance at local social and business functions on the Big Island as well as on O'ahu, where on several occasions I saw Neal Abercrombie. I usually avoided him. He was easy to spot, usually wearing a lived-in-looking suit or aloha shirt and his scruffy beard. He would be talking, always talking; no, it was more like bragging. Abercrombie was usually surrounded by liberal academia types and not well regarded by locals. I could not bring myself to acknowledge his position as a representative or an ambassador of Hawai'i. On the Big Island, Abercrombie was known as a hippie agitator and doper. A friend of mine who attended the University of Hawai'i on the Manoa campus at the same time as Abercrombie told me that he (Abercrombie) was "a weird little man dressed in African garb." That's how he's remembered.

Abercrombie made no secret of his love for communism and socialism and frequently met with the disenfranchised hippies who came to the Big Island from elsewhere, just as Abercrombie had — in his case, from New York. They came from somewhere else and imposed their will, their ideology, and their lack of morals on an unassuming and good-natured local citizenry. Abercrombie and a handful of hippies tried to get legislation passed to allow nudism at a particular stretch of beach. The free-love, free-everything group of Abercrombie followers contaminated popular Spencer Beach Park, a favorite place for family gatherings and camping. We were turned away by beach closure signs announcing staph infection outbreaks, and later, needles found on the beach would again shut down use of the park. Locals quit going and, like us, found other beaches to frequent, staying away from those with hippies and "pastafarians" — the blond dreadlocks.

So, how could a socialist/Marxist/communist come from some-place else and become the governor and impose his will, his ideology, and lack of morals on the people of Hawai'i? Abercrombie did it by using Obama's blueprint — Alinsky tactics — a means to an end, the end being the destruction of America as we know it.

Chapter 16

"I'll Hunt You Down and Cut Your Heart Out!"

When the little hapa-haole girl was eight years old, she was invited to a birthday slumber party. She didn't know the friend from school who invited her all that well, but she was happy to be asked to attend. Her mama took her shopping for a pair of pajamas because the girl's regular sleeping attire of undershirts and panties just wouldn't do. Her mama also bought her a small suitcase with a picture of Walt Disney's Sleeping Beauty on it, and her pajamas, toothbrush, hairbrush, and birthday present for Gwen fit perfectly inside.

The party that afternoon was a lot of fun, and the girls laughed and giggled at the silliest jokes. The hapa girl laughed along, but she spoke very little. She was the fifth wheel and didn't have a partner who would whisper in her ear or whose ear she could whisper into the way the other girls had.

Gwen's father was the ringmaster of the party. He was so funny and made everyone laugh when he instructed them on how to play the party games. He worked in a bakery, and the cake he made for his daughter was the biggest and most beautiful cake the little girl had ever seen. The roses were so real looking, it was hard to believe they could actually be eaten. But eat them they did, and the hapa girl got her favorite pastel blue rose with green leaves put on top of her piece of vanilla cake. It was the best party she had ever been to.

When the sleeping time of the slumber party came, the hapa girl went into the bathroom to change into her pajamas while the other girls changed in Gwen's bedroom. They giggled and laughed at seeing each other bare-chested and naked, but the hapa girl couldn't do that. Her mother had instilled in all her daughters a strong sense of modesty, and bare chests and private parts were just that — private. She wanted to fit in and to be just one of the girls, but she wasn't just one of the girls. They were all haole with blonde hair and blue eyes and she wasn't. She was deathly afraid that they would laugh at her if they saw her naked. It was safer to excuse herself to the bathroom and avoid any shame.

The four haole girls paired up to sleep. Two were on the twin bed and two were on the bottom of the bunk bed, and the little hapa girl would sleep alone on the top bunk. She laughed at the jokes and antics of the other girls but otherwise was left out of the banter. Earlier, she had tried to initiate a joke during the party, but her small voice was cut off and drowned out by a louder, popular girl. She felt humiliated, and she knew humiliation only as shame. She fell asleep thinking about morning and pancakes with whipped cream and berries.

She was shocked awake by a rough hand reaching into her pajama bottoms, but before the hand could get into her panties she clenched herself into a ball and rolled toward the wall, away from the offending hand. The hand persisted, forcing its way into her panties and closer to her private area. She kept her legs clenched tight, and the force of her trying to pull away ripped a button off her pajama top, but she didn't know it at the time.

"What are you doing in there?" a voice asked. It was Gwen's mother at the doorway. Her husband spun around. The offending hand was gone.

"I was just checking on the girls."

"Liar! Liar!" the girl screamed in her head.

"Well, you don't need to be in there," Gwen's mother said.

It was the middle of the night, but the girl knew the man had to go to work very early in the morning because he was a baker, and they started working before it was even daylight. She knew the man wouldn't be back because he had gotten caught. She heard his wife ask him again what he was doing, and he told her he was covering up one of the girls. Again, "Liar! Liar!" screamed in the girl's head.

She lay wide awake curled up as close to the wall as she possibly could and waited for the other girls to wake up.

When morning came, she didn't say a word and silently played with her plate of pancakes and blueberries. When she was asked if she wanted whipped topping on her berries, she shook her head "no."

She didn't want to be the first to leave, which would bring special attention on her, so she waited until someone else left first, and then she walked home.

Her mother went through her Sleeping Beauty suitcase and found the top with the missing button. It was obvious to her the button had been ripped off. She thought her daughter might have been playing rough at the pajama party, but she asked about it anyway, and the girl confessed. She didn't cry. She just told her mother the truth: the man tried to put his hand in her panties, but Gwen's mother said something and he stopped.

"Did you scream?" her mother wanted to know.

"No."

"Why didn't you scream?"

"I don't know."

"Well, next time you scream. Did his wife know what he did?"

"No."

"So nobody knows?"

"No."

After careful thought, the girl's mother instructed her not to tell anyone because if her daddy found out he would beat up Gwen's father, and the whole town would know. Worse, her classmates would know. It would be a shame too big to live with.

Over the years the girl found out something about herself that made her unique. She never screamed. Even when someone came up behind her and scared her, she never screamed, and she never told anyone when she was slapped so hard she was knocked to the ground and raped. After all, she had deserved it — he said she was a "cock-teaser."

She never told anyone about all the times in over twelve years of marriage that she was slapped or beaten by an alcoholic husband who begged forgiveness immediately after meting out physical punishment. After all, she was to blame for much of it. Why did she do things to make him so angry and drive him into a rage? It was best just to try to get along and if that meant drinking a bottle of wine every night to be able to stand his racist rantings and verbal attacks on her family and friends, then so be it.

They had married in the Ali'iolani Hale, where the statue of King Kamehameha the Great stands upon a pedestal with one arm outstretched in a beckoning gesture and a spear in the other. The Ali'iolani Hale for years served as a judicial building where judges were available to perform marriages. Later it would be the State Supreme Court.

After tying the knot, the couple lived in Kailua on the windward side of the island where the hapa girl worked at a nearby garden store and her husband worked at Pearl Harbor as a civilian shipfitter's apprentice while working toward an engineering degree. After five years, they transferred to the mainland. The haole husband had always felt he was being discriminated against. Koreans, Japanese, Chinese, Filipinos, Hawai'ians, and combinations of all the above didn't like the haole boy. He was in the minority and never got the breaks the other races got. When they moved to the mainland, it was the blacks who got all the breaks. He was discriminated against by everyone, and every day brought a new outrage, and his wife drank to drown out the rants.

There were good times in the twelve years. The couple had chosen to be DINKs, Double Income No Kids, and they traveled and pulled their boat to the Florida Keys every year, diving for lobsters for dinner and collecting shells. The hapa girl had a knack for spotting shells — the live conchs blending into the sea floor and giant horse conchs buried deep in the sand with only a small telltale sprig of coral visible above the surface. She quit lugging her scuba gear along because it was a hassle, and she chose instead to free dive for shells, sometimes fifty feet deep for the buried helmet shells.

She loved the ocean, but she loved horses more. After years of begging for one, she finally bought a horse, and it was totally on her own. She wasn't allowed to use "their" money — the combined salaries of the DINKs, so she saved up her extra earnings from part-time jobs and selling blood and hair samples at a medical lab in the city. A friend and fellow horse owner worked at the research facility and knew when they would need samples so they would be the first ones in line. Eventually, money from selling blood and hair would pay for a saddle and bridle. The hapa girl would smile and boast that her saddle was bought with "blood money."

The hapa girl was twenty-eight years old when she finally got her own horse, but she wouldn't have it for long. Her husband was jealous of her horse. He never wanted her to have one.

He didn't want her going to community college in Hawai'i, so she didn't. He didn't want her going to college when they moved to the mainland, so she didn't. It made sense that he should get his college degree first, and besides, she liked her jobs even though he complained all the time. He really just wanted her to stay home and take care of the house and him. When he started complaining every day, every single day, about the time she spent with her horse, she started fighting back.

He didn't like losing control. As she asserted herself they fought more frequently, and she took solace in the company of her horse. "Brighty" was pastured at a nearby ranch within walking distance, and the horse always nickered when she saw her person coming. The hapa girl would drive up in her pickup truck after work, and Brighty would be at the gate waiting for her. The hapa girl loved her horse more than she loved her husband, but when they had a showdown over keeping her horse or going home to Hawai'i to visit her daddy when he had a heart attack she sold her horse and went home — alone.

Her family had missed her. It had been eight years since she moved away, and they were glad to finally see her after all those years. They didn't know how unhappy she was until she broke down and cried that she didn't want to go back to the mainland. She never told them that it was her husband that she didn't want to go back to, but her family would support her in any decision she made. There was always a place for her in any of her relatives' homes. She went back to her husband to face the music. She reasoned that they were headed in different directions. She kept the real reasons to herself. She no longer wanted to live with a domineering man that controlled every aspect of her life. His jealousy drove his actions. He never wanted her to be better educated than he was. He resented her success when she climbed the rungs of the corporate ladder. He loved her but wanted to keep her in a box and let her out only when it suited him. He took out his frustration by picking fights that escalated until they ended in physical altercations. He would always win. He towered above his wife and outweighed her by a hundred pounds. She explained away bruises on her face by claiming a fall or clumsy accident, and when she got Brighty she blamed it on her horse. Once she got back from Hawai'i there was nothing joyful in her life anymore. Brighty was gone.

There was no reason to stay in the twelve-year marriage, and she begged for a divorce. She wanted to go home to her family. She was stunned when he agreed to a divorce, but there were conditions: "Don't plan to take anything with you, or I'll hunt you down and cut your heart out."

⸺⸙⸺

Fred was the first cop I ever knew socially. He was a friend of my family, and I felt a sense of security knowing him. Not only would he look out for me, but all of his brothers in blue would as well. They were family and took me into the fold. When we began dating we were both over thirty years old starting over with pretty much nothing to show for our lives at least materially. He'd been taken to the cleaners by his ex-wives, and I pretty much gave everything to the cleaners. Fred knew I had a constant fear in the back of my mind that my ex-husband might one day come after me.

The day before the horrific tornado hit nearby Joplin on May 22, 2011, I received an e-mail from one of the CIA Columbia trial transcript members on Pastor Manning's committee that I met while I was in New York City. Kurt sent the results of an inquiry from an online detective site that he subscribed to. It confirmed Obama's social security number as being "active" and issued in Connecticut. To check the accuracy of the site, I had Kurt plug in my social security number and that of my ex-husband which was still stuck in my head thirty years later. Mine came back "active" and issued by Hawai'i but the other was "inactive" because the holder was dead. I couldn't believe it. Kurt did some more checking and told me that the my ex-husband had been dead for two years!

I ran and told Fred, and we both sighed a breath of relief. I never had to worry ever again, at least not about the tyrant who controlled my life for twelve years and longer because of fear of retribution for leaving him. But there was another tyrant affecting my life, and I would push back with everything I had, having decided long ago never to be a victim again.

Chapter 17

Samuel Adams, Thomas Jefferson & Thomas Paine

The Tea Party movement was really picking up steam and patriots were watching Glenn Beck's show on FOX and listening to his radio show. It seemed to be the only place we had to go where we felt we belonged. He told us that we were not alone, and he encouraged us to send our photos. He was working on a surprise that would be unveiled soon. I sent a photo of Fred and me. Alan sent his. Thousands of people sent photos. Tens of thousands sent photos. Glenn Beck showed us all that we were not alone — there was the proof — our photos artistically assembled to read, "We the People."

On September 12, 2009, at the nation's Capitol, we spoke as one, exercising our First Amendment right to peaceably assemble and petition our government for a redress of grievances, of which there were too many by then to keep track of.

I arrived on Thursday afternoon and checked into the Marriott at Metro Station. My three roommates had yet to check in. They were coming from Oklahoma City. We'd only spoken on the phone or communicated by e-mail, and I was looking forward to meeting them in person.

I had booked a room two months earlier and sent out e-mails offering to share the room and soon had roommates. They met up with a larger contingent from Oklahoma, and I didn't see them much because I had volunteered to meet up with Tim Cox and other volunteers for GOOOH.

We met in the lobby of the Marriott near Freedom Plaza where the march would begin the next morning. Several people showed up to pick up brochures to hand out and talk about GOOOH with Tim. It was there that I met Jim Linn, who was dressed in Colonial finery; from buckled shoes to his powdered wig, he was the embodiment of Samuel Adams.

In 1776 Samuel Adams said, "If ever a time should come, when vain and aspiring men shall possess the highest seats in Government, our country will stand in need of its experienced patriots to prevent its ruin." Here we were — the "experienced patriots." It was up to us to hold our elected representatives accountable or to replace them, every last one of them if need be. GOOOH was the mechanism by which we would do it.

Supporters of FairTax had scheduled a rally in front of the Internal Revenue Service that Friday afternoon. I told Tim that I needed to leave right away to make it there on time for the start, but would be back as soon as it was over. Jim wanted to go with me so we caught a cab and got to the IRS building in time to see a crowd gathering. I felt so special — here I was arriving with a founding father! Right away, I saw some people I knew from other rallies, and they introduced us around. It was a few minutes past two. It looked like only about 100 people there, which I thought was disappointing. Then a huge crowd that had assembled on the other side of the building came around the corner with banners and signs. As more arrived by car and got dropped off or joined us from elsewhere, we grew to about 200. There was a short program, and the speakers used a bullhorn to talk about FairTax. A young man, who everyone recognized, spoke and later posed for photos. It was Jonathan Krohn, a conservative prodigy who spoke at CPAC and at thirteen years old had already written a book. There he was, and I was a fan. Sam Adams took my photo with Jonathan. I boasted. "How cool is that?" I said to Fred over the phone.

We had to stay on the sidewalk and walk through the parked cars to get from one side of the crowd to the other because we weren't allowed on the little strip of cordoned-off park bench area at the base of the steps or on the steps at all. There were four or five IRS police or guards standing on the landing of the steps outside the entrance doors. They just crossed their arms and talked among themselves. At first they didn't wave back when we waved at them, but later they were waving back and we took that as a good sign. I think they decided that we weren't so bad after all.

Jim and I returned to the Marriott by cab. I was having so much fun watching people react to seeing one of our founding fathers step out of a cab or walk down the street. When we got back to where Tim was meeting with people we were ready for something to drink. I went downstairs to the hotel bar and bought several bottles of Sam Adams beer and passed them around, making sure Jim got a bottle. I had to get someone to take our photo. Here I was having a Sam Adams with Sam Adams. I mean, really, how cool is that?!

Yvonne Donelly with the 9.12 project in Washington, D.C., spoke to Tim on Thursday night and on Friday called in to Glenn Beck's radio show for her regular update on the planned rally:

(Excerpt)

Glenn: *What's been going on? I know there have been meetings and get-togethers, and people from 9.12 projects and Tea Parties all over the country are starting to gather. A lot more coming in today, but what happened yesterday and last night?*
Donelly: *Well, I met with a representative from the Central Illinois project, 9.12 project, where they have a large, impressive group. I met with some people last night, I met with an individual from a very . . . I'm meeting just amazing people, as you would expect, from goooh.com. We've got to look into this. Very interesting.*
Glenn: *What is goooh.com?*
Donnelly: *Goooh.com is this very interesting gentleman by the name of Tim Cox, I believe his name is, and he is funding an organization, Glenn, all on his own . . . all his own money. It's a nonpartisan organization to pretty much replace all the representatives and letting the American people decide who goes in through a questionnaire ballot. We just started looking into it last night, but a very impressive gentleman, and funding it with his own money.*
Glenn: *And are you sure the address is right? Goo.com?*
Donnelly: *Yeah, but it's goooh.com. (Pronounced "go.")*
Glenn: *Ah, I've read, I have read, goo . . .*
Donnelly: *Oh.*
Glenn: *Yeah, oh. Getoutofourhouse.com.*
Donnelly: *Oh, yeah, yeah, yeah, yeah.*
Glenn: *I've read that book.*
Donnelly: *You have?*
Glenn: *Yeah, I've read that book. I don't agree with everything in it, but it's a very interesting, very interesting concept. Yeah, very good.*
Donnelly: *Absolutely! That's what I said. I just started looking into it and so very interesting, but not, you know, certainly don't know all about it . . . but a very great gentleman who was funding it all on his own*

evidently, and, you know, he's meeting with people here. So I met with
him last night and met some other 9.12ers. So it's great.
Glenn: *Great, okay. Activities tomorrow in Washington . . .*

Yvonne Donelly came back on Friday night to speak further with
Tim and talk about her call to Glenn Beck. Wow. It was exciting. Glenn
Beck talked about GOOOH and Tim Cox. Maybe that would be the
break we needed . . . but it wasn't to be. Beck, like all the biggies, had
his own agenda.

Tim appeared on Fox & Friends Sunday on December 20, 2009,
with Alisyn Camerota. We hoped this would be the big break for
GOOOH, but it wasn't. Tim was invited to a whole host of radio talk
shows, but not Rush Limbaugh, not Hannity, not Glenn Beck. I was
able to talk about GOOOH at least once with Andrew Wilkow on The
Wilkow Majority, a conservative radio show host in New York City, and
his tag line of "We are right! They are wrong! End of story!" But, again,
no break into the mainstream.

Tim worked tirelessly and the number of hits to the website grew
steadily, but we would need a lot more, and fast, for the plan to work
before the primaries and filing deadlines in mid 2010.

At the 9.12 march, Tim, me, Sam Adams, and several other
volunteers handed out over 25,000 GOOOH brochures and thousands
of cards until we ran out. We stopped along the way to the Capitol,
while Sam Adams was interviewed by reporters. The most notable was
a reporter from The Associated Press. The others were relatively
obscure news agencies and online conservative news sites and blogs,
but we were thrilled that they asked Jim for an interview and that he
could promote GOOOH.

We never got close to the steps of the Capitol where the program
was staged. The people who'd planned the event never expected the
crowd to be so large as to be completely out of hearing distance.
Occasionally, depending on the way the wind was blowing, we could
hear singing and sometimes someone talking on a microphone, but
there was no way we could understand what was being said. As people
left when the program was over, we could work our way a little closer
to where the stage was. The whole time people just walked around
reading signs and milling throughout the throngs of patriots, friendly
and peacefully.

People stayed just to experience the once-in-a-lifetime event, and many, having come not knowing what to expect, said they would certainly be back the next year with their families. The sentiment was heard everywhere.

At one point I saw a Hawai'ian flag and worked my way through the crowd trying to reach the group gathered around it. By the time I sighted it again it was a lot farther away, and I gave up trying to reach it for fear I would lose my way back to Tim and Sam. That night Tim told me he met a woman from Hawai'i at Freedom Plaza who said she knew me, but when they couldn't find me in the crowd she left to get back to her group. I never found out who that was.

As the crowd thinned I noticed people picking up the tiniest shreds of paper and litter, and if there had been any cigarette butts before, there were none to be seen on the grounds as we left. Everything looked pristine, although the trash bins were overflowing with rubbish.

People were talking about how the police and park workers were trying to keep the crowds contained to the areas where Freedom Works had a permit to assemble, but there were just too many people. The barricades had to be moved back, and eventually the cops manning the barricades just kind of disappeared.

There weren't near enough porta-potties, johnny-on-the-spots, chem-lavs, loan-a-luas, drop-zones, load-er-ups, pee-pees, oui-ouis, tanks-alots, gotta-goes, urin-bizzes, doodie-calls, whizzers-on-wheels, or whatever you call them in your neck of the woods; there weren't enough, so people were allowed to use the toilets in the Smithsonian Institute.

Tim, Sam, and I stayed near the Peace Monument, also known as the Naval Monument, on the west side of the Capitol. Tim continued to talk to people who wanted to know more about GOOOH. Jim and I sat at the base of the monument, and people came up to take photos of him. I volunteered to take their photograph so they could be in the picture with Sam Adams.

When we started on the march from Freedom Plaza, Tim was carrying the bulk of three cases of brochures. We distributed at least one case to his volunteers before we started, and I took the equivalent of half a case, stuffing most of them into my backpack and kept a supply in my camera case where they were handy to grab and hand out. Jim would get stacks from Tim's supply and distribute them along the way. It was exhausting, not just carrying the heavy promotional materials but also walking the long distance from Freedom Square to the Capitol, but I wouldn't have missed it for the world. Several times I tried to call Fred to share the exhilarating experience with him but was unable to get through. I had told friends I would call from the rally but again tried and failed but had no problem reaching anyone the following day.

I was exhausted and I knew Jim was too. His buckled shoes were authentic but new, and his feet hurt from blisters after the long walk up Pennsylvania Avenue to the Capitol grounds. Tim looked as if he was still going strong, though, and we stayed as long as there were people wanting to know about GOOOH. Eventually we started back and hailed a cab.

Tim treated us to a tour of the capital that evening on a trolley bus that started at dusk so we could see the lights of the buildings and monuments at night. Our tour guide was a friendly fellow. I read between the lines of his comments and decided he was one of us — a conservative. We passed by the House of Representatives office building. On a Saturday night it was pretty well assured there were no Congress people working, but most of the offices had the lights on. In fact, all the buildings had offices with the lights left on and no one inside. The very worst offender with almost all the lights on and no one in sight was the Department of Energy building. I swear; I'm not making this up. Our tour guide was very dismayed. We were disgusted.

The trolley made a long stop at the Jefferson Memorial where there was a snack and drink vendor, but Tim, Jim, and I went directly to the monument. I'd been to D.C. a few times before when I was representing Hawai'i hotels and once to attend a travel trade show when I worked for Hyatt Regency Waikoloa. I had also visited Washington as a child when Daddy brought me and my older brother for a visit, but this time was really special. We made history on September 12, 2009, and I had high hopes that our message would reach our representatives and send a stinging warning to the administration that we had had enough, and we weren't going to take it anymore, but when I looked up at the bronze statue of Thomas Jefferson my confidence was shaken, and I had to hold back tears. Dust covered Jefferson's face and shoulders and cobwebs drifting from the ceiling were attached to his head. I was profoundly saddened. This is how Obama and his anti-American administration regard our founding fathers, our Constitution, our exceptionalism, and I would not stop telling everyone I knew that he was a liar, a thief, a usurper, a traitor, and a fraud.

The trolley dropped us off close to our hotels, which were a couple of blocks apart. Tim and Jim walked me back to my hotel. I would see Tim again when he came to Muskogee to conduct a mock candidate selection session, and I would see Jim again at future events, and in lots of photos on the Internet, and on the news when he was Sam Adams.

The morning after the march I stayed in bed watching FOX News and let my roommates shower and get ready before me since they had a schedule to keep. I had a later flight than anyone else. My three roommates from Oklahoma City were members of the 9.12 group there. Jean, Carma Neta, and I were in regular contact through e-mail and phone before the D.C. trip and long afterward, running into each other at different events. I didn't know Jean's friend, Carol, as well as the others, but she was lots of fun, too. It had been like a teenage slumber party the three nights we stayed together. I was traveling by myself so we said our good-byes that Sunday morning, and they left to check out. I drank the coffee that Jean made for me as she did each morning, which made me feel very special.

There was just a little coverage of the 9.12 Tea Party on FOX. I had hoped they would report it extensively, but the establishment media considered it more of a Glenn Beck show than newsworthy reporting. The live coverage on Friday night where most of the bus groups were staying was pretty exciting. There was an impromptu gathering out in the bus parking lot where the Tea Party Express was parked. Sean Hannity had a film crew there, and we were live on his show. We shouted and hollered — no, actually we screamed — when he greeted us on the monitor. It was fun. We were packed like sardines around the lighted set, and I wasn't worried that the crowd would get unruly. There were some anti—Tea Party hecklers on the sidelines swearing and calling us names. When no one would take the bait, one girl ran away in tears — her ranting at us was met with laughs and cheers. I loved it!

"You people are horrible!" she cried as she ran away.

I had arranged with Mark Hughes to call in to his radio show, "Eye on Muskogee," on Sunday morning and instead of taking a cab to the Capitol building, since I had lots of time before I called in, I took a leisurely walk and snapped photographs along the way. Pennsylvania Avenue was deserted. It was eight o'clock on a Sunday morning, and very few people were out and about. I saw one homeless person lying on a bench covered with newspapers; otherwise, my walk was very pleasant, and it was difficult to believe that just the day before there were wall-to-wall people taking the same walk I was now taking. The only difference was that I was walking on the sidewalk. The day before I was told by a cop to get off the sidewalk and march in the street. He said we only had a permit to march on the street. I had wondered why there was no one on the sidewalk walking. Only standing was allowed.

Capitol police took their permits seriously. I would find that out six months later at the "Code Red" rally when I was nearly arrested for standing in an area I didn't have a permit for.

I returned to the area near the Peace Monument and the Reflection Pool, where we were the day before, and found a nice shady area on the grass to sit and do the interview with Mark. I called in right on time, and Mark was eager to have our listeners hear all about the wonderful historical event and more about GOOOH, which Mark enthusiastically endorsed.

On my walk back to the hotel I stopped at the Newseum, which is the building on Pennsylvania Avenue that has the giant inscription in the marble wall several stories high that reads: "Congress shall make no law respecting an establishment of religion, or prohibiting the free exercise thereof; or abridging the freedom of speech, or of the press; or the right of the people peaceably to assemble, and to petition the Government for a redress of grievances." I took several photos of the First Amendment's text thinking that building must really irk Obama when he sees it. After all, try as they might, they could not silence the nearly two million people who took their grievances against him and his Democrat-controlled Congress right to their face, but Obama, narcissist-in-chief, fled town in search of those who would worship him and satisfy his ego.

The Newseum gets around 800 front pages from 84 countries and posts them daily on its website, www.newseum.org, and a dozen or so from around the United States are posted outside the building on the ground floor. The New York Times had an article and photo of the 9.12 rally on the lower front page, and the Washington Post also had a small story, but most had nothing, at least not on the front page. I saw a couple studying the papers. Since they were wearing patriotic colors, I asked them if they had come for the Tea Party, and they had, so they came over to talk to me. I pointed out the papers that had stories, and they, like me, were surprised to see that the New York Times, a decidedly liberal paper, actually put us on the front page, and the article was rather complimentary.

The following week I attended the Camdenton Tea Party at the county courthouse, handed out 200 or so brochures, and had a table to sell books and answer questions about GOOOH. The organizers had paid to fly in Oklahoma Rep. Charles Key to speak. It was there that I gave him a second book. He said it didn't look familiar, so I knew he wasn't interested in finding out what it was about, but I did my part. I tried.

September was a busy month. The Thursday after the 9.12 Tea Party and the rally at Camdenton was the scheduled GAB meeting in Grove at which I was shunned. Less than a week later Tim came to Oklahoma to conduct the mock Candidate Selection Session in Muskogee. I had booked a room in the community center and paid the rental in advance. Not knowing if a lot of people would show up and if we would need a sound system and mic for Tim, I kept one reserved and ready. Thirty or so people showed up. Some were already members, and the others would become members. They, too, saw the genius in the GOOOH plan.

A fellow FairTax leader, Elza Jones, came all the way from Oklahoma City, and I was able to finally meet him in person. He had been so helpful to my FairTax efforts by e-mail and phone, and it was good to finally meet him. Jim Conroy was there too, as was Carol Chouinard, FairTax Director of OK District 2.

Earlier I had picked Tim up at the Tulsa airport. Shortly after we arrived at the community center, Fred and Alan showed up in Alan's truck. I was really happy that they took such an interest in GOOOH. Alan was thrilled to meet Tim in person, and Tim later told me he was very impressed with Alan. Alan and his friends were conservatives, at least they finally figured that out. They started out not giving a rat's ass about politics, but after seeing such disturbing actions by Obama and his bevy of czars, they started getting involved and educating their peers about what was really going on.

Early on Alan, like Fred, initially thought I was off my rocker, but it didn't take long for them to see the truth in what I was telling them. Their own research convinced them we had people deliberately ignoring our rule of law, and worse, deliberately trying to shred the

Constitution and change our country into something we would no longer recognize.

"Mom, you have no idea how many of us are out there," Alan said.

Alan was referring to the growing number of his generation that had become engaged, telling others that Obama was a fraud. They ridiculed the "mindless obots" through their social networks. Alan enjoyed sparring with the mindless idiots. His argument could not be broken, and I was extremely proud of him.

There was another young man at the GOOOH meeting. He was very nice looking and well dressed, and I thought he might be around nineteen or twenty years old. I was always pleased to see the younger generation involved in politics and planned to tell him so when I got the chance.

We broke up into groups of six for the selection process. We had our worksheets and documented how we would vote on the issues presented. Everyone had two minutes to stand and give an introductory speech and mention the issues most important to them. All participants then rotated places until each person met with the other five mock candidates — the vetting process. Tim then entered the information, and one person from each group went on to a second round and so forth in the elimination process. An actual session would begin with ten groups of ten and continue until one candidate is left to become the GOOOH candidate to go on the ballot. We had to work with a scaled-down template, but the person who emerged was quite clearly the best choice to go on the ballot. The winner was the person I had selected to best represent me and apparently the others felt the same.

After the meeting I looked around for the young man I wanted to meet, but he had already left. I would find out later that his name was Jeremy Vaught, (not his real name) founder of the Muskogee Tea Party, and that his father was a state senator. Jeremy had a political blog, and when I checked it out I was impressed with its professionalism and canny insight into local politics. My admiration would be short-lived, however. It only lasted about a week — which was how long it took for the young Vaught to start circulating attack e-mails about me and GOOOH. By the time I received a copy of what was being said, there was a long string of back-and-forth dialog with other Republicans criticizing my candidacy for the U.S. House of Representative. I had changed my political affiliation from Republican to Independent when

I learned about the GOOOH plan. That apparently was the first volley in a battle I didn't know I was in.

Eventually the e-mail found its way to Charlie Woltz, Route 66 Tea Party's Thomas Paine, and he was outraged at what was being said about me. He responded with a scathing message and copied me. I wasn't surprised to see that one of the bloggers on the e-mail string was the leadership of GAB in Grove, but it did surprise me that the person who had started the whole thing was Jeremy Vaught, who I'd never even officially met. Apparently he was on my Route 66 Tea Party contact list. I knew at least one other person criticizing me, but there were names I didn't recognize at all. I didn't bother to respond to any of the criticism or insults since Charlie pretty well slammed them and put them in their place.

Their nasty e-mails were meant to intimidate me and stop me from challenging the Republican candidate but it had the opposite effect. I wasn't going to back off. I wasn't going to sit down and shut up. I had only just begun to fight.

Chapter 18

Running the Good Race

October 2009 found me busy attending meetings and rallies throughout the state and into neighboring Missouri looking for contacts in Joplin, my old stomping grounds. I had joined the Southwest Missouri Conservatives group after finding them through Meetup, the internet place to go to find like-minded individuals. At the October 5 meeting, which was my first and also my last, I was able to get in a short announcement about GOOOH and pass out flyers. Their agenda was already prepared in advance so I didn't get to say a whole lot, and when I asked about speaking at a future meeting I was told, "It would be considered." I felt some "bad vibes" from the Republican leadership that what I was offering didn't fit their agenda. Nevertheless, a couple of women thought GOOOH was great and took extra flyers for their friends at home.

On October 10, 2009, I met up with Carol Chouinard at the Tulsa State Fair. It was the first time in many years that FairTax didn't have a booth, so Carol and I went around passing out brochures. She did FairTax; I did GOOOH. We were a team. We are a team still.

There weren't many people at the State Fair interested in spending any time learning about GOOOH or FairTax. People were there to have fun and for the exhibits, to which I wandered away from Carol for a while to see. Horses and riders were gearing up for barrel racing competition in the exhibition barn. I watched for a while admiring the beautiful and well-groomed horses and the lovely young ladies sitting atop expensive hand-tooled saddles. Bling was everywhere. Hats, belts, bridles, saddles, and breast collars (on the horses) glittered with rhinestones and silver. Horses with tails touching the ground would take off like a rocket and stop on a dime. It was exhilarating to watch and as much as I would like it to be me atop one of the beautiful horses, I never got the "butterflies in the stomach" the way I would get when it was, "surf's up!"

Carol and I were a team, and she would have loved to get to all the events on our planning calendar, but she was running her own company, and it was impossible to do everything. I didn't work, so I continued driving to conservative venues, paying for the trips, the transportation and lodging with the allowance I got every two weeks. I made several trips to Tulsa in October 2009. There was a Can You Hear Me Now? rally in front of Channel 2, NBC's affiliate in Tulsa, on the 17th. Approximately 200 protesters showed up with signs promoting FOX as the only place for "fair and balanced" news. Other signs were in protest of all the other "lamestream" media. We got some car horn honks and some "thumbs-ups," but we also got the occasional middle finger. Mostly we got nothing. Not even looks. It was as if people just didn't want to know there was a problem or care what the problem might be. Apathy, it was everywhere, and there was hate. The middle fingers were bad enough, but someone threw a whole bunch of what looked like square plastic chips at us, but the wind blew them back in the direction of the car from which they were thrown, and they landed on the street. A woman carrying a sign walked over to take a closer look.

"They're condoms," she said.

I couldn't believe it and looked for myself . . . sure enough, they were condoms.

We would laugh about it later when we were asked how the protest went. Condoms! Not many other Tea Party participants can claim they had condoms thrown at them.

We had hoped to get on the news, but the only reporter to show up was a conservative blogger. I was really glad that I went because I was able to put faces to the names of several people I'd been sharing valuable e-mails with. I met supporters of Randy Brogdon for governor who later supported me in my official candidacy for the U.S. House, and they also supported my efforts to expose Obama as the perpetrator of the biggest fraud ever to hit the world stage. At the time I hadn't yet officially filed to run for congress and continued to promote the GOOOH program, considering myself a potential candidate through the plan. Lots of familiar faces were at the Channel 2 protest including Jim Conroy with his FairTax gear, who I was always glad to see. A new face was there also, a man who took a very keen interest in GOOOH, and his passion to promote it made him a great ally.

Mike Kurtz and his wife, Cris, founders of USA Patriots and Of God & Country in Tulsa, are the owners of Kurtz Design Studio and known for their exquisite graphic arts designs. Their professional careers often take a backseat to their tireless work as Tea Party leaders and founders of the Tulsa Tea Party. The Kurtzes would later design and produce my campaign material and cover for this book.

I attended one of the Kurtz's Of God & Country events. It was a professional educational presentation of the role religion played in the founding of our country. The event in Tulsa, held at a large church complex, was attended by hundreds of people, maybe as many as 500. There I met more people that I knew previously only by their e-mail names or addresses. The organizers allowed me to put GOOOH brochures at the entrance and inside the hall. There were several conservative groups that had tables set up selling fund-raising items and flyers announcing other religious events and organizations.

Mike and Kris kept me apprised of Tea Parties and conservative events in Tulsa, and I did my best to get to every one because the contacts I was making were the potential for new members of GOOOH which was a top priority for me.

As I promoted GOOOH, I began finding that a disturbing number of people I spoke to would dismiss GOOOH for "splitting the conservative vote" and siding with Republican candidates. It was difficult breaking through their mindset of resistance to something new. They weren't yet fed up with both parties as so many of us were who switched party affiliation to Independent or none. I called Tim to discuss these challenges and share a thought that had been dogging me for some time.

"What do you think about me actually running for office? I mean, officially filing to run against Dan Boren?" I asked.

"I think you should," Tim responded. "There are other GOOOH members running simultaneously as both Independent and potential GOOOH candidates. By promoting themselves they have more opportunity to get the word out about GOOOH and when critical mass is reached and candidate selections begin they will be better known which would be an advantage."

That was exactly what I had been thinking. All along I had met people who encouraged me to run. They would support me, they said.

They were sick of the two-party system and wanted new blood, new ideas, and new solutions, but especially they wanted someone who would honor their oath to the Constitution, something sorely lacking in Washington. Honor is a word void in American politics, and the Obama administration is DISHONOR on steroids. Most of the people I met through Tea Parties, FairTax, and GOOOH had never been active in politics, including myself, but here I was, suddenly contemplating a life immersed in the cesspool of American politics. I wasn't alone. Around the country others were stepping up, coming from all backgrounds and professions. It was especially gratifying to see those with military experience come forward. They understood honor. They understood love of country. My heart swelled with pride when I watched a video of Allen West that was going viral on the Internet. What we all had in common was summed up in two words: Constitutional Conservative. Col. West was running for Congress from his district in Florida. (West would gain support from the Tea Party movement and from patriots everywhere. He won the U.S. House seat in the mid-term election and joined Michele Bachmann's Tea Party Caucus in Congress, but he would disappoint Americans throughout the nation when he took the politically correct stance of ignoring the eligibility issue and ignoring Terry Lakin).

Critical mass needed for GOOOH to work would be half a million people registering and supporting the system with a $100 donation each. GOOOH would then fund a single national campaign to promote the 435 candidates selected to run against the party politicians. I knew this was the only way we would be able to defeat Dan Boren, who at the time had $1.3 million in his war chest. Having a dad who was a former governor and U.S. Representative gave him quite an advantage. That his dad was a member of the Council on Foreign Relations didn't hurt either.

I had a lot of misgivings, but promoting myself as a GOOOH participant took some of the edge off the pressures of running a traditional campaign like fundraising and jumping through party hoops. Fred and Alan were very supportive of everything I was doing and gave me encouragement. They loved Tim, and they gave whatever help they could give me to help make GOOOH a success. I asked Fred, "What if I was really elected to go to Congress? What would you think?"

"I think that would be really great," he answered. "You would do well."

Then I asked Alan, "What would you think if I got elected to go to Congress?"

His face lit up. He had an immediate reaction. "Mom, I would be so proud of you!"

That was all I needed to jump headlong into a new endeavor: Miki Booth for Congress, Independent, Constitutional Conservative, state leader of GOOOH, District 2 community coordinator for FairTax, founder of Route 66 Tea Party, District 2 community coordinator for the Patriotic Resistance now Patriot Action Network, all volunteer, all self-funded.

I went to the Federal Election Commission website (www.fec.gov) and printed out the campaign guide for candidates, 111 pages, and read it through. Since I was running for the first time and had no political financial history and relationship with lobbyists, there wasn't much I had to disclose. The whole theme of the guide, if there was one, was ethics, ethics, ethics. Uh-huh, I'm not making this up.

For those reading this book who don't like endings revealed prematurely, I offer my apology: Boren won.

I was asked by Tulsa Today (tulsatoday.com), an online news service, to recount my experiences running for office. My account explains some of the mechanics of officially running for a seat in the U.S. House of Representatives.

RUNNING THE GOOD RACE
Written by Miki Booth
Thursday, August 26, 2010

(Editors Note: The following is a personal reflection by a critic turned Republican candidate for Oklahoma's 2nd Congressional District. Battered from pillar-to-post by leftist critics and having withdrawn from that race before the primary, today Miki Booth is departing by bus to reach the Restoring Honor event Saturday in Washington. Her effort for love of country continues.)

"Some call her the homely Sarah Palin or the wild woman of Wyandotte, but Miki Booth hopes she'll soon be called congresswoman as she wants to pony up to D.C. via Oklahoma's District 2, while embarrassing the state on a larger stage."

This is the type of hateful rhetoric I expected when I threw my hat into the political ring. I was prepared for a whole lot worse since I had already become a controversial figure on the national stage by asking, "Where's the birth certificate?"

I didn't just question Obama's eligibility to be president, I held up my husband's and son's birth certificates from Kapi'olani Hospital on C-SPAN to prove by comparison that the Internet copy of Obama's certification of live birth was a fraud. My appearance and speech in Nashville at the National Tea Party Convention in February garnered overwhelming support for my candidacy. People want someone in Congress to champion an investigation into Obama's hidden records (from birth through college to campaign donations).

In January of this year I crossed the threshold of $5,000 in donations and/or expenses and went from testing the waters to officially filing for candidacy for Oklahoma's 2nd District of the U.S. House of Representatives. I did withdraw from the race before the primary in order to endorse and support Dr. Charles Thompson, but I will always hold the title of "former candidate for U.S. House of Representatives" whether I run again or not.

"Why did you run?"
"Was it worth it?"
"How did you do it?"
"How long have you been in politics?"
"Would you ever run again?"

These are some of the questions I'm still asked on almost a daily basis. The answer to why is far more complicated than the physical act of becoming an actual candidate. You can find most everything you need to know for filing candidacy on the Federal Election Commission website, fec.org or contacting your party's state officials for guidance. Of course, I did things the hard way as an Independent, having had it with both parties, and most recently changed from Republican to no affiliation, and before I was a Republican I was a Democrat, again for complicated reasons, and then back again to the Republican Party where I am today.

The guide on the website answered all the questions I had, and so I basically got to work assembling a team of friends and supporters, those who asked or encouraged me to run. From there they put together a committee to elect me and filed the Statement of Organization (FEC Form 1) and shortly thereafter I filed the other necessary form, Statement of Candidacy (FEC Form 2) — all that's easy enough. Very shortly thereafter the information appeared on the website and tracking my opponents became a daily task.

The most important thing about running for public office is money. Not only do you need a lot of it, you need to keep close track of where it goes, which is why so much emphasis is put on the treasurer and record keeping. We hired a CPA for impeccable financial records and would do so again.

I didn't read the guide cover-to-cover, but a lot of what it contains has to do with ethics. I think that's why we see so much corruption in Washington. The career politicians have long forgotten the rules they're supposed to abide by and made up their own on their way up. They've also forgotten the oath they pledged to support and defend the Constitution. Forgotten? How can that be? They take the oath at the start of each new Congress — the entire House of Representatives and one-third of the Senate.

The current oath was enacted in 1884: "I do solemnly swear (or affirm) that I will support and defend the Constitution of the United States against all enemies, foreign and domestic; that I will bear true faith and allegiance to the same; that I take this obligation freely, without any mental reservation or purpose of evasion; and that I will well and faithfully discharge the duties of the office on which I am about to enter: So help me God."

Take, for example, Charlie Rangle in his twentieth term. Forty years in Congress pledging his loyalty to the Constitution, twenty times in front of a public audience, yet arguably the most unethical congressman in D.C. and systematically shredding the Constitution and the protection it affords us against a tyrannical government.

Closer to home, Dan Boren has taken the oath three times, yet he voted 98 percent of the time with his party including all the bailouts and spending bills. He has the distinction of receiving the most money from oil company donations. He hasn't been a representative for the average resident of District 2. Many of us have a collection of matching form letters if we were lucky enough to receive any kind of response from him at all on any question we asked him.

Early on in my campaign I wrote a letter to Rep. Boren challenging him to a debate and to a marksmanship contest. Dan Boren is on the board of the National Rifle Association (NRA). Although he's a proponent of the Second Amendment for hunting and sport, he doesn't talk about it in the context of the Constitution, which many of us believe is our last defense against a tyrannical government — a government of cram down legislation, auto company takeovers, bank bailouts, and anti-business agendas led by Dan Boren's party.

The Constitution clearly gives federal government eighteen enumerated powers and that which it does not, are reserved to the States or to the people. As the Tenth Amendment states: "The powers not delegated to the United States by the Constitution, nor prohibited by it to the States, are reserved to the States respectively, or to the people."

Campaigning for office is all consuming, and I was torn between going to Washington to fight or continue my fight here at home championing FairTax and GOOOH, the plan to replace all 435 members of Congress with individuals like myself who believe money and influence should be taken out of the equation to run for office. Without GOOOH an Independent candidate like me would stand no chance and split the conservative vote. When it didn't appear the GOOOH plan would reach the number of participants for implementation in 2010, I changed parties and ran as a Republican by changing party affiliation on the Statement of Candidacy (FEC Form 2).

Preparing a business/action plan is the key to success for any endeavor, and as a career businesswoman and former sales director, I began work on just such a plan. I planned my work and had every intention of working my plan, but it seemed like every day, every single day, Obama, his administration or Congress pulled a shenanigan that infringed on our freedom and liberty, and I just could not sit still or shut up.

I never wanted to have anything to do with politics. When I was a little girl I looked up the word and the definition that stuck with me was "shrewd." I'd always heard and believed you just vote for the less crooked politician and Hawaii had a slew of them influenced by unions and, yes, organized crime. Half the time I never even voted.

But in 2008, here I was retired in Oklahoma screaming at the TV like so many Americans, angry, frustrated and paying attention to politics for the first time in our lives. I joined the rank of Tea Party leaders. My political activism grew, and I attended every freedom rally I was able. Soon I was invited to speak throughout Oklahoma and the three states that adjoin District 2. The subject that most people wanted to know about is the matter of eligibility, and I have the proof that Obama is not only an illegitimate president, he may be an illegal alien.

Running for office interfered with my efforts to expose Obama and his corrupt administration, so I made the decision to bow out and support the candidate I felt would have the best chance of defeating Boren. I endorsed Charles Thompson, a Constitutional Conservative, retired military major, small business owner and veterinarian. We've had the opportunity to debate all the candidates, and Dr. Thompson far and away is the best person to represent Oklahomans in Congress.

I'm back to my role as a vocal critic of Barack Hussein Obama and his team of czars, socialists, communists, tax cheats, crooks, cronies, and union thugs — now exposing his Muslim upbringing and Arab/Islamic ties that have infiltrated every aspect of American life.

Lately it seems the Obama facade is beginning to crumble. It was only a matter of time before their programmed response to the question of eligibility (laugh and move on) would no longer be acceptable. Would I run in 2012 if Charles Thompson isn't able to defeat Boren in November? Yes, in a heartbeat.

I will always appreciate every supporter, every group that provided an opportunity to speak, and to the founding principles of the United States of America for which I am proud to stand.

Sincerely,
Miki Booth

I'm getting ahead of myself on many things that happened in the time frame herein, but the aforementioned information regarding my challenge to Boren has an update from a February 24, 2011, town hall. Dan Boren never replied to my challenge for a debate and marksmanship contest. I figured he's a good shot, he's hunted big game, and is on the board of directors of the National Rifle Association, but he never responded to my challenge. I received an e-mail form letter a couple weeks later, which merely thanked me for contacting him.

January 30, 2010

Rep. Dan Boren
U.S. HOUSE OF REPRESENTATIVES
216 Cannon House Office Building
Washington, D.C. 20515

Dear Rep. Boren,

It is with great pleasure that I announce my candidacy to challenge you for the District 2 House of Representatives seat of the 112th Congress. In the spirit of competition and sportsmanship I further challenge you to 1) a rifle marksmanship contest and 2) a debate.

1. Rifle marksmanship contest — venue of your choosing.

2. Debate on issues relevant to District 2 voters — venue of your choosing.

Your diligent efforts protecting our Second Amendment rights are commendable and appreciated. However, our interpretation of the right to bear arms seems to differ in that I believe the framers of the Constitution armed us in defense against a tyrannical government. It's good and well we can hunt and target shoot but if you've discussed guns in the context of the Constitution, I must have missed it. Your record of voting 98 percent of the time with your party leads me to believe you might have not read the Constitution because it appears you are not guided by it.

Although I don't have a written record of my rifle shooting skills, I did drop a coyote at about 200 yards a couple of weeks ago, so you can be assured I am qualified to challenge you in a shooting match.

I am very concerned about the direction our country is headed, and most people in District 2 share my concerns. I believe it is imperative for us to talk about the challenges we face and offer solutions to the dire troubles our country is in.

I look forward to receiving a quick reply to my challenges and allowing We the People of District 2 an opportunity to see the caliber of their candidates.

Respectfully,
Miki Booth
cc: Distribution

Response from Congressman Dan Boren
Tue, February 16, 2010 10:03:20 AM

From : Congressman Dan Boren
iamaoko2@ mail.house.gov

Dear Mrs. Booth:

Thank you for contacting me to share your views on the issues that are important to you. I always value hearing from my fellow Oklahomans.

It is an honor to serve and represent the State of Oklahoma in Congress. I carefully take into account the input I receive and the concerns I hear from my constituents. Rest assured that I will keep your views in mind as I vote in the U.S. House of Representatives on issues important both to Oklahoma and our nation.

Again, thank you for contacting me with your concerns. If I can ever be of future assistance, please do not hesitate to contact me.

Respectfully yours,
Dan Boren
Member of Congress

DDB: EM

During my campaign I was asked frequently if Boren ever replied to my challenges and just as frequently told that he would never acknowledge my challenge because he has never agreed to a debate with anyone. Ever. Undeterred, I kept sending him e-mails.

One Friday evening I drove across the state line to Seneca, Missouri, to the only Dairy Queen in the three-state area to bring home burgers and fries for dinner. Our big dog, Brandi, sat on the front passenger seat in her usual position, with front feet planted on the floor and nose against the dashboard. It was a Friday tradition to take Brandi out for ice cream. She knows when it's Friday, and she knows the words "ice cream." Even the employees at Dairy Queen know not to put a spoon in the cup of vanilla ice cream since Brandi's paws make it difficult to manage an eating utensil.

On this particular Friday as Brandi was licking her vanilla treat, I heard a caller on the Mark Levin show say that the number to the Capitol switchboard was toll-free: (800) SOB-U-SOB. I could hardly believe it. That was just too funny, too rich, so I got out my iPhone and dialed: 1-800-SOB-U-SOB. A woman answered, "Capitol switchboard."

It took me off guard, but I quickly recovered and asked for Rep. Dan Boren's voice mail. After his recorded announcement and the beep, I left him a message: "Hi! This is Miki Booth. I still haven't heard back from you regarding my challenge to a debate and marksmanship contest. Please give me a call back so we can work out a time and place for the event," or something to that effect. Whenever I had an opportunity to speak at Tea Parties and at debates I would take out my phone and call Boren using 1-800-SOB-U-SOB and on speaker phone the audience could hear Boren's greeting and then hear me leaving a taunting request for a debate and shooting contest. It was fun for me, and the audience loved it. I'd check the number periodically to make sure it would work for my presentation and after about a month of calling, the federal government changed the number.

On February 24, 2011, after a postponement due to the historic blizzard that left at least two feet of snow across most of Oklahoma, Dan Boren held a town hall meeting at the community center in Grove. I got the notice from the GAB group, and they requested we wear our GAB shirts if we had one. I donned mine and drove to pick up my bundles of the Banner newspaper so I'd be able to distribute them at the meeting. I got there after the meeting started and went to the back of the room. Someone motioned to me that an empty seat was available, so I sat down a few rows from the back.

Boren placed some large graphs up on easels and described government spending with color-coded segments of a pie chart. Most of us knew the income-to-spending ratio, and when Boren asked the audience if we thought the government should stop spending, all hands in the auditorium went up. Over 100 people were there. Many were members of the Republican Party who followed the philosophy of the Tea Party movement. A lot of new people came to the meeting to hear Boren and get what was happening in Congress from the horse's mouth.

Boren wanted ideas from the audience on how and what to cut. When he was asked why we were still giving foreign aid to countries that don't even like us, his answer irritated my sensibilities. He said that foreign aid didn't amount to all that much in the great scheme of things, and if foreign aid were cut off that would mean funding to Israel would be cut off as well because it is all in the same pot.

My hand shot up, and he pointed at me saying, "Yes, ma'am."

I looked around behind me to make sure I was the one he'd called on so I wouldn't look like a fool if I started talking, and it wasn't me he'd acknowledged. I was always sensitive to "making ass" especially when I knew there were people in the room who didn't like me very much, and I was nervous, but I had to address the foreign aid statement.

I spoke. Again it was more of a statement than a question, but I had developed a thicker skin.

"I just learned that we are spending six million dollars to restore mosques and other Islamic sites around the world. That has got to stop for the sheer principle of it, and I take offense at the liberal tone of your statement implying that we have to keep funding everybody for the sake of Israel. I say cut off foreign aid. Our country is in trouble and we need that money for us. Surely we can continue to help Israel, not only with funds but also with the entire might of our military and our country." Boren responded that I made good points.

Of the five congressional districts in Oklahoma, four remained in Republican hands and in the fifth, District 2, Boren would win a fourth term. He escaped the shellacking Democrats took in the midterm election because he satisfied his conservative rural base when he voted against both cap and tax and Obamacare. He appeared on national news saying, "You can cut my arms off, but I won't sign that healthcare bill." He was conservative. He was reasonable. He was given another chance.

He did well at the town hall. Even when critics cited his past voting record and his loyalty to Nancy Pelosi, he was able to slough it off by pointing out that that was then, and this was now.

A GAB leader told me that she thought for sure I would bring up the birth certificate issue and was surprised that I did not. I told her I never knew what kind of crowd I was addressing and wasn't up to a tar and feathering, a veiled reference to the last GAB meeting I attended. It was then that I saw a large crowd still gathered around Boren, and I wanted to shake his hand and thank him for cosponsoring FairTax and ask him if he was still the only Democrat to sign on. I stood at the outer circle of people listening to Boren talk, waiting for an opportunity to reach over, shake his hand, and leave. I was running on a tight schedule that day.

Someone asked Boren what the deal was with the governor of Hawai'i saying he can't find Obama's birth certificate. Boren laughed, but before he could answer I interjected with, "Can I answer that?"

I said, "Abercrombie was my representative and senator from the Big Island. He's a doper, toker, socialist-commie hippie and tried to pass legislation for a nude beach on the Kona Coast. This is Obama's friend and cover for his lies and anti-American activity."

Boren laughed and said, "Abercrombie is known to be a 'toker' now and then."

I had everyone's attention. I told them, "Obama's birth story is a lie."

But Boren said that when the issue comes up with congressional leaders, their opinion is that it's a distraction, and they have a lot of pressing issues to work on.

"My name is Miki Booth," I said. "Do you know who I am?"

He answered, "Yes, I know who you are. You ran against me, and I still have a card pinned in my office of you and that gun. What is . . ."

"You mean my 'Yellow Boy,' the Henry rifle?"

"Yeah, you challenged me to a shooting contest."

"And you never responded. How come you never took me up on the challenge?"

"Because I knew you could probably beat me," he laughed.

I reached to shake his hand. "Thank you for supporting FairTax," I said and turned to walk away. I was already late to a meeting but stopped to answer a lady's question about the birth certificate posted online. I told her that it was not a birth certificate but a certification of live birth and that it certified only that a live baby was born. "Coulda been born in a marijuana patch," I told her, "but he wasn't born in a Hawai'i hospital, and the certification posted on the Internet is a forgery."

Chapter 19

Black Robes and Firing Back

One of the first places I announced my candidacy officially running as an Independent was at an event in Tulsa where several area pastors spoke. There I learned about the role of religious leaders in the first American Revolution, the pastors who had the ear of the people during the War for Independence. The British referred to them as the "Black Robes," the preachers who wore black smocks over their everyday clothes as they spoke to the members of their congregations. They were the ones who led successful attacks against advancing British troops, and the Red Coats despised them.

At the Black Robes meeting, the pastors loosely formed a "Black Robes Brigade" among themselves. If there was a leader, it appeared to be Rev. Paul Blair, pastor of Fairview Baptist Church in Edmond, Oklahoma and founder of Reclaiming America for Christ, which with many other organizations banded together and boycotted the February 2011 CPAC due to its inclusion of the gay conservative group GOProud.

Blair, I learned, was a former football star in Oklahoma, and he looked the part. Tall and impressive, he was very recognizable with dark hair and mustache, and I would later easily pick him out of a crowd and report to him things going on that I was involved in such as the CIA Columbia trial, LTC Terry Lakin, the Boren challenge, Obama's hidden records and phony birth certification, and any other tidbits of information that came to mind.

Besides Rev. Blair, there were many more speakers, some of whom I did not know at the time but would see at many subsequent conservative events. Someone requested that if any people in the audience were running for office, they should stand up, which I did. I received much applause when I stated who I was running against because thus far no one had come forward to announce a challenge to Boren. That wasn't unusual. The attendees at the meeting were from Tulsa, a different district, and Rev. Blair and many others had driven from

Oklahoma City, yet another district not familiar with District 2 where I was running. Two or three others also stood and announced their intention to run in their own districts challenging Republican incumbents.

I remember well a woman who was running for U.S. representative in District 1, Tulsa. She stood out like a sore thumb because she was unmistakably from the Middle East. She wasn't well received and didn't win, but Fran Moghaddam, an Iranian, was a conservative Christian and raised more than $15,000 that sources say came from her wealthy family. Every two years since she began running, she did a little better. I also met Nathan Dahm that night. He had the backing of the Tea Party movement except in one or two areas where incumbent John Sullivan was favored. Sullivan had nearly a million dollars to spend on his campaign plus special-interest and party influence, so he was easily able to defeat Nathan's $28,758 even with the support of the faithful Tea Party patriots campaigning for him. It mirrored the situation with Randy Brogdon running for governor. The well-funded, special-interest, Republican Party RINO favorite, Mary Fallin, beat him.

The featured guest at the Black Robes Brigade meeting was the last speaker at the event. Charl van Wyk, missionary and author of, Shooting Back: The Right and Duty of Self-Defence. I was unaware of the massacre that happened in South Africa on July 25, 1993, so I listened with rapt attention and astonishment to the incredible recollections of Charl van Wyk.

It was during Apartheid and a particularly dangerous time in South Africa when four men, members of the Azanian People's Liberation Army, attacked the St. James Church in Kenilworth, Cape Town with automatic weapons and hand grenades. Approximately 1,000 congregants were in the church, and the assault left eleven dead and fifty-eight injured. Undoubtedly there would have been even more casualties but Charl van Wyk pulled out a gun and shot back.

"Grenades were exploding in flashes of light. Pews shattered under the blasts, sending splinters flying through the air," he recalled. "An automatic assault rifle was being fired and was fast ripping the pews — and whoever, whatever was in its trajectory — to pieces. We were being attacked!"

Had van Wyk been unarmed like the other congregants, the slaughter would have been much worse.

"Instinctively, I knelt down behind the bench in front of me and pulled out my .38 special snub-nosed revolver, which I always carried with me," van Wyk recalled. "I would have felt undressed without it."

When van Wyk shot back at the attackers, they fled.

Four of the people killed were Russian seamen attending the service as part of the church's outreach program. Another seaman lost both legs and an arm.

When van Wyk concluded his program, many of us stood in line to meet him. Eventually I got to say hello and shake his hand. He engaged me in conversation, asking about my candidacy for the U.S. House and about the process of running for office. I was beaming. Charl van Wyk was actually talking with me. I was cognizant of others wanting to meet him too, so I told him that I must go get a copy of his book so he could sign it for me, but when I got to the books table they were all gone.

Chapter 20

The Palintologists

The Tea Party Express bus came to Oklahoma City on Wednesday the 4th of November 2009. On my way to the capitol to attend the rally I stopped and picked up Carol Chouinard, district director of FairTax, at her home near Tulsa. I was able to find a parking space very close to the rally, which made it easy to unload the FairTax and GOOOH brochures. The crowd was still growing, and Carol and I set up our lawn chairs to use as a base of operations to hand out brochures and designate a place to regroup. Nearby were friends I'd made at the D.C. march who were part of the 9.12 Oklahoma City group, Carma Neta Morris and Jenny White of R.O.P.E. (Restore Oklahoma Public Education.)

There were about 2,000 people and as dusk fell I could barely recognize the people on the stage, but I could hear them speaking. They introduced a speaker, a representative of FairTax, Elza Jones, who had come to the GOOOH mock selection meeting in Muskogee. When he was finished speaking, I worked my way to the stage at the top of the Capitol steps, but when I got there Elza was nowhere to be seen. There were just too many people. (I would see Elza later when he came to a 9.12 OKC meeting where I gave a GOOOH presentation and a campaign speech.)

After the crowd thinned out, Carol and I discovered that the Tea Party Express had tables set up selling assorted merchandise. We met Ron and Kay Rivoli who were traveling with the bus and provided musical entertainment. I was a huge fan, having bought their latest CD that featured the song "Press One For English." Ron and Kay signed a photograph for me. I was tickled knowing how much Fred was going to like it.

Also there, selling buttons and Gadsden flags, was Kenneth Gladney, a black conservative who was beaten by Service Employees

International Union (SEIU) thugs following a town hall meeting in St. Louis.

"The criminal attack was inspired by the DNC and BarackObama.com propaganda," wrote an eyewitness on the St. Louis Tea Party website. Days before the attack on Gladney, the White House had promised to counter opposition to his policies by punching back "twice as hard."

Typical of SEIU's thug mentality, the attack was planned and intended to create a riot to discredit the American political resistance. The Alinsky tactic from Rules for Radicals "Agitate to the point of conflict," repeats over and over and even reached a boiling point in Madison, Wisconsin where it was the unions against common sense, the unions against reason, the unions against fiscal discipline, and the unions against Gov. Walker. They might have lost the battle when Walker signed the bill to end collective bargaining, but they haven't lost the war, not by a long shot, not as long as Obama, the head agitator, keeps them inspired, encouraged, and funded. The Obama inspired-attack on the Wisconsin capitol resulted in millions of dollars of damage to the marble inside and outside the building.

Kenneth Gladney autographed a "Don't Tread on Me" flag (which I later auctioned for much-needed campaign funds), and Carol and I took photos with him and the Tea Party Express bus. I gave Kenneth and the Rivolis several of Tim Cox's GOOOH books that they promised they would distribute on the buses. Would they be on board with us or side with the Republican Party and ignore GOOOH? We're still waiting to find out.

By early December 2009 Kurtz Design Studio was busy at work creating a logo and designing promotional material for my campaign. In the meantime I used some of my own graphic arts experience to design some temporary things I would need right away such as calling cards and T-shirts for volunteers to wear. I hired a professional photographer to take shots for the Kurtzes to use in their creations. When Fred and I tossed around ideas for photos, we agreed that the best way to show my support for the Second Amendment would be to show that I was a gun enthusiast, so I chose Fred's .45 caliber "Yellow Boy" rifle. The nickname was given to the 1866 rifle for its bright brass frame and was one of the most popular rifles of the time for its easy handling, especially on horseback.

I saddled up Cheyenne after giving her a thorough brushing and combing out her mane and tail while I waited for the photographer to arrive. Earlier, Fred had polished "Yellow Boy" to the highest sheen possible. I wondered if I should also get some pictures with my favorite gun, a Smith & Wesson .357 magnum that I had owned since 1975. I decided that the .45 caliber rifle would match Cheyenne better. Our message was, "It's Time for a Reckoning," and this Constitutional Conservative was ready to ride — taking the fight to Washington.

Sarah Palin came to nearby Fayetteville, Arkansas, for a book signing to promote Going Rogue: An American Life. Fred desperately wanted to meet her and get an autographed book, but he had to work that Thursday in December 2009, so I agreed to go and stand in line for a signed book, shake hands with Sarah Palin, and get a photograph perhaps. I had a T-shirt with an iron-on campaign poster on the back that I planned to wear. I designed it to look like a wanted poster with a sepia effect and blurred edges. In the center was a black-and-white photo of me standing and holding "Yellow Boy" and the text read, "U.S. House of Representatives — Oklahoma Dist. 2." "MIKI BOOTH, Constitutional Conservative" stood out in bold type. "Limited Government, Low Taxes, Free Market and Personal Responsibility" was listed on the right, and on the left was Elizabeth Jones-Weaver's contact information. My fellow Smart Girl Politics member had agreed to help me with my campaign. The bottom of the poster featured GOOOH, FairTax and my website URL.

I found out several of my friends from Grove were planning to go too. There were seven of us total including Elizabeth and her daughter, Chloe, so I went to work making T-shirts for everybody so we would match.

Earlier during the presidential campaign, my sister in Alaska sent me a T-shirt with "Palintologist" and a dictionary-looking definition of the word as I described earlier. I got the bright idea to put it on the front of the T-shirts with my poster on the back. I bought red T-shirts including a small one for Chloe (who suggested we make one for Piper and Sarah Palin too) and bought enough printable iron-on sheets to put "Palintologist" on the front in white ink. The finished product was striking. The white wording on the dark red background stood out and attracted a lot of attention as we stood in a serpentine line of 500 people waiting outside Sam's Club in the freezing cold for hours. I was about 130th in line, and when Elizabeth and Chloe arrived they were well into the 200's but I gave up my place in line to be with them. Our shirts were a sensation. People asked where they could buy one.

When the rest of my group showed up they barely made the 500 person cutoff. I'd been really worried that they might not make it at all. I gave my Grove friends their T-shirts, and we had two extras, a small one for Piper Palin and one for Sarah.

To break the monotony of standing in line, Elizabeth led a cheer and the other group of my supporters joined in, chanting, "Hey, Miki, you're so fine . . . you're so fine you blow my mind! Hey, Miki! Hey, Miki!" The 1982 song recorded by singer and choreographer Toni Basil was remembered by many there, and some chimed in while others clapped out the rhythm.

Before long, many people waiting in line knew that I was running for office, and there were people there who had driven to Fayetteville from my district. It was so wonderful to hear them pledge their support for me. They were all Sarah Palin supporters, but a few anti-Palin protesters showed up and made a lot of noise. They were on private property, however, and so were quickly removed, much to our delight.

When I first arrived at Sam's Club and was walking to the rear of the building to get in line, I passed two men who were obviously a news team, one with a mic and another with a large video camera. They read the poster on my back and hurried to catch up with me to request an interview. They were from Finland and were following Sarah Palin to document her book-signing tour. The men wanted to know what the poster meant. I told them I was running for office in Washington, D.C., and the information was my campaign platform.

"Why do you have a gun on your back?" one of the men asked.

"It's to show that I support our country's Second Amendment right to keep and use guns to protect our lives, our freedom, and our property. It's my right to protect myself from government tyranny, like what happened during the Revolutionary War," I explained.

"But why do you have a gun?" he asked again.

So I tried again. "See me holding my rifle?" I asked. "That makes me a free citizen. If I let the government take my gun away from me, then I become a slave. If the government makes them illegal and tries to take them away from the people of America, then they will have to fight us because we will not be slaves. Our country was bought and paid for by the blood of our founders and generations of patriots who fought and died for our freedom. Barack Obama is a tyrant, and we reject tyranny. We reject him and his anti-American policies."

I doubt they showed my interview in Finland. I might've come off a little too radical for their tastes.

The bus carrying Sarah and her entourage finally arrived amid cheers and whistles. As she appeared at the open door of the bus and made her way down the steps, camera phones seemed to come out of nowhere to catch footage or a snapshot of Sarah. From where I was standing I saw dozens of them in the air, held high by outstretched arms aimed at Sarah Palin. It would have made an interesting photo, I thought.

Sarah held her son, Trig, while she made her way along the line of people, shaking hands and thanking them for coming. She worked her way toward the building and stopped to speak to reporters before disappearing from view into a back door of Sam's Club. Soon the line began moving. There were a couple of women dressed to look like Sarah Palin, and they got a lot of attention. Reporters worked their way along the lines of people looking for someone interesting to interview and focused on Chloe. Eight-year-old Chloe made us beam with pride as she spoke clearly and confidently to the interviewer. She charmed the local TV news crew and impressed everyone around her. It was no surprise to anyone to learn she was homeschooled.

Chloe told the reporter that she loved Sarah Palin, and that she was also there for me, and so their attention turned to our group all wearing the matching red Palintologist shirts. The reporter asked where the shirts came from and was told that I had made them. I turned around so the news crew could video both sides of my shirt, and I answered some of their questions before they moved on. Both Chloe and I were on the local Fayetteville news that night, I was told later.

We finally got out of the cold wind and into the building where we were ushered down a curtained corridor to a security area where we put our belongings into a bin to go through x-ray screening and walk through a metal detector just like at the airport. Just past the security point, our pre-purchased books we got at Sam's Club were taken from us and exchanged for cards printed by Sam's Club with all the book-signing event information. Those who brought their books from elsewhere to be signed kept theirs. We gave the "Palintologist/Miki

Booth for Congress" shirts to an attendant who assured us that Sarah Palin and Piper would get them.

It was the first time for many of us to attend such an event. Security was tight and we took baby steps along the curtained path as we inched along. We could see people in line ahead make a left turn, and we wondered if that was where we would finally see Sarah Palin, but when we got up there we saw that there was yet another turn in the curtained hallway. We got to a staging area where we were informed about how we would meet Sarah and what the protocol was. At this point we could see a large lighted room ahead where there was a table stacked with books and people talking to someone, but we couldn't hear much until we actually got into the room where they limited the number of people inside at a time. When we finally got in, Elizabeth and Chloe went first to the table full of books, and a man had them stop there until the two people ahead of them got their books and handshakes from Sarah and moved on to the curtained exit.

Elizabeth augmented her household earnings by designing and making her own line of jewelry using local freshwater pearls found in the Poteau River near their home. She had made a set of matching necklace and earrings of the unique pearls especially for Sarah and sent them to her a few months earlier. She was thrilled when she received an unexpected handwritten thank you card from Sarah in reply, and they had something to talk about. Sarah remembered and said she treasured the gift.

Elizabeth got a special hug from Sarah, and Chloe got Sarah to sign her favorite animal book. Sarah said she loved the Palintologist shirt, and Elizabeth introduced me, whereupon Sarah reached over and shook my hand, saying, "Thank you for your boldness." Elizabeth, Chloe, and I all turned our backs to Sarah to show her the poster of me with the "Yellow Boy." She said, "I love that," and reached over to tug on Elizabeth's shirt to see the poster better. The photographer shooting the obligatory souvenir photo, which I later purchased online, captured Elizabeth bending over and Sarah Palin touching her butt.

Sarah's father was standing at the exit, and Elizabeth and Chloe got a hug from him. I gave him a big smile, shook his hand, and made my way through the curtained hallway. After a couple of turns I found myself in the refrigerated foods section of Sam's Club.

We milled around talking to other supporters and fans and after a while I went outside to see if the rest of my group had gotten into the building yet. There was still a line outside, but no red Palintologist shirts were visible. The line was moving slowly, and I knew it would be a long wait before they appeared in Frozen Foods.

Back in Sam's Club there were lots of people at the snack bar area, and everyone was sharing their stories of meeting the rock star, Sarah Palin. People asked where they could get a shirt like mine, and I handed them my business card–size campaign cards. I told them to check on my website later where I would have them for sale. The Kurtzes were already printing a batch of T-shirts with my new logo, and I just decided on the spot that I would have them print a batch of red Palintologist shirts too.

An Associated Press reporter asked for an interview, which I was delighted to give. I'd been called a "publicity whore" by an anonymous Obama robot (Obot) and smiled to myself knowing that more coverage of me in the media would get their heads spinning.

The first questions had to do with why I liked Sarah Palin and what I had in common with her. The reporter questioned me in depth about my campaign, and when I talked about Obama, the reporter furiously scribbled some things on his small spiral notepad. He was very interested in what I had to say about Obama, which was extensive.

The reporter told me he was from Oklahoma and would like to stay informed about my bid for the U.S. House. He wrote his name and phone number on a page of the notepad and tore it from the spiral binding. I took his info and tucked it into a pocket, not thinking a whole lot about it. I actually doubted that he was an AP reporter. He showed me no credentials. He had no recording device of any kind. No camera, nothing except a tiny notepad and his scribbled notes.

When the rest of my support team finally emerged from the maze, they said that Sarah had commented on meeting the others of the Miki Booth for Congress group. Everyone was hopeful that Sarah would endorse my candidacy as she had already used her "kingmaker" touch on other political hopefuls. Unfortunately, more times than not, she chose to support RINOs over Tea Party candidates.

The following day the AP story was picked up by media worldwide:

FAYETTEVILLE, Ark.

Lynn Giese calls Sarah Palin the best thing that's happened to the U.S. in a long time, and the 57-year-old housewife says she'd work tirelessly for the former Alaska governor were she to run for president in 2012.

"I'd do anything, go anywhere," said Giese, of Bokoshe, Oklahoma, while waiting in line at a Sam's Club in Fayetteville where Palin signed copies of "Going Rogue," her best-selling memoir.

She'd also have support from Kayla Hogue, a 20-year-old student who came to the same event sporting a button melding a photo of Palin and Ronald Reagan. And Bob Rutz, 78, first in line at Palin's book signing a day earlier in Springfield, Montana, who said, "I'm hoping she'll be drafted (to run)."

These are the foot soldiers in Palin's army: thousands of devoted fans who show up to catch a glimpse of the one-time GOP vice presidential nominee on her book tour and urge her to seek the nation's top job.

In Fayetteville, hundreds of people — some camping out in frigid weather nearly a day before the event — formed a line that snaked around the back of the store. They wore camouflage fatigues and suits, work boots and dress loafers, ball caps and cowboy hats, and T-shirts that read, "Palintologist."

But while huge crowds greet her with roars of "Run Sarah Run!" as she tours the country in a bus, many national Republicans look on nervously, worrying the unparalleled enthusiasm she generates among some conservative voters isn't enough to power a Republican victory over President Barack Obama in 2012.

"People look at her and see themselves: patriotic, religious, family oriented outsiders looked down on by a liberal elite," said Jim Broussard, a political science professor at Lebanon Valley College in Pennsylvania. "But what makes her so attractive to her base makes her less attractive as an actual candidate, because you can't win with just your base."

In an increasingly urban multicultural country, the hordes coming out to see Palin are overwhelmingly white, conservative, and from small towns (not surprisingly, since her book tour largely avoided cities.) They often express disdain for Obama, the mainstream media and the culture of Washington, which they said doesn't reflect them or their concerns.

"B.O. scares me," said Miki Booth, 59, of the president, adding that Palin "is as American as it gets."

Palin played into that fear on a radio show Thursday, telling host Rusty Humphries that voters "rightfully" have questions about the legitimacy of Obama's birth certificate. The so-called birther conspiracy around Obama's U.S. citizenship has been widely discredited, and state health officials in Hawaii have repeatedly confirmed that the president was born there in 1961.

I was wrong. He was an Associated Press reporter.

Chapter 21

Obaachan's House

The little four-year-old half-Japanese girl, her older brother, and her mother had gone to live in Massachusetts near her father's family when he was deployed to Korea. Her Daddy's family were staunch Catholics and although they were kind to "Tommy's new family," they insisted on everyone being Catholic. That meant his new wife, who had been raised a Buddhist, had to convert to Catholicism and get married again in the Catholic Church. That meant the two children had to go to Catholic school and catechism on Saturday. It was all very complicated for Tommy's new wife, but her husband was not a devout Catholic and did not press his new wife to conform to his religion. The children, however, would go to Catholic school.

The girl and her brother attended a school nearby — the brother in first grade, the girl in kindergarten. The other kids in the Catholic school were really nice, and the girl already had a best friend who lived next door to the house she moved into. Everything was good. She enjoyed school.

Then one day the Sister handed out sheets of manila construction paper for the children to draw pictures on. The girl enjoyed drawing, but that day something kept her attention away from the task at hand. There was a wart on the knuckle of her left thumb, and she had picked at it until it bled. The blood kept oozing out, and she began blotting it on the construction paper. Soon a pattern appeared and she was inspired to form a picture with the little round blood blots.

She was deep in concentration creating her "drawing" when suddenly she heard a shout that came from right above her head.

"WHAT ARE YOU DOING?" screamed the nun. The little girl was startled and then frightened of the black-and-white-robed teacher hovering over her.

The nun snatched the drawing up off the desk and walked away, leaving the little girl confused about what was going on. Within seconds the nun returned. She had a wooden ruler in her hand and used it to rap the little girl sharply on the knuckles of her right hand. Once, twice, three times while she kept a grip on the girl's arm to keep her from pulling her hand away.

The girl's mother was called, and she went to the school to take her daughter home. The little girl had been crying the entire time she waited for her mother. She pleaded and cried, begging not to be sent back to school. Although her brother would stay, the girl would not return to the Catholic school.

She heard her parents arguing. They were talking about her, "Oniichan," eldest daughter. Her mother won the arguments. The girl would not go to Catholic school, and her mother would not attend Easter Mass.

Her father insisted that everyone had to go to church on Easter Sunday. Even if they didn't attend Mass regularly, it was mandatory that they do so on Easter and Christmas. The little girl went shopping with her parents to find the perfect Easter dress, bonnet, and gloves to wear to church with her daddy and brother. She got an added bonus — a little purse decorated with pastel-colored plastic flowers. It was the perfect accompaniment to carry the coin she would put in the offering plate when it passed in front of her, an offering for God's house.

All dressed in her Easter finery, gloved hands holding the flowered purse, she was carried from the car by her Daddy while he held her brother's hand. They walked up the many steps and entered through the large open doors of St. Bernard's Catholic Church in Worcester, Massachusetts.

The little girl had never seen anything so spectacular. The inside of the church was like a castle decorated with the most ornate statues and windows she had ever seen. When the priest spoke, his voice echoed throughout the gigantic chamber that was filled with what looked to her like a million people. She didn't understand what the priest was saying, but it didn't matter — everywhere she looked was something incredible to see. There were even people who smiled at her as she looked around, and she smiled back at them.

Then it was time to give the offering. Helpers of the priest walked down the aisles and passed a metal dish down through the benches, and people put their money in and passed it to the next person. The dish would soon come to her, and she opened her purse to get the dime her father gave her to give to God. She looked in the purse. It was empty. The plastic purse was fastened together by staples. There were gaps in the sides and on the bottom, and the dime had fallen, unnoticed, through one of those gaps. She stared into the empty purse. She had no money to give to God. She panicked as the dish came closer and closer and she started to cry. The closer the dish came, the louder she wailed. Somehow her father knew what had happened, and he tried to console her, telling her it was okay. He put money in the dish and passed it on. He tried his best to get his daughter to stop crying, but to no avail, so he picked her up, took his son's hand, and they left the church, never to return.

The girl's parents continued to argue. Her mother was unhappy. She had no friends or anyone to talk to.

The family moved back to Hawai'i, and there was less pressure to belong to a particular religion or church. There were so many races, cultures, and different religious beliefs. There was something for everyone or none at all, and that was okay, too.

March 11, 2011: One of the largest earthquakes ever recorded hit Japan and triggered a massive 23-foot tsunami. It left catastrophic devastation and horrific images played over and over on every news channel. It got worse every day as officials learned the overwhelming scope of destruction and loss of life.

We got calls at home, e-mails, and messages on Facebook. Was our family okay? Do they live near the disaster? Have you gotten in touch with anyone? Friends checked in on us and sent kind words and prayers for the people of Japan. Some asked what I thought they could do to help.

"Give to the Red Cross," was my answer.

Days after the disaster in Japan, FOX News contributor Fr. Jonathan Morris, a Roman Catholic priest, had the audacity to say that Japan was the most apolitical, non-religious country in the world.

I couldn't believe what I was hearing. Does he think that if it's not Catholic, then it's not a religion? How dare he deny Buddhism as a religion. Japan is a freedom-of-religion country with all religions including minorities like Christianity, Sikhism, and even Islam, but Buddhism is the religion of Japan.

My mother grew up Buddhist, as did everyone in her family for 600 years. My mother and father were married in a Shinto ceremony. They were then married a second time in the American Consulate in Japan. The Catholic Church said those marriages didn't count and required them to be married for a third time, in the Catholic Church, but that never happened, so in their eyes, my five brothers and sisters and I are illegitimate.

The shrines that dot the landscape throughout Japan are Buddhist. They are peaceful places of worship and meditation and an important part of Japanese culture and history. All my life I've experienced social harmony within my family and among Japanese communities in Hawai'i, and during the time I spent in Japan I knew the quiet resolve and inner peace of these honorable people.

I watched the news and the disturbing images of the horrific tragedy. I was heartbroken. I saw my mother's eyes in the elderly women's faces, their hands held up to their faces in shock and disbelief, their lives forever shattered, their loved ones missing and very possibly dead. How can they cope with such loss? I wondered.

Food, water, and gasoline shortages were immediate. People not familiar with Japan speculated about riots and looting. Instead, the world learned about Japan's calm in the face of extraordinary tragedy. American news reported that shelters were peaceful and orderly. Visitors from other countries were amazed at the volunteer efforts made with little help from officials and the ease by which they set up emergency operations. They brought prepared meals for strangers and made them comfortable until assistance could come.

A friend of mine in Hawai'i sent me an e-mail he received from a friend visiting there. He shared it with me, and I sent it on to all my contacts. It describes how she saw people dealing with the situation. (The e-mail is just as I received it and unedited.)

"hi everyone, yesterday we walked to the market to shop for some non perishable food products and naturally we were among long lines of people doing the same. what i wanted to share today is something from the hearts of the admirable Japanese. everyone was calm and patient and no "attitude" was felt. in their teachings of community welfare, these people consider the whole rather than themselves. one woman who was

finally joined with her missing father said, "I am happy, but cannot fully rejoice because others still are missing their loved ones."

the electric company announced a rationing of power to 9 districts including ours. but the rolling black outs were cancelled because the people "voluntarily" stopped using non essential power. i come from a country where most people expect the other person to comply and will not give up their own comfort. another remarkable thing is that their was not one incident of looting in the areas where there is very little food for thousands and again they wait patiently and orderly in line to get whatever they are able.

please continue to pray for the nuclear reactor situation to be remedied. thank you"

After my mother passed away, I didn't stay in contact with her family in Japan. Her address book and contact information were written in Japanese, which I couldn't read. Her three brothers and their families lived in the Tokyo area and on the northern island of Hokkaido, where I was born. These places are not near Sendai, the "ground zero" of the devastation, but we worried nonetheless and prayed for their safety.

In 1962 my mother got sick while my father was working overseas. It was a difficult time for all of us. My brother Tamé, the "ichiban-son," the eldest son, was only fourteen years old and unable to care for the rest of us while our mother was in the hospital. We didn't know it at the time, but her recovery would be long, and she would be in and out of hospitals. My father and grandmother arranged for all of us to stay with her in Japan, and my father would return to Kwajalein to work.

I was thirteen at the time, but much of the responsibility of watching out for my brothers and sisters fell on me, "Oniichan," eldest daughter. I worried constantly for my mother. I was afraid she was going to die. Immediately after arriving in Sapporo, on the northern island of Hokkaido, my mother was again hospitalized. "Obaachan," our grandmother, had more than enough space in her home for all of us to live comfortably. Her room on the ground floor was large, and she had a miniature shrine for my grandfather where she prayed daily. The shrine was shiny black lacquer with gold edging and printed Japanese characters. There was a bowl filled with sand to hold the incense sticks, and a compartment that held a small bone from Grandfather's neck or so my older brother told me, and I had no reason to doubt him. I knew that the rest of Grandfather's skeleton was kept at a cemetery a long drive away because I visited there a few times. As with many Japanese graveyards in Hawai'i, the people buried there would be dug up and the bones moved to mass graves as land became too precious to be taken up by dead people.

My grandfather's bones, along with many others', were disinterred to make room for commercial expansion and relocated to another cemetery where Grandmother would pay to have a place where she could visit his bones interred in a container just large enough to hold them, buried, with a shrine on top, a little bigger than the one she had at home. Eventually, when she could no longer pay for the bones of "Ojiisan," my grandfather, to be kept at the faraway site, he was moved, for the last time, to a cemetery near Tokyo where my uncles owned space. The Konno sons, proud descendants of Samurai, were highly educated and held important positions — not in government but as businessmen. They honored their family, those past, present, and future. They provided for their mother, too, supplementing her government income from her deceased husband's high-ranking position as superintendent of a major high school.

Obaachan's house was larger than the houses around it. She was living in a newly constructed neighborhood of about ten houses. There was only one house larger than my grandmother's and one apartment building located next door that was a dormitory for young men working for the Toshiba Corporation. There were many sounds that I loved hearing while I lived in Grandmother's house. One was the rattling and clicking of the mahjong tiles being shuffled on a table by the young Toshiba men whose window faced my own upstairs window. Another sound came from Obaachan's room when she rolled her Buddhist prayer beads together in her hands, the beads counting the number of times she recited a mantra as she meditated, and I loved to hear the trains go by on the tracks on the other side of the Toshiba dormitory. (When Fred and I bought the land in Oklahoma where we would settle for good, I got an added bonus — a train track a mile away. When the wind blows to the north or when the air is still, I can hear the rumble of a passing train, and the whistle announcing its arrival warning to the small town nearby — a sound that reminds me of Japan.)

All around the small grouping of houses was farmland, and a high school was separated from the little community by an empty field used for outdoor school activities. We formed a baseball team with the kids who lived in the neighborhood. Our ages ranged from our neighbor, "Yochan," two houses down, who was fourteen and the same age as Tamé, to the brothers who lived in the biggest house, who were nine and ten.

We played ball in the huge field after school and on free days. Soon it became apparent that I could run the bases faster than anyone else on the team. As word spread, kids from all around came to the field, and we would have running races. They were highly competitive and loved physical activity. We taught them "kick the can" and other games they continued to play long after we moved back to Hawai'i. I was unbeatable at running until my youngest brother, Hitoshi, started winning, and then he became the one to beat. I was glad. It took the pressure off of me, and I drifted away from the races so I could spend time doing what I'd rather be doing and that was visiting the friends I'd made on a nearby farm.

I don't even remember their names now, but the older girl was my age and her younger sister was my little sister's age, and they became best friends. The farm girls worked hard. They always had too many chores to do and rarely took part in the fun we were having on the nearby field. I loved helping them do the chores. They had sheep, and I would bring dry oatmeal from Grandmother's house to feed the animals by hand. Their muzzles tickled my palms as they ate. It was a good feeling, just like feeding horses.

They grew mushrooms, some in the earthen room where they stored vegetables and apples, and some on stumps and fallen trees in the wooded area of their farm. There was a huge apple orchard, and I helped tie baggies on the fruit as they began to ripen. At first my friend's father didn't want me to do the high branches atop the tall ladders, but I showed him I wasn't scared and assured him that I wouldn't fall. He laughed and thanked me for helping. The time to bag the apples was short, and there was a lot to do, so all help was appreciated. My brothers and sisters helped indoors making the bags. They cut large rectangles of newspaper and used a paste made of rice to seal the edges and fold in a wire at the top to twist the baggie closed at the apple's stem. The bugs would not be able to damage the apples at the prime ripening stage. All the apples ripened at once and needed to be picked quickly and all hands were needed. Everyone who helped in making the bags or putting them on the apples turned out to help with the harvesting. I was comfortable at the top of the high ladder and concentrated my efforts on picking the topmost apples while others picked the lower branches. I would fill a basket to the top and lower it by the attached rope to someone waiting below who would arrange the apples in boxes to be taken to the cool earthen cellar. Later, we would watch men carry the boxes of apples and stack them on a truck to be taken to the green grocer.

My younger brothers and sisters enrolled in the local elementary school and became more fluent in Japanese than me and Tamé. My older brother explored the big city of Sapporo, sometimes with neighbor Yochan, sometimes alone. He would walk through farms and the nearby small villages to get to the outskirts of the city, board a bus, and travel to the heart of Sapporo, to the "telebi" (television) tower that looked exactly like the Eiffel Tower in France. The surrounding park would play host to the Sapporo Snow Festival, a weeklong event in February that now draws about two million people each year to Odori Park, where hundreds of snow statues and ice sculptures line the street around the park.

Tamé would take me on tours of places he had discovered. Obaachan always gave us yen to spend. On the first trip I took with Tamé to the heart of the city, he introduced me to a girl my age from Russia. Her family lived there and she spoke Japanese fluently but knew no English. My Japanese was limited and halting, but she understood me. I thought it was remarkable that we could meet on middle ground — an American and a Russian unable to understand one another in their home languages but getting on famously in Japanese. When my father came for a visit he was eager to meet the Russian girl and her family, and arrangements were made to meet at a restaurant in Sapporo. My father shocked my brother and me when he spoke Russian to the girl and her father. They got along very nicely, and while the three of us kids listened in amazement, my father and his new cohort shared another thing they had very much in common — vodka, and lots of it.

My father took Tamé and me to the Sapporo Beer factory, a beautiful brick building obviously steeped in a rich heritage, where we toured the facility as special guests of one of the managers. We walked along the huge tanks, which varied in size and shape according to the stage of the brewing. After the tour we went to a nicely appointed lounge where my father drank beer and visited with members of the Sapporo Beer staff. My father spoke little Japanese, but the men spoke understandable English, and there was a lot of laughing and enjoyment in their conversations. Tamé and I drank cokes with Japanese writing on the bottles.

When it was time to leave, one of the managers came to me and held out a box wrapped in decorative paper. He bowed low from the waist, both hands holding the box as he invited me to accept it.

"Onegaishimasu," he said while bowing. "Please," was his meaning, "accept my gift."

I stood, and as low as I could bow, deliberately trying to bow much lower than he, accepted his gift. "Domo arigato gosaimasu," I said, thanking him as humbly as I knew how.

The box was heavy. What could it possibly be?

We all politely bowed to one another as we departed for home. It would be impolite to open the gift in their presence, and so the box sat on my lap while we took a taxi home. Mom was there to listen to our accounts of the brewery tour, and then everyone focused on the box, the omiyagi gift — a traditional gesture of gratitude that I still held in my hands. I removed the tape, trying to keep the wrapping intact so it could remain part of the presentation. I lifted the lid and spread the tissue paper away from the object to see a heavy glass candy dish shaped like a star, the symbol of Sapporo Beer. The glass had marbling and swirls of red and yellow — the colors of the familiar logo. It was beautiful and a treasure I would keep for years until I married a controlling man who decided for me that it wasn't worth taking up space in our small studio apartment in Kailua and gave it away.

Whenever my brother took me with him to the city of Sapporo we would always go to a ramen house for a bowl of noodles and order a "cider," a carbonated beverage very much like 7-Up or Sun Drop in a bottle with a marble at the bottom. The bottles would be washed and used again at the bottling plant, and some of the marbles and bottles would be worn and dull from repeated use. We didn't know the purpose of the marble, but we would never see that oddity again, not anywhere but in Japan.

Tamé took me to a bar, saying there was no age limit to drink a beer. I hadn't believed him and so he proved it by taking me to a bar. I declined a beer but had a coke instead. The men in the smoky bar paid us little attention. Our friend and neighbor, Yochan, took to calling us Henna-gaijin, "strange foreigner," when we did or said something that struck his Japanese sensibilities as odd or silly. I was sure he would call us that when we told him we went to a bar and he did.

All of us kids would be sent to buy things from time to time. There was a small store within walking distance but more for convenience items like paper goods, ice cream, and candy than regular grocery shopping. A few times a week, Grandmother would go to a large market for fruits and vegetables, fish and meats. My sisters would go with her, walking the half mile to a bus stop and riding to the stores at the outskirts of the city. They would always bring with them net or crocheted bags rolled up into tiny balls that fit into themselves and fastened with a button. Grocery bags were not unknown, but most shoppers would bring their own bags or satchels to carry their purchases home. Fish and meats were wrapped in pink or white butcher paper, and expensive products were always wrapped like gifts, using paper designed to uniquely identify the store.

I never minded being asked by Obaachan to run to the store for pan (bread), which was about a mile away. The walk took me through the garden of a friendly farmer, who told me to help myself to anything I wanted that was ripe for picking. He would wave at me when I was headed to get the bread that would be sliced on the spot for me, and he would catch me on my way back and put plums or carrots or potatoes into my bag to take back to my "Baa-chan." When the concord grapes were ripe, Tamé and I stood at the vines popping one after the next into our mouths and marveling at the most delicious fruit we'd ever eaten in our entire lives. We picked bunches of the huge grapes and took them home for the others. My younger brother, Tadashi or Tad, after devouring his share of the purple bounty, insisted we take him to the vines so he could feast as we bragged we had done.

The farmer was pleased to meet our younger brother, and Tad began helping the farmer with chores like fertilizing the gardens and picking the ripe vegetables and fruit. Tad became the provider of the vegetables, I was the bread-getter, Tamé ran for ice cream or sweets, the tofu man would come by in his pushcart every other day, and the coal truck would come regularly to keep the bin outside the back door full of wood and coal.

When it was cold, Grandmother would make a fire in the wood heater. She would ask us older kids to bring in firewood. Sometimes she would need small pieces and shreds of wood for tinder to get the fire going. Tamé and I both proved we could use the large hatchet without cutting our fingers off, so she reluctantly turned the job over to us.

Furo, bath day, was usually only once a week, but with the arrival of the six Snyder children the frequency ratcheted up to whatever was necessary to ensure we went to sleep under the luxurious futon blankets free of dirt and grime. Tamé and I learned from Obaachan how to make a fire under the wooden tub, the furo. Outside the tub was a tiled area with a drain where we would wash and rinse using plastic containers to douse ourselves before getting into the steaming furo. Everyone would have to take turns soaking in the hot water of the furo, so we made sure our bodies were clean before getting into the tub. In a regular Japanese household the men would bathe first, then children according to age, with women going last, but there was no way that Tamé, the oldest male in the household, would get that honor as long as the rest of us kids had anything to say about it. After Obaachan bathed, it was a free-for-all, which I usually won.

Where our neighbors and friends spent more time indoors studying, we were outside playing in the field and taking long walks and hikes. My sisters were the exception. They were always together and liked the same things. More studious than me and our three brothers, they picked up the language easily and spoke fluently by the time we left Japan.

I didn't go to school as they did, but I was invited regularly to the nearby high school, where I was an unofficial English teacher. Tame' and I were given the option of enrolling in the high school since it was thought that we would only be in Japan for a couple of months. Neither of us wanted to go to school so we decided we would help Obaachan which was the other option. The "couple of months" turned into eight before Mama was well enough to travel, and homeschool material was sent to us from Hawai'i so we wouldn't fall behind.

The students at the high school vied for my attention; they wanted to practice correct pronunciation. English was mandatory in school. Many knew how to speak it, but they'd never heard it spoken properly having learned from Japanese teachers and instructors who also had learned it from Japanese teachers and instructors, and so down the line. They especially wanted me to hear their l's and r's and compare them to mine. It was an adventure. Even my mother still had challenges at eighty years old, fifty-five years in the United States, with her l's and r's, although it was not as pronounced as in her youth.

For about two years before she died, I would take her in a wheelchair to the casino where Fred worked, and I would park her at her favorite slot machine. One of Fred's security guards upon hearing we were on our way would remove the chair and put a cup of ice water and a coffee at the machine, basically reserving it for Mom. She had her oxygen bottle and some cookies or candies and played at twenty cents a whack. It was entertaining, and I would sit and play the next machine to be with her to laugh and cheer if she got a hit or laugh and swear if she kept losing. It was a long-running game of me teaching her to swear.

"Say 'holy crap!' " I would tell her, and she'd reply, "Hory clap! This is a bum machine. Only take my money! Ruse, ruse, ruse. Hory clap!" She'd laugh and people would hear us having the time of our lives. They would smile. It was a good time.

I would show the Japanese students how to pronounce the letters by having them watch my mouth, my tongue touching the back of my upper teeth.

"El, el, el," I enunciated and they would repeat, "Elu, elu, elu."

"See, watch," I would instruct and they would watch closely as I breathed, "Arrrr, arrrr, R!" which they would do rather well, sounding a bit British when they said words like "car" or the question, "How are you?"

It gave me hope, but we were back to square one with words like "run" and "sorry" which came out "lun" and "solly."

It would take a better teacher than me to work it out.

Our friend and neighbor, Yochan, and his sister, Mariko, had a new reel-to-reel tape player. They had recorded a lot of rock-and-roll songs from a radio station that played all the current popular songs from the United States and beyond, songs that they learned to sing by replaying the tape over and over.

Yochan wrote the songs down in his neat Japanese hand but wanted to see the words in English and understand the meaning of the songs.

"Tie Me Kangaroo Down, Sport" by Rolf Harris was popular, and Yochan asked me to explain what the song was about. Since I was a huge fan of Australia and had had a pen pal from Melbourne for years, I knew a lot of things peculiar to the continent. The old stockman dying in the Outback, his mates gathered around him listening to his last wish that his wallabies, kangaroo, cockatoo, koala, abbos, and platypus duck be set free.

"Play your didgeridoo, Blue" and "keep playin' till I shoot thru."

And then he died.

Fred "tanned his hide when he died, Clyde, and that's it hangin' on the shed!"

"Ohhhhh, ohhhh, wakata, hai, wakarimasu." Yochan understood.

Another song was easy to interpret the meaning, but pronunciation was a different story. We worked on it diligently and sang it over and over along with the tape recorder.

"Risten to the lythm of the fawring lain, terring me just what a foor I've been . . ."

I was closest to my younger brother, Tad. We had similar interests and never argued, and we did stuff together that was challenging and interesting such as going on long hikes up the nearby mountains. The trails leading to the tops of the two largest mountains in the area were marked with wooden signs that my brother could read. They were mile markers, locations, and warning signs. We chose the higher mountain to climb one day. It would be a challenging climb. Tad and I started out early in order to get back before dark. Many times, we had to stop and catch our breath before continuing. We carried containers of water and some dried fish to snack on. People passed us on their descent, smiling and nodding — fellow adventurers. We cheered and jumped up and down when we reached the top. There were others at the summit, some taking photos of the breathtaking scenery below. Tad and I sipped our water and ate dried fish. We headed back and raced each other downhill to stay in the lead, neither of us wanting the branches-in-the-face slaps that the follower was sure to get.

Laughing and joking, we were off the mountain in no time, and it was still early — too early to go home when we still had lots of energy, water, and dried fish.

"What you think, Tad?" I asked. "Want to climb two mountains in one day?"

He was game. "Yeah, let's go!"

We hiked to the other big mountain and raced for the top, sometimes me in the lead, sometimes Tad. We were half way up the trail when we noticed there were no more people coming down.

"Maybe we should turn back," Tad said.

"Nah, we can't be that far from the top. Let's keep going." I was confident that if we kept up our pace we could be up and back before dark. I was wrong. The beautiful blue and orange sunset was brilliant from the top of the mountain, but that meant the sun would soon set, leaving us in darkness. When we started down, the shadows of the pine trees already made it difficult to see which way the path led. Before long, we were inching our way down the mountain in total darkness. This was bad. We would be home later than we'd ever been before, and nobody knew where we were.

My brother never complained, never blamed me for getting us in the mess we were in. He held my hand as I led him through some of the steepest and rockiest parts of the trail. I knew he was thinking about what would happen to us when we got home. I was thinking those thoughts myself. Mom was convalescing at home. I hoped she wasn't worried. Maybe she didn't even miss us yet, but I knew Obaachan did.

Once we reached the bottom and were out of the dense pine and evergreen trees. The moon lit our way home and we hurried. As we approached our house, we could see Obaachan standing outside the back door under the porch light. She saw us and waved and then went into the house. Oh no, I could imagine all kinds of things going on inside.

"Were the police called to report two missing kids?" I wondered. Obaachan didn't have a phone, but a neighbor two doors down did and she had used it on occasion.

When we went inside, everything was normal. The other kids were watching TV, eyes glued to the black-and-white set. Chibiko Taisho (The Little Rascals) and Lassie, dubbed in Japanese, were on every evening.

"C'mon, Lassie!" little Timmy would say. "Oide, Lasshie!"

Tad and I looked at each other, waiting for the boom to be lowered, but it never came. I finally asked, "Baa-chan, were you worried about us?"

"Ie," she said. No, she wasn't worried. She knew we had gone to climb the mountain and figured it took us longer than we all thought. Neither Tad nor I ever told her that we had actually climbed two mountains that day.

I heard from Tad a few days after the tragedy in Japan. He told me he couldn't even watch the news on TV. The images were too distressing. It was especially hard for him to see the elderly people, loss and fear etched in their faces. We grew up in a culture that honors the elderly, and the tradition of the younger generations caring for the elderly completes the reciprocal cycle of responsibility, generosity, and love, the way Mama would care for Obaachan and the way I would care for Mama.

Two years before we left Hawai'i to move to Oklahoma hoping one day to retire, I was working for Hilton Hotels in Hawai'i, my office located in the Hilton Waikoloa Village on the Big Island of Hawai'i. Fred was retired from Hawai'i County Police Department and working full time as a private investigator on O'ahu. Alan was in seventh grade at the private Parker School in Waimea (Kamuela). Because Fred worked and lived on another island during the workweek, flying home on weekends, and my job frequently took me on mainland trips to call on clients, my mother moved in with us to care for Alan.

Mom and Alan were very close. She was more of a parent than either Fred or I were at the time. She cooked his special requests for Japanese foods and taught him to speak a little Japanese. When a new boy from Japan entered his class, Alan reached out and befriended him and introduced him to his Grandma, and he in turn introduced Alan's "Baa-chan" to his parents. Before long, Alan and his new friend, Tom, were inseparable.

Tom's father was a landscape project engineer for a new resort hotel being built in the area. They expected the job to keep them in Waimea and Tom in school at Parker for at least a year. It was unclear if they would then return to Japan or find another project in Hawai'i, but at least for now Alan and Tom would spend a lot of time together playing video games, rollerblading, riding horses, and flying kites at the beach down near the thermal energy lab on the Kona Coast.

Their favorite pastime, though, was playing Nintendo. Tom would sit on the edge of Alan's bed and Alan would be on the floor, controllers in hand as they fixated on the game in front of them. They were both good boys who played well together.

Alan wanted Tom to go with us to Honolulu when we took a weekend trip where we would stay at the Hilton Hawai'ian Village on Waikiki Beach. I had to be there for meetings, and Fred and Alan would swim in the ocean or the pool or do any number of fun things at the famous resort. Mini-vacations such as this were few and far between, and Alan and his dad were like little kids turned loose on the playground.

Alan understood that his friend's parents wouldn't want him traveling by air to another island and be gone for a whole weekend. His parents would worry, we told Alan, just as we would worry about him taking such a trip away from us. Tom was an only child and so was Alan.

Fred and I were having coffee in the lobby of the Tapa Tower where our room was located. We would be checking out in a few hours and had left Alan to sleep in. If he woke up, he would know where to find us. I was reading the Honolulu paper and on the second page were news briefs from the outer islands. I read the news from the Big Island: a boy had been struck by a car and killed as he was riding his bike.

"How horrible," I thought. The roads around Waimea were narrow and winding, with no real shoulders to speak of. I read on . . . it was Tom.

"Oh God, please, no, no, please, God, don't let it be true."

We were devastated and sat in silence for a long time. There was nothing to say.

I broke the silence, "How do we tell Alan?"

Alan brought home a flyer with Tom's photo on it announcing a memorial service at his home. Mom, Alan, and I would go, but Fred was working in Honolulu so it would just be the three of us. The morning of the service as we were leaving the house, a sparrow flew into the open door and flitted into the laundry room and then flew through the kitchen and living room and down the hall to the bedrooms. We all followed, waiting for it to land so we could figure out the best way to get it to fly back outside. The bird made a right turn at the end of the hall, into Alan's bedroom, and landed on his bed.

Alan looked at us and said, "That's Tom's spot! That's where Tom always sits. Mom, do you think that's Tom?"

I was astonished. I couldn't say I'd never seen a bird fly into the house before, but certainly it was very unusual, even more so to fly directly to that spot. We stood looking at the bird. No one moved and then the bird decided to leave. It flew over our heads and retraced its flight the way it had come, down the hall through the kitchen and out the open laundry room door.

Alan was convinced, "That was Tom. He came to tell us not to worry about him. He'll be okay."

"Yes, Alan," I told him. "I believe that was Tom." And Mom believed it too.

At Tom's home, people were lined up at the front door making a slow procession into the living room, where on the mantle of the fireplace was an urn with Tom's ashes that would eventually return to Japan. On one side of the urn was a bag of McDonald's burger and fries, Tom's favorite food. On the other side was his game machine with a stack of game cartridges, items to give comfort to his spirit. There was a guest book to sign on a table on the right of the room, and on the left, Tom's parents and two relatives from Japan sat in chairs acknowledging condolences and words of comfort. In the middle of the room was a table with a candle burning and incense sticks for those who would follow the Buddhist ritual of lighting incense to honor the deceased and drive away bad feelings.

I waited to see if Tom's father would hold his hand out for me to shake, as he did the men. He didn't, so I just bowed to show my respect. He bowed his head and then looked at me with a pained expression on his face. His wife sat next to him with her head down, her hands on her lap, and she openly wept. I reached down and touched her hand. She looked up and saw that it was the mother of Tom's best friend. She took both my hands in hers and laid her cheek on our clasped fingers, her never-ending tears flowing between them. I knelt down in front of her determined to stay as long as she wanted me to. Except for their family, I was perhaps the only one there who understood what she might be going through and how special Tom was. Ours was his "home away from home," just as theirs was to Alan. We had a bond. What if it had been Alan? My heart ached with awful regret. I wished to God I'd allowed Alan to invite Tom to go with us to Honolulu. Tom's mother never knew what might have been.

Alan stayed outdoors with other classmates from Parker School, waiting under the canopy where picnic tables were arranged for the food that would be served. It was the saddest day of my life. Everyone was weeping. Some had silent tears running down their faces while others held tissues to their eyes and sobbed. Tom's father and his relatives from Japan were stoic. After everyone had walked through the room and exited to the backyard, Tom's mother allowed herself to be taken to her room to rest. Only then did she let go of my hands, and I went to look for Alan. He didn't want to stay to eat and neither did I.

My mother spoke with the two woman relatives from Japan for a little while and then we all three departed and silently drove home.

Chapter 22

Kaluakauka — The Doctor's Pit

Waimea or Kamuela, as the town is known by both names, sits at the foot of a mountain chain of rolling green hills. Many people who have been to Ireland say Waimea is very reminiscent of the Emerald Isles "across the pond," as we say in Oklahoma, for its green hills and rock walls.

We moved to Kamuela from Hilo when Fred was promoted to sergeant and transferred to the Waimea Police Station. "Kamuela" is the Hawai'ian word for Samuel, and the town is named after a local politician, Samuel Spencer, for whom Spencer Beach Park, mentioned earlier as the beach chronically contaminated with staph bacteria, is also named, or it can be in honor of the other "Kamuela," Samuel Parker, grandson of John Palmer Parker, who married Princess Kipikane, granddaughter of King Kamehameha the Great. She was awarded 600 acres of land, which over time became Parker Ranch, arguably the largest privately owned cattle ranch in the United States.

The Parker Ranch was born nearly two hundred years ago when John Palmer Parker arrived on the Big Island after jumping ship. The daring young Boston entrepreneur and seaman struck a bargain with Kamehameha I that would change the face and culture of the area called Waimea. King Kamehameha hired Parker to capture and domesticate the wild cattle that roamed the Big Island, and the young man soon became the manager of the king's herds. Marrying the King's granddaughter didn't hurt his social status or accumulating wealth, either.

Cattle had been introduced in Hawai'i in 1793. Captain George Vancouver of the British Royal Navy picked up cows in Monterey, California to give to King Kamehameha as gifts on his second trip to the islands. The cattle were a scruffy long-horned breed descendant from the first cattle introduced in Mexico by Spaniards in 1521.

The first cows soon died or were killed and eaten. When Vancouver landed additional cattle at Kealakekua in 1794, he strongly encouraged the king to put a kapu (off limits) on the cows forbidding molestation of the animals in order to grow a herd. The herd grew until nearly thirty-thousand wild and semi-wild cattle roamed the island.

By the time King Kamehameha III came to power in 1825, wild cattle were creating havoc, trampling gardens and eating thatching on houses as well as injuring and sometimes killing people. The king lifted the kapu and encouraged hunting the cattle. The king hired bullock hunters from overseas to help control the wild cattle. Many hunters were former and escaped convicts from Botany Bay, Australia.

One escaped convict was strongly suspected in the death of Dr. David Douglas of Scone, Scotland. Dr. Douglas died at the young age of 34. He had already made quite a name for himself as the first botanist to explore the wilds of the Pacific Northwest and California, discovering and documenting hundreds of species of plants many of which are now named for him. Called "the patron saint of the botany of the Pacific Northwest," counties are named for him in Oregon, Washington and Idaho as well as Douglas Lake in British Columbia and Mt. Douglas in the Canadian Rockies. Most notable is his discovery of the fragrant evergreen popular at Christmastime named for him — the Douglas fir.

Fred and I had heard of the unsolved mystery of the death of the doctor found at the bottom of a bullock pit, his head bearing blunt force injuries. Was it possible that Dr. Douglas fell into the pit with a trapped bull? The blows to his head could be from the horns or hoofs of a fear crazed wild bull, but they could also be the work of a murderer bent on taking the roll of money the doctor was known to carry.

Douglas always traveled with his little Scottish terrier, Billy, and due to a series of unforeseen circumstances, the doctor and his dog would debark a ship at Kawai'hae on the northeast side of the Big Island, walk a trail from Hawi along the Kohala Mountains, into the Waimea Valley toward Hilo where along the way, he would meet his death.

He was buried at the KawaiaHa'o Church in Honolulu, but over the years the exact location on record was lost. A tombstone erected later to his memory was eventually brought into the church to protect it from further weathering and is mounted on the church's vestibule.

We heard that there was a marker made of lava rocks erected near the spot where Dr. Douglas died and so we planned a family picnic and trip to look for that marker. The only clue we had to its whereabouts was to take Mana Road from Waimea along the base of Mauna Kea toward Hilo approximately 15 miles through 16 gates, or was it 16 miles through 15 gates? The dirt road traced the same ancient footpath that Dr. Douglas walked July 12, 1834, when he met his fate.

Another clue we had was to look for a wooden sign reading "Kaluakauka (the Doctor's pit)" but we were warned it might not be there because last anyone saw of it reported that it was "weather worn and falling apart."

There was yet another clue we could look for and someone just mentioned that they had heard from someone who heard it from someone ... and on down the line that the lava rock marker was surrounded by gigantic Douglas Fir trees. We found that to be incredible, if true, because Douglas fir trees would not grow in tropical climes. But we also knew that the Big Island was special, having nine of the world's eleven temperate zones — in other words, all of them except Arctic and Saharan, the coldest and the driest, respectively.

The Alpine zone, where firs and pines would do well, could be found on the higher elevations of Mauna Kea, (the highest mountain in the world measured from its base on the ocean floor) on the island's windward side where they get the most rain. Hawai'i imports more Douglas fir, Noble Pines, Blue Spruce and other evergreens for Christmas trees every year from the Pacific Northwest than any other state but, except for the Douglas Fir, the trees do not have much fragrance. Locals grow other species of fir and pine to sell at Christmastime, and the spindly Norfolk and Cook pines grow abundantly throughout the islands, but the Douglas Fir is fey, and the three of us, Fred, me and Alan would go on a quest to see if the story of the Douglas Firs growing where Dr. Douglas was killed was, indeed, true.

We set out early to get back before evening clouds shrouded our route in fog. Weather moves in fast at the higher elevations, and if we got caught in the clouds we risked straying off the road, taking a wrong turn or running headlong into an oncoming vehicle. We picked a day when no rain was expected. Mana Road was impassable during heavy rains, and the ruts in the road even in good weather usually required a 4-wheel drive vehicle which we didn't have. A cooler packed with drinks and a picnic basket rode in the back of my Nissan pick-up truck, while Alan and Tesi, our poi (mixed breed) dog from a Hilo rescue center, rode behind Fred and I in the small club seat area of the cab.

The ride was rollicking and rolling, and we laughed as we bumped along over the ruts and deep potholes. At one point Fred stopped and shifted to reverse and started backing up. "What are you doing?" Alan and I wanted to know.

"We missed one," Fred answered, referring to a pothole.

Alan and I cracked up.

We stopped to let a flock of wild turkeys make their way across the road in front of us, and Fred took lots of video of the normally secretive birds. We were close enough to hear them "talking" for the camera.

It was most convenient that the front seat passenger get out to open the gates, and so the job fell to me, and I loved doing it. It was very "ranchy," something horse people love to do. I would "ride the gate" closed after Fred pulled the truck through, and eventually Alan saw that I was having too much fun so he insisted I ride in the back so he could open and close the fences, but then he lost track of the number of gates we went through, which was his assignment. We laughed having fun every minute of the adventure we were having.

All the land we crossed through was part of Parker Ranch although some parcels were privately owned, and the cattle and horses belonged to, and were controlled by, particular families not all of which appreciated strangers passing through their property. We were aware of this and made sure no gate was left open and no taking of the precious native koa wood, which was no longer plentiful on the only island that once had complete forests of it and sandalwood, which was harvested to near extinction. Like the advice we would give to visitors to Hawai'i, "Take nothing but pictures, leave nothing but footprints," we were the visitors on Mana Road and heeded those words.

We stopped at the side of the road in a pretty area of lush native pili grass and gnarly koa to have our picnic. Alan and Tesi explored the surroundings while Fred and I spread a large blanket out to sit on and eat our snacks. A slight breeze always seems to travel up the slopes of the dormant volcano, and the occasional cold gust made us glad we had dressed warmly. When the wind dies down and the sun warms, there is no better feeling in the world than lying on a blanket in the warmth of the sun and listening to Hawai'ian music. We could have stayed there all day, but we were on a quest and under a time constraint so we loaded up the truck and continued our journey. We had stayed on our picnic much longer than we should have.

After going through approximately nine gates, or perhaps ten, we encountered our first vehicle. The army surplus jeep coming our way had only one occupant, a young man. He looked friendly and so Fred signaled him to stop. We asked him how far it was to Kaluakauka, the doctor's pit, but the young man didn't know. He said he thought it was easier to get there from the Hilo side, at least that was how he remembered getting there a long time ago.

We thanked him and resumed our journey. Alan asked us if we saw the rifle he had in the back of the jeep and, of course, we did. We were armed too. We hardly went anywhere without Fred's service revolver and sometimes we were doubly armed, like we were that day when my Smith and Wesson .357 came with us.

Rifles in vehicles are common, not like on Oahu. The Big Island is a hunting mecca. The largest and least populated island in the chain, Hawai'i boasts an assortment of game species, ranging from feral pigs, sheep and goats to turkey, pheasant, francolin, chukars, and dove. On our drive we saw just about every type of game bird imaginable, but had it been hunting season we probably wouldn't have been so fortunate.

Just inside the property of gate twelve or so, we stopped and looked down a steep hill which had such deep ruts and patches of mud we had to seriously consider turning back. Although we got to that point without four-wheel drive, the hill in front of us posed too big a challenge and a huge risk. If we got stuck in one of the deep washouts or sloppy mud holes there was no telling how long we would have to wait for someone to come along. It could be hours, a day even, since the scant number of residents choose Hilo to conduct business and shopping which, from the point we had reached, was more accessible.

A possible option was to go off the dirt road and cross through a pasture but again, without 4-wheel drive we might get stuck in soft dirt and no telling what was under the lush pasturage so we turned around and headed home. We were disappointed but at least we found out Kaluakauka was reachable from Hilo, and we could try that another day. In the meantime, just getting home safely was foremost in our minds since the low clouds of afternoon had already moved in and slowed our progress home.

To be continued . . .

Chapter 23

Hunting Vermin

Spring in northeast Oklahoma seemed to arrive overnight. The "greening" certainly was very noticeable from one day to the next. Fred used the hand mower to cut some of the lespedeza grass already growing higher than our ankles around the steps to the back deck. The horses love the lush clover with the little purple flowers, and Cinnamon, the turkey, daintily picked the blossoms off, enjoying the springtime delicacy. It wouldn't be long before the lespedeza gives way to Bermuda grass that will grow out of control and become an unwanted invader, choking garden plants and flowers.

It was too pretty a day yesterday, March 23, 2011, to stay indoors and get wrapped up in distressing e-mail and frightening warnings of financial terrorism, FEMA fusion centers, underground cities being built for a secret society in anticipation of America's meltdown, and, of course, the never-ending anti-American actions of Obama and his cult fueling our fears of the impending manufactured meltdown of our once-proud representative republic.

Some days it's just too overwhelming for me. I look at the number of e-mail messages waiting to be downloaded and know there is so much important information to be forwarded, some messages needing to be sent to people who don't get the information from any other source. I feel as if I'm shirking my responsibility if I don't spend my day communicating back and forth with the hundreds and potentially thousands, even hundreds of thousands, of people just like me who will not let our country go down without a fight.

Yesterday I just couldn't even turn on my computer and get bogged down in it. I went outside and worked in the yard, getting the flowerbeds and garden ready for spring planting. To plant a garden is to believe in the future, reads a small plaque on my desk. I would plant my garden as I did every year for fresh vegetables, but my belief in the future was very, very shaky.

I came in the house for a break after digging holes for new fruit trees and conditioning the vegetable garden. I checked my iPhone for messages and listened to one from Victoria from Richmond Patriots.

"You might have just gotten your wish," her message said, alluding to my wish for someone famous to question Obama's legitimacy. "Donald Trump was on The View saying Obama needs to show his birth certificate." She finished out the message relating the exchanges between Trump and the ladies of The View, tossing in, "Whoopie pulled out the race card, saying, 'If he were white, he wouldn't be asked for his birth certificate.' "

I was stunned. Who would have guessed it would be Donald Trump challenging Obama? I could hardly believe it. I called Fred and told him. When I repeated Victoria's message about Whoopie saying, "If he were white . . . " Fred said, "HELLO! News flash for Whoopie: he IS white!"

Had my prayers been answered? Only time would tell.

I went back outside to work in the dirt and feed worms and grubs to the chickens and kept an eye on Hoku while he feasted on the lush lespedeza in the front yard. I felt hopeful that the truth about Obama would finally hit the mainstream.

That night Hannity became a birther, supporting Trump and million of Americans who agree that Obama should show his birth certificate. But after the segment aired on FOX & Friends the next morning, Steve Doocy parroted the same misinformation, the same lie that continues to shield Obama's fraud. He said, "During Obama's campaign he did show his certificate of live birth." Doocy, Gretchen, yes, you too! He showed a CERTIFICATION and a forgery at that! O'Reilly, you pinhead, WISE UP! Megyn Kelly, too — enjoy your irrelevancy! The talking heads sickened me. I was fed up with all them.

For three years I was a vocal critic of Barack Obama. He was not and never was eligible to be put on the 2008 ballot as a presidential candidate. He may be a citizen, may even be a native-born citizen, but he is not a "natural-born citizen" as specified by the Constitution — is not, never was, and never could be, but nobody would listen to me. I'm a nobody, and Obama is the most powerful man in the world. I certainly had a lot of other issues with Obama and remained a very vocal critic during the initial stages of my congressional campaign and knew that as a member of the House of Representatives I could bring those issues to the fore from inside "the belly of the beast."

I'd been hearing rumors of a phony birth certificate and a Kenyan birth but didn't pay a lot of attention to them because it was common knowledge that Obama went to Punahou School and his grandmother worked at Bank of Hawai'i, so I figured he may well have been born in Hawai'i. I didn't pay a lot of attention, that is, until Thanksgiving 2009.

It had become our tradition to have friends over for the feast and combine the holiday with Alan's birthday, which sometimes falls on the same day but is usually within a day or two. The conversation turned to Alan's birthplace, Kapi'olani Hospital, which Obama claimed was his birthplace as well, although even his family and Obama himself was confused about which hospital he was born in. *

A UPI article dated November 4, 2008, read "Obama described his birth at Queen's Medical Center in Hawai August 4, 1961," but the article was later changed to read, "Obama described his birth at Kapi'olani Medical Center for Women and Children in Hawaii August 4, 1961." The subtle change might have disappeared to history but for Dr. Jerome Corsi's thorough documentation of Obama's dubious life narrative. Corsi, author of Where's the Birth Certificate, includes screen captures of United Press International's original text in exhibits number 74 and 75. Statements by Obama family members also identified Queens as Obama's birth hospital.

I pulled out both Alan's and Fred's birth certificates, since Fred was also born in Kapi'olani. Wondering what difference there would be between ours and Obama's led us to the computer, where we found the copy of Obama's posted online. With the exception of the Kenya birth records, the image of Obama's certification of live birth was consistent: We were looking at a CERTIFICATION OF LIVE BIRTH, where Fred's and Alan's were both entitled CERTIFICATE OF LIVE BIRTH.

"Holy crap!" I said out loud. I got it! We all got it! We now saw what everyone was talking about — Obama's certification is not proof of a hospital birth, no evidence whatsoever of his being born in Kapi'olani, as Fred and Alan clearly had been.

Within a day or two I got in touch with a friend in Hawai'i whose granddaughter had been born in Japan and had a Hawai'i Department of Health document. It was a CERTIFICATION attesting to the fact that a live baby was born and not proof of being born in a Hawai'i hospital.

Armed with my newfound knowledge, I made copies front and back of all the birth records, including Fred's father's "Certificate of Hawai'ian Birth," which is needed to prove Hawai'ian ancestry for inclusion in programs and services reserved only to Hawai'i's indigenous people. The Office of Hawai'ian Affairs (OHA) clearly lists short-form birth certificates and CERTIFICATION OF LIVE BIRTH, such as Obama's as NOT ACCEPTABLE PROOF.

Even before this latest revelation of fraud, I was filled with an anger I cannot describe, only that I've felt it before and recognize it as a rage brought on by someone or something that deliberately victimizes me or my loved ones. I could either fight it or sit back and take it. My days of letting thugs get away with stuff was long over, and I took the birth certificates and other documents of possible fraud (anomalies), such as Obama's Selective Service form and the two different DNC presidential nomination forms signed by Nancy Pelosi, and put the copies in plastic sleeves, stuck them in a three-ring binder, and took them with me everywhere I went. Visual proof of Obama's fraud would convince even the most skeptical liberal, I hoped, as long as they were willing to consider the evidence.

I received a notice that the Muskogee Tea Party would have an event at the civic center. The program would include an "open mic" for general topics. Anyone interested in speaking would be allowed two minutes to address the attendees. Remembering that the organizer, Jeremy Vaught, had a problem with my running against his Republican choice for Congress from our district, I penciled in the date, making sure I wouldn't miss the event.

In the meantime I worked on presentations of FairTax, American Grand Jury, Miki Booth for Congress, and GOOOH, two minutes for each one. Depending on how many people lined up to speak, I would try to get them all in.

As I got ready to go to the Tea Party, I dressed according to the order of my topics. In other words, I put my GOOOH shirt on first, then donned a FairTax T-shirt, and over that put on a Miki Booth for Congress shirt with the newly designed logo of a sheriff's badge imprinted with "U.S. Congress" and "It's Time for a RECKONING" next to my name.

I would start out talking about Obama's crimes and my desire to expose him by bringing the fight to Washington. If I had more time, I would talk about my involvement with American Grand Jury and hand an exemplar of Grand Jury Presentments to someone willing to take the step and teach others to serve presentments to government officials detailing Obama's criminal activities. If I didn't have time in the first two minutes, I would try for two more. After that, I would peel my Miki Booth shirt off and wear my FairTax shirt to represent the plan that would abolish the IRS and the 60,000-plus-page tax code and implement a simpler, transparent way of paying taxes. I would then try for two more minutes to talk about GOOOH. My plan set, I drove the hour and a half to Muskogee.

I recognized the young Vaught and guessed an older woman and teenage girl to be his mother and sister. Not only did they not acknowledge me, they made it a point to ignore me as well. The elder Mr. Vaught, a state senator, was really decent. He introduced himself, and we chatted politely. I was more than willing to be friends with the young Vaught, but he had decided to regard me with contempt, evidenced by childish snickering with his mother and sister whenever I was in their proximity.

Vaught opened the program and laid out the rules for the speakers. I was the second one up and introduced myself. "Hi. My name is Miki Booth, and I'm a community organizer from Hawai'i," then, "Obama is a usurper, a traitor, a fraud, and a liar!" to which the entire room exploded into applause. Everyone there knew it or at least knew that something was very wrong with the man who was catapulted into the White House under a cloud of suspicion. No one had ever done what I just did, and I had no idea how the crowd of over 100 people would react to someone accusing the most powerful man on earth of crimes that in another time were punishable by death.

I had everyone's attention and held up the three birth records from Hawai'i and explained the differences and their significance. I held them out to a person in the first row to examine and pass along while I answered questions from the audience. A woman stood to ask a question when the timer went off. I looked at Vaught for direction as another women shouted from the audience, "Let her talk!" "Give her my two minutes," another shouted.

Vaught allowed me to answer one last question, and then I went back to the line where there was one person waiting. Between speakers, Vaught added some snippets of information, quoting a founding father or reading a noteworthy article, something to make for an interesting patriotic program.

When I got my second turn at the mic, I introduced myself with, "Hi. My name is Miki Booth, and I represent American Grand Jury."

I explained the purpose of the organization and encouraged people to visit the site and become members. I held up a set of Presentments and explained that any citizen can serve them on any government official, essentially "serving" them notice of criminal charges, which the government then bears the responsibility of investigating and adjudicating. I showed the page signed by the plaintiff, one Walter Francis Fitzpatrick III, and encouraged someone, anyone, to step forward and help Walter Fitzpatrick and all Americans who believe we are still a nation of laws, and Obama had to be brought to justice. "Every day that justice is delayed," I told them, "is justice denied."

I don't remember the name of the man who stepped up and promised he would serve the presentments and join American Grand Jury, but everyone applauded his commitment. While everyone was still clapping, the timer went off. I turned and looked at Vaught. I swear he was absolutely glaring at me. I was having fun.

My next turn at the mic would be for FairTax, so I stepped out into the lobby and pulled off my "Miki Booth for Congress" T-shirt to expose my FairTax shirt. There was no one else in line, and the last speaker was still talking, so I sat down to wait my turn.

Vaught returned to the mic. I was sure he was dismayed that no one else had lined up to speak, just me this time. I was grinning inside, knowing I was irritating the crap out of the young Tea Party leader. I absolutely couldn't believe my good fortune when he asked the audience if they'd heard about FairTax. Some hands went up, and Vaught encouraged people to learn about the tax plan that would replace the current tax code. He didn't offer a whole lot of information about it but said it was a good thing to get involved with.

And then it was my turn again. "Hello," I said. "My name is Miki Booth, and I'm the District Two community coordinator for FairTax."

And so it also went with GOOOH, but I held off until the last minute to see if Vaught would mention GOOOH in any of his snippets because he had been at the mock candidate selection session and, in fact, had spoken with Tim Cox. GOOOH threatens party politics, and the entire Vaught family were Republican Party animals.

The last two weeks of December 2009 found me traveling to Poteau, Oklahoma, where I joined with a group that met regularly on

Saturday mornings to talk politics. They were strong in the Tea Party movement and, like me, were fed up with party politics. They were a mixture of registered Independents and Republicans, and even some Democrats came on board; they were so upset with Obama and his administration. I received a lot of support from people in Poteau and made the eight-hour round trip many times in 2010.

Dewey Harrison, his wife, Joanie, and Dick and Ardith Wilkerson were especially kind and helpful to me in the early stages of my campaign. Dewey, a teacher and professional auctioneer among other things, held a fundraiser where we auctioned off a number of items such as Kenneth Gladney's autographed Gadsden flag and several of the current bestselling books by authors such as Sean Hannity, Glenn, Beck, and Mark Levin, but the one that brought the highest bid was Jerome Corsi's Obamanation. It also brought out a lot of laughs. Fred had covered Obama's face on the cover of the book with duct tape and drew a smiley face on it. I later bought the book again when I met Dr. Corsi on the WorldNetDaily cruise and elicited a laugh from him when I told him what Fred had done to the other copy I had. I couldn't stand looking at Obama's face, I told Corsi. He wanted to know how much his book had auctioned for and seemed pleased that we'd gotten thirty bucks for it.

When I was a little girl in Kaneohe, we used to have shooting contests in the back yard, and I was always the best shot. With a BB gun or .22 rifle I could outshoot my brothers and even my dad. They nicknamed me "Annie Okole," playfully calling me the Hawai'ian word for "butt." Throughout my lifetime I would shoot on occasion, and even killed a dog that was in a chicken-killing frenzy, but any competitive spirit I might have had for shooting went dormant the older I got. So when a challenge presented itself, it was a test that I had no idea how I would fare in.

On January 9, 2010, a Saturday, Fred was at work and I was home alone when I got my chance and wrote about it in an e-mail to my family and friends:

This morning has been full of action and adventure. Several times this morning Brandi exploded with loud barking and running back and forth to the doors to be let out. She only gets that excited when she sees coyotes. We've lost many of our chickens to these predators, and I'm still sad about losing "Tecate" our Polish Crested rooster a few years ago. I actually watched as a coyote came within a few feet of our house to grab him. I enjoy all the wildlife around our place and wouldn't mind the coyotes if they earned an honest living, but when they steal chickens that's crossing the line.

So when I spotted a pack of four or five coyotes, I let Brandi out to bark and chase them since sometimes that's enough to drive them off. But they stood their ground and Brandi knew she was outnumbered so she came home, and I got out my Ruger mini-14 semi-automatic. I fired a few shots in their direction, and they scattered and ran in the opposite direction. A few minutes later Brandi threw a fit telling me the coyotes were back. This time they were much closer and coming our way. I got the mini-14 again and snuck out the laundry room door so Brandi and Sheila wouldn't interfere or get in the line of fire.

So, I'm standing on the deck in 15 degree weather, lots of snow on the ground and wearing a nightshirt and house slippers. Then I spot two coyotes on the back berm of the frozen pond, and then they disappear. I walk off the deck to get closer for a better look, and they appear and disappear again behind snow drifts and depressions in the ground but still coming my way. Figuring that I could steady my rifle against Fred's motorcycle hale (house) I crept up alongside the building, right into foot-deep drifts, and my house slipper got sucked off my foot, first one, then the other. I take a few more steps forward, thinking if I can't see them they can't see me creeping up. Then I see one of them appear about 200 yards away, and I get it in my sights and remember to not breathe and to squeeeeze the trigger. Bang! The coyote drops in its tracks and never moves again. The other coyote runs zig-zagging back across the pond and stops at the top of the berm. I took a shot but didn't hit it, and it ran off.

I realized then that my bare feet are in horrible pain, and my nose has been running with snot freezing on my face, and I can't feel my lips. I'm running for the house, and Brandi and Sheila are still frantically barking and howling in the house, totally P.O.'d that they weren't allowed in on the action. I yell at them to "stop it!" but it comes out like "smophit" 'cause my lips are frozen numb.

After thawing out and donning Arctic clothing, I got my camera and a .22 magnum six-shooter in case the coyote was alive and suffering. It wasn't.

That was my validation. I could still shoot. My dad had taught me well. It bolstered my confidence to challenge Boren to a marksmanship contest, and it didn't even bother me that he was on the board of the NRA.

I made more trips to Poteau in January and stayed busy going to events as far away as Oklahoma City, which is outside my district, but the contacts I made at events like Clouds Over America featuring the John Birch Society ("Less government, more responsibility, and — with God's help — a better world") were invaluable. There were people I began recognizing from events in Tulsa or the 9.12 OKC group and through them continued to meet people who lived in my district and pledged their support or donated.

At the "Clouds" event I met Charlie Meadows of Oklahoma Conservative Political Action Committee (OCPAC). He looked through my binder of information and took an interest in my campaign. I was pleased to receive advice from someone I considered the foremost authority on Oklahoma politics. He told me the same thing my detract-tors were saying: "You'll never make it as an Independent." He encouraged me to change my affiliation, and he was willing to help me. He was impressed with the photo of the coyote I'd shot two weeks earlier. He showed others the photo and the copies of the Hawai'i birth certificates. He was a good man to know.

On February 1, the first day of the Oklahoma legislative session, I was back at the capitol and by that time knew many of the Tea Party and conservative leaders in the state. Amanda Teegarden of Oklahomans for Sovereignty and Free Enterprise (OK-SAFE) was there with flyers, the result of much hard work and diligence by Amanda, listing the bills conservative Oklahomans should support and which bills were hurtful to our sovereignty and needed to be quashed.

After the short program featuring legislative speakers and signing petitions, I headed upstairs to find my state senator, Charles Wyrick, and representative, Larry Glenn, both Democrats. I interrupted Sen. Wyrick's lunch, but his secretary said that few constituents ever visit, and the senator would surely want to speak with me.

Sen. Wyrick set his lunch aside and invited me to sit and talk about what was on my mind. I told him I was with the Tea Party group downstairs and presented him with the paper listing the bills that he would be voting on and asked him to support those listed on the front of the sheet. He scanned through them and then began explaining to me that it wasn't so simple to say "support this bill or don't support this other" — that every bill needs to be thoroughly read through and given careful consideration.

I read his body language and between the lines and felt as if he was lecturing a little girl who had walked in with demands she knew nothing about. After a few more minutes of talking at me the way politicians do, he paused long enough for me to place a business card on his desk, the one where I'm holding a rifle and reads, "Miki Booth, Constitutional Conservative for Congress."

The senator continued to monopolize the conversation, but his tone definitely changed. Now he was talking about how hard his job was. He had a ranch to run in addition to being a senator, and with the commute to Oklahoma City and his responsibility at the capitol, he made the equivalent of only five dollars per hour. He'd considered many times whether he should just give it up. It was an awful lot of work and perhaps not worth it.

I actually felt kind of bad. The senator didn't get to finish his lunch. He was called to session and already late.

Knowing that Rep. Larry Glenn was probably in session I went to find his office anyway. I familiarized myself with the layout of offices and looked at the nameplates to see if I recognized any familiar names. I found Rep. Glenn's office and walked in. There was no one in the office that he shared with another representative. There was a photograph of Obama in the hallway of the double office. At the time I didn't have a camera phone. If I did, I surely would have taken a picture of the 8 x 10 color photograph of Obama affixed to the wall with pushpins and thumbtacks.

New York 25 July 1787

Dear Sir

I was this morning honored with your Excellency's Favor of the 22d Inst: & immediately delivered the Letter it enclosed to Commodore Jones, who being detained by Business, did not go in the french Packet, which sailed Yesterday.

Permit me to hint, whether it would not be wise & seasonable to provide a strong check to the admission of Foreigners into the administration of our national Government, and to declare expressly that the Command in chief of the american army shall not be given to, nor devolved on, any but a natural born Citizen. ___

Mrs Jay is obliged by your attention, and assures You of her perfect Esteem & Regard—with similar Sentiments the most cordial and sincere I remain

Dear Sir

Your faithful Friend & Servt

John Jay.——

His Excellency General Washington

QUEEN KAPIOLANI
1834 - 1899

This Certifies

that ALAN   PALIKO   BOOTH   *was born to*

Miyuki and Frederic Booth II   *in this hospital*

at 7:55 A. m. Tuesday *the* 24th *day of* November *1*981

Sex: Male *Weight:* 8 *lbs.* 9 *oz. Length:* 20 *in.*

President   *Attending Physician*

Souvenir Certificate of Birth

Kapiolani-Children's Medical Center
Honolulu, Hawaii

A BRIEF HISTORY OF THE HOSPITAL

On June 14, 1890, King Kalakaua and Queen Kapiolani opened the Kapiolani Maternity Home of the Hooulu a Hoola Lahui Society "for the purpose of benevolence and charity and for the special object of providing a maternity home where Hawaiian women can receive proper care and treatment during the period of childbirth, and for such other benevolent and charitable purposes as may be consistent with the maintenance of such Maternity Home".

Later, in 1918, the name Kapiolani Home of the Hooulu a Hoola Lahui Society was changed to Kapiolani Maternity Home.

Dictated by the requirements of its constantly growing clientele, Kapiolani Maternity Home in 1920 purchased and moved into the premises of the August Dreier homestead located nearby on Beretania Street. A sanitarium was added, and, for the first time, a charge for services was asked of those patients who could afford to pay.

On March 26, 1929, Kapiolani Maternity Home moved into its newly erected, modern maternity hospital. The cost of constructing the hospital building was in excess of $100,000 and was located on property purchased from Dr. John M. Whitney on the corner of Bingham and Punahou Streets, the hospital's present location.

On May 6, 1931, by further amendment of the charter the name of the hospital was again changed, and it became known as Kapiolani Maternity and Gynecological Hospital.

On September 28, 1971, the Board of Trustees changed the name of this institution to Kapiolani Hospital.

In keeping with anticipated changes in the delivery of health care in the future, and in the interest of cost containment, Kapiolani Hospital joined with Kauikeolani Children's Hospital on September 15, 1978 to form the Kapiolani-Children's Medical Center.

King Kalakaua
David Mahiulani Lumialani
"The Merry Monarch"
(1836–1891)
Founder of
Kapiolani Hospital KCMC

Queen Kapiolani
Esther Julia Napelakapuokakae
(1834–1899)
Founder of
Kapiolani Hospital KCMC

Queen Emma
Kalanikaumakaamano Rooke
(1836–1885)
Founder of
The Queens Medical Center

King Kamehameha IV
Alexander Liholiho Iolani
(1834–1863)
Founder of
The Queens Medical Center

Victoria Kawekui Lunalio Kalaninuiahilapalapala Kaiulani Cleghorn

"I must have been born under an unlucky star,
as I seem to have my life planned out for me
in such a way that I cannot alter it..."

...Princess Kaiulani,
Rozel, Jersey,
summer of 1897

Alvin T. Onaka stamp of Mar 15, 2011, Mar 17, 2011 &
Mar 28, 2011 DO NOT HAVE THE MISSPELLED "TXE" OR
THE "SMILEY FACE" FOUND ON OBAMA'S LONG FORM
BIRTH CERTIFICATE DATED APR 25, 2011

MAR 17 2010

I CERTIFY THIS IS A TRUE COPY OR
ABSTRACT OF THE RECORD ON FILE IN
THE HAWAII STATE DEPARTMENT OF HEALTH

Alvin T. Onaka, Ph.D.
STATE REGISTRAR

OHSM 1.1 (REV. 10/08) LASER This current version of the short form was revised one month before the
2008 pres. election. Parent's place of birth was added and title of form changed to "certificate" instead of
"Certification" like Obama's due to complaints from HI birth certificate requestors being denied legal
instruments by departments and organizations citing the lack of information on a "Certification" didn't
prove you are who you say you are. Onaka and "globalists" behind the fraud with help from the Clinton
cartel changed the requirements in the US Dept of State to accept ANY certified document issued by a state
to be acceptable for obtaining a US passport.

PHOTOS

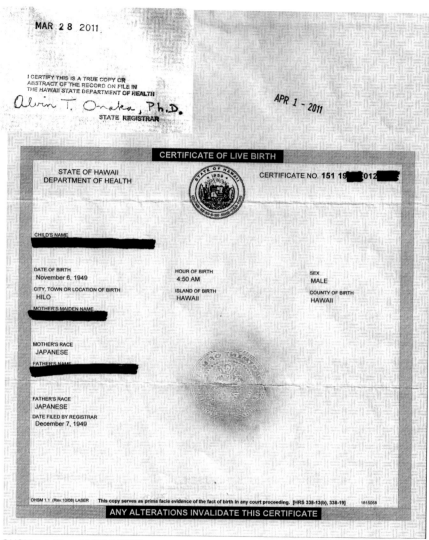

OHSM 1.1 (Rev. 10/08) LASER

This is the same form used for Alan but parents' place of birth has dropped off. Why? Is it so it will look more like Obama's? This low standard is now accepted at the State Dept. to get a passport. Does the passport application still ask for parents place of birth? If so, it appears they don't ask for proof.

CERTIFICATION OF LIVE BIRTH

STATE OF HAWAII
HONOLULU

DEPARTMENT OF HEALTH
HAWAII U.S.A.

CERTIFICATE NO. ▮▮▮▮▮▮▮

CHILD'S NAME
BARACK   HUSSEIN   OBAMA II

DATE OF BIRTH
August 4, 1961

HOUR OF BIRTH
7:24 PM

SEX
MALE

CITY, TOWN OR LOCATION OF BIRTH
HONOLULU

ISLAND OF BIRTH
OAHU

COUNTY OF BIRTH
HONOLULU

MOTHER'S MAIDEN NAME
STANLEY   ANN   DUNHAM

MOTHER'S RACE
CAUCASIAN

FATHER'S NAME
BARACK   HUSSEIN   OBAMA

FATHER'S RACE
AFRICAN

DATE FILED BY REGISTRAR
August 8, 1961

OHSM 1.1 (Rev.11/01) LASER   This copy serves as prima facie evidence of the fact of birth in any court proceeding. [HRS 338-13(b), 338-19]

ANY ALTERATIONS INVALIDATE THIS CERTIFICATE

OHSM 1.1 (Rev. 11/01) LASER   This is the "document"which former White House Press Secretary Robert Gibbs said is Obama's birth certificate.

On April 27, 2011, just days after Jerome Corsi's book "Where's the Birth Certificate" came out, Obama released an alleged long form birth certificate claiming he waived his right to privacy and asked Hawai'i's Dept. of Health for 2 copies of his long form certificate. His ill-fated decision to pass off a forgery didn't silence critics and instead led to even more evidence of lies and cover-up. They tried to sell the short-form as "all anyone can get." The Obama Campaign stated recently and reiterated their claim in June of 2008 that the campaign requested Obama's birth certificate in 2008, received it from Hawai'i and posted it on their website. Why then, is the stamp on the back dated June 6, 2007-a year before they asked for it? In 2001 it was Alvin T. Onaka who made the decision to stop issuing long-form birth certificates in Hawai'i but DOH employees ignored the policy and continued to issue long-forms. When the democrat-led Hawai'i government was sworn in, a complete crack-down ensued to protect Obama's birth story in his manufactured historical narrative.

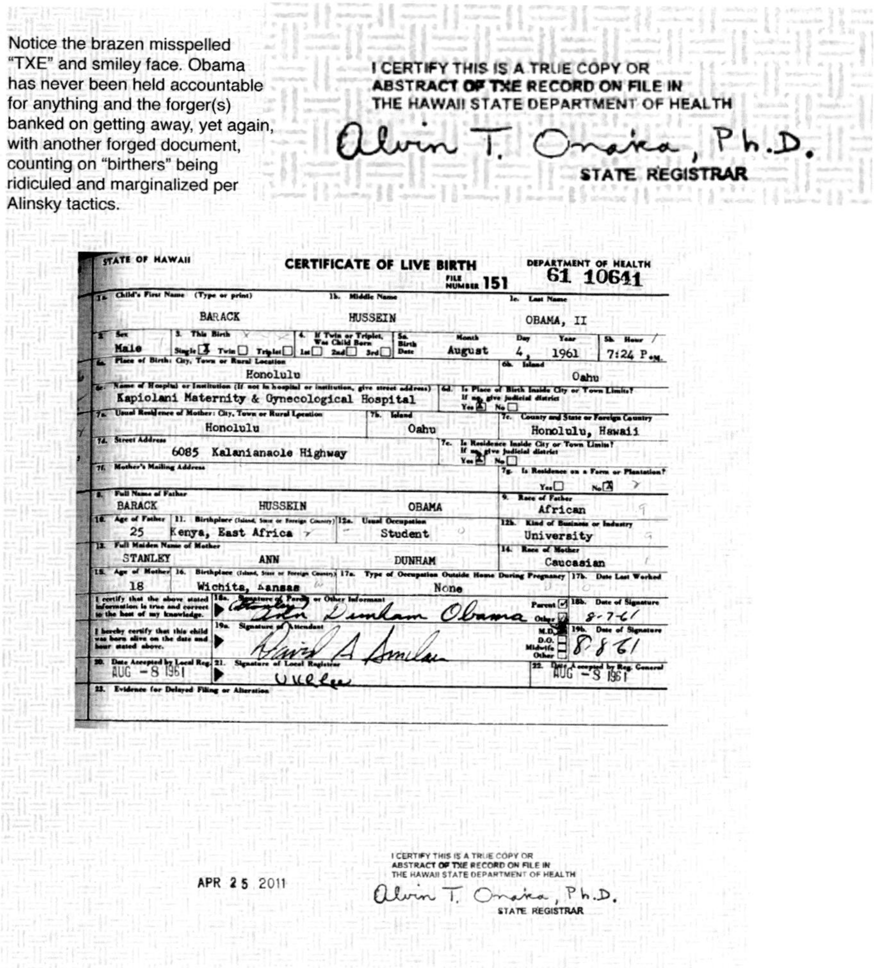

Notice the brazen misspelled "TXE" and smiley face. Obama has never been held accountable for anything and the forger(s) banked on getting away, yet again, with another forged document, counting on "birthers" being ridiculed and marginalized per Alinsky tactics.

I CERTIFY THIS IS A TRUE COPY OR
ABSTRACT OF TXE RECORD ON FILE IN
THE HAWAII STATE DEPARTMENT OF HEALTH
Alvin T. Onaka, Ph.D.
STATE REGISTRAR

STATE OF HAWAII — CERTIFICATE OF LIVE BIRTH — DEPARTMENT OF HEALTH
FILE NUMBER 151 — 61 10641

1a. Child's First Name (Type or print): BARACK
1b. Middle Name: HUSSEIN
1c. Last Name: OBAMA, II
2. Sex: Male
3. This Birth: Single [X] Twin [ ] Triplet [ ]
4. If Twin or Triplet, Was Child Born: 1st [ ] 2nd [ ] 3rd [ ]
5a. Birth Date: Month August, Day 4, Year 1961
5b. Hour: 7:24 P.M.
6a. Place of Birth: City, Town or Rural Location: Honolulu
6b. Island: Oahu
6c. Name of Hospital or Institution (If not in hospital or institution, give street address): Kapiolani Maternity & Gynecological Hospital
6d. Is Place of Birth Inside City or Town Limits? If no, give judicial district. Yes [X] No [ ]
7a. Usual Residence of Mother: City, Town or Rural Location: Honolulu
7b. Island: Oahu
7c. County and State or Foreign Country: Honolulu, Hawaii
7d. Street Address: 6085 Kalanianaole Highway
7e. Is Residence Inside City or Town Limits? If no, give judicial district. Yes [X] No [ ]
7f. Mother's Mailing Address:
7g. Is Residence on a Farm or Plantation? Yes [ ] No [X]
8. Full Name of Father: BARACK HUSSEIN OBAMA
9. Race of Father: African
10. Age of Father: 25
11. Birthplace (Island, State or Foreign Country): Kenya, East Africa
12a. Usual Occupation: Student
12b. Kind of Business or Industry: University
13. Full Maiden Name of Mother: STANLEY ANN DUNHAM
14. Race of Mother: Caucasian
15. Age of Mother: 18
16. Birthplace (Island, State or Foreign Country): Wichita, Kansas
17a. Type of Occupation Outside Home During Pregnancy: None
17b. Date Last Worked:
I certify that the above stated information is true and correct to the best of my knowledge.
18a. Signature of Parent or Other Informant: Ann Dunham Obama — Parent [X] Other [ ]
18b. Date of Signature: 8-7-61
I hereby certify that this child was born alive on the date and hour stated above.
19a. Signature of Attendant: David A Sinclair — M.D. [X] D.O. [ ] Midwife [ ] Other [ ]
19b. Date of Signature: 8-8-61
20. Date Accepted by Local Reg.: AUG -8 1961
21. Signature of Local Registrar: UKLee
22. Date Accepted by Reg. General: AUG -8 1961
23. Evidence for Delayed Filing or Alteration

APR 25 2011

I CERTIFY THIS IS A TRUE COPY OR
ABSTRACT OF TXE RECORD ON FILE IN
THE HAWAII STATE DEPARTMENT OF HEALTH
Alvin T. Onaka, Ph.D.
STATE REGISTRAR

This manufactured document was posted on the White House website on April 27, 2011. Graphic arts and document specialists continue to step forward challenging the authenticity of the document and attesting to "amateurish" manipulation, most notably the 28-page Affidavit of forgery by Douglas Vogt. Document, scan and print experts Paul Irey, Mara Zebest and Karl Denninger have also weighed in. Hawai'i's department of health continues to stonewall legal attempts to obtain the original document for forensic testing. Alvin Onaka, Registrar, HDOH and Loretta Fuddy, director of health, refuse to provide access to the original, citing privacy laws but Atty. Orly Taitz, plaintiff, filed an appeal stating that there cannot be a consideration of privacy, as Obama already released the document in question, and it is available to the public at large on the web site WhiteHouse.gov.

STATE OF HAWAII
DEPARTMENT OF HEALTH
RESEARCH & STATISTICS OFFICE

CERTIFICATE OF LIVE BIRTH

STATE FILE NO. 151 · 81 015124

1. CHILD'S FIRST NAME	MIDDLE NAME	LAST NAME	2a. DATE OF BIRTH (MO., DAY, YR.)
ALAN	PALIKO	BOOTH	November 24, 1981

			2b. HOUR	3. SEX
			7:55 A. M	Male

4a. HOSPITAL — NAME (IF NOT IN HOSPITAL GIVE NUMBER AND STREET)	4b. CITY, TOWN OR LOCATION OF BIRTH	4c. ISLAND	4d. COUNTY OF BIRTH
Kapiolani/Children's Medical Center	Honolulu	Oahu	Honolulu

5a. I certify that the stated information concerning this child is true to the best of my knowledge and belief. (Signature)	5b. DATE SIGNED (MO., DAY, YR.)	5c. NAME AND TITLE OF ATTENDANT AT BIRTH IF OTHER THAN CERTIFIER (TYPE OR PRINT)
David A. Sinclair MD	11/26/81	

5d. CERTIFIER — NAME AND TITLE (TYPE OR PRINT)	5e. MAILING ADDRESS (STREET OR R.F.D. NO., CITY OR TOWN, STATE)	5f. ATTENDANT — M.D., D.O., MIDWIFE, OTHER (SPECIFY)
David A. Sinclair, M.D.	1441 Kapiolani Blvd. Hon. HI	M.D.

6a. REGISTRAR (Signature)	6b. DATE RECEIVED BY LOCAL REGISTRAR (MO., DAY, YR.)	6c. DATE ACCEPTED BY STATE
DEPUTY *P. Gonsalves*	NOV 27 1981	NOV 27 1981

EVIDENCE FOR LATE FILING OR ALTERATION

7a. MOTHER — FIRST NAME	MIDDLE NAME	MAIDEN NAME	7b. AGE (AT TIME OF THIS BIRTH)	7c. STATE OF BIRTH (IF NOT IN U.S.A., NAME COUNTRY)
MIYUKI		SNYDER	31	Japan 73

8a. RESIDENCE — STATE	8b. COUNTY	8c. CITY, TOWN OR LOCATION	8d. NUMBER AND STREET OF RESIDENCE	8e. INSIDE CITY LIMITS (SPECIFY)
Hawaii	Honolulu	Wahiawa 08	1512 Glen Avenue	YES OR NO Yes

9. MOTHER'S MAILING ADDRESS STREET OR R.F.D. NO.	CITY OR TOWN	STATE	ZIP
1512 Glen Avenue, Wahiawa, Hawaii 96786			

10a. FATHER — FIRST NAME	MIDDLE NAME	LAST NAME	10a-1. LAST NAME AT BIRTH	10b. AGE (AT TIME OF THIS DELIVERY)	10c. STATE OF BIRTH (If not in U.S.A., Name Country)	10d. ACTIVE MEMBER U.S. ARMED FORCES?
FREDERIC	NEWTON	BOOTH II	BOOTH	32	Hawaii	YES ☒NO

11a. I certify that the personal information provided on this certificate is correct to the best of my knowledge and belief. (Signature of Parent or other informant)	11b. RELATION TO CHILD
Miyuki Booth *Frederic N. Booth II*	Mother & Father

12a. RACE — MOTHER Caucasian/Japanese	12b. IS PERSON OF SPANISH ORIGIN? YES 1☐ PUERTO RICAN 2☐ MEXICAN 3☐ CUBAN 4☐ CENTRAL S. AMERICAN 5☐ OTHER & UNKNOWN SPANISH ORIGIN NO 6☒	13a. RACE — FATHER Caucasian/Hawaiian	13b. IS PERSON OF SPANISH ORIGIN? YES 1☐ PUERTO RICAN 2☐ MEXICAN 3☐ CUBAN 4☐ CENTRAL S. AMERICAN 5☐ OTHER & UNKNOWN SPANISH ORIGIN NO 6☒

I CERTIFY THIS IS A TRUE COPY OF THE RECORD ON FILE IN THE HAWAII STATE DEPARTMENT OF HEALTH

DEC 29 1981

George H. Tokuyama
STATE REGISTRAR

190

STATE OF HAWAII
DEPARTMENT OF HEALTH
OFFICE OF HEALTH STATUS MONITORING

CERTIFICATE OF LIVE BIRTH

STATE
FILE NO. **151**

95 005

1. CHILD'S FIRST NAME	MIDDLE NAME	LAST NAME

2. HOSPITAL OR FACILITY NAME (If Not Institution, Give No., Street, Zip)	3. TYPE OF FACILITY - Hospital, Freestanding Birthing Center, Clinic, Doctor's Office, Residence, Other (Specify)	4. DATE OF BIRTH (Mo, Day, Yr)
TRIPLER MEDICAL CENTER	HOSPITAL	APRIL 12, 1995

5. CITY, TOWN OR LOCATION OF BIRTH	6. COUNTY OF BIRTH	7. ISLAND	8. HOUR	9. SEX
HONOLULU	HONOLULU	OAHU	5:24 AM	FEMALE

10. CERTIFIER'S SIGNATURE I certify that this child was born alive at the place and time and on the date stated. (Signature) ► *Shelia R. Richardson*	11. DATE SIGNED (Mo, Day, Yr) APRIL 14, 1995	12. CERTIFIER'S NAME & TITLE (Type or Print) SHELIA R. RICHARDSON, BIRTH CERT. CLERK

13. ATTENDANT'S NAME IF OTHER THAN CERTIFIER (Type or Print) DAPHNE L. JONES, CPT, MC	14. ATTENDANT'S TITLE - M.D., D.O., C.N.M., OTHER MIDWIFE, OTHER (Specify) DR OF MEDICINE

15. REGISTRAR'S SIGNATURE (Signature) ► *N. Shina*	16. DATE RECEIVED BY LOCAL REGISTRAR APR 17 1995	17. DATE ACCEPTED BY STATE APR 17 1995

EVIDENCE FOR LATE FILING OR ALTERATION

18. MOTHER - FIRST NAME	MIDDLE NAME	MAIDEN NAME	19. AGE AT THIS BIRTH	20. STATE OF BIRTH (If not in U.S.A., Name Country)	21. ACTIVE U.S. MILITARY? (yes / no)
			33	HAWAII	NO

22. RESIDENCE - STATE	23. COUNTY	24. CITY, TOWN OR LOCATION	25. NUMBER & STREET OF RESIDENCE, ZIP	26. INSIDE CITY LIMITS? (yes / no)
HAWAII	HONOLULU			YES

27. MOTHER'S MAILING ADDRESS - STREET OR R.F.D. NO.	CITY OR TOWN	STATE	ZIP

29. FATHER - FIRST NAME	MIDDLE NAME	LAST NAME	29. AGE AT THIS BIRTH	30. STATE OF BIRTH (If not in U.S.A., Name Country)	31. ACTIVE U.S. MILITARY? (yes / no)
			34	PENNSYLVANIA	YES

32. SIGNATURE OF PARENT OR INFORMANT I certify that the personal information provided above on this certificate is correct to the best of my knowledge and belief. (Signature) ►	33. RELATION TO CHILD MOTHER

34. RACE - MOTHER Caucasian, Japanese, Etc. (Specify) HAWAIIAN/CHINESE/KOREAN/GERMAN/ENGLISH/PORTUGUESE	36. SPANISH ORIGIN? (If yes, specify Cuban, Mexican, Puerto Rican, Central/S. American, Other & Unknown Spanish Origin)
35. RACE - FATHER Caucasian, Japanese, Etc. (Specify) BLACK	NO (MOTHER) NO (FATHER)

I CERTIFY THIS IS A TRUE COPY OR
ABSTRACT OF THE RECORD ON FILE IN
THE HAWAII STATE DEPARTMENT OF HEALTH

Alvin T. Onaka, Ph.D.
STATE REGISTRAR

MAR 15 2011

Long-Form Certificate of Live Birth from the state of Hawaii received in March 2011 by the requester. Note: The "THE" on Onaka's stamp is not misspelled and does not have a "happy face". Note also that race is listed as "Black" not "African".

191

CERTIFICATE OF LIVE BIRTH
TERRITORY OF HAWAII
DEPARTMENT OF HEALTH
BUREAU OF VITAL STATISTICS

REGISTRAR'S No.   BIRTH No. **151 - 49 06982**

1. PLACE OF BIRTH	2. USUAL RESIDENCE OF MOTHER (Where does mother live?)
a. COUNTY Honolulu	a. STATE T.H. b. COUNTY Honolulu
b. CITY (If outside corporate limits, write RURAL and give judicial district) Honolulu	c. CITY (If outside corporate limits, write RURAL and give judicial district) OR TOWN Honolulu
c. FULL NAME OF HOSPITAL OR INSTITUTION (If NOT in hospital or institution, give street address or location) Kapiolani Mat. & Gyn. Hospital	d. STREET ADDRESS (If rural, give location) 1929 Vancouver Drive

3. CHILD'S NAME (Type or print)	a. (First) FREDERICK	b. (Middle) NEWTON	c. (Last) BOOTH, II

4. SEX Male	5a. THIS BIRTH SINGLE [X] TWIN [ ] TRIPLET [ ]	5b. IF TWIN OR TRIPLET (This child born) 1ST [ ] 2ND [ ] 3RD [ ]	6. DATE OF BIRTH (Month) July (Day) 17, (Year) 1949

FATHER OF CHILD

7. FULL NAME	a. (First) FRANCIS	b. (Middle) NATHANIAL	c. (Last) BOOTH	8. COLOR OR RACE Caucasian
9. AGE (At time of this birth) 30 YEARS	10. BIRTHPLACE (District, county, state or foreign country) Honolulu, Oahu, T.H.		11a. USUAL OCCUPATION TELLER	11b. KIND OF BUSINESS OR INDUSTRY BANK

MOTHER OF CHILD

12. FULL MAIDEN NAME	a. (First) VIRGINIA	b. (Middle)	c. (Last) WHITE	13. COLOR OR RACE Caucasian
14. AGE (At time of this birth) 24 YEARS	15. BIRTHPLACE (District, county, state or foreign country) Washington, D.C.			

16. CHILDREN PREVIOUSLY BORN TO THIS MOTHER (Do NOT include this child)
a. How many OTHER children are now living? 1	b. How many OTHER children were born, alive but are now dead? 0	c. How many children were stillborn (born dead after 20 weeks pregnancy)? 0

17. INFORMANT'S FULL NAME   Virginia White Booth

I hereby certify that this child was born alive on the date stated above. AT 8:00 a.m	18a. SIGNATURE _ccmoGmston_	18b. ATTENDANT AT BIRTH M.D. [X] MIDWIFE [ ] OTHER (Specify)
	18c. ADDRESS 881 South Hotel Street, Honolulu, T.H.	18d. DATE SIGNED 7/19/49

19. DATE REC'D BY LOCAL REG. JUL 25 1949	20. REGISTRAR'S SIGNATURE _LHLehing_	21. DATE ON WHICH GIVEN NAME ADDED BY
DATE RLC'D BY REG GEN JUL 25 1949		Deputy Registrar General

THIS CERTIFIES THAT THE ABOVE IS A TRUE AND CORRECT COPY OF THE
ORIGINAL RECORD ON FILE IN THE BUREAU OF HEALTH STATISTICS,
TERRITORY OF HAWAII DEPARTMENT OF HEALTH

C. L. Wilbar Jr.
PRESIDENT

12-14-50
DATE

DEPUTY REGISTRAR GENERAL

PHOTOS

Application No. 28717

Certificate No. 38453

TERRITORY OF HAWAII
OFFICE OF THE SECRETARY
Certificate of Hawaiian Birth

TO ALL TO WHOM THESE PRESENTS SHALL COME, GREETING:

Whereas, Application has been made for the issuance of a certificate of Hawaiian birth to

FRANCIS NATHANIEL BOOTH

now residing at _____ Honolulu, Oahu, Territory of Hawaii

Satisfactory Proof has been submitted to show that __ he __ was born in Hawaii on __ June 8, 1919

and the photograph attached hereto is a good likeness of __ him __ at this time.

Physical identifying marks _____ Mole on right bicep.

It Is Hereby Certified, That _____ FRANCIS NATHANIEL BOOTH

was born in Hawaii and is entitled to a certificate of Hawaiian birth. This certificate is not transferable.

In Testimony Whereof, the Secretary of the Territory of Hawaii has hereunto subscribed his name and caused the great seal of said Territory to be affixed.

Done at Honolulu, Hawaii, this twenty-second day of August A. D. 1949

Secretary of Hawaii.

38453

OCT 2 1 2004

I CERTIFY THIS IS A TRUE COPY OR ABSTRACT OF THE RECORD ON FILE IN THE HAWAII STATE DEPARTMENT OF HEALTH

Alvin T. Onaka, Ph.D.
STATE REGISTRAR

193

King Kamehameha Day Parade 1984
Kona, HI

Fred at the Beach ??

NOT! There's no beach in Oklahoma!

Freddie
"Boot Boot"
HPD Solo Bike

4th of July
2011

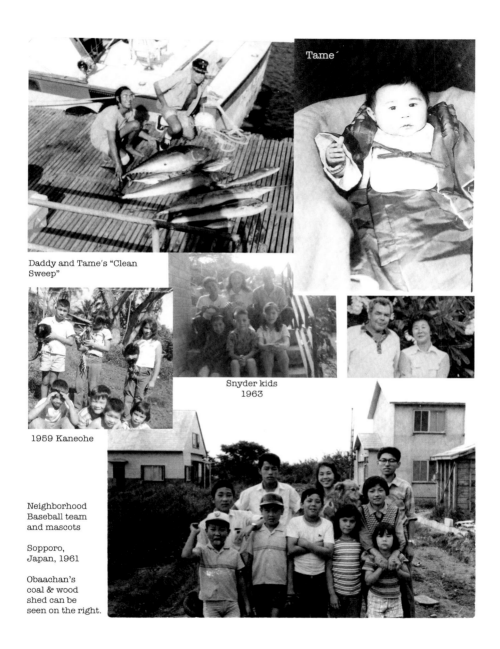

Daddy and Tame's "Clean Sweep"

Tame

Snyder kids
1963

1959 Kaneohe

Neighborhood
Baseball team
and mascots

Sopporo,
Japan, 1961

Obaachan's
coal & wood
shed can be
seen on the right.

Ashes at Sea, Kona Coast

First Mate Tame' on my birthday fishing trip Dec. '86

Captain & Owner of "Sea Strike" Dale Leverone on back deck.

Kailua-Kona Pier

Me and Dale with a "mahu" marlin (short-nosed spearfish)and a striped marlin. March 1987

Capt. Tame' on bridge

L-R: Me, Elizabeth Manning, Capt. Pamela Barnett, Pastor Manning in front of Columbia University.

(Photo by Carl Mehr)

Pastor Manning, Elizabeth, and following are on Morningside Drive and the main street behind us has two names 110th Street and/or Cathedral Parkway.

(Photo by Carl Mehr)

PHOTOS

Gathering for the march around Columbia University on Day Three of the CIA-Columbia Sedition Trial.

New York City - May 17, 2010

Photos courtesy of Fred Booth

American Grand Jury contingent
L-R: Rudy Badzik, Bill Miller, Bob Campbell, Neil Turner, Rudy Folds and Carl Mehr in front of Columbia University.

Fred's cousin, David Booth Ramsey entertained us at his home in Brooklyn and took us sightseeing.
Neil, Rudy, Bill, David & Rudy

May 20, 2010

THE BLOOD OF JESUS

ATLAH

World Missionary Church

James David Manning, Pastor

THE BLOOD OF JESUS AGAINST OBAMA
HISTORY MADE 4 NOV 2008 A TALIBAN
MUSLIM ILLEGALLY ELECTED
PRESIDENT USA HUSSEIN

Praise
Robinson

Mother
Keturah

Praise,
Mother
Keturah and
I went
shopping in
Manhattan
for a perfect
dress for
Mother to
wear in a
wedding
party and we
found it
wouldn't you
agree?

Mother Keturah sent me one of
her famous "Gospel Pies"

Sweet Potato Pie
Ingredients
Sweet Potatoes, Eggs, Milk,
Butter, Cinnamon, Lemon Extract,
Sugar, Flour, & Shortening
Mother Keturah's Gospel Pies 212-368-8382

On May 18, 2010 Obama and Columbia University were found guilty of all charges in the CIA-Columbia Trial held at ATLAH Church in Harlem. After the guilty verdicts I joined several members of the church and marched in celebration. I'm pictured here, from left to right, with Minister Esther Payne, Virtuous Charity Manigault, Virtuous Debbie Meyers, Mother Shekinah Sills and Elder One Whitaker

RESTORING HONOR
Lincoln Memorial
August 28, 2010

Clockwise from upper left: Dr. Alan Keyes, former UN Ambassador, WND Tea Party at Sea; Sam Adams & Button Gwinett (Jim Linn & William Temple) at 1st Nat'l Tea Party Conv., Nashville, TN; Joe the Plumber, Carol & Mike McLean, Jerry Nielsen, Me & Fred at Midwest FairTax rally, Columbia, MO; Paul Ryan, OK Council of Public Affairs OCPA 2010 Dinner; Me, Chloe, Elizabeth Jones & Sarah Palin- book signing, Fayetteville, AR; Charles Thompson, Candidate for OK Dist. 2 US House of Representatives & Carol Chouinard, Dist. 2 Dir. FairTax OK; Thomas Paine (Bob Basso), Oathkeepers rally, Fayetteville, AR (Photos courtesy of Fred Booth) Palin photo by Shaleah Craighead

Clockwise L-R: David Kawika Pa'a'aina, Ret. Navy SEAL, 40th Castle HS reunion; David Kuplelian, Author of The "Marketing of Evil", WND Tea Party at Sea; Run for Liberty, Paul Both (runner), Chris Swenson (bike) & Michael Cernak (support), Joplin, MO; Dr. Jerome Corsi, Author, "Where's the Birth Certificate?", WND Tea Party at Sea; Gov. Mike Huckabee being presented with Tim Cox's GOOOH book (Which he ignored) Tulsa, OK

(Photos courtesy of Fred Booth)

Jack, Andrew, Pili, Holly & Terry

LTC Terry Lakin

Even 5 months in prison didn't dampen Terry's resolve and commitment to his decision..

Popping up on trucks in Ohio & Michigan...

Terry with his sons, Andrew and Jackson with Miki Booth at Terry's Welcome Home Celebration at Baltimore International Airport, May 14, 2011

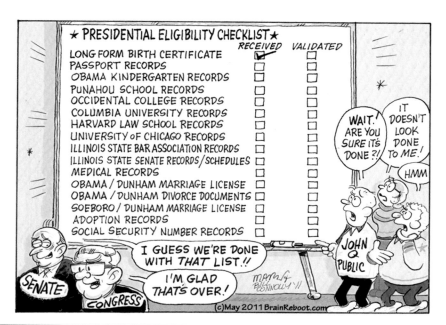

Renown leaders of the Constitutional eligibility movement aka 'birthers' meeting in CA
L-R: Jeff Lichter, David Larocque, Neil Turner, Gary Wilmott, Orly Taitz (Photo courtesy of Gary Wilmott)

Rogues' Gallery

"YES, HE WAS BORN IN THE UNITED STATES AND YES HE IS ELIGIBLE TO SERVE AND PERRY, TRUMP AND OTHERS SHOULD STOP ASSOCIATING THEMSELVES WITH THIS IDIOTIC FRINGE GROUP OF BIRTHERS" Karl Rove, Oct 24, 2011.

Brian Schatz was Chairman of the Hawaii Democrat Party in 2008 and is now the Lt. Governor. The Post & Email has contacted him by letter and telephone to ask why eligibility wording was removed from the party's nomination certificates in 2008, but his office refuses to respond.

PINHEAD NOT PATRIOT. Bill, we're looking out for the U.S. Constitution, not for you! Who paid you to scrub the stolen CT social security number question from your Mailbag?

Rogues' Gallery

PUBLIC ENEMY No. 1
Karl Rove
for attacks against the Constitution using propaganda and Alinsky tatics.

On Oct 26, 2011, at 11:51 AM, Miki Booth wrote:
Born to Citizen parentS. Matters less where the child is born as in the case of military parents ie John McCain. Article II, Section I, Clause 5 requirement that president and VP (devolved) be natural born Citizens. Founders wanted highest standard of citizenship for the highest office in the land, to ensure the pres and VP would have allegiance only to the US.
Let me clue you in, Mr. Rove, at the time of Obama's birth his father was a British subject and subject of the UK Colony later called Kenya. My husband and son were both born in Kapiolani Hospital and it makes no difference whether he born there, his Certification of Live Birth and the Certificate of Live Birth posted on Apil 27 are both forgeries.
Miki Booth
On Oct 26, 2011, at 4:07 PM, Karl Rove
<karl@rove.com> wrote:
No US court has ever held a child born to a US mother on US soil to be anything other than a natural born citizen. Never. And no they aren't.
Mr. Rove, You are thinking of native born citizen. Yet, again, you make a statement w/o facts to back it up. Name one court case defining natural born citizen and don't rely on CRS propaganda. Miki Booth Sent from my iPhone. (No answer forthcoming from Rove)

"Is Mr. Trump going to ask the candidates whether they agree with him that Barack Obama was not born in the United States?" Rove asked. (Huff Post Politics Dec. 6, 2011) Clever wording, Rove, but we are on to you.

Is Governor Abercrombie a socialist like Obama?

Rogues' Gallery

Sen. James Inhofe (R-OK) served four terms in the U.S. House of Representatives before his election to the U.S. Senate in 1994. Prior to that, he served as a state legislator. He refuses to meet with his constituents but instead champions causes in Africa. Why did he propose an end-run around the Constitutional requirement for President?

Bobby Titcomb's photo after his arrest on April 4, 2011.

Dr. Chiyome Fukino lied on national TV and MSNBC with Michael Issikoff when she said that the "Certification of Live Birth" is all a person can obtain from the Health Department.

November 2008, our country elected as its president, a man who not only had no verifiable qualifications for the job, but was also constitutionally ineligible to hold it. The only proof he offered the public was an image that was thoroughly debunked as a computer-generated abstract that was not what it was purported to be.

What Is the Birther Summit?

In the time since that election, a groundswell of Americans asked for nothing more than an independent investigation into a document that nobody had any empirical evidence even existed, and were stonewalled at each step.

On April 27, 2011, Barack Obama released to the nation yet another computer-manipulated image that he proclaimed was the document that, previously, the American people were told could not be obtained, while he also directed a veritable fortune to be spent to keep from revealing it. Once again, forensic document experts weighed in on the authenticity of that image, and handily dismissed it as a forgery as well. The release of that image also produced another valid question. If that were the "real" birth certificate, why would he have fought so expensively to obfuscate it, since there was little additional information included on it that the first image lacked?

Very possibly, the reason that the obvious forgeries were foisted on the American people was to keep public discourse away from the constitutional issue that plagues Barack Obama—that, according to the historic definition of "natural born Citizen," he is not constitutionally eligible to be president because his father was never a citizen of the United States, let alone at the time that Obama, Jr. was born.

To the repeated demands of the people over this constitutional calamity, and the subsequent crimes committed to veil the truth, our leaders in Washington have responded with outright deception, and continue to provide cover in an attempt designed to prevent any action on their parts to uphold their oaths of office to support and defend the Constitution.

LTC Terry Lakin, an 18-year honorable Army flight surgeon who could not, in good conscience, deploy to a foreign war until he had confirmation that Barack Obama was a legitimate Commander-in-Chief (something that the April 27, 2011 document would have purportedly answered), LTC Terry Lakin was stripped of his military career and sentenced to prison in Leavenworth. (http://www.terrylakinactionfund.com).

Having been ignored by their leaders for far too long, the American people are demanding to be heard. Out of those demands was born the Birther Summit, an event presently being planned for the voice of the people to be united into a single unavoidable chorus requiring our

officials to do the jobs for which they were elected, and fully investigate Barack Obama's eligibility, based upon the sparse documentation he has provided.

In the coming weeks, this website will become the gateway to the Birther Summit, providing everything from relevant information to online registration to attend the event. Please bookmark it, and return often!

Summit Facts

Countless multitudes of Americans have literally been screaming for nearly three years for our government to properly, and honestly, address what we all know has been the biggest fraud ever perpetrated upon our nation. Our government officials have merely ignored our demands for governmental redress of our grievances, forgetting that government derives every bit of its authority from We the People.

We have tried to be heard by our elected officials and by our courts, and so far, not a single plea has actually been heard . . . until NOW!

If you are as frustrated about Washington's stonewalling tactics as we are, then the Birther Summit is your chance to be heard, to be seen, and to be reckoned with. Your letters, your emails, your faxes, and your phone calls have likely never even been seen by those to whom you've written them, for it is apparent that our members of Congress have form letters they have directed their staffers to send in response to anyone asking our legitimate questions.

Those unresponsive career politicians now need to be confronted by you ... by us... in person!

As long as the complicit media broadcasts its false message that we are just a small group of "conspiracy theorist nut cases," the elitists in Washington will continue to ignore us. Those abrogators of our Constitution need to come face to face with the America to whom they are supposed to report . . . the America that has given them their jobs.

The Birther Summit is your chance to make a difference!

The Birther Summit will be a two-day event, with an optional third day for the Summit's foot soldiers to team up into groups, and personally take the Summit's Declaration to the "battle zone."

DAY 1 will be a "working conference" of the national leaders and spokespeople of the eligibility movement. Their names are all very well known to you, and this group will hammer

out a unified, cohesive message to issue to Congress and every citizen of this country. That message will be our Declaration of Constitutional Dependence, and will address every facet of Barack Obama's constitutional ineligibility to hold the highest office in the country, and the lengths to which he has gone to hide that fact.

DAY 2 will start with a massive rally at which many of the previous day's conference attendees will address the huge crowd assembled to make our presence known to Washington and the rest of the country. The rally, with poignant messages from some of our leaders, will culminate in the reading of our Declaration of Constitutional Dependence. We have asked the one individual we all immediately recognize for the vast sacrifice he made on our country's behalf—LTC Terry Lakin. Stay tuned.

Following the rally, we will take our message to the streets in a unified march, protesting Washington's continued cover up of the fraud that has been perpetrated upon us.

DAY 3 will be the day for the Summit's attendees to deliver our message in a more personal way, by teaming up and visiting the offices of every member of Congress.

When the dates, times, and places are finalized, we will offer online registration for the Birther Summit. Join our email list today, and we'll keep you informed about this exciting, historic event!

Website:
http://www.birthersummit.org

Handbook for taking over the government

RULES FOR RADICALS

by Saul D. Alinsky

RULE 1: "Power is not only what you have, but what the enemy thinks you have." Power is derived from 2 main sources - money and people. "Have-Nots" must build power from flesh and blood. (These are two things of which there is a plentiful supply. Government and corporations always have a difficult time appealing to people, and usually do so almost exclusively with economic arguments.)

RULE 2: "Never go outside the expertise of your people." It results in confusion, fear and retreat. Feeling secure adds to the backbone of anyone. (Organizations under attack wonder why radicals don't address the "real" issues. This is why. They avoid things with which they have no knowledge.)

RULE 3: "Whenever possible, go outside the expertise of the enemy." Look for ways to increase insecurity, anxiety and uncertainty. (This happens all the time. Watch how many organizations under attack are blind-sided by seemingly irrelevant arguments that they are then forced to address.)

RULE 4: "Make the enemy live up to its own book of rules." If the rule is that every letter gets a reply, send 30,000 letters. You can kill them with this because no one can possibly obey all of their own rules. (This is a serious rule. The besieged entity's very credibility and reputation is at stake, because if activists catch it lying or not living up to its commitments, they can continue to chip away at the damage.)

RULE 5: "Ridicule is man's most potent weapon." There is no defense. It's irrational. It's infuriating. It also works as a key pressure point to force the enemy into concessions. (Pretty crude, rude and mean, huh? They want to create anger and fear.)

RULE 6: "A good tactic is one your people enjoy." They'll keep doing it without urging and come back to do more. They're doing their thing, and will even suggest better ones. (Radical activists, in this sense, are no different that any other human being. We all avoid "un-fun" activities, and but we revel at and enjoy the ones that work and bring results.)

RULE 7: "A tactic that drags on too long becomes a drag." Don't become old news. (Even radical activists get bored. So to keep them excited and involved, organizers are constantly coming up with new tactics.)

RULE 8: "Keep the pressure on. Never let up." Keep trying new things to keep the opposition off balance. As the opposition masters one approach, hit them from the flank with something new.

(Attack, attack, attack from all sides, never giving the reeling organization a chance to rest, regroup, recover and re-strategize.)

RULE 9: "The threat is usually more terrifying than the thing itself." Imagination and ego can dream up many more consequences than any activist. (Perception is reality. Large organizations always prepare a worst-case scenario, something that may be furthest from the activists' minds. The upshot is that the organization will expend enormous time and energy, creating in its own collective mind the direst of conclusions. The possibilities can easily poison the mind and result in demoralization.)

RULE 10: "If you push a negative hard enough, it will push through and become a positive." Violence from the other side can win the public to your side because the public sympathizes with the underdog. (Unions used this tactic. Peaceful [albeit loud] demonstrations during the heyday of unions in the early to mid-20th Century incurred management's wrath, often in the form of violence that eventually brought public sympathy to their side.)

RULE 11: "The price of a successful attack is a constructive alternative." Never let the enemy score points because you're caught without a solution to the problem. (Old saw: If you're not part of the solution, you're part of the problem. Activist organizations have an agenda, and their strategy is to hold a place at the table, to be given a forum to wield their power. So, they have to have a compromise solution.)

RULE 12: Pick the target, freeze it, personalize it, and polarize it." Cut off the support network and isolate the target from sympathy. Go after people and not institutions; people hurt faster than institutions. (This is cruel, but very effective. Direct, personalized criticism and ridicule works.)

BARACK OBAMA (D)

Top Contributors

University of California	$909,283
Goldman Sachs	$874,207
Harvard University	$717,230
Microsoft Corp	$714,108
Google Inc	$701,099
JPMorgan Chase & Co	$581,460
Citigroup Inc	$581,216
National Amusements Inc	$543,859
Time Warner	$508,148
Sidley Austin LLP	$492,445
Stanford University	$481,199
Skadden, Arps et al	$473,424
Wilmerhale Llp	$466,679
UBS AG	$454,795
Latham & Watkins	$426,924
Columbia University	$426,516
Morgan Stanley	$425,102
IBM Corp	$415,196
University of Chicago	$414,555
US Government	$400,819

214

Chapter 24

Sooner Bags Seat at National Tea Party

February 2010 is when things really got interesting and very hectic but sometimes a lot of fun, too. Just a few days after the start of the state legislative session and my trip to Oklahoma City, I was again traveling. This time I was headed to the National Tea Party Convention in Nashville, Tennessee. I had a suitcase full of T-shirts that I hoped to sell and raise enough funds to print the "push" cards needed for my campaign. Cris and Mike Kurtz of Kurtz Design Studio had designed a very attractive and eye-catching promotional piece for me in which I pledged the following:

LIMITED GOVERNMENT
I pledge to get government out of our business, schools and homes.

FREE MARKET
I pledge to decrease regulations that inhibit jobs and increase incentives to promote jobs.

FAIRTAX
I pledge to move FairTax legislation forward and replace punitive taxes with a national sales tax.

STRONG NATIONAL DEFENSE
I pledge to make real homeland security the utmost priority.

SECOND AMENDMENT
The cornerstone to our freedom is the right to bear arms and the one right that protects all others.

STATES' RIGHTS ARE FOUNDATIONAL

I will fight to protect our constitutional rights as individuals and our constitutional rights as a State.

The GOOOH and FairTax logos appeared on both sides of the push card.

On the flight to Nashville from Tulsa, Cheryl, friend and fellow Route 66 Tea Party member, and I stopped to change planes in Memphis. I turned my phone on to call Fred while I waited to board the next flight and saw that I had missed calls from Cris Kurtz. A reporter from Tulsa World, Randy Krehbiel, wanted to interview someone from Oklahoma who was going to the Nashville convention. I was the only person she could think of, and she gave me Krehbiel's contact information. I called him and straightaway he wanted to know if I thought the price of the convention and hotel rooms was awfully high.

His approach kind of took me aback until I remembered that Tulsa World is a decidedly liberal paper, and Randy Krehbiel definitely leaned left in his political reporting. But since I hadn't even reached Nashville yet, I agreed to call him the following day after the official start of the conference.

When I called the next afternoon, I never let on that I was running for office. I figured Krehbiel would be looking for negative angles on the convention, and there was already controversy, not only about the cost but also about politicians being part of the program. Michele Bachmann and Marsha Blackburn had both been removed from the program for that reason. The liberal media did their best to malign Judson Phillips, convention organizer, "with a cacophony of criticism" according to Luke O'Brien, AOL News, and posted on far-left websites like the Huffington Post. Hit pieces were everywhere, a situation deliberately intended to discredit both Phillips and the Tea Party as a whole — the same full-on assault Sarah Palin received for her conservative efforts. I knew Krehbiel would be hungry for any negativity he could draw out of me. So I gave simple and straightforward answers, and I couldn't resist "talking up" Sarah Palin and FOX News, which always irritates liberals. I was pleased that Randy quoted me on both subjects, and man, did liberal heads spin. For fun, I added some of the comments after the story below:

Sooner bags seat at group's Tea Party
A Miami, OK, woman is attending the convention for conservatives.
By RANDY KREHBIEL World Staff Writer

A Miami, Oklahoma, woman is attending the convention for conservatives.

Five hundred fifty-eight dollars and ninety-five cents is a lot of money for Miki Booth, but she knew she had to come up with it somehow, and she did.

On Thursday, Booth and her friend Cheryl flew to Nashville, Tennessee, for the National Tea Party Convention at the Opryland Hotel.

"The tickets (to the convention) were quite high, but to me this is important," said Booth, a retiree from Miami, Oklahoma, and the organizer of the Route 66 Tea Party.

The price of the convention $558.95 including taxes and fees, plus $110 a night for lodging has been controversial among Tea Partiers, who tend to be working-class people without deep pockets. Organizers also have been criticized for trying to make a profit on the event.

Booth, who worked in the hotel industry in Hawaii before moving to Oklahoma, said she understands that conventions are expensive to stage. For her, she said, the trip has been worthwhile.

"The gathering is not so much for participants as it is organizers," she said Friday in a telephone interview. "I think they might have made a mistake calling it a convention. They should have called it a conference."

Along with seminars on local organizing and voter registration, the convention schedule includes sessions with such titles as "Why Christians Must Engage," "Five Easy Fixes to the High Cost of Mass Immigration," and "Defeating Liberalism Via the Primary Process."

A speech Saturday morning is titled "Correlations Between the Current Administration and Marxist Dictators of Latin America."

The headline event Saturday features an appearance by former Alaska governor and Republican vice presidential nominee Sarah Palin.

"She's a true American," Booth said. "She's not so political. She talks right to our hearts."

Booth, though, seemed most interested in making new contacts and seeing old acquaintances she has made through her involvement in Tea Parties and FairTax, which advocates replacing the federal income tax with a national sales tax.

Booth describes herself as someone who "never paid much attention" to politics until the past few years.

"I'm one of those to blame for what's happened," she said. "Lots of times I didn't bother to vote."

FOX News, she said, changed her life. "I used to watch CNN all the time," she said. "All that was on it was which celebrities were getting divorced and international news. Once I started watching FOX, they were reporting things I just couldn't believe were going on."

I read the comments following the story for a time; they added up to hundreds. I picked a few of my favorites to share:

Polyphonte: FOX News, she said, changed her life. "I used to watch CNN all the time," she said. "All that was on it was which celebrities were getting divorced and international news. Once I started watching FOX, they were reporting things I just couldn't believe were going on." End quote. This literally had me rolling. I almost feel sorry for sheeple like her.

Lovene: These tea baggers are likely scared, not smart and easily fooled by charisma: Sarah Palin and lies: FOX news and Rush L. This scares ME. They know things aren't working and not properly identifying the cause. As some other guy said, I'd like to see an IQ poll on these poor people. They are so deluded. You can throw some religious extremism in the mix and might come up with a disaster that could truly take us down. In a leader we need more than homesy talk and winks. We need someone with a knowledge of constitutional law, the ability to see the problems of the whole world, common sense and a good work ethic. Does anyone really believe those baggers will come up with that person? Friends, we need to do something proactive. Please tell me what we can do. HELP!!!

I was surprised to read some of Randy's comments and replies to postings. He did not "pile on" as would please the rabid left but instead wrote thoughtfully.

Tulsa World Staff Writer Randy Krehbiel: In my view, the power paradigm in America is shifting, and it scares a lot of people. The people who are used to being in charge can feel the ground moving under their feet, and it makes them uneasy, even if they can't identify exactly why they're uneasy. Add to that the worst economy in most of our lifetimes and a national debt at or near historic highs in terms of its share of gross domestic product and you get some pretty freaked out people.

In talking to Miki Booth and others, I venture to say that the true Tea Partiers are disproportionately self-employed and/or small business owners, or retired. They hate Democrats but distrust most Republicans. According to Miki Booth, most of the people at the convention appeared to be in their fifties or older (which, to be fair, may be what you'd find at just about any convention). Still, it's kind of interesting to me that they seem to be from the same generation as the anti-war protesters of the late 1960s and early 1970s.

It was inevitable that his saying we hate Democrats would draw fire.

Elusive: *The Tea Party participants will have the last laugh at the polls. I'm pretty shocked at your statement, Randy, that they hate Democrats. That simply isn't true, perhaps the person you talked to but not the majority, there are many Democrats that belong to this organization that are not happy with what our government is doing.*

Randy Krehbiel: *Elusive, by Democrats I mean Democratic office-holders. By and large, the Tea Partiers at least say they are independent but clearly they're not going to vote for many Democrats. They don't even seem to like Dan Boren, whose voting record is probably the most conservative for a D in Congress.*

Someone going by the name Mennis Diller had something to say, and it sounded kind of like Dennis Miller so I included it here. I like his cheeky style.

Mennis Diller: *I have to say it is amusing to watch all this pants wetting from the left. We were drug through the long primary last year watching the political theatre of Obama vs. Clinton. All the "super delegates" in the "Democratic" party install a candidate. The convention turns into a "catharsis" LOL. It appears your catharsis has come un-done. Incidentally, someone told me awhile back that every time the media and the haters on the left make their derogatory remarks about "teabags" that it just makes them more determined.*

Randy, by your analogy it would appear that the Route 66 bunch from the seventies has a real problem with Haight Ashbury bunch running the Democrat Party! LOL

Redbeard: *The Tea Partiers might have more credibility if they stopped calling Obama a Marxist and hinting that he wasn't an American citizen. Obama is as much an American citizen as Palin is.*

Mennis Diller: *Redbeard, that is a good nugget of wisdom for anyone wanting to have credibility. Thank You*

There are a lot of comments intended to insult, but they pretty much just fall to the wayside as the bloggers go on to banter hate-filled messages among themselves. But when I read a message from people like Shakin' the Bush, I get the motivation and the inspiration to do what I do.

Shakin' the Bush: *Miki Booth, THANK YOU for going to this event. Pay no attention to the raging liberals and their posts here. It is people like you who will help steer this country back on course. Keep up the good work!*

Chapter 25

"This Piece of Junk"

Oklahoma firecracker takes on Obama eligibility
Candidate for Congress: "If he claims he was born at Kapi'olani, I want him to show proof."

Posted: February 09, 2010
By Chelsea Schilling
© 2011 WorldNetDaily

NASHVILLE — *Just as a tea-party convention crowd gathered to discuss strategy for the movement, one woman stepped forward to the microphone — holding up two Hawaiian long-form birth certificates and a copy of President Obama's purported short-form certification of live birth — and, referencing the short form, she told the crowd, "This piece of junk is what you get when you don't have one of these!"*

The crowd went wild, clapping and cheering.

When the forum was over, Tea Partiers scrambled around a table to see and photograph her original documents.

The woman, Miki Booth, originally from Hawaii, is running for the U.S. House of Representatives in Oklahoma's second district as an Independent Constitutional Conservative. She had presented original long-form birth certificates belonging to her son and husband, dated 1981 and 1949.

"They are the 'vault' copies of the original ones filled out at the hospital and sent to the Hawaii State Department of Health Vital Statistics Office," Booth told WND. "It is from this office that the newspapers get their stats for births, deaths and marriages to announce in the newspapers."

Her husband, Fred, and son, Alan, were born at the Kapi'olani Medical Center for Women and Children in Honolulu, Hawaii — the same hospital declared as Obama's birthplace in a purported letter from the president.

"If he is going to claim he was born in Kapi'olani like my husband and my son, then I want him to show proof," Booth said, explaining that a certification of live birth only shows that a live baby was born — and not necessarily in Hawaii.

"What he's given us perpetuates the mystery of what he's covering up and gives us more reason to not trust him," she said.

Booth presented this 1981 long-form Hawaiian birth certificate belonging to her son. It contains information about the doctor, birth hospital, time of delivery and other information.

Asked what she thought of the crowd's overwhelmingly positive reaction when she presented the documents, Booth said, "I was pleased but not surprised, since I get that reaction every time I do it. I think people really appreciate when someone shows them they're not stupid. They know what's going on."

Most of the convention attendees appeared to rally around WND founder, Joseph Farah, as he presented his speech at the national convention Friday referencing the eligibility issue. They gave him a standing ovation at the end of his speech; however, a small number of people suggested the topic shouldn't have surfaced at a Tea Party event.

"I would say those people have bought into the notion that it's a dead issue since it was 'proved' to them that Obama was born in Hawaii," Booth explained. "What proof were they convinced by? Bill O'Reilly saying so? Newscasters saying so? ACORN saying so? The Internet copy?"

Booth also presented this 1949 long-form Hawaiian birth certificate belonging to her husband. It contains information about the birth attendant, birth hospital, time of delivery and other information.

She continued, "I wonder if these same people think we shouldn't question his record of what passport he traveled to Pakistan with — or his Occidental records of foreign student funding and his Columbia records or his Harvard records or his Punahou records."

As WND reported, when Farah discussed the eligibility issue — explaining to the crowd that the president refuses to produce documents proving he meets the Constitution's natural-born citizen requirement — the crowd cheered wildly, whistled and applauded.

Booth added, "The people I hang with enjoyed and appreciated Joseph Farah's speech, and we are with him all the way."

The eligibility issue was a hot topic at the convention even before Farah arrived to present his Friday evening keynote speech. Prior to Booth's presentation of the Hawaii documents and Farah's speech, other convention attendees had expressed concern about Obama's eligibility documentation as well. One Tea Partier asked Judicial Watch president, Tom Fitton, whether his organization would sue the White House for documentation of Obama's eligibility.

"On the birth certificate, we are not pursuing that. I don't think, at this point, that is going to be a fruitful pursuit," Fitton said. "My suggestion to activists is that they go back to their states and ensure that the secretaries of each individual state next time around have the certification process and candidates for the presidency certified for eligibility."

The crowd reacted to his suggestion for a more stringent certification process with booming applause.

Booth wasn't always skeptical about the president's background. She said she and her husband, a 25-year veteran police officer from Hawaii, were registered Democrats when the Obama campaign sent them a promotion card requesting a $75 contribution in 2008.

"His platform sounded great, and I was ready to send the check," she said. "Then I heard he was from Hawaii, so I was thrilled and went online to find out what I could about him."

She said her family originally took issue with his admitted history of cocaine use.

"I spent all my life as a law-abiding citizen and married a cop who enforced our laws," she said. "I just couldn't accept the notion that it would be OK for the leader of our great nation to have done hard drugs."

However, that wasn't her biggest concern.

"What really frightened me and sent me on a mission to warn others was when I found out about his connections to Bill Ayers and Rashid Khalidi," she said.

"I lived during the time when Ayers bombed the judge's house, and protesters waged war on our law enforcement."

She continued, "As I connected the dots, I was hit with a cold stab through the heart when I thought, this is a deliberate plan to destroy our country from within."

Booth founded the Route 66 Tea Party last year, became community coordinator for District 2 Oklahoma's ResistNet and FairTax groups, and held rallies to promote pro-American programs and protest Obama's healthcare "reform."

"*I believe in limited government, a free-market system, a strong national defense, states' rights, and our right to bear arms against a tyrannical government as our founding fathers intended when they wrote the Constitution,*" *she said proudly.*

Booth is also a member of "Get Out Of Our House," or GOOOH, pronounced "Go." According to its website, GOOOH is "a non-partisan plan to evict the 435 career politicians in the U.S. House of Representatives and replace them with everyday Americans just like you ... GOOOH is not just another political party. It is a system that will allow you and your neighbors to choose, among yourselves, the person who can best represent your district."

Booth said the GOOOH system is a plan by Tim Cox of Liberty Hill, Texas, a man who spent his career creating systems for Dell and developed credit card readers for gas pumps. She said candidates answer 100 questions on how they would vote on particular issues.

"*That becomes your platform and also documents how you would vote, because it becomes a contract, and you will be held accountable,*" *she explained. "There will be a timeline for candidate selection sessions where all members will go through a process of selecting their peers or be considered themselves, and someone will bubble up to the top after the session is completed. That person will be the GOOOH candidate to go on the ballot."*

She said when the organization reaches half a million people who invest $100 each, there will be a $50 million pot to fund national campaigns for those candidates — $1 million in each of the 50 states.

"*I went home and asked Fred, 'What would you think if got elected to go to Congress?' " He said, 'I would be so proud of you.' "*

Even if GOOOH doesn't make critical mass by reaching the 500,000 membership mark, Booth has every intention of continuing her fight for the House seat currently held by Rep. Dan Boren, a Democrat.

In a January letter, Booth, a passionate supporter of Second Amendment rights, challenged Boren to a debate and rifle marksmanship contest.

"*Our interpretation of the right to bear arms seems to differ in that I believe the framers of the Constitution armed us in defense of a tyrannical government,*" *she wrote. "It's good and well that we can hunt and target shoot, but if you've discussed guns in the context of the Constitution, I must have missed it. Your record voting 98 percent of the time with your* party leads me to believe you might have not read the Constitution because it appears you are not guided by it."

She added, "I did drop a coyote at about 200 yards a couple of weeks ago, so you can be assured I am qualified to challenge you in a shooting match."

Booth recently shot a coyote dead on the spot from 200 yards away with open sights. It was trying to eat her chickens. She said, "I wouldn't mind the coyotes if they earned an honest living. But when they steal chickens, that's crossing the line."

Booth speaks to many groups while she campaigns, and she always starts out her presentation by introducing herself in this way:

"I'm Miki Booth. I'm from Hawaii, and I'm a community organizer."

"I show them the birth certificates, explain them and then hand them out for closer scrutiny," she said. "Overwhelmingly, I'm accepted as being on their side, and I'm appreciated for my willingness to expose myself and my family to criticism and possible danger."

She continued, "Alan and Fred are proud of me for doing it, and they know the danger. But we'll do anything to help our country."

Cheryl and I arrived at the Opryland Hotel and Convention Center on Thursday evening, too late to attend the evening mixer, but the official program didn't start until the next morning anyway.

When I checked in, there was a message from Jim Linn (Samuel Adams) asking me to call as soon as I arrived. The person who took the message wrote the number down wrong, so we didn't connect right away. Jim was the only person I knew who would be there, and I was distressed about not being able to reach him. The event had sold out. There would be over a thousand people at the banquet with Palin. With that many people, I wondered how I would ever find Jim.

I felt bad because he wasn't even sure he wanted to go to the convention in the first place, and if he did it would just be to check it out; he would leave his Sam Adams costume at home. I had persuaded him to go and insisted it would be a shame if he didn't bring Sam Adams so he did. And now I couldn't find him.

I studied the message; the numbers didn't look right. Wondering if they might be transposed, I dialed after changing a number in the sequence.

"Hello?" It was Jim!

What a relief. But Jim hadn't been pining away waiting for me. No, sir. Samuel Adams met Button Gwinnett on the convention floor, and they had a lot of catching up to do since signing the Declaration of Independence two hundred and thirty-four years earlier.

Friday morning, Cheryl and I picked up our registration packets, helped ourselves to a continental breakfast, and went into the main banquet room to find a place to sit down to eat and plan out the sessions we wanted to attend.

As soon as we entered the room, I saw a couple sitting at a nearby table wearing FairTax gear. There were empty chairs at their table so I motioned Cheryl over to sit with them. I sat down next to the man and he said,

"Miki! There you are!"

I drew a blank. I was totally confused for a moment and then realized the woman next to him, standing up to give me a hug, was Carol, so he had to be Mike McLean. I was flabbergasted. I hadn't recognized Mike with the hat on, but I was still confused.

"How did you know I was here?" I asked Mike.

He showed me my business card.

"Samuel Adams gave me this," he said.

Jim had a stack of my business cards and had been handing them out at all the tables. Jim was a huge supporter of FairTax as well as GOOOH, and meeting the McLeans tied us all together. Suddenly I felt as if I knew lots of people at the convention. It was really going to be a good time.

Later that morning, Cheryl and I carried armloads of T-shirts down to the main conference room to sell. Panelists and speakers were scheduled throughout the day and Judson Phillips, organizer of the convention, was speaking, along with a panel of others, and taking questions from the audience. I was sitting with Jim when Judson said that people running for office should come up and speak too. I pulled the Hawai'i birth certificates out of the binder and said to Jim, "I guess it's now or never."

"Yes," he answered. "Get up there."

From the back of the room I made my way to the microphone. I was absolutely trembling inside. I had never spoken before such a huge crowd. Waiting in line was agonizing. All the people asking or answering questions were so articulate. I didn't do well speaking "off the cuff" or talking about myself. But once I started talking, my nervousness went away, and I did talk about myself and I was well spoken and articulate. I asked for help. I needed, I said, to raise money for my campaign and had T-shirts for sale for $15 each. I pointed to the table where Cheryl sat with the T-shirts. I said I needed to raise $497.16 to buy push cards. They were ready to go to the printers, but I didn't have the money to pay for them.

Then I said, "I have something from Hawai'i I want to share with you."

C-SPAN captured me holding up Obama's certification of live birth and calling it a "piece of junk."

Immediately after speaking, I handed out the copies of the birth certificates to anyone who wanted to take a closer look. I was approached by a very pretty blonde lady who asked if she could photograph them, and, of course, I gave permission to anyone to photograph even though nothing was redacted on either Fred's or Alan's. After all, we had nothing to hide. I was interviewed by reporters and gave an exclusive to the pretty blonde lady from WorldNetDaily.

People came up and handed me twenty-dollar bills. The stack in my hand kept growing. I was overwhelmed but so happy. Everyone knew Obama was a fraud, and their support for me proved it. While I was talking to reporters, Cheryl was selling T-shirts, and some people just gave her money without taking a T-shirt. Those who bought a shirt rarely asked for the five dollars in change. A man handed me a $100 bill and hugged me. Not one person who gave me money for my campaign was from my district or even from Oklahoma. Not one could vote for me.

Judson Phillips gave us a wonderful opportunity when he asked for people running for office to stand or hold up their hands, and about nine people complied. Judson told the crowd to look around at the candidates and help them out with donations.

"These are the people you need to help," he had said, and that sure helped me.

When Cheryl counted the money, we had enough for the push cards with almost $500 extra. I called Cris and put in my order.

I then met Button Gwinnett (real name William Temple), who could easily be found in the middle of a crowd bantering with Samuel Adams in an Old English accent. The two men dressed in colonial garb were a huge hit at the convention, and Button was already well known as a highly visible leader of the Tea Party movement, an iconic figure. Button Gwinnett was a member of the Georgia State government at the time he signed the Declaration of Independence.

William Temple, vice president of the Golden Isles Tea Party of Brunswick, Georgia, has been getting inquiries almost on a daily basis asking him to attend an event somewhere in the country. He has a number of different accents to go with his numerous historical costumes, and he draws a large crowd to hear his speech when he yells, "Hear, hear!" as he holds a musket or other antique firearm high in the air.

On Friday evening as we broke to get ready for the dinner banquet at the convention, I received a call from Carol Chouinard. She had been listening to Neal Boortz on his radio show. He made the statement that he should have been invited to the Nashville convention and was disappointed that he was not. As a premier supporter and the foremost champion of FairTax, Boortz felt he should have been on the program to promote the legislation. Carol and I agreed.

I told Carol I would get hold of the organizer and find out if there was a reason FairTax was not participating and try to get Neal on the next day's agenda.

There were a few people still inside the information booth, and someone got an assistant to Judson Phillips, the convention organizer and decision maker, to talk to me. He in turn got in touch with Judson, who scrambled to see if there was a slot on the agenda to slip Neal in. The only opportunity that would work was in the morning between 9:00 a.m. and 9:30 a.m. and by shifting one of the speakers.

I ran back to my room to change to dinner attire and called Carol. We brainstormed, trying to figure out how to get in touch with Neal. While Carol called the contacts she had and sent e-mails to others, including Ken Hoagland, FairTax spokesman, I called Mike McLean, who was already at the banquet hall, so I raced down to meet him. Time was of the essence, and unfortunately radio personalities are next to impossible to reach unless you have a personal connection with them.

Mike had a few contacts in his cell phone. He tried and got in touch with someone who had the number of Congressman John Linder's chief of staff but didn't expect to find anyone in their offices on a Friday evening. Linder coauthored The FairTax Book with Boortz and introduced the legislation in 1999 during the 106th US Congress and reintroduced the same bill in each subsequent session of Congress.

Mike's contact would keep trying to reach someone who knew how to get in touch with Neal or Rob Woodall.

(Linder's chief of staff at the time, Rob Woodall, would be elected to fill Rep. Linder's seat upon Linder's retirement. Woodall, of Georgia, and Sen. Saxby Chambliss, also of Georgia, are sponsors of H.R. 25/S. 13, respectively. Woodall was instrumental in getting a record number of co-sponsors for FairTax on the very first day of the 2011 legislative session.)

I reported to Judson that we were doing our best to contact Neal Boortz and would let him know the minute we heard anything back. I called Carol, but there had been no callbacks or responses to her e-mails.

At the Friday dinner Cheryl and I sat at a table with a couple who used to live in Hawai'i, so there was much we could "talk story" about. No one at our table had been present when I'd spoken that morning, so I passed my binder around, and they were amazed at the information inside and asked a lot of questions. They hadn't even been aware of any birth record controversy.

Judson came by my table and asked if I'd heard anything yet.

"No, not yet," I was disappointed to say.

When the program started, Judson made the announcement that efforts were being made to have Neal Boortz on the program the following morning, which elicited a lot of applause. I learned later from many people that they hadn't even thought of FairTax but felt that the convention was the perfect place to talk about the plan.

Later, during dinner, Judson came over to me with a big smile on his face. "We got in touch with him. He's going to try to get here."

I grinned. I was so pleased. But Neal Boortz was in Georgia and if the window had closed on travel possibilities, FairTax would not get a spot at the first national Tea Party convention.

The following morning Judson announced that Neal Boortz was unable to be there as hoped but would definitely be at the next national convention.

On March 1, 2011, I received a call from William Temple asking for my assistance to be a state contact for a planned Tea Party rally scheduled for September 28 to October 2, 2011. Titled "Freedom Jamboree" the event will be at the Woodlands Racetrack on the Kansas side of Kansas City. I agreed to help get the word out to Tea Party leaders in

Oklahoma and went to the website, freedomjamboree.com, to register and purchase a table in anticipation of promoting my book and having a place for Terry Lakin information and perhaps Terry himself.

It wasn't until we hung up that it occurred to me that I had been speaking to Button Gwinnett, so I called him back and asked, "Is this Button?"

He replied, "Yes," so I asked if he remembered Jim Linn's friend who organized the get-together in the pub at the national convention after the Sarah Palin banquet. "Indeed I do!" he answered. "I'm sorry, dear lady, for not recognizing your name."

I hadn't recognized his either, so we were even.

"Jim's going to be at the jamboree, too, so we'll all be together again," he said enthusiastically.

William Temple's plan for the gathering was right in line with my own thoughts of how to make this event even more successful than the 9.12 2009 event in D.C. Locating it in the center of the country and near (but not directly in) a major metropolis opens it up to far more people who will drive to the event. Campgrounds abound near the racetrack, and hotels and motels are offering special rates. Tour buses and groups can easily access the location, unlike the prohibitive nature of transportation in D.C., and the cost of lodging will be less expensive than in D.C.

The very best thing is that the organizers and participants will be the true grassroots, We the People, not the commercial Tea Party groups bent on co-opting us. Neither will political groups be given a platform on the program, though they may purchase booths.

The Freedom Jamboree is billed as "The National Tea Party Straw Poll Convention." No presidential candidate can win without the support of the grassroots. Invitations will go out to the candidates to participate in the straw poll.

As plans were being made for the Freedom Jamboree, the second national Tea Party Convention, I sent William Temple an e-mail, "Don't forget about FairTax."

Chapter 26

The Hotel Executive

OK Candidate Releases Son's 1981 Hawaiian Certificate of Live Birth
DOCUMENT CONFIRMS INVESTIGATORS' SUSPICIONS, EXPOSES DOH AS LYING
By John Charlton

(February 10, 2010) — *Miki Booth, a native Hawaiian and candidate for the U.S. House of Representatives for the State of Oklahoma, shocked and awed supporters of Barack Hussein Obama during the recent Tea Party Nation convention in Memphis, TN, when she publicly disclosed the certificate of live birth for her son, Alan Paliko Booth, born on November 24, 1981, at 7:55 AM, at Kapi'olani Children's Medical Center, the same hospital that Obama has claimed to be his own place of birth, nearly 20 years before.*

The actual document contains a wealth of information such as the signature of the attending physician or midwife, a field for evidence presented for an Amended Birth Filing, race of parents and child, and a signature and date stamp, certifying the copy as an authentic representation of the information on file with the Hawaii Department of Health.

Importantly, the actual document, which you can view through this link, *contains the fields, "Date received by Local Registrar" and "Date accepted by the State" and the name of the local registrar. In recent months, Miss Janice Okubo has insisted that the terms mean the same thing and that she has no knowledge of what terms were used previously to the alleged Obama certification of live birth.*

The now widely recognized, crude forgery which Obama claims to be his own certification of live birth bearing the date of 2007 but without the seal and confirmatory signature of the state registrar, does not contain information regarding witnesses to the birth or the date the filing was accepted by the state.

This has led private researchers to speculate that Obama's original vital records, which Dr. Fukino claims to have seen and which she herself admits are several, might contain a delayed birth filing, an amended birth filing, adoption record, or other changes regarding the name of the child and parents and location or nation in which the child was purported to be born.

The details of this actual 1981 "long form" "birth certificate" indicate more precisely the possible motives Obama might have for refusing to disclose his own real certificate, that is, if he was, in fact, born in Hawaii in the first place because the actual form might indicate:

1) Race of Child: Negro or White — in the former case, Obama's racism might take offense; in the latter case his race politics might be undone. An at-home birth filing, reportedly, contains the race of the child.

2) Race of Parent: Father might be indicated as Negro rather than African, which would gut the prima facie evidentiary value of his own alleged birth certificate.

3) Parents might not be who they are claimed to be — there has been a lot of speculation on that;

4) Place of birth might have originally been Mombassa, Kenya, as Obama's co-grandmother and he, himself, have in the past claimed; if so, Obama is perhaps not even a U.S. citizen.

5) No father might have been indicated originally, because Obama's mother might not have been sure who the father was at the precise moment of the original filing — which would reflect badly on his mother's morals and cast doubt upon any evidentiary value of whomever was subsequently claimed to be the real father; because doubt in such cases is prima facie evidence that there was more than one man who could have been the father.

6) Name of child might not be Barack Hussein Obama, II, which, in the absence of name changes, would make Obama's usage of his current name unlawful.

The Post & Email

After the "Oklahoma Firecracker" story in WND and The Post & Email report, I started getting a lot of calls and e-mails to be a guest on radio talk shows. Oklahoma's KTOK radio show, The Manning Report, TruNews, and The Dave Levine Show were a few I appeared on closely following the story. Pastor Manning of ATLAH Church and Dave Levine had me on their shows a couple of times. Then there were some shows I'd just as soon forget. I didn't like being set up for people to take pot shots at, and I cut off any further contact with those. Dave Levine remains a good friend and partner in the immigration battle to stop illegal invaders. Pastor Manning and The Manning Report continues to stay on the cutting edge of breaking Obama crimes and political shenanigans.

In March I stayed very busy and put a lot of miles on my Dodge Caravan traveling around my district campaigning and speaking at Tea Parties and other meetings. The mileage on my van was well over 200,000 miles, and along with some challenges with mechanical functions, the driver's side window didn't work so I always had a small stress factor going on whenever I drove long distances — and even short distances, for that matter — wondering when and where the breakdown might occur. Not just a mechanical breakdown but an emotional breakdown. It happened before.

In 2004 I lost my job. It wasn't just any run-of-the-mill job; it paid me close to $50,000 a year plus bonuses, which was really good money for the area, and the only high-paying hotel executive position in the entire four-state area of Oklahoma, Missouri, Kansas, and Arkansas at the time.

I was hired on April 1, 2000, to direct an established eight-member sales and catering team at the Joplin Holiday Inn and Convention Center. My responsibilities would also include marketing and advertising for the 262-room, 50,000-square-foot convention hotel facility. Shortly after taking the position, I joined the Joplin Convention and Visitor's Bureau Advisory Board and became chairman two years later. I also joined Soroptimist International, a sorority of businesswomen considered to be the equivalent of Kiwanis but reserved for women only. Within three years I attained the vice presidency of the club.

Two years into my tenure a new general manager arrived at the property and things began to sour. He brought a management style of cronyism and closed door meetings. Turnover was already high at the hotel and with the new arrival it got even worse. Within a year all the department heads, with the exception of myself, had been fired and replaced with cohorts from the general manager's former hotel or someone of his choosing. The manager, Dean (not his real name), was difficult to figure out. He seemed likable but behind closed doors he browbeat and intimidated employees into quitting. As workers resigned, word circulated around the departments that the general manager was a pathological liar. Employees had no recourse. Missouri is a right to work state and, in my opinion, that is as it should be. However, no one with authority over another should ever be allowed to abuse an employee, but it was happening on a daily basis, and morale around the hotel was in the toilet. I didn't know just how bad it was until members of my sales team were targeted for removal. One by one they told me horror stories of their closed door meetings with the general manager. There was nothing I could do. It was a "he said, she said" encounter, and he held all the cards. It was all about control.

It took about a year, but Dean finally got rid of me. I was the last hold out, but I went down in a blaze of glory. I was called to his office over the resignation of my most successful sales manager. In the privacy of his office he sat across the desk from me and lie after lie spewed forth from his mouth. He accused me of things so absurd it was breathtaking.

I stood there absolutely stunned that someone could so blatantly make up stuff, and I challenged him with, "You're a liar!"

He kept lying with such bald-faced audacity, it boggled my mind. I'd had enough.

"You're a fucking liar, and you know it!" I said as I took off my magnetic nametag and threw it at him.

I walked out and drove to the corporate office in Springfield, Missouri. I talked to the head of Human Resources. I said I wanted my job back and that the general manager was a sociopath and needed to be fired and investigated for human rights and worker's rights violations including age discrimination and sex discrimination as well as a multitude of other violations.

The CEO for the hotel chain called me when I got home. He said they considered my complaint, but they would not hire me back.

They got rid of the aging woman sales director and hired a young man at $15,000 less in base pay. Fifteen thousand dollars that went straight to their bottom line, and hired someone they could control.

Chapter 27

The Wahiawa House

The atmosphere at home was quiet. Very little was said beyond, "I quit my job." Mom and Tamé started spending more time sequestered in their rooms. Everyone was worried. Fred had quit the sheriff's department several months earlier and tried selling health insurance on a commission basis, which had yet to earn him any income to speak of. We had his Hawai'i State retirement income, but losing my $50,000 annual salary plus bonus left us with little hope for continuing the lifestyle we had become accustomed to.

Mom and Tamé were living off Mom's Social Security and her retirement benefits from Dad. Her monies went to pay for their expenses, with a huge chunk going to my brother's methadone treatments, a daily dose of pink liquid that kept him relatively pain free, relatively balanced emotionally, and off of street drugs. They had come to live with us in 1999. Tamé had been on methadone for several years and living with Mom in Hawai'i. They moved to Vegas when both had health issues that made it difficult to live without help, so they went to stay with my youngest sister and her family.

When I visited them in Vegas in early 1999, I was appalled at the poor air quality of the area. From high above as my flight came in for a landing I saw a brownish cloud hovering low and ominously over sin city. My mother had been diagnosed with COPD, a condition that resulted from years of smoking that developed into chronic bronchitis, asthma, and emphysema, requiring oxygen when her symptoms were especially bad. To make matters worse, smokers and cats lived in the household and I knew that couldn't be good. It had been three years since I last saw my mother, and she had aged so much I wanted to cry.

Mom came to visit us the first year we lived in Oklahoma. She looked good then and still had a lot of peppy energy. We had a good time with plenty of laughs and gossip from Hawai'i to catch up on, but now she was small and brittle. She was caving in on herself, her back hunched from osteoporosis.

I made a decision right there to take her away from the conditions that were hastening her deteriorating health. Yes, Tamé would come too — whoever got Mom had to take Tamé. It was understood. When I got back home, Fred and I went looking for an instant house, something big enough for all of us, and we found just what we needed in a double-wide trailer home, a pretty model that when the two sides were attached would have over 2,000 square feet of living space. The split floor plan separated the house into two living areas that would work perfectly for our needs. Outside our bedroom suite was the living room that opened up to the dining area and kitchen. On the other side of the house was the den with the fireplace, two bedrooms divided by a full bath, and another room that could have been a fourth bedroom or small deck. We chose the deck. Beyond the large kitchen with island was a utility room and the powder room or half bathroom.

When it was finished and ready to move in, Fred and I sat on the carpet looking out through the lanai glass doors. There was no lanai, though, just a grassy area with a pretty valley down below. We were amazed at how quickly the house was readied and how afordable compared to Hawai'i. Structurally, it wasn't much sounder than most of the average family dwellings in Hawai'i, the island-style homes which are single-wall construction with no insulation or heating and air. Of course, rich people can have anything they want but most regular people in Hawai'i in our day lived in houses made of wood with just the width of a board separating the indoors from the outdoors, and care had to be taken not to remove the nail used to hang a picture or you would have a peephole to the outside.

"If our house and land here were picked up and moved to Hawai'i," Fred would say, "it would be worth a million dollars or more." And he was right.

Jimmy Buffet had a song. I forget how the rest of it goes, but he says, " At least I don't live in a trailer," meaning that would be the epitome of loser-dom. But I loved my trailer — I would joke that there are no trailers in Hawai'i, so I'm ignorant of any stigma attached to living in one. Indeed, people for years have wanted trailers and manu-factured homes to come to Hawai'i for less expensive housing options. At one time it almost happened. Someone brought the first mobile homes to Hawai'i on a barge, but it mysteriously burned and sank off the islands. They got the message and never tried it again — the powerful builders unions owned the new-home market, and you'd be taking your life in your hands if you didn't learn that lesson the first time.

By the time Fred and I left in 1995, the median price of a single-family dwelling was over $300,000. If you didn't inherit a house or hadn't bought long before, your chances of ever affording a home of your own was pretty slight. That's why so many people like us left the islands for better opportunities and lifestyles on the mainland. They called it brain drain — the best and brightest young islanders left when the rich of the world wanted their piece of paradise and could afford to pay for it. Financially we were displaced.

Fred was supposed to inherit his parents' house in Wahiawa, an attractive two-story home with a detached carport on a quiet street in an established neighborhood. The house stood out from the others not only because it was a rare two-story but also because the eaves had oriental up-curved tips. The unusual paint combination of ivory with turquoise trim drew compliments from people passing through the neighborhood. Fred and his only sibling, an older sister, grew up in the home and both graduated from nearby Wahiawa High School. Fred's dad, a strong disciplinarian, was a vice president of First Hawai'ian Bank, and his mother was a stay-at-home mom, only no one called them that then. She was the typical housewife who cared for the home, did the shopping, cooked the meals, and raised the kids.

Brother and sister were close. They both had issues with their mother, an alcoholic, for as long as they could remember. They tiptoed around the house fearful of making noise and drawing her hateful wrath, screaming obscenities and upsetting their father. Fred's sister eventually married and moved to the Big Island, where she would raise three children of her own well away from their dysfunctional mother.

On and off over the years their father brought them together to talk about his will. It had been easily settled. Fred wanted the house and his sister wanted the bank accounts, investments, household furnishings, jewelry, gold, and coin collections, in other words, everything except the Wahiawa house. The house and the assets were of nearly equal value and as the house appreciated so did the assets. By 1995 the combined value of the house and assets totaled over $800,000.

Alan was twelve when his grandfather died. Fred was a sergeant at the Waimea Police Department on the Big Island, and I worked at the new Hyatt Regency Waikoloa managing the Japanese market. We flew to O'ahu for the funeral at Punchbowl National Cemetery of the Pacific where we had buried my father four years earlier. Fred's mother was a basket case and it was evident she had spiraled down to the lowest point alcoholics could go without being dead. She was wheelchair bound, and her husband had been feeding her unlimited amounts of vodka to keep her at a level where he could tolerate her growing madness.

The house was in ruins. The roof leaked. Kitchen cabinet doors were missing. Parts of the wooden floor and beams had been ravaged by termites. Worst of all, the house was infested with fleas. "How could it get this bad?" I asked Fred and his sister.

I returned to the Big Island shortly after the funeral while Fred stayed on O'ahu to help his sister find someone to be a live-in caregiver for their mother. It didn't take long to hire someone and get them moved into the house. Their mother could tell the help what needed doing. Both children beat a hasty retreat back to the Big Island.

The arrangements soon fell apart. Mrs. Booth was impossible to live with. She was an abusive drunk from the get-go. Nobody could live with her. She was a tyrant and throughout the night would shout obscenities in a voice so loud and ugly she sounded like the devil incarnate.

"The help" as Mrs. Booth liked to call the care-giver, told the children an astonishing story: Mrs. Booth was two people — she was a horrible, hateful drunk one moment, and the next she was this syrupy sweet little woman with a melodic voice. There was only one word to describe what was going on with her, "bizarre."

The children were back to square one, but Fred's sister figured out the perfect solution where her mother could stay in her own home. Fred brought his sister's proposal to me. Since it was going to be our house I could go to take care of my mother-in-law. Alan could move with me, and Fred would put in for a transfer back to Honolulu Police Department, and even if he wasn't able to transfer he would be retired in about a year. It made perfect sense to the Booth children. I wasn't so sure. Since Fred's last promotion and assignment to Waimea, we'd rented out our Hilo house and moved to a rental on the wet side of Waimea that had a one-acre pasture lush with California grass. If we moved to O'ahu, what would we do with the two horses we now owned?

Sunshine and Hari joined our family when we moved to Waimea. Both horses had never been ridden, but I broke and trained Sunshine for Fred and a few months later when we purchased Hari, he became my horse, and I broke him to ride. On nice days Fred and I would ride the trails and pretty pastures near our home while Alan would follow on his bike. One day we would get a horse for Alan, we promised, but for now two horses were as many as we could handle comfortably. Alan could ride with his dad or alone on Sunshine — she was that trustworthy, as quarter horses generally are. Hari, my registered Arabian, didn't have a bad bone in his body, but he spooked easily.

I loved my horses and my job at the Hyatt. I had a beautiful office and enjoyed dealing with the Japanese clients and guests. I didn't want to leave. It had been a struggle to get where I was — managing the Japanese business.

Management in the sales office didn't understand the nature of Japanese business, the largest and most profitable segment of tourism to Hawai'i, and the Hyatt wanted in on the action but had been largely unsuccessful.

The sales managers hired for the different market segments were at the top of their game in Chicago and the big cities. But when they were rewarded with a position in paradise, they had no knowledge of Hawai'iana and, therefore, were unable to sell "the experience" instead of just rooms. I was hired well after the majestic grand opening of the first "mega-resort" in the world, as the Hyatt Regency Waikoloa was billed. At a cost of over $356 million to build, the resort would later sell to Hilton for a fraction of the price, a mere $65 million, and Hilton would turn the still brand new property into a great success.

I was hired by Hyatt's sales director to coordinate the managers and help them sell the resort experience by coaching and organizing their efforts.

It was during a brainstorm session called by the director to discuss ideas to develop the Japanese business that the other major chains in Hawai'i were enjoying, and which Hyatt was woefully missing out on, that I spoke up and laid out the mistakes that the new administration was making. "First off," I told them, "you have to stop treating them like second-class citizens."

"What can you tell me about the Japanese market?" the director of sales wanted to know, and when we walked out of the brainstorm session I was the newly appointed Japanese sales coordinator.

Fred's sister pressured him. "Nobody can take care of family like family," she repeated over and over. Fred and I agreed that was true, though I would be the only one giving anything up. But I was the only one who could talk to their mother without it turning into a screaming match, or in Fred's case his mother screaming and berating him until he quietly walked out, having learned long before that you couldn't argue with her — or his father either, for that matter.

My salary paid to keep Alan in private school. If we moved to Wahiawa, I wanted Alan to go to Trinity Lutheran School. The school's playground butted up against the Booths' backyard, the main buildings practically next door. Fred's mother agreed to pay for his tuition.

We checked out stabling facilities for our horses and Mokuleia Stables had vacancies, so we arranged to have a trucker friend pick up the horses in portables stalls and put them on a barge to Honolulu, where someone would pick them up at the dock and deliver them to Mokuleia. Our furniture and household belongings were shipped to Honolulu and temporarily put into a storage facility. Fred would stay with a friend in Waimea until his transfer came through or he retired, whichever came first.

We settled into a routine at the Wahiawa house. Alan was in school, and the horses were adjusting to their new surroundings at the Mokuleia facility so I went to work renovating the house after a new roof was installed. I tore out carpet squares from the kitchen and Fred's old bedroom. I demolished the kitchen by ripping up the faded black laminate counter top and throwing it out along with the particleboard beneath it. Since Fred's mother slept until noon, I could get a lot of stuff thrown out before she started hollering, "What was that?" and "What are you throwing away?" She wanted to know exactly what I was doing and to explain any noise I made. Alan was thankfully in school much of the day and playing outside with friends until dinnertime. Once he brought a friend inside and they went up to play in his room, which was Fred's dad's old room. Mrs. Booth had taken over the den when she could no longer manage steps. I had her former room, the master bedroom. The Booths had had separate rooms for as long as their kids could remember. Their mother had lived downstairs for years.

I cautioned Alan and his friend to keep the noise down so they wouldn't disturb Mrs. Booth. They played quietly with Nintendo games, and when they were finished they trotted down the stairs, which were exposed to the den where Alan's grandmother slept on a punee (day bed).

"GOD DAMN IT TO HELL!" the devil bellowed. Alan and his friend scattered. His friend ran out the front door, and Alan ran to me in the kitchen and hugged me around my waist, burying his face in my clothing.

"It's okay, Alan," I told him. "Go outside and find your friend. Explain to him that your grandmother is sick. It's probably best not to play in here anymore."

"What is wrong with you?" I demanded of Fred's mother.

I saw the other person that "the help" had talked about — the syrupy sweet little lady said in a singsong voice, "Oh, did I say something wrong? I'm SOOOOOO sooooorrrrryyyyy. Tee-hee."

Yes, she actually said "tee-hee," a little "oopsie" when she did a "no-no" like defecate in her clothes — which was mortifying for her at first, but by the time she went to the hospital to dry out or die, she was wetting the bed and making "poopie" in her diapers on a regular basis. It was nothing to her, I would clean up. I loved her and she said time and again she loved me more than she loved her daughter. She loved me until she came home from rehab and Fred and I declared her home "alcohol-free."

During the two months Fred's mom was in the hospital and rehab, Fred retired and came to live with us in the Wahiawa house. He helped me finish the remodeling projects I had going. I'd totally gutted the kitchen and with the help of a local retired builder, renovated and transformed it into a room anyone could be proud of. But my mother-in-law wasn't impressed. She sniffed her nose in the air when friends complimented. She was miffed that I had gone ahead with the renovations using our own money when she refused to spend the funds needed for repair and upgrading. She wrote checks to the carpenter for his work but refused to pay for materials. She and her daughter were both concerned that I was "feathering my own nest." It would be Fred's house, and I shouldn't be using his sister's money to fix it up for me. Thinking along those lines, his sister and mother were unhappy about the conditions I had set down before agreeing to quit my job and move into a situation that drastically changed our living conditions. The new roof and Alan's tuition weren't the only expenses I wanted my mother-in-law to agree to. The house had to be tented to kill the cockroach and flea problem and especially the termites. Extensive damage had already been done to some areas of the house. An old rotting oriental rug covered a floorboard that was so ravaged by termites, the ground below was exposed.

Before agreeing to move into the Wahiawa house Fred and I discussed the many pitfalls. We had grave concerns about how his mother's smoking would affect Alan's asthma, a condition he developed shortly after he was born.

When Alan was a newborn, we left Kapi'olani Hospital a day early so we could celebrate Thanksgiving with Fred's parents. His dad made his traditional turkey in the Weber grill, basting it with butter and wine. I chatted with him outside while he attended the turkey — a little wine for the turkey, a little wine for us, a little wine for the turkey, a lot of wine for us.

I loved being around my-father-in-law. He was so kind and loving and hugged me easily. He was glad Fred had finally found someone right for him. He didn't have kind words for Fred's ex-wives or for Fred's multiple marriages and neither did Fred's mother, but now they were happy, "He did it until he got it right."

Three-day-old Alan sat in an infant carrier on the dining room table covered by a Hawai'ian baby quilt someone gave us at our baby shower. Fred and his mother talked story, and she cooed at Alan while he slept, her left hand holding a little fist, her right holding a cigarette at arm's length.

The formal dining table was set with the family silver and fine crystal goblets for water and wine. A beautiful antique cabinet was filled with fabulous silver-inlaid crystal champagne glasses we would later use to toast the turkey. The ambience of the formal dining room reflected a grandeur of a time past, a time of the last Hawai'ian princess, Kaiulani, heir to the throne. Victoria Kaiulani Cleghorn, crown princess of the Kingdom of Hawai'i, lost her birthright when a small group of businessmen overthrew the Hawai'ian monarchy in 1893. Kaiulani was stranded in England, where she had been attending school, until she was able to make a trip to America where she unsuccessfully pleaded her nation's cause. She returned to Hawai'i to comfort her people and show solidarity with her aunt, deposed Queen Lili'uokalani. Princess Kaiulani died of a broken heart, it's said, at age 23 in 1899, shortly after her country's annexation to the United States.

The same year the princess died, two men, brothers and soldiers in the U.S. Army, from "Kingston on the Hudson" in New York, arrived in Honolulu and took their assigned posts in Diamond Head crater. The Booth brothers were part of a large influx of military might arriving in Hawai'i during the Spanish-American War. There had been proposals for annexation during that decade, and on July 7, 1898, with the excuse that Hawaii was needed as a naval military base for the war against Spain, the U.S. annexed Hawaii.

The Booth brothers were two generations removed from Manchester, England and were distant relatives of John Wilkes Booth. Their father, Nathaniel Booth, of Kingston, New York was preparing for a "pleasure excursion" to Canada, west of Niagara Falls, when word reached him that his distant cousin had shot President Abraham Lincoln.

Frederic Newton Booth remained in the islands and his brother returned home to New York. Frederic married Dorcas Fern, of half-Hawai'ian ancestry on September 13, 1905. Only one child was born to Dorcas and Frederic Newton — a son, Francis Nathaniel Booth, Fred's father.

Fred's grandfather on his mother's side was Navy Captain Charles White, who was stationed at Pearl Harbor when it was attacked by Japan. After the attack on Pearl Harbor, Capt. White's wife, Genevieve, and daughter, Virginia, were sent home on the Lurline to Seattle for the duration of the war.

After returning to Honolulu, Virginia married Francis and became parents, first to a daughter and two years later to Frederic the Second, named after his grandfather who'd arrived in Hawai'i in 1899, the same year Princess Kaiulani died of a broken heart.

Chapter 28

Mokuleia Ranch

Thanksgiving at the Booths' home when Alan was three days old is especially memorable for the good time and excellent feast. The dining room was a special world of its own, with family heirlooms dating back more than a century from Manchester, England. Fred's family had put down roots in this beautiful home in Wahiawa Heights near Schofield Barracks. Fred's father was assigned to manage the First Hawai'ian Bank branch on the Army base. Prior to settling in Wahiawa the family had lived on the island of Lana'i, the "Pineapple Island," the smallest island in the Hawai'ian chain. While on Lana'i, Fred and his sister lived the rural life, riding horses on the red-dirt roads of the pineapple fields and the lush green pastures of California and pili grasses.

Their father was the bank manager, and they lived in quarters attached to the back of the bank, so their dad needed only to walk through a door to be home for dinner after work. The only town and located at the highest point in the center of the island, Lana'i City sounds like a metropolis instead of the tiny little town that it is. Fred loved the quiet country life, and having a horse to ride tethered just outside his back door was really great for a young kid. The horse belonged to a local family, a bank customer, and on loan to Fred. It would do until the day he could get a horse of his own.

Fred's father was promoted once again and sent to manage a branch in Honolulu. The family moved from Lana'i and bought their first house in the beautiful shadows of the old banyan trees on Nu'uanu Pali Drive on the leeward slope of the Pali Ridge. When Fred's father was transferred to the bank at Schofield Barracks, he had to sell the Nu'uanu home because the bank's policy said you had to live in the neighborhood of the branch you managed. It was after his father sold the Nu'uanu property and bought a new home in Wahiawa that First Hawai'ian Bank rescinded the "ridiculous policy." Fred's father bemoaned losing the valuable Nu'uanu home until the day he died. He was a frugal man, and losing his valuable investment of the Nu'uanu home left him somewhat bitter at the bank he worked for "all his life."

Alan's first Thanksgiving ended as many Booth family get-togethers did, with Mrs. Booth in a drunken stupor shouting obscenities. Fred's dad looked at us hopelessly and half-carried, half-dragged his wife to her bed. Fred and his dad then tore the house apart looking for a liquor stash. They hunted everywhere, including the tank of the toilet where a bottle was found once before but apparently no longer served as a good hiding place. Eventually they gave up. No vodka bottles anywhere, full or empty. Fred and his father laughed a stilted laugh. She was amazing. Where was the liquor and how did she get it?

A baby shower was held for me at the rental home Fred and I moved to early in my pregnancy. Fred's parents were there with many other guests and created an uncomfortable situation. Fred's father was trying to limit what his wife was drinking, and she got mad and argued loudly with him. He gave up and gave in by letting her have her way. The party resumed, and Mother drank and passed out long before the last guest left. When Father went to pick her up off the couch to get her to their car, he discovered that my new sofa was sopping wet with urine. There wasn't much to say. Even apologies get old after a while. We just had to live with it or not.

Alan liked his new school when we moved in to take care of his grandmother, and he made new friends in the neighborhood. Part of the Schofield Army base butted up to our dead-end street and someone had cut holes in the chain-link fence that was topped with razor wire. The kids would sneak in through the cut fence and hide to watch military maneuvers. It seemed there were always soldiers jumping out of planes or helicopters and floating to the ground under a round white canopy. They would disappear from the kids' line of sight when they landed in the tall, dry grass that covered the landscape of East Range. Sometimes Alan would come home from great adventures and reveal treasures he had found. Once a partially filled box of MREs (Meals Ready to Eat) was left abandoned after a group finished some sort of training exercise. Alan and his friend divvied up the treasures, and it was a special treat for him to dine on the nifty military meals. On many occasions Alan would come home with empty shell cartridges. When he found enough clips, he put the sections together and filled them with the spent cartridges to wear over his shoulder like a bandolier.

When I first learned that Alan was trespassing on government property, I scolded him and warned him never to go there, but Fred said that that was where he grew up, exploring and playing. East Range had been his back yard. I was persuaded to let Alan play, but his dad warned him, "Don't get caught!"

My days in Fred's mother's house settled into a routine rather quickly. Sunshine and Hari, our horses, had arrived by barge, and a hired hauler delivered them to Mokuleia Stables. We couldn't afford a private paddock for them, so they were turned out into a huge pasture to run with the herd. Every day I would quickly do my chores and then make a lunch for my mother-in-law, arrange it on a tray with a jelly jar filled with vodka, and deliver the tray to the TV table in front of her, making sure everything was arranged conveniently within her reach — cigarettes, lighter, ashtray, Kleenex box, nail clipper, and glasses. "Anything else?" I would ask. "I'll be back in three hours. You gonna be okay till I get back?"

"Yes, Mike." She called me Mike, a pet name. She had a pet name for everything, and when she used cute little colloquial sayings to add to a story, she was as charming as anyone I'd ever known. But the bursts of anger of "GOD DAMN IT TO HELL!" chilled me to my bones, and it was happening more and more frequently.

My daily getaways kept me sane. Tesi and Moki, the dogs, watched me intently, waiting for the signal to go to the car for the exciting ride to Mokuleia. I put the top down on Fred's dad's 1965 Mustang convertible, and the dogs took their favorite positions, Tesi in the front seat next to me and Moki in the backseat lying on the horse blanket next to my saddles and tack. I kept grain, a grooming caddy, and other supplies in the trunk of the Mustang, which became the vehicle for going back and forth to the stables. Since I rarely used my mother-in-law's Cadillac, she gave it to her daughter, who in turn took it to the Big Island and sold it.

Moki loved going to Mokuleia with Tesi and me, but her trips with us were short-lived. Mother was lonely and wanted her dog to stay home with her. Moki couldn't understand why she could no longer go with us. She pined, and that pissed Mother off and she screamed at Moki to "get away from the door." I could hear her yelling as we pulled away in the Mustang.

There was always someone to go riding with at the stables. Although we weren't allowed to ride mauka (mountainside) beyond the fenced area of the Mokuleia Ranch, we could ride the dirt roads that cut through the sugar cane fields and across Farrington Highway to the beach. The first time Hari saw the ocean, he freaked out at the waves. I drummed my heels against his sides, encouraging him closer to the water's edge. He craned his neck to get a better look at the water receding past his hoofs, firmly planted in the sand. He became disoriented and started to fall over but at the last second got his bearings and leaped in the air to get away from the moving water. He tossed his head and snorted loudly while I laughed hysterically and held on for dear life. It was a fun time until someone complained about horses and dogs on the beach and a cop showed up to chase us away.

Mokuleia Ranch is part of the original Dillingham Estate established in 1897. Benjamin Franklin Dillingham on his third sailing voyage to the islands in 1865 broke his leg when he fell from a horse and, after convalescing in Hawai'i, decided to stay. He built a fortune with his business acumen, founding O'ahu Railway and Land Company and interests in the sugar industry. King Kalakaua and Queen Lili'uokalani were among those he was friends with. He disapproved of the overthrow of the kingdom and imprisonment of the Queen, but welcomed annexation in 1898.

In Hawai'ian ancient times the concept of owning land was unfamiliar to its inhabitants, but there was a complex system of land division controlled by the highest chief or king, who held it for the population under their control. A whole island was divided into parcels, wedge-shaped tract that ran from the top of the mountains to the sea, called ahupua'a.

Under King Kamehameha III, who reigned from 1825—1854, a great division of lands was proclaimed, called "The Great Mahele," which changed the feudal ownership of lands to modern land titles. Native Hawai'ians — by this time, a population reduced by hundreds of thousands, due to diseases introduced by foreigners — knew little of the bureaucracy that stood between them and their right to claim land and were thus greatly dispossessed, leaving foreigners in control of 90 percent of the land by the end of the nineteenth century.

Dillingham married the daughter of a prominent missionary, Rev. Lowell Smith, who was among the first groups sent from the American Board of Commissioners for Foreign Missions of the Protestant Church to bring Christianity to the islands. It was the children and grandchildren of these original missionaries who claimed power in business and politics and led the overthrow of the Hawai'ian kingdom. A provisional government was put briefly in place until annexation in 1898.

During the provisional government, the Dillingham family took advantage of the "Great Mahele" decreed by King Kamehameha III and acquired the ahupua'a known as Mokuleia.

Today, Mokuleia Ranch is owned by Korean developers with plans for a major resort and golf facility. But because of a moratorium put forth by local residents, the Korean owners have been forced to sit on their hands and in the meantime continue to manage the existing businesses such as leasing pasture space to dairy farmers, growing and selling coconut and royal palm trees for landscaping, running the polo fields and stabling facilities, and maintaining the grounds of the massive estate.

The developers own the entire ahupua'a, all the way up to the top of Peacock Flats, the summit where the eerie cry of wild peacocks can be heard clear down into the valley below. Few people have been to Peacock Flats, and most residents of O'ahu have never heard of it. A state-owned road runs from Farrington Highway near Waialua on the north shore up along the inside of the Mokuleia property, winds its way clear up to the summit and along Makua Rim before descending to Ka'ena Point Satellite Tracking Station, which is off limits to anyone without proper credentials. A hiking/camping permit from the state forestry division will allow access to the area, which makes for one mean hiking excursion; The road is so poor and washed out that only a four-wheel-drive vehicle can get from one side to the other.

During the time we boarded Sunshine and Hari at the Mokuleia stables we could only wistfully look up at the ridges and slopes of the mountain and dream of riding our horses up to Peacock Flats and looking down at the shoreline from the lofty elevation. The State Forestry Division was very stingy and selective about who would get permits to go hiking up to the summit, and the military on the other side guarding the satellite station was just as secretive and stingy. Few permits were ever approved except for those who knew somebody who knew somebody.

But the most possessive and jealous guardian of the Mokuleia ahupua'a was the management of the ranch. Ruling on behalf of the owners from Korea, the office manager decreed most of the ranch off limits except for very limited areas specifically designated for riding. The more we were cautioned against trespassing, the more we wondered if they were hiding something they didn't want to public to know about.

Fred retired and moved into his mother's house with us. We continued renovating, and work went along faster with Fred doing the heavy lifting. We didn't like being accused of "feathering our nest," so we took Fred's retirement lump-sum payment to make repairs, purchase materials, and replace items. The psychedelic orange, blue, and black drapes from the '6os were thrown out and replaced with new. When the bank had renovated and got rid of the '6os look, the old drapes made their way into the Booths' Wahiawa house and remained there until we moved in. Chairs and lamps of the era also lived there until they were given to the Salvation Army. An old sofa and matching easy chair of turquoise brocade were still very attractive although they clashed terribly with the psychedelic drapes, but the sofa had to be thrown out due to microscopic pieces of glass from angel hair used for Christmas decorations years earlier. Visitors in the past had complained of being bitten by mosquitoes or some unseen bug while sitting on the couch. I discovered the embedded glass by breaking out in hives whenever I touched the couch.

Fred's mother eventually had to be hospitalized; she was so run down, weak, and emaciated, she was no longer able to get out of bed. Her refusal to leave her home and go to the hospital no longer kept me from doing what I thought was best, and I called for an ambulance. After several days of hospitalization, she was finally stabilized and moved to a rehab facility connected to Kuakini Hospital, where she underwent physical therapy for nearly eight weeks. Fred and I visited her daily or took turns, so never a day went by that we didn't check in on her. She was hateful and sullen, ugly and mean-spirited. She wasn't allowed to smoke or drink, and she resented everything and everyone.

Before she was discharged, we spoke with a psychiatrist who had assessed her condition. We had to take charge, she told us. Mother was suffering from dementia. She said things and laughed at things that were inappropriate. The psychiatrist's advice was to put her in a nursing home, but we felt we would be criticized for taking over her house. The psychiatrist insisted that when we took her home we should stay firm and not allow her to fall back into the habits that had gotten her hospitalized. No smoking. No alcohol.

Easier said than done. "THIS IS MY HOUSE! I MAKE THE DECISIONS! IT'S MY MONEY! GOD DAMN IT TO HELL!" The devil bellowed.

Fred had submitted applications and resumes to a number of possible employers on O'ahu, and we hoped something would materialize soon so we could find a live-in housekeeper for his mother and move out. Mother's condition had improved sufficiently for her to get around with a walker. We heard her moving around downstairs in the night, swearing and huffing and sniffing with reproach at the liberties we had taken on her house. She was most vicious in her attacks on Fred. He never said anything to her in reply, but he would look at me with crossed eyes and goofy facial gestures that caused me to double over in repressed laughter and flee the room.

Fred and I went to the stables every day to ride together in the designated riding areas. Alan, Tesi, and Moki went with us too until Mother came back from rehab and Moki was once again relegated to the den at Mother's feet.

One day, completely out of the blue, the Mokuleia property administrator approached Fred and offered him the job of ranch manager. The position included the manager's ranch house to live in, with all utilities paid and a nice salary. The responsibilities included, but weren't limited to, overseeing the entire land area of nearly 3,000 acres and upkeep of the buildings, grounds, infrastructure, and machinery. Fred would supervise a number of managers who in turn supervised employees ranging from cowboys to groundskeepers and mechanics.

It was great. We could hardly wait to move out and into a life we had only dreamed about. Immediately after we broke the news to Fred's mother she began whining that we were abandoning her. But we had spent two years taking care of her, and no amount of guilt-tripping on her part was going to keep us from pursuing a future of our own, especially to live on a ranch — my life-long dream.

I had learned new skill sets during the time I spent renovating Mother's house. One of them was tiling, and I had transformed the kitchen of the Wahiawa house into a showplace. I scraped, puttied, drywalled, painted and stained, tiled, grouted, and buffed. Fred told me often how proud he was of me and my work. I was proud of myself; I'd never done any of that kind of work before. I needed the skills — the ranch manager's house at Mokuleia was a shambles. No one had lived in it for years. The glory days of the Dillingham estate were long past, and many outbuildings and servant homes had been claimed over the years by fluctuating weather patterns and hidden from view by tall California grass, and a variety of choking vines, and heavy growth of haole koa and tangled hao.

The ranch manager's house, the luna's house, was built in more recent times along with several other homes occupied by families who worked the grounds. Everyone wore many hats, and they were always on call when work had to be done. The work was never ending. Nothing new had been built in years. Fred was given the option of two houses to live in. We inspected them both and although a huge home at a higher elevation had a beautiful view of the coastline and the sugar cane fields below, it was more deteriorated than the house without a view that was nearby the original Dillingham home and carriage house. We chose the latter, which had four bedrooms and two bathrooms. After a good cleaning and removing dead leaves and spider webs, it was well on its way to being livable. It was a typical island-style home with single-wall construction. The slight termite damage was quickly fixed by one of the ranch hands, who was asked to assist me in repairing where it was needed. Fred went to work for the ranch right away, and I made preparations to leave the Wahiawa house and move to the ranch. Fred's mother interviewed prospective live-in companions but rejected the first few. I saw a pattern forming and advised my mother-in-law that we were definitely moving out and if she didn't settle on someone to move in with her, then we had no choice but to place her in a nursing facility. Her attitude changed and she settled on a woman she could easily manipulate and immediately sent her off to buy cigarettes and vodka.

We didn't have much furniture in storage, having sold off a lot of what we had before leaving the Big Island, so we purchased items to furnish the ranch house. I took the home furnishings I'd bought for the Wahiawa house, lamps, rugs, and our personal wall coverings and artwork. I put the decrepit furnishings we had removed and stored in the attic back in place, but I had thrown the itchy sofa and psychedelic drapes away and she was furious, demanding I leave the drapes and sofa I had bought in replacement.

I continued to visit her, making the trip to Wahiawa and doing chores that "the help" was incompetent to do to Mother's satisfaction. She made no attempt to hide from me the fact that she was back smoking and drinking, and I didn't really care. Fred and I worked at getting her to agree to an excursion to see our new house and have dinner. She finally accepted the offer. We picked her up and brought her to our new home. She was livid and huffed and sniffed as we pushed her along in a wheelchair. She saw the items that had graced her house for a short while, the beautiful oriental carpet, the shell lamps that took the place of the '6os fandango lights, the new living room suite, and large elegant artwork of horses, but what she resented the most was the koa coffee table that she had complimented and commented on time and again as it sat in the formal living room of the Wahiawa home and was now the centerpiece of Fred and Miki's ranch house.

She didn't want to stay for dinner. She was tired and wanted to go home. She had very little to say to us after that, and I quit going to visit her. I used the time instead to raise chickens, ride horses, explore, hike, and entertain Alan's friends and our visitors with cookouts and parties. One of the cowboys loaned Alan a mellow horse, and we had the best fun ever packing a picnic and riding our horses up to Peacock Flats. As ranch manager, Fred had a duplicate set of they keys needed to open the locked gates of the state-owned road to the summit. We would sit on our horses at the top of the mountain and look at the windward side of O'ahu and then turn and see the leeward.

Life was good, but Fred was unhappy. The job was a nightmare. All the facilities were old and run down, and the administration was micromanaging to the point of being ridiculous. They questioned every purchase right down to screws and washers from the hardware store in Waialua and inquired why two trips were made in one day or why it was necessary for two people to make a run into town.

Fred was told to tell me not to ride outside the designated riding areas although our horses were now in paddocks and pastures next to our house, and that policy didn't make sense. Fred joked that I was expected to carry my horse the half mile to the riding stables. Fred worked the cattle with other cowboys, and they showed him areas of extraordinary beauty seen only by a few. There were hundreds of head of cattle over a thousand acres, and I would ride with Fred looking for missing cows or breaks in the fencing where wooden posts and gates had fallen into disrepair and were hanging loosely. Like hell I would let Fred ride alone where anything could happen to a lone rider.

But every day, every single day, it was something. The Korean owners wanted expenses kept to a minimum. Lawyers were working to get the moratorium lifted. Every day they didn't break ground on their new resort was a day of wasted money maintaining the status quo. If duct tape, WD-40, or baling wire could fix it, so be it. Work orders and purchase orders sat on the desk of the administrator . . . and sat and sat.

I had never seen Fred so unhappy and quiet, but Alan and I loved our life. He was attending the Catholic school in Waialua and had friends who came to visit him on the ranch. There were children of other workers who lived on the ranch as well, and they took Alan and his friends to explore bunkers, buildings, and abandoned houses that hinted of a glorious past — 1920, 1930, 1940, rich people sitting on rockers on the lanai sipping highballs and rehashing the morning polo games.

But war came to the islands and everything changed. Walter Dillingham had taken over his father's enterprises. The O'ahu Railway and Land Company rail line evolved into Hawai'ian Dredging Company and the Dillingham Corporation. In the 1920s, a communication system and dirt airstrip was built along the original rail line. By 1941, the Army leased the land and established Mokuleia Airfield. Curtiss P-40 fighters were deployed from Mokuleia when the attack on Pearl Harbor took place.

The fighters that took off from nearby Haleiwa airstrip destroyed several attacking aircraft. The Haleiwa strip was abandoned after the war and became a hangout for outlaw races for cars and motorcycles. Much of the asphalt crumbled away and yielded to patches of grass and weeds, and eventually the area was fenced in for use as a beach park for the law enforcement community — a private getaway where we could shoot our personal firearms without drawing the ire of the local community.

By the end of the war, Mokuleia Airfield could handle the "Superfortress" B-29 bombers. In 1948, the airfield was inactivated and renamed Dillingham Air Base after Walter's son, a B-29 pilot, Capt. Henry Gaylord Dillingham, who was killed in action over Kawasaki, Japan on July 25, 1945. Today the airstrip is operated by the Hawai'i Department of Transportation under a lease from the U.S. Army and is a popular location for gliding and skydiving operations.

The Dillingham Mokuleia estate is currently marketed in many different venues. The equestrian center has stabling facilities and polo grounds, where games are played on a regular basis and are famous for Prince Charles's visits. The original home of several generations of Dillinghams and the surrounding palatial grounds is rented out for weddings, photo shoots, and movies. In 1994, the film Picture Bride was shot at the ranch, and Alan got to hang out with the main characters, well-known Japanese actress Yuki Kudoh and Tamlyn Tomita of Karate Kid fame. The story is about a sixteen-year-old girl who journeys to Hawai'i in 1918 to marry a man she hadn't met. The "picture brides" of Hawai'i met their potential husbands through photographs and letters. Oftentimes when the bride arrived in Hawai'i, they were terribly disappointed. They found themselves trapped into a life of farm labor and married to a man who was himself a worker in the cane fields.

Prior to the start of filming, the project director considered Fred for the role of the luna, the plantation field overseer. They liked Fred's look: not quite a haole—more like Portagee, slightly darker, mustachioed, and sat a horse well, fitting of a field boss. "Who is that?" they wanted to know.

But the part of the luna was already cast, and Fred missed out on his opportunity to become a movie star. We teased him, and he loved it. But he hated his real job as luna of the present-day Korean-owned plantation.

It was calving time at Mokuleia. Fred and the cowboys rounded up the "heavies" — the cows ready to calf. They were herded into pens located mauka of our house. The pitiful mooing and moaning disturbed me, so Alan and I left for the day. By the time we returned, the pens were empty, but there would be more the next day, and so the process went. The cows were owned by a dairy farm over the ridge on the other side of the mountain in Waianae. They would take the cows by truck back to the farm and after calving the cows were separated from their calves and milked commercially. The female offspring were kept for future stock, and the males were sold off to cattle ranchers.

Rounded up with the heavies were cows that had already dropped calves. They were herded into the pen next to our house and the last of the adult cows and female calves were taken away, leaving the male calves. Since the dairy didn't want them, they didn't care whether they were sold or given away to local workers to raise for beef. I felt bad for the little male calves taken from their mothers and put into the backs of pickup trucks with makeshift containers and was glad when they were all gone. The ranch was peaceful and quiet again save for trade winds caressing the fronds of the coconut trees.

One evening as we were eating dinner we heard what sounded like a goat bleating. We wondered aloud what it could be. Whatever it was, it was distressed and the crying persisted. Fred and I left our dinner half-eaten to go find out what it was. We took flashlights and walked toward the cattle pen, where the cries were coming from. We shone our flashlights around the pen, which appeared empty at first, but then the beams landed on the little white face of a tiny calf. It stopped crying and looked at us with huge black eyes that blinked in wonderment. The baby Holstein was no more than a day old. No one wanted him. He was too little.

Fred scooped the baby up in his arms, and we brought him into the house. We knew he was starving, and we weren't sure what to do. The feed store, where we could buy special formula powdered milk and bottles to feed him with, was closed until morning.

The calf was content to suck on Fred's thumb while I heated some milk. With a little trial and error and Fred's thumb stuck down in a pan of milk, the calf was able to suck enough of the milk to satisfy his hunger and immediately afterward curled up against Fred and went to sleep.

We'd never seen such a white calf before. Most Holsteins have an even mix of black and white, but this little guy was almost completely white. "Let's call him Kea," Fred said, Hawai'ian for "white."

I was already at the feed store in Waialua the next morning when the owner arrived and opened the door. He helped me get what I needed: powdered milk and a big plastic milk bottle with a huge screw-on nipple top. When Kea got bigger, we would get a bucket with an attached nipple to hold more milk volume, but for now the quart-size bottle would do.

I raced home and mixed up a batch of formula for Kea. He ate enthusiastically, and it was fun to feed him, so someone always wanted to be the one to feed Kea. It was usually Alan, but visitors would be given the honor. We always knew when it was time to feed Kea; he had an "I'm hungry" sound that was unmistakable.

There's nothing cuter in the world, I think, than a little calf running and jumping in the air with sheer delight to be alive. Kea would play his game of nudging someone until they got up to chase him, and then he'd fly across the yard with his tail straight up in the air, leaping and bucking, circling, and returning, only to take off galloping again. He would slowly walk up to the chickens and reach his nose out to smell them, and if they squawked he would race off in the opposite direction leaping and bucking. Most of the time he would just hang around, content to be near his people.

I made a garden for the first time in my life. The soil around the house was rich and dark, unlike the red, iron-rich dirt that covered most of the island, and was ideal for pineapples and sugar cane. The ranch dirt was easy to work, and I planted corn, okra, tomatoes, and sunflowers, which all grew well and year-round.

Things weren't all that great for Fred, though. The constant micromanaging, nitpicking, and stinginess of the administrator had him quiet and withdrawn. I knew what he was going through. I made a sign for him to hang up in his office. I'd read the sentiment somewhere and decided it fit his situation perfectly. It read, "We have done so much, for so long, with so little, we are now qualified to do anything with nothing."

The administrator saw the sign and didn't like it. She demanded it be removed. Fred, she said, was disrespectful, and so things got worse. The administrator couldn't hide her contempt for Fred, or for me either, for that matter. She knew I'd been riding all over the ahupua'a in direct disobedience of the ranch's decree.

"Lucky she doesn't know about the wild pig you shot," Fred said to me. "She'd go ballistic!"

He was referring to a trek I took up the mountain where I shot a feral pig. Our neighbor, one of the landscapers, helped me dress the pig, and I gave him half. He taught Alan how to make a snare, and it worked very effectively; we always had fresh pork.

We had been living on the ranch for about eight months when the phone rang. It was a call that changed everything. Sean Ross, a partner at Hawai'i's premier private investigations firm, Goodenow Associates, called for Fred. I answered the phone.

"Your mother-in-law told me you guys moved to Mokuleia Ranch and Fred's the ranch manager," said Sean, "Wow, I guess he's not interested in coming to work for us."

"Wait," I told Sean. "I think Fred wants to talk to you."

Within two weeks we were headed back to the Big Island. It was impossible to stay on O'ahu. Not only would our horses have to be boarded again at great expense, but we now had a cow that would need a place to live, too, and chickens. We had six full-grown hens that were family pets and gave us eggs every day. Rent was exorbitant, and prospects for a job for me were next to none. Goodenow would eventually be opening an office on the Big Island, which Fred would manage, but that was in the future. His assignments in his new job as private investigator would be on O'ahu primarily and on Maui and the Big Isle as needed. It only made sense that we move back to the Big Island, where we could keep our family and pets intact, but we'd have Fred only part-time at least for the time being.

I'd read in the newspaper that Hilton had acquired the Hyatt Regency Waikoloa property for a fraction of what it cost to build. Most of my hotel career had been with Hilton, and I thought I would have a good chance of getting a job there. I couldn't believe my eyes when I read the name of the new director of sales, who happened to be an old friend of mine and fellow sales manager. I called him and said I needed a job. He asked me what I wanted.

"Would you rather have the Japanese market again or would you like domestic wholesale?" he offered.

I chose domestic explaining that the volume of Japanese business they would get when it became a Hilton would really need someone more fluent in Japanese than I was. So, domestic wholesale it was. I would start immediately after getting resettled on the Big Island.

As it turned out, the house we'd rented when Fred was a sergeant in Waimea was again available for rent, so we packed up our belongings into a container and hired our trucker friends to move us back to the Big Isle. The livestock hauler we'd used before coordinated with another who would pick the horses up at Kawaihae Harbor and bring them to us. This time we had little Kea put in the trailer with Sunshine and Hari and watched the three of them disappear down the road on their way to Honolulu Harbor. When we got to the baggage claim at Kona's Keahole Airport, Tesi was brought to us in a pet carrier from cargo. We kept looking for the two pet containers that carried our chickens while we also kept an eye out for our luggage coming down the conveyor to the carousel. Then we heard our chickens squawking and looked up to see them coming down the belt with everyone's luggage. It was a sight not seen every day, and I didn't know whether to be embarrassed or laugh along with everyone else as we sheepishly claimed our noisy luggage.

We did everything in reverse of what we had done over two years earlier when we'd moved in with Fred's mother. When she found out our situation, she wanted Fred to move in with her while he was working in Honolulu. He chose not to. Instead, he moved in with my youngest sister and her husband in Waianae. It enraged his mother and sister.

"How could he abandon her?" his sister asked anyone who would listen.

They blamed me. "She put him up to it," they said.

Back on the Big Island, Alan enrolled in Parker School for his middle-school years. It was then he met Tom, who would be his best friend until the tragic bike accident took his life. We settled into a routine, and Mom moved in with us to take care of Alan while I was at work or away on one of the many trips I would take to the mainland calling on tour company wholesalers of hotel rooms in the major cities.

Once back on the Big Island, I bought a pickup truck that would be my vehicle. I would drop Alan off at Parker in the morning and Mom would pick him up when school got out. Fred, on Oahu, had claimed his father's Mustang convertible and he tooled around Honolulu in his flashy classic car wearing equally flashy aloha shirts. He was too noticeable to be a private investigator, at least so the crooks thought.

Chapter 29

Aloha, Hawai'i

It was a different world at the former Hyatt. Under Hilton management the property flourished and occupancy skyrocketed. My job as leisure sales manager required being at the top of my game. I was fortunate to have an equally sharp assistant who helped me plan and implement new policy and procedures for a market that was chomping at the bit to contract for discounted rooms at the hottest property in the Hilton chain. The international tour companies wanted blocks of rooms too, and I was assigned that market in addition.

I was paid well, and on my trips back and forth to the mainland flying to major cities around the contiguous United States, I was usually upgraded to first class, using miles or a bump from a friend. Fred earned a decent salary too, but even with both our incomes we were stretched thin paying high rent in Waimea, a mortgage on the Hilo house, private school tuition for Alan, and renting pasture space for Sunshine and Hari. We had given Kea away to someone we knew who promised he would remain a pet.

At Christmastime, I worked evenings for the local supermarket in their electronics division. With a background in cameras, I sold a lot of them along with video recorders and sound systems. My employer gave a nice discount, and the last Christmas we had in Hawai'i was nice because of that, but we were stretched thin financially. Fred was flying back and forth from Honolulu, and I would pick him up at Keahole Airport on Fridays and drop him off Monday mornings to return to work. It was nice having him home on weekends. There was lots of work for him on Maui, and jobs on the Big Island came up now and then, but they were few and far between.

I remember the many trips taking Fred to the Kona airport on Monday mornings. He had to leave on the first flight to get to the Goodenow office on time for work. I'd always seen the signs along

Queen Ka'ahumanu Highway cautioning drivers to beware of donkeys crossing. The wild burros that inhabited the stark lava fields, created by flows over the centuries, were descendants of donkeys that worked hauling coffee beans over the decades and got loose to join the wild herds. The donkeys or "nightingales," so named for the braying sound that carries across the Kona night, are an icon of the Kona coffee trade.

The first time I saw them it was in the near-dawn darkness on a Monday morning, I thought they were just more shapes of a'a and pahoehoe lava. I saw some movement and realized I was looking at an entire herd of donkeys.

"Look! Look!" I shouted at Fred, but he didn't see them. Eventually he would be able to make out their shapes in the dark, and it was a thrill to see them nearly every Monday morning on Queen K Highway as we neared the airport.

We had looked for the donkeys for years. We'd heard there was a large herd, but few people ever see them until one is killed on the road. The police would usually be called because of damage to the driver's car that hit one. If the animal was still alive, they would have to shoot it, and if it's a recent kill and still in good condition, it would end up being smoked meat, which I've enjoyed on many occasions.

After dropping Alan off at Parker School, the route I took to work had me driving down the winding road toward Queen K Highway. From the higher elevation of the upper road, I would frequently see whales breaching or slapping their tails on the surface of the water. It was always thrilling for me to spot them. I felt I was being rewarded for living a good life. I was blessed to have keen eyes and an uncommon ability to spot interesting things before anyone else saw them. Like having the "squid eye," finding an octopus of which would become taco poki (marinated octopus, seaweed, onions and other ingredients) for pupu before dinner. At work, I would point out whales to the travel agents on familiarization tours of the Hilton Waikoloa. My clients would return to their reservation cubicles on the mainland and book a customer's vacation by relating their experience of watching whales from the lanai of their ocean-front rooms.

On my frequent business trips I had the responsibility of representing not only my own hotel but the other Hiltons in Hawai'i as well. Hilton Hawai'ian Village on Waikiki and Turtle Bay Hilton on the north shore of O'ahu were both beautiful and iconic resorts, and I was proud to present them to eager agents who would in turn sell them to vacationing customers. Hawai'i was competing against cruises and cheaper Caribbean trips, but Hawai'i was holding its own with Japanese visitors and a growing clientele internationally and especially the U.S. West Coast.

There was little confidence that an office on the Big Island would open any time soon, so Fred and I were looking at living on separate islands for some time to come. We assessed our situation, and Fred considered taking another job to help with expenses. That's when we asked ourselves what our plans were long term. I didn't want to give up our horses even though I had no time to enjoy them. We weren't going to take Alan out of private school. He was our only child, and we were not going to have him go to the public school in our district, notorious for having the highest rate of teen pregnancy in the nation. Into our conversation always came the fact that Fred would inherit the Wahiawa house one day, and we would move back to Oahu and sell our Hilo house, which had been a hit-and-miss situation with renters.

Fred's sister called to report that Mother was in bad shape again. She had gotten a call from the latest live-in help that Mother had a black spot on one of her toes and wanted to know what she should do. Since it apparently wasn't painful, Fred's sister had said let it go but keep an eye on it. The black spot spread quickly and turned out to be gangrene due to lack of circulation. Mother's foot had to be amputated. Fred's sister went to O'ahu and called Fred to blast him for not running to his mother's bedside. As far as Fred and I were concerned, Mother should be in a nursing home.

When Mother was admitted to the hospital for the amputation, it looked as if she would be in for a while. Her condition was dire. She had regressed to a point worse than at any time in the past. It was possible she wouldn't leave the hospital, she was that bad. When she heard that her foot had to be amputated, she lost all will to live.

The first thing Fred's sister did when her mother was removed from the house was to take Moki to the vet and have her put to sleep. Fred and I took that as a sign that his sister was sure their mother wasn't coming back. She was right. Within a few weeks, their mother was dead.

Fred had been summoned to the hospital when he was told his mother had only a day or two to live.

"Get here to the hospital. This may be the last time you'll get to see your mother alive," his sister cried with great angst bordering on melodrama. Her husband and three children were already on their way and would arrive at the hospital at any time.

Fred called me at the hotel we were staying in Honolulu at the time. When Mother passed I drove to the hospital to find Fred's sister and her family standing around Mother's dead body, crying inconsolably. I was struck with the irony that in life they had nothing but contempt for their "stingy" grandmother who gave them "crap" for Christmas and birthdays. And now here they were, ready to claim their fortune of over $400,000 of their grandmother's assets. I didn't say a word, but I looked at Mother and felt a cold chill. Her face was frozen in a sardonic grimace, her mouth open as if silently screaming. No wonder the children were crying. Their grandmother looked horrific, and I silently cursed Fred's sister for not fixing her mother's face before her children arrived. Was it intentional, I wondered, or does she really hate her mother as she's stated time and again over the years?

Weeks after Fred's mother's death, Fred was again summoned, this time to the family house to meet with his mother's lawyer along with a friend of Fred's father from the bank, and his sister. Fred's mother had changed her will around the time we moved to the ranch and out of her house. She wanted Fred to get nothing. Fred's sister was to inherit all the Booth assets including the house. They wanted to make sure Miki Booth would never set foot in the Wahiawa house again. Even Alan would not get the $5,000 each grandchild was to receive. So deep was their hatred for me that they punished Alan. No matter that he was told time and again by his grandmother that he was her favorite grandchild. No matter that she spoke venomously of her daughter and her family for being unsophisticated and downright crude.

Fortunately, Alan never knew about the $5,000 and knew little about Fred's father willing the house to us. He was just a young boy and didn't need to know that his parents were hated by the only family his father had.

The funeral was held before the reading of the will. Alan stayed home with my mother, his Obaachan on the Big Island, and I flew to Oahu for the funeral that took place at Punchbowl National Cemetery of the Pacific. Quite a few people came, mostly friends of Fred's. Fred didn't speak about his mother as he had for his father years earlier when he'd shown me a side of him I didn't often see; he was an impressive public speaker. His sister brought a large calabash-type koa bowl for the expected condolence cards and checks. It bothered us later that at the end of the service Fred's sister commandeered the bowl full of money when most of the donations were from Fred's friends and acquaintances. The ceremony was short, and a nice black-and-white photo of my mother-in-law was propped up against a container that held the cremains, which would be interred with her husband's ashes in the columbarium at Punchbowl.

Fred called me after the meeting to break the unbelievable news to me. Certainly his sister wouldn't take everything, I thought. She, better than anyone, knew how twisted her mother's mind had gotten in her final years. Fred's sister and her husband insisted they had to "honor her wishes." Fred would get nothing.

"What did we do to deserve such harsh punishment?" Fred asked aloud to no one in particular. "All we did was fix up her house."

Life went on, but our future was shattered. There was so much we had counted on, and much of Fred's lump-sum retirement had gone into the house to make it livable, and more than that, the house had appreciated to well over $400,000. We hoped Fred's sister would let him have something besides the Mustang and a clock, but a fine clock it was. Although it didn't work, it was an heirloom of fine porcelain originating in Manchester, England making its way to Kingston on the Hudson and eventually gracing the mantle of the fireplace in the house in Wahiawa, Hawai'i.

We took a two-week vacation to Oklahoma where I had lived before and spent the first week in a rented cabin on Grand Lake O' the Ozarks in the northeastern corner of the state. "Green Country," as the area is called, skirts the Ozark hills of Arkansas and Missouri. Grand Lake is over sixty-five miles long from where two rivers, the Spring and Neosho, meet to form the uppermost part of the lake to the country's longest multi-arch dam, which creates electric service for much of the state. The lake boasts over 2,000 miles of shoreline, and the nearby town of Grove has been discovered by Rand McNally and is advertised as one of the best places to retire.

We rented a boat and a waverunner, and Alan and Fred fell in love with the lake experience. I knew they would. In the '70s my ex-husband and I had a lake cabin there, and I learned to water-ski and fish for crappie and bass, a different fishing experience from a lifetime of big game fishing in Hawai'i. It was fun, peaceful, and relaxing, something I spent a lot of time doing by myself, fishing and collecting arrowheads on a small island that was once a high bluff where over a thousand years ago natives chipped arrowheads and spearheads out of flint.

We spent the second week of our mainland vacation with a rental car driving to Slidell, Louisiana, where we stayed with friends. They took us to New Orleans and showed us the sights. On the way back to our friends' house, we stopped at the window of a drive-thru daiquiri stand. Fred and I gaped in amazement as my friend who was driving ordered four large daiquiris in Styrofoam containers. Fred wondered whether frozen daiquiris-to-go were promoting drinking and driving, which, of course, was against the law, so we transported our drinks home, tempted to sip, but waited until the car stopped in the driveway. When we told friends about the daiquiri drive-thru, they were skeptical.

Once back home in Hawai'i, we talked more and more about moving to the mainland. It was clear that if we stayed in Hawai'i we would have to work for the rest of our lives. We had little retirement money anymore, having spent much of it. While in Oklahoma, we looked at some homes and land. Incredibly, you could buy a decent house for $50,000, some even lower than that.

All I wanted was acreage and a couple of horses. We could certainly have that in Oklahoma. Fred loved the idea of jumping in a car and driving in any direction to go someplace he'd never been before, unlike driving around and around the same islands. Alan liked the idea of having a boat and waverunner. He was all for leaving his childhood home for new adventures on the mainland. It was decided. It was a good time for the change. Alan would complete eighth grade at Parker, spend the summer on the lake in Oklahoma, and start ninth grade at Grove High School.

We left our horses, Sunshine and Hari, with people who would ship them once we got settled, but after months of paying mortgages on two places, the lake cabin we bought and the Hilo house, our savings were depleted, and we took a loss on the Hilo house due to a slump in the Hawai'i housing market caused by the crash of Japan's economy. We had to sell our horses in Hawai'i. We never rebuilt the funds needed to air freight or ship them to Oakland, California, and truck them to Oklahoma, which at the time would have run about $5,000 for both horses.

Alan thrived at his new public school. He made friends easily, and his best friends from high school are still his best friends today, fifteen years later. It worked out well that both Fred and Alan enjoyed their first winter. I had worried that they would have misgivings once they experienced severe Oklahoma weather and possibly even tornadoes. We all missed the ocean, though, and I especially missed the mountains that were always part of the backdrop no matter where or on what island you happened to be.

Fred went to work as a sheriff's deputy, and I found work at a local resort on the lake as a sales manager. Alan made the honor roll four years in a row and the dean's list at Northeastern Oklahoma A&M College, where he earned an associate of science degree before going on to Northeastern State University in Tahlequah, Oklahoma.

Life was good. Much of the unpleasantness we'd experienced over family betrayal no longer stung, and we had moved on to a life less complicated and free of the hurt and anger that had filled the last months of our life in Hawai'i.

Fifteen years after leaving our island home we have a million-dollar trailer home on sixteen fine acres with horses, chickens, happy rescued dogs, Cinnamon Turkey, and Ping, the cat. There's a fine porcelain clock sitting on the mantle of the fireplace in the den of our gorgeous trailer. It's all a matter of perspective, and the best revenge is living well, so they say.

My mother came to visit for a couple of weeks while we were still living in the lake cabin. She was getting around pretty well, although osteoporosis had taken its toll and she was slowly caving in on herself. We were the same height and clothes size for most of my adult life, but now she had lost so many inches of height I was looking down at her. It hurt, and I wondered how many good years she had left to take care of herself.

In Hawai'i she had the added burden of taking care of my older brother, Tamé. After years of drug abuse and subsequent suicide attempts, he was put on methadone, and the daily dose kept him from seeking street drugs.

Tamé was always a hard worker and excellent fisherman, but his acquaintances and lifestyle revolved around "getting high" or drunk or both. Tamé's first accident, a motorcycle wreck that wasn't his fault, resulted in constant back pain and a steady marijuana and painkiller habit. Like most hard-core drug users, he began with marijuana. There's no doubt he was dealing with severe pain but was able to function at his jobs, getting stoned only when work was pau (finished).

His dependency escalated, and there were always contacts who supplied whatever he needed. He crashed a few times overdosing on cocaine and heroin. Suicide attempts, according to his friends. They wanted me to help him. They wanted my mother's contact information. "No," I said to them. "Do not call my mother." They got hold of her anyway and she went along, enabling him for years. He always had a place to stay, food to eat, and money for drugs. As long as my mother was around to take care of her "Ichi-ban," number one son, she enabled him to maintain the path he was on, not by choice but by circumstance.

During Tamé's good years of fishing in Kailua-Kona, he hung out with business leaders and prominent local residents. He dated the prettiest girls and was well liked. People enjoyed being around him. He was quick-witted and funny — hysterically funny. But drugs were ever present in his life and those are the people he got together with after hours. Marijuana is easily obtained in Hawai'i, and even tourists openly ask for directions to the nearest dealer. I remember hosting a luau when I worked for Kona Hilton. A young man asked me, "So, where's the buds?" I answered that my husband was a cop and told him he really didn't want to ask me that.

When the Exxon Valdez disaster occurred in Alaska, Tamé was recruited by a workboat firm with tugs in Hawai'i. The boats immediately set out from Honolulu Harbor to assist with the cleanup. Tamé was "head cook and bottle washer," as the old salts would say. He functioned in all capacities to keep the tug shipshape, and because he was an exceptional cook, as are all the men in the Snyder family, he usually did the cooking.

From tropical waters wearing little but a pair of shorts, Tamé was transformed into an arctic sailor outfitted with clothing needed to survive Alaska's cold weather. It was a different world and Tamé took in the adventure with excitement and determination, but his letters home reflected at times great sadness and futility.

Once back home in Hawai'i, Tamé stayed with the workboat firm and set out on a job to recover a scientific buoy that had broken loose from its mooring near San Diego and was headed toward Hawai'i. The tug located the buoy off Kauai, and the crew attached a steel line to winch it onto the back deck of the tug. The buoy weighed around 2,000 pounds, hardly a challenge for the huge tug. While being winched, the buoy caught on the stern of the tug, unbeknownst to the winch operator. The tension on the cable built, and when the buoy cleared the obstruction it sling-shotted onto the deck, hitting Tamé full force. The impact crushed bones in Tamé's legs and shattered his pelvis.

Tamé was medevaced to Wilcox Hospital on Kauai by helicopter, where he stayed until he was eventually moved to Honolulu to begin physical therapy. From there it was all downhill for him. If he needed painkillers and dope for his injuries sustained when he was a teenager, he would surely need them hard-core from then on out.

He returned to the Big Island, and unable to work or fish anymore, he fell back in with the doper crowd, but he had friends who truly cared for him. One woman brought him into her rented apartment in Kona, and we all sighed with relief that they could each look after the other. Tamé was on the road to stability. His lady friend was as damaged as Tamé, and they each understood the trials and tribulations of injury and illness. A cancer survivor, Tamé's new partner was dependent on a myriad of drugs and painkillers, which she shared when Tamé was in particularly intense pain.

The personal injury lawyer, who specializes in federal lawsuits and helped my mother sue Tripler Hospital for my dad's death, approached my brother to file a maritime injury lawsuit. The lawyer had come to Hilo to take my brother's and my deposition for my mother's lawsuit when he found out about my brother's accident at sea. At the deposition we learned that the government was saying my father died because of complications caused by his excessive drinking. My back went up when I heard this, and something triggered in me, and I said to myself, "They're not going to get away with this."

Hawai'i had become a litigious society, but our family never entertained the idea of suing anyone for bad things that happen. Conversely, others have sued our friends and acquaintances, effectively ruining their lives. But now I was "all in" to use a lawyer and his investigators to find out what really happened to my father.

Eventually the government settled when the medical records revealed that during my father's heart surgery, power went out and no one "bagged," manually ventilated, my father for at least six minutes when he was unconscious resulting in anoxia to the brain. Daddy was irreversibly brain damaged during the operation. Mom got some money. The government has a set amount for things such as this. I don't remember how much she netted after attorney fees, but whatever it was, my brother helped deplete it with his drug addiction.

Tamé got about $250,000 from his maritime accident. He and his live-in girlfriend, whose cancer had returned, were married and renting our Hilo house at the time Tamé finally received his compensation. They began looking for a house and found one with several living areas. "What do they plan to do with all those bedrooms?" Fred and I wondered.

"A bed-and-breakfast for a source of income?" I asked, but immediately wondered out loud, "or a place for their druggie friends to crash?"

But before they bought the house Tame's wife was again diagnosed with cancer. They found a cancer clinic on the West Coast, and Tamé's wife made several trips for treatments. Tamé insisted she fly first class. He bought her a new car. He was good to her. He made sure she visited her daughters on the mainland. On one such visit while she was off-island, Tamé got together with his fellow drug addicts and partied to the tune of several thousand dollars. When his wife returned and found out what he'd done, she formulated a plan for her self-preservation.

With her daughter's help, they emptied the bank accounts and shipped the car to the West Coast under the guise of a "fender-bender" being repaired. And she was gone without a trace. All the money was gone. Tamé sold his new Harley and other toys to fund his search to get his money back. He traveled to Reno, where a private investigator had tracked her. When he ran out of money, there was no place to go except back to his mother, the only one who would take him in.

———— ⊗⊗⊗ ————

A couple of years after we moved to Grove, Oklahoma, Fred and I found a beautiful piece of property. It was mostly pastureland with many large old pecan and black walnut trees. There was a perfect place for a house to sit overlooking a "holler" created by a river wash that was now a "wet weather creek," meaning it flowed only when there were heavy rains. There was also a stock pond for cows which occupied the fenced-in property until we purchased the land. The pond was filled with sun perch and bass. None of us were really fond of eating fresh water fish so we threw them back in the pond after the fun of catching them. Fred would make sure the tine of the hook was bent down so the fish would come off easily after we reeled them in.

By sheer coincidence I became reacquainted with relatives of my ex-husband who owned three horses but because of illness in the family were unable to properly care for them. One of the horses was rideable, and I offered to purchase it since I was looking for a riding horse I could keep on our fenced-in land. But even though the owner was in a wheelchair minus his feet due to diabetes, he didn't want to give up any of his horses regardless that his wife was burdened with the responsibility of caring for them. When he passed away, his wife offered the three horses to us. All she asked was that they be given the care they needed: regular veterinary checkups, worming, and farrier work.

We had sold our Hawai'i horses. We just didn't have the money to ship them and found buyers who we knew would be good to Sunshine and Hari. I had saved up a thousand dollars for a horse and gladly gave it to the owner for three. Soon a large trailer arrived with Amigo, a very old quarter horse, Sugar (renamed Sugarfoot), and Cur (renamed Hoku, Hawai'ian for star.)

The horses had been together for years in Colorado and had moved to Oklahoma when their owner became very ill. Whenever horses cross state lines, they are required to have the proper paperwork from a veterinarian certifying the horses are free of certain deadly blood-born and other diseases. The travel papers and recollections of the former owners were the only historic facts we had about our new charges. They were their own little herd and each had its own personality. Sugarfoot reminded us a lot of Sunshine. Not only did they look alike, chestnut color and white blazes, they had the same personality — friendly, and they enjoyed being scratched. Sugarfoot was mixed quarter horse and Arabian, with four white-stocking legs that unfortunately were deformed and that we knew would be problems for her in the future. Hoku, which I just couldn't bring myself to call "Cur," looked a lot like Hari, a bay Arabian with a bright white star on his forehead and, typical of the breed, a streak of naughtiness. Hoku was always looking for a treat. He was the friendliest of all. Amigo had had a long life. According to the papers, he was nearly thirty years old. Already a ripe old age for a horse, Amigo would live another four years before he told us he didn't want to get up anymore.

Our horses were "easy keepers." They did just fine on their own, eating the lush pasture grass in spring and summer, and bales of hay in winter. We visited them on pretty days and learned that Hoku could be pretty ornery when ridden. I lost count of the times he acted up and I ended up on the ground, so I gave up my English saddle and started using the Western saddle that Hoku was used to, although it made no difference as far as his orneriness went, but at least I didn't end up on the ground as often.

Life was good. We didn't miss Hawai'i all that much. We were looking forward to the day when we could build a house on the beautiful sixteen acres and move in to live with the horses. That day came sooner than later when I visited my mother in 1999 when she was living with my younger sister in Las Vegas. When I flew into Vegas that day and saw the brownish pollution that hung in a cloud over the city, I thought, "No wonder Mom has breathing issues, how can anyone be healthy inhaling that?"

After talking to my mother I called Fred and he agreed we should have her move in with us. He had misgiving about Tamé, but I assured him that Tamé would be fine — he had reached a level of trustworthiness on the methadone program by staying illegal-drug free. His status was reached after more than two years on the program in Honolulu and carried over to a clinic in Vegas. It worked the same way from Vegas to Tulsa. Instead of daily doses at the clinic, Tamé could pick up a week's worth at a time after the clinics worked that out between one another.

While Fred held down the fort, I took time off my job as a sales manager and once again flew to Vegas. This time I rented a U-haul, and we filled it with Mom's and Tamé's belongings. With Tamé in the passenger seat we headed to Oklahoma. I would return one last time to bring Mom home. During the two-day trip in the U-haul I got to know my brother again, but he was a changed person. Instead of the gregarious, fun-loving and sometimes audacious older brother I had before, I was sitting next to a quiet stranger who deferred to my every decision and seemed grateful to do so. He no longer had the means or the desire to call the shots, not even for himself.

We spent the night at a motel in Albuquerque and the following morning over breakfast discussed some logistics about the move and Tamé's required weekly trips to Tulsa for his methadone, a 150-mile round trip not including tolls. He came clean that he didn't have a driver's license because of fines he had outstanding at the Hawai'i DMV. That explained why he hadn't offered to drive the U-haul.

Almost immediately after getting home I flew back to Vegas to bring Mom home with me. She wasn't doing well, having just gotten out of the hospital again a few days earlier due to COPD. It was a relief to land at the Tulsa airport and head home in my van.

The following day we all piled into the van and went to inspect our new home. It was huge and beautiful and new. While we sat around in lawn chairs in the heated trailer and visited, snow began to fall. Huge flakes quickly covered the ground and began to stack up. Several inches were on the ground as we got in the van to head the twenty-five miles back to the lake cabin. While we crept along, following in the ruts of a large truck, we passed cars in the ditch — the result of miscalculations on the hidden road. When we reached the cabin, the snow was nearly a foot deep. That night Mom struggled to breathe. We called an ambulance to take her to the hospital. There was no way our van could make the trip.

By the time Mom was released from rehab and outfitted with oxygen bottles and medications, we were completely moved into the new house and prospects of renting the lake cabin quickly were good. Tamé and Mom were a joy to have in our home. Tamé stepped in and did all the grocery shopping and cooking. Mom did dishes and kept the kitchen spotless. They had the house to themselves all day when Fred and I worked and Alan was in school, and they would retire to their rooms early so we could have the den and the rest of the house to ourselves in the evenings. We got chickens for them to have a hobby, and Mom would feed them twice a day, rain or shine, sleet or snow. Tamé built coops and demonstrated a great skill for carpentry and mechanics. He maintained all our machinery, vehicles, and electronics. When I bragged on him, he would demur: a jack of all trades but master of none was he.

Life was good. Tamé had reached another level of trustworthiness. Instead of a once-a-week trip to Tulsa for his methadone, it became once a month. I no longer had to drive him to get his doses. We paid his fines in Hawai'i, and he got an Oklahoma driver's license. Mom had bouts with asthma and other health issues from time to time, but mostly she got around well enough to feed the chickens, with Tamé doing the work she couldn't do. She ordered him around and he grumbled, but they had an indescribable bond. One without the other could never survive. The arrangement wasn't without conflict. Tamé was a perfectionist and at times got into arguments with Fred, who was usually easygoing but sometimes just couldn't stand my brother and so we lived with tension. Because of Tamé's long history of abusing drugs, he was emotionally immature and unstable, but for the most part Mom kept him in line by ordering him to his room when he got loud and argumentative.

My brother loved me and was proud of me. He liked to tell stories of when we were kids, and Fred especially was surprised to learn things about me that even I had forgotten. One such story was when I was about eleven. Tamé and I were at a luau and a man who was drunk came up behind me and grabbed my chest where breasts were supposed to be. I spun around and punched the man in the mouth, breaking a tooth and cutting the knuckles on my hand. Tamé said, "There was blood everywhere! You couldn't tell who was bleeding worse, Miki's hand or the pervert's mouth!"

He told that story many times and would even grab my hand to show the scars on my knuckles and warn people not to mess with me. He told about me in high school. How his friends all wanted to get fixed up with his sister. "She was so cute," he would say about me. "Everyone wanted to go out with her."

Sometimes his stories were kind of exaggerated, but hey, it was good for my ego.

I lost my job in 2004. Mom and Tamé had lived with us for five years by then. We were all worried. Fred had quit the Sheriff's Department, disgusted with the politics that went with the job. After weeks of job hunting and depleting our savings to pay bills, Fred and I were both frantic. There were just no jobs to be had that paid decently. We would have to commute from Tulsa or move to where the jobs were. We had to do something.

At one time I'd been offered a job representing a Hawai'i hotel group which required relocating to a major mainland city. I figured the only way I could find such a position now would be to travel to Hawai'i and meet with industry people to see what was available. I made some calls to old friends and contacts and soon had appointments for interviews.

I arrived in Honolulu the day before my first appointment and visited with friends before checking into a hotel. I hadn't been sleeping well, unable to fall asleep because my thoughts were always racing, not knowing how things would turn out. Would we have to move back to

Hawai'i? Would I find a job at all after spending so much money to get here? What would we do about Mom and Tamé if we had to move? Where could they go? What about the horses? What about the chickens? Tesi? Alan? Ping the cat?

The stress was too much for me to handle. I suffered a physical and emotional breakdown and was admitted to Queens Hospital in Honolulu. Fred got the call that scared him more than anything else he could remember in his lifetime and immediately left For Hawai'i. He couldn't imagine what might have happened. I was fine when he saw me last.

I was diagnosed with bipolar disorder. The doctor spoke to both of us explaining that the stress I was under probably brought on the symptoms which were extreme mood swings from deep depression to manic outbursts of rage. The inability to reconcile the two conditions basically caused what I call a "meltdown." Medications were prescribed, but the best therapy was Fred's good news: he just got a new job, and I wouldn't have to worry about working at all.

Chapter 30

A Blessing in Disguise

I was really happy to finally not have to work anymore. Fred had a good job that paid well. I missed out a lot on Alan's formative years sometimes working two jobs while Mom took care of him. Now that Alan was grown up and on his own, I could spend lots of time with his grandma who'd raised him. My mom was aging and barely able to get around without oxygen, but she still had good days after working the soreness out of her joints each morning. With my brother's help she took care of the chickens and did dishes after meals. Tamé cooked, but I was slowing taking that responsibility away from him to give him more freedom to visit the few friends he had. I started taking Mom to the casino where Fred worked and shopping at Sam's Club, pushing her in a wheeled cart. She was always saying she was ashamed to be out in public. That her clothes were boroboro, worn out, and her hair needed coloring and all kinds of reasons for me to be embarrassed being seen with her.

Every morning it took a while for her to get the kinks worked out, but after eating breakfast and taking all her medications she would be ready to go holoholo (leisure outing) all kine places: casino, go kau kau (eat) lunch, go stoah (store), whatevahs (whatever). We had so much fun together, spoke "pidgin" (a dialect) and made light of just about everything. We called my appointments with the psychiatrist and psychologist "visits with the headshrinker." Mom would laugh and call it "headshrink day," which Fred didn't like but enjoyed hearing us laugh. Mom was my best friend and my illness was a blessing in disguise. I was giving back to my mother all the doing she gave to us and especially to Alan, for which I was very grateful. She raised him and did a very good job of it.

In 2006, my mother turned eighty years old. Almost a year earlier I'd started putting together plans for her birthday and combining it with a family reunion. My brothers and sisters, their children, and even some of Mom's great-grandchildren would be there. As the months crept closer to the event, we wondered if Mom would live to see her eightieth birthday. She had had some hospitalizations and a lengthy stay in rehab after a bad fall, as well as visits to the emergency room struggling to breathe. But we went on with the secret plans, and everything turned out like magic. Mom had no idea her eightieth birthday would be so special. When it was over and everyone had gone back home, she talked about it continuously. No one ever gave her a party before. It was the most fun she had in her life. She was truly surprised. We laughed as she recounted the moment when she discovered the secret: One minute she was talking to my sister from Alaska on the phone and all of a sudden my sister was standing next to her in the kitchen on a cell phone.

"How come you're wearing such boroboro clothes?" my sister asked while tugging on my mother's pants.

"Adah, waaaaaaat!?" Mom said, looking at my sister in disbelief. She kept talking on the phone and my sister talked back on her cell while we all howled with laughter. In all, there were about twenty-five of us. Mom was the oldest at eighty, and the youngest was her three-year-old great-granddaughter from the Red Hill area on O'ahu. Our house was full and some family members stayed at a nearby hotel where I had a block of rooms at a special rate.

Event planning was my forte, and two days earlier the luau food I ordered well in advance arrived in Styrofoam coolers packed in dry ice. There were thirty large frozen lau laus filled with pork, beef, butterfish, and luau leaf wrapped in ti leaves and tied with the stem. There were two big bags of frozen poi that we would steam to reconstitute to a smooth "two-finger" texture. Fred and Alan drooled. Poi was one thing we'd rarely found since leaving Hawai'i. The fresh ti leaves were wrapped separately and taped to the outside of the coolers so as not to freeze. We used the leaves to wrap around a huge pork butt after it was scored and rubbed with Hawai'ian salt and liquid smoke. Heavy foil was wrapped around the leaf-covered butt and, without an imu (fire pit) to cook in, roasted in the oven until it was so tender you could shred the meat with a fork.

We also cooked chicken and long rice, sweet potato, and made rice using the extra big rice cooker hardly ever brought out from the furthest reaches of the lower cabinet until an occasion such as Mom's luau.

"Shhhhhhhh Shizukane!!!" The invitations read. "Keep quiet — it's a surprise party." And a surprise it was for Mom. Even her huge full-sheet birthday cake with the shizukane theme in frosting surprised and delighted her no end when it was brought into view. The $1,000 cash contributed by all her kids and presented in a decorative treasure chest secured with a tiny lock was probably the best-thought-out gift for our mother. What does one get for an eighty-year-old woman who has every creature comfort and needs very little else? Well, you give cash so she can go HOLOHOLO!!!! CASINO!!!!

After everyone was gone, Mom and I spoke reflectively about the party and having everyone together for the first time in years. "I hope I make it one more year. I want to have one more party like that before I die," Mom said. But it wasn't to be. She passed away three months before her eighty-first birthday.

That last year was especially hard on all of us. It started getting bad even before Mom's party. Tamé had fallen in with bad company. Actually, he sought them out and the fault might have been mine. Before I lost my job, Tamé was the acting head of household, and Mom was totally dependent on him. Fred and I were at work all day and when we came home, dinner was ready for us. Tamé did everything, and he was a perfectionist. He really felt displaced when I relieved him of many of his duties. His feelings were easily hurt, and he would bottle up his emotions until they exploded in an unexpected barrage of angry words. He would then storm out the door and drive off and stay gone for hours, coming home with glassy eyes and reeking of marijuana. To say anything would start a fight of epic proportions, so we'd leave it to Mom to talk to him. We could hear her blasting him in her room. He was risking losing his methadone if he tested positive for drugs. If he were kicked off the program, he would surely seek out illegal drugs. Mom paid a lot of money for his methadone, and Fred and I had put up with a lot, not just the seven years he was with us and stable on methadone, but all the years before when he'd destroyed his own life and took my mother with him.

When Mom was deteriorating in the last months of her life, Tamé clearly couldn't handle it. He left for hours every day and came back stoned. For years now, he had gone to the Tulsa methadone clinic on a monthly basis. He was trustworthy. He bragged that he had been testing negative because he knew how long pot would stay in his system, and he made sure he didn't smoke before his scheduled visit. Fred and I tried to avoid any discussions with my brother. He was completely out of control, and Mom would get so upset when she heard us fighting. It all came to a head when I discovered Tamé was selling or trading Mom's OxyContin pills. Worse, Mom knew and enabled him to do it.

I told him to get out and he left, but the following day he was back begging me to let him stay because he had nowhere else to go. After that he stayed with Mom, hardly leaving the house. He took care of Mom's chickens and quietly went about his chores. He seemed to get a grip on the fact that Mom was dying, and he made her last weeks and days pleasant, comfortable, and loving. She went to the hospital and soon afterward hospice care took over and did all the necessary things to bring Mom home to die. She had a strong heart and she lived days beyond everyone's expectations of when she would pass. Fred and I went out for the first time in a week. It was nice to get away from the death vigil and have dinner out. Surely Mom wouldn't pass while we were gone.

On the way home, about five miles from our house, we saw there had been a bad wreck. Just as we approached the scene of the accident, the police turned off their lights and drove off, and the road was opened to traffic flow. Whatever had been there had been removed. Skid marks, deep ruts in the dirt shoulder, and pieces of metal and glass were all that was left.

"That's a strange place for an accident," I said to Fred. He agreed. There was high visibility for miles. I didn't think much more about it until we arrived home and saw that my truck was gone. I immediately knew that Tamé was in that accident. He would never have left Mom unless she was dead.

"Call the Highway Patrol," I said to Fred. "Tamé was in that wreck."

"You don't know that," he replied. "What's Judy's number? What's his friend's number?"

I got angry. "Just find out something!" I snapped and went into Mom's room.

I lowered the rail of the bed and sat down next to Mom. She looked peaceful. My tears started to flow as I stroked her hand and spoke to her silently. She was in heaven with God, I knew, for surely such a good person who brought joy and comfort to many people, not just her family, and never asked a thing for herself would be accepted into God's grace.

Where's Fred? I wondered. Why doesn't he come in here? I expected him to be with me but he still hadn't come into the room, so I went to look for him. He was on the phone.

"What did you find out?" I asked.

"He's not at the neighbors'."

"I know that! Did you call the Highway Patrol?"

"No. What's his friend's phone number?" Fred asked.

Now I was angry. Why wouldn't he listen to me? "CALL THEM!" I demanded. "FIND OUT ABOUT THAT WRECK!" I stormed away, returning to sit with Mom, and then the dogs started barking. Someone was at the door. I could see through the glass of the storm door that Fred was talking to two men on the front porch. I recognized the sheriff's deputy as someone Fred used to work with. The other was a highway patrolman. They all looked at me through the storm door, and Fred nodded his head, "It was Tamé."

I opened the door and spoke. "Is he dead?"

They all affirmed that he was. My next question: "Is anyone else hurt?"

Fred made a strange noise. "That was the second question I asked too," he said.

We were assured that no one else was hurt. The accident involved a semi-trailer. What they described was hardly an "accident." The driver of the semi tried to swerve away from a head-on with a small white truck. The semi was able to avoid a direct hit, but the small truck ended up under the trailer and against the back wheels, crushing the driver. When the sheriff's deputies arrived, they all recognized the brother-in-law of their former undersheriff, Fred.

They came in and asked for a photo ID. Although the deputy recognized Tamé, the highway patrolman wanted to positively identify my brother for his report. I found Tamé's wallet with his Oklahoma driver's license and showed it. "Yes, that's him," the patrolman stated.

The deputy stayed and helped us make the necessary calls to hospice. When they arrived, they made the call to the mortuary, and by three o'clock in the morning Mom was placed on a gurney and covered with a plush, dark green blanket. I stopped the funeral director and asked if the tulips I had cut for Mom could go with her. "Of course," he said, and I gathered the dozen bright red tulips from off the otherwise empty hospital bed and placed them on the green covering. "Goodbye, Mom," I whispered, and she was gone.

The time I'd been spending with Mom and my memories with her since losing my job was something no one could ever take from me. We were both up in years and had our ailments that curtailed a lot of activities we could have enjoyed, but we had fun where and when we could find it. While Mom was still able to walk short distances with her "chicken stick," a staff that doubled as a cane and implement to discipline rowdy roosters, she would walk around the yard checking on the progress of plants and visiting the horses when they were near the gate. She would have to stop frequently to catch her breath, but sometimes she made it all the way to the small park I made for her. Over the years we'd planted several trees and flowering shrubs. The area was once part of the horses' pasture, but I'd moved the hot-wire posts to create a new fence line, making space that Fred then had to mow since it added to the yard. He would moan every time he saw a new tree or plant go in, since he would then have more to weed-whack around the base of the plant. I put in several blueberry bushes, but each time Fred would mow, he'd pretend he didn't see them or thought they were weeds and mow over them. They eventually stopped trying to grow and became part of the lawn. Fred won that one.

When Mom passed away, I did what she wanted me to and that was to plant a tree in her memory and return her ashes to Hawai'i to be with Daddy at Punchbowl National Memorial Cemetery of the Pacific.

I planted a large Autumn Blaze maple for Mom and a different maple for Tamé, which was not quite as big as Mom's but was beautiful. My sisters pitched in with some money, and we purchased a granite marker to go under Mom's tree. It reads simply, "Love might be a tree, rooted in time for all eternity." Under the shade of the maple also sits a bench where we can rest and be close to Mom's memory.

Six months later, when Fred, Alan, and I left on our long-planned Hawai'i trip to attend my Castle High School fortieth class reunion, we took Mom's and Tamé's ashes home. We stayed at the Makaha Resort near Waianae, where the class reunion was to be held. We met my brother Tad and his son, Kaui, at Daddy's grave, to the right of the memorial where the thirty-foot statue of Lady Columbia stands on the prow of a ship. Daddy's was one of the last burials before the cemetery was full and a new veterans' cemetery opened in Kaneohe.

Visiting Daddy at Punchbowl always brought back some troubling memories. Daddy's ashes should have been scattered at sea, and all his Pearl Harbor Yacht Club buddies were ready to join a regatta that would escort the family for a scattering at sea. But that didn't happen. One member of the family wanted a Catholic funeral and another agreed. They eventually talked Mom into it, and so we had a full-on funeral with all the expenses that go with it. It didn't matter that he wanted his ashes scattered at sea.

Tad, Fred, and I went to the administrative office at Punchbowl to deliver Mom's ashes. The small staff there welcomed us; we were expected. The funeral home had called ahead and made all the necessary arrangements. There were so many things the average person would never think about when a loved one dies that we were very grateful to everyone who helped us through the rough time; the hospice people, the funeral home person, the people at Punchbowl. Notices were put in the Hawai'i, California, and Oklahoma newspapers, anyplace where we had family, anyplace we wanted, actually. The funeral home took care of that.

As we filled out paperwork at Punchbowl, we were stymied about what to put for Mom's religion. Daddy had a cross on his bronze marker, but we weren't sure that we wanted to write "Catholic" in the space for Mom's religion, especially since she embraced Buddhism in her last years of life. The ladies in the office suggested putting a Buddhist "wheel" on the marker.

"Can we do that?" we asked.

"Of course," we were told. "It's very common here," someone said, meaning the cemetery. So it was arranged. A new bronze plaque would be made with Mom's and Daddy's names, a cross, and a Buddhist "wheel." I haven't been back to see it, but a Catholic family member did and went ballistic, never to speak to me again.

Fred, Alan, Sandy, my best friend from intermediate and high school, and I flew to the Big Island with Tamé's ashes. Sandy and Tamé had been sweet on each other in high school. We had many stories to share about my brother, and it was fun remembering. Alan found out some really great things about his uncle that tempered his memories of living with a substance abuser.

We kept our room at Makaha Resort and stayed one night at the former Kona Hilton, where I was employed for two years as sales manager. Many of the employees I'd worked with twenty years earlier were still there, and it was a wonderful reunion, full of hugs and alohas. The following morning we met Dale Leverone, captain of the charter boat Sea Strike. I'd called Dale earlier to let him know about Tamé. He was surprised. Rumors of Tamé's death had been circulating for years around Kona. I guess when Tamé came to live with me, he totally dropped from sight. Dale had no idea Tamé was in, of all places, Oklahoma. Dale offered his boat to take Tamé's ashes out to sea off the Kona Coast.

We ate breakfast at the Hele Mai restaurant and listened to the waves crashing against the seawall while we ate before leaving for Honokohou Harbor. We met Dale at the Sea Strike. He was ready to go and equipped with everything needed for a full-day charter, which would cost the average tourist over $800, but we were ohana, family, and the trip would be manuahi, (free). Of all the fishing boats and charter captains on the Kona Coast who knew and liked Tame, Dale Leverone was the closest to him and a friend of mine. The two times I went out off Kailua-Kona and caught big game fish was on the Sea Strike. Tamé had captained the boat while Dale functioned as first mate. It was Tamé's birthday present to me, and I caught two marlin, the first weighing in at 164 pounds and the other at 72. It was December of 1986, and catching not one, but two, blue marlin on my "special day" drew attention and congratulations at the Kailua pier. Most astonishingly, it was the first time I didn't go out next to the rail throwing my guts out. It was thrilling and I bugged my brother and Dale to take me out again, and a month later they did. Dale had used the photo of us with our catch in the Kailua-Kona Activities Guide. I was a minor celebrity since so many people already knew me from my position at Kona Hilton. I'd also appeared in Japanese magazines and on local TV shows and in the news as a leader in the hospitality industry. It didn't come easy. Public speaking and appearing on TV made me so nervous I would get nauseous and throw up in anticipation, but was fine when the time actually came to speak.

On the second trip fishing, I caught two more marlin, a 52-pound Striped Marlin and a 26-pound Pacific Short-nosed Spearfish. The latter is just like a marlin but lacks the spear. The species is rather scarce, and Hawai'i is one of the few places they're caught. Of the four marlin I fought, the short-nose, or mahu-marlin, as locals call it, was the toughest fighter I encountered. Sometimes you never know what you have until it's brought to the side of the boat, and for sure Tamé and

Dale didn't know what I had at the end of the line until we saw it brilliantly shining while swimming alongside the boat.

Word spread around Kailua that I was good luck. "Take Tamé's sister fishing," they said. "For sure you gonna catch fish!"

But Fred was promoted to traffic division, and we moved from Kona to Hilo, and I never got to go fishing again with my brother.

The urn with Tamé's ashes rode in the fight chair as we headed out to sea. A framed photo was propped up next to the urn, with leis around it. The morning was bright and sunny, the ocean calm. But not taking any chances, I remembered to apply a transdermal patch behind my ear to ward off motion sickness. Alan bought a couple of six-packs of Longboard Island Lager, which is the best-selling draft beer in the state and brewed in Kailua-Kona. Dale and Fred put fishing lines into the water to troll while we cruised to one of Tamé's favorite fishing areas, and we honored Tamé's memory by christening the rod and reels with the local beer. Tamé had a special dance he did while splashing beer around, which was kind of like a crazy native dancing around a cauldron of missionary soup. If a bone through the nose had been stylish at the time, Tamé would have been wearing one.

Dale throttled back down to an idle, and we assembled at the transom to say goodbye to Tamé. Everyone said a few words. I opened the container and poured the ashes into the water. As they sank, the sky and the sea came together and created refracted rays that gave brilliance to the ashes as they drifted downward. It was a color of blue that only a fisherman has ever seen. It's the sparkle and hue of a live fish before it's taken from the water.

Dale had thoughtfully picked loose flowers to sprinkle upon the surface of Tamé's watery grave. The ashes were gone. Only the flowers remained, and they drifted further and further away.

There were no tears shed. Tamé would have expected a party, and so we partied. We broke out the cold beer and toasted, drank, and fished. Although we didn't catch anything that day, it was a glorious and memorable time spent on the Sea Strike.

We flew back to O'ahu, rented another car, and drove to our room at Makaha Resort, where we'd left most of our belongings before leaving for the overnight trip to the Big Island. Our Castle High School forty-year reunion was everything Sandy and I had hoped it would be. We hadn't seen most of our classmates since graduating and would never have recognized them without the name tags.

While in Hawai'i we also attended a planning meeting for my other alma mater, Aiea High School Class of 1967 forty-year reunion. Although I couldn't be there for the event, I was thrilled to be among my Aiea classmates again. They were the surfers and friends of an older me. The Castle crowd was from small-kid days, but Aiea held wonderful memories of being a surfer and having friendships with others who understand what that means.

I reunited with my best friend from the glory days of surfing Rest Camp. Mavis and I had totally lost touch with each other, but after a few phone conversations and seeing her in person, it was as if we'd hardly been separated a year, much less forty. We were treated to the best Hawai'ian style potluck imaginable at the planning meeting, and Alan and Fred were in local-food heaven.

One of our class leaders and event planner for the reunion party and trip would become a good friend and ally in the years to come as I stumbled and fell into the role of a community organizer from Hawai'i.

Chapter 31

Code Red Rally

After we said goodbye to Tame´ and Mom and returned home from Hawai'i, we went back to our routines. Alan was back in Tulsa, Fred went back to work, and I was alone again. On pretty days I spent hours grooming the horses, working in the yard or taking a ride in the woods with my dogs. They took turns leading and following depending on where an intriguing scent took them. Except for the animals, I had little responsibility, and I liked it that way. I was finally living the quiet existence I'd always wanted to have.

Fred and I had no political leanings. In Hawai'i we rarely voted. Our attitude, like many others, was that all politicians are crooks so you could vote for your favorite criminal. We didn't bother. Moving to Oklahoma changed us a little. If Fred wanted to work for the sheriff's department, he needed to be a Democrat, especially if he ever considered running for sheriff, which he did. Most people in our county were registered Democrats just so they would be able to vote at all.

In December of 1999 Fred was working as a detective for Jack Harkins, Ottawa County Sheriff. We were at a Christmas party at a friend's house when Fred got the call that Sheriff Harkins had been killed by his wife. The news was stunning. There had never been any indication of problems in the sheriff's personal life. Fred would be the lead detective investigating the killing, so we left the party together to make the long drive to the Harkins residence.

Mrs. Harkins had been angry about custody issues regarding their grandson. When her husband refused to use his high-profile position to influence the court, she killed him in a fit of rage, driving a steak knife into his heart. She immediately called 911 and confessed. She was sentenced to a year in jail, which was later suspended, creating a furor among the deputies who regarded Jack Harkins with great respect and admiration. After a long succession of corrupt and indicted sheriffs,

Harkins had been elected for his background in private-sector business instead of politics as usual.

"She got away with murder" was the prevailing sentiment.

Harkins had served more than two years of the four-year term, and, therefore, the three county commissioners would select a candidate instead of holding a special election. It was then that Fred and I registered to vote as Democrats. Fred and others submitted résumés. Fred was by far the most qualified applicant and chosen by two of the three commissioners, but cronyism ruled the day when the third commissioner, who later resigned under a cloud of controversy, held out for his candidate.

A compromise was reached. Dennis King would be sheriff, and Fred would be the undersheriff. But King had someone else in mind to be next in command and so created a second undersheriff position. Fred would be in charge of law enforcement, and Larry Glenn would oversee the jail facilities. King would win the next election cycle and, no longer under any agreement with the commissioners, demoted Fred back to chief of detectives and promoted Larry Glenn to official undersheriff. Sick of the politics, Fred would eventually quit the department, but for the time being he was a Democrat, take it or leave it, and so was I.

Sometime around spring of 2008 we received a campaign card in the mail promoting Barack Obama for president. The nice-looking man in the photo sounded very good to me. His message of hope and change to bring our country together was a good message. The United States was slipping into mediocrity, and the candidate promised to make America strong and its people united. I read every word on both sides of the glossy mailer and set it aside to write a check for $75 as the campaign requested. I never sent a check. The more I learned about the flashy candidate, the more frightened I became of him.

On the morning of March 19, 2010, I received a call from Gary Jones, Oklahoma State GOP chairman. We had a long conversation, and Mr. Jones was successful in talking me into running as a Republican instead of an Independent. He said I was a very viable candidate, and he wanted me to come to a GOP dinner being held in Muskogee that evening. J. C. Watts, former Oklahoma University quarterback and U.S. congressman from Oklahoma's 4th District, was the keynote speaker. The candidates running for the U.S. House from District 2 would be speaking as well, and that included me if I wanted to. Mr. Jones said he would announce my decision to run as a Republican, and several people he wanted me to meet would be there. I told him I would go to Muskogee to meet him but wasn't able to stay for the dinner because I was meeting a group of people that evening in Tulsa and driving to D.C. for the "Code Red" rally — our last attempt to kill the Obamacare bill.

Gary Jones would be at the dinner early and so would the event planners and District 2 candidates. My opponents would be there in advance to set up booths, and the event planners and hosts would be putting up the final touches for the $100-a-plate GOP function. I was meeting the "Code Red" group at six o'clock in the evening in Tulsa, so I had ample time to meet Mr. Jones and the dinner hosts before the start of their event.

Few cars were in the parking lot of the meeting hall. It was the same building where the Muskogee Tea Party and GOOOH meeting were held so I was familiar with it. I walked in, dressed totally inappropriately for a banquet dinner in my jeans and T-shirt, but I wasn't staying. I dressed instead for a 1,300-mile non-stop drive to D.C.

I saw two ladies carrying boxes into the banquet room and recognized them as Jeremy Vaught's mother and sister. The younger woman turned and saw me, did a double take, hustled over to her mother, and whispered in her ear. Mrs. Vaught whipped her head around and looked at me. They whispered conspiratorially and threw their heads back and laughed loudly. When their son arrived, I watched them point me out and all three laughed. People began arriving and I introduced myself to a friendly face who said he would point Gary Jones out to me when he arrived. I went outside to wait and recognized one of my opponents, Howard Houchen, who shook my hand. I found him to be very friendly and funny — someone I thought would be fun to hang out with. Dan Arnett, a tall, nice-looking young man, showed up and introduced himself. We were all running against Dan Boren, and I was pleased to finally meet Howard and Dan in person and soon would have the opportunity to debate them. We talked and joked for few minutes. Both men knew about the Code Red rally and wanted to go, but chose instead to attend the dinner. J. C. Watts arrived and came over to talk to us. He towered above me and brought himself down to my level when he shook my hand and spoke to me. I'd never met J.C., but I recognized him the minute he stepped out of his car. Howard and Dan told him I was another candidate for the 2nd District and that I'd challenged Boren to a debate and shooting match. J. C. burst out laughing and I thought, "Man, what beautiful white teeth he has," and made a mental note to tell Fred about that. J. C. asked me to keep him posted on my challenge to Boren. They all thanked me for going to protest the bill, and we all went inside the building.

Gary Jones had arrived, and the nice man who looked for him brought him over to meet me. After our long telephone conversation earlier that day, we both felt we already knew each other. Mr. Jones would announce my candidacy change to GOP at the dinner. He wanted to introduce me to the hosts and head of the Republican Party of Muskogee, the Vaughts. I let him know I already knew them and left for Tulsa.

When I got home from the Code Red rally I wrote the following letter:

March 25, 2010
Dear Editor,

I am among a large contingent of Americans who are fed up with the politics of both parties and changed affiliation to Independent or none. In January I threw my hat into the political ring by registering to run as an Independent candidate for the U.S. House of Representatives in District 2 Oklahoma, the seat currently held by Dan Boren.

There are four Republicans that will be on the primary election ballot, and as of Friday I became the fifth by announcing my decision to return to the Republican Party. Today the change is reflected on the Federal Election Commission website, fec.gov.

Last Saturday, March 20, was a critical day for America. Thousands answered the "Code Red" call to get to our nation's capital to protest the massive entitlement bill that we cannot afford and most Americans don't want. This massive 2,000-page monstrosity being hawked as "healthcare reform" is nothing more than a government takeover of one-sixth of our economy and heavily laced with "goodies" and paybacks to Democrats in Congress, their allies and supporters.

I was one of the 40,000 or so Americans that stood outside the Capitol building shouting, "Kill the Bill!" and "USA!" We don't want our country turning into a socialist nation, and yet this is where we are rapidly heading under the dictates of this president, his administration, and a far-left "progressive" congress. No matter people from all 50 states and a group of us from Oklahoma that drove non-stop the 1,300 miles to make a last plea to stop the takeover, we ultimately lost the healthcare battle.

But we haven't lost entirely. All indications are good for conservatives to reclaim the Senate and the House in November, but party politics could ruin our chances if Republicans don't change the way they do business. And by this I mean it's less about money than it is adhering to the Constitution as the law of the land: the difference between attending a $100-a-plate fundraising dinner in Muskogee or driving 1,300 miles non-stop to defend the Constitution of the United States of America.

Respectfully submitted,
Miki Booth
Candidate for U.S. House of Representatives
Wyandotte, OK

Conservative newspapers printed it for supporting the Constitution. Liberal newspapers printed it for slamming the Republicans. It got a lot a play. I was pleased.

U.S. House Members Break Gallery Rules and Use Alinsky Tactics to Silence Opposition

HEALTH CARE PROTEST RALLY ATTENDEE SAYS BEHAVIOR OF DEMOCRAT HOUSE MEMBERS "MAKES ME SICK AND DISGUSTED"
by Sharon Rondeau, The Post & Email

(March 24, 2010) — Miki Booth, candidate for Congress from the second district of Oklahoma, drove all night last Friday to be in the nation's capital over the weekend for a final rally against socialized medicine, which one poll says 59 percent of Americans oppose but the Obama regime has now pushed through anyway.

Ms. Booth reports that the Capitol police were less than cordial. When she and several other anti-healthcare-reform protesters were standing together in a small group, the police told them to move, stating, "The other group has a permit." Miki told them that she was there as a *private citizen, and the police's response was, "If you're standing here together, you're a crowd, so you'll have to move. I'll give you three warnings and then I'll arrest you." With the exception of a Capitol policewoman, pictured above, Miki reports that the group of seven from Oklahoma of which she was a part was constantly told to, "Get off the sidewalk!" They were then told to get off the road.*

At one point, when Miki asked the police where they could go if neither the sidewalk nor the road were allowed, she was told to, "Go over there behind that tree." She said she observed a Capitol policeman carrying a shotgun, and others had assault rifles. She also reported a stark difference in the way black Capitol policemen treated black and non-black demonstrators. Miki said she observed no police harassment of those who supported illegal immigration and the healthcare bill.

Miki estimates that there were over 40,000 people demonstrating on Saturday against Obamacare. On the north side of the Capitol on Saturday night, thousands were chanting "Kill the Bill!" and "We will remember in November!" when Congressman Steve King (R-IA) emerged with a bull horn. He spoke to the crowd, thanked them for their support and stated that congressional Republicans "were inspired." He added, "You're so loud they can't hear themselves in there!" King then shook hands with many of the healthcare bill protesters as he made his way across the street.

On Sunday, the pro-illegal-immigration group, La Raza, which had not been there Saturday, set up a stage complete with a sound system and entertainment. Miki said that some of the members supporting La Raza began taunting members of her group, and at one point a fight almost broke out. She said for the most part, those supporting the U.S. Constitution's limits on congressional power "did not take the bait." In some instances, the constitutionalists presented a "calm, rational plan" to those who supported the healthcare bill rather than succumb to the taunting.

Miki reports that no one from the "mainstream media" reported on those protesting the healthcare bill; however, they were spotted at the La Raza activities on Sunday. Miki saw only Internet reporters covering the protests in which she and approximately 40,000 others against healthcare reform were involved.

Early on Sunday afternoon, having noticed the prominent brown and yellow flag of the Tulsa (OK) 9.12 Project, Congresswoman Virginia Foxx (R-NC) asked the capitol police to move the barricade to the congressional members'-only entrance of the House Gallery and invited Miki's group to observe the pre-vote proceedings. Miki handed the congresswoman a brochure and a "push" card detailing her campaign for Congress for Oklahoma, and Ms. Foxx reportedly replied, "This is providential."

Miki observed a statue of Father Damian* in the long hallway that led to the House chamber. She said that "there were guards everywhere." Once in the House Gallery, Miki said that the rules of that chamber were enforced strictly, but only for some.

Seated in front of her group were four men who were the object of Congressman Barney Frank's (D-MA) attention throughout the entire time that they were there. The rules in the gallery of the House chamber were clear: no leaning over the railing, no talking while someone was speaking on the House floor, and guests had to remain seated during the presentations. Miki reported that the men sitting in front of her were exchanging conversation and greetings with Barney Frank constantly throughout the House proceedings as well as leaning over the railing, something that was clearly posted as not permitted. Miki observed no guard attempting to bring them to order despite the rules.

However, Miki saw that when a Republican House member spoke, many of the guests in the gallery applauded, but because the chamber rules prohibit applause, guards swooped down "like ducks on a June bug," telling them to stop clapping. No such discipline was imposed on Rep. Sheila Jackson-Lee (D-TX), Nancy Pelosi (D-CA), and Louise Slaughter (D-NY), who reportedly maintained their own conversations and social interactions while Republicans were trying to speak on the floor. Booth feels that "this is part of their whole battle plan — using Alinsky tactics to marginalize the opposition. She also said that Congresswoman Slaughter could not put a coherent sentence together when it was time for her to speak.

Republicans repeatedly asked for order to be restored in the chamber as Democrats laughed and waved to people up in the balcony of the gallery. Miki reports that the Democrats were so loud that at several points, the House secretary had to bang his gavel three times so that the person trying to speak could be heard. As a Republican from California was addressing the House members, the four men seated in front of Miki's group had their own conversation amongst themselves. Booth said she was especially appalled at the behavior of Congressman Anthony Wiener, whom she said was "the biggest offender" by his entrance to the

House during the proceedings, making "big gestures" to people, and never sitting down. She said that while the Republicans were "respectful" when others were speaking, the Democrats were loud and disrespectful as they were seen "fleeting around" within the chamber of the U.S. House of Representatives.

Miki heard some Republicans mention the U.S. Constitution in their addresses, but she said she did not hear one Democrat do so.

As the final vote came late, Miki and some of her Oklahoma delegation had already begun the 1300-mile trip home. During that time, she received a call from one of the Oklahomans who had remained in Washington and was told that the bill had passed. In response, Miki said, "I felt terrible about it. I knew they were going to do it. But I detest them for what they're doing to us, and it makes me sick and disgusted. I'm not going to let them get away with this."

When Virginia Foxx was taking me through the security checkpoints in the Capitol she said, "This is providential," when I told her I was running for a seat in the House. I believe she wanted me to bear witness and tell everyone I spoke to as I campaigned, about the Constitution and the People's House being trashed and treated with contempt and disrespect. Writing this book is the only way I know how.

Father Damien de Veuster, a Roman Catholic priest from Belgium, dedicated his life to patients of Hansen's disease (leprosy) who had been placed under quarantine on the island of Moloka`i. He cared for the physical, spiritual, and emotional needs of those in the leper colony and after 16 years of ministry, contracted the disease and died on April 15, 1889.

Chapter 32

Dr. Manning's CIA-Columbia Sedition Treason Trial

Columbia Trial Has Ended with "Guilty" Verdict
*COLUMBIA UNIVERSITY AND OBAMA ACCUSED OF LYING AND
DEFRAUDING THE AMERICAN PEOPLE*
by Sharon Rondeau
The Post & Email

*(May 19, 2010) — According to eyewitness Miki Booth, the Columbia
Trial ended yesterday with a verdict of "guilty" on all charges after a
three-hour deliberative period. The Post & Email has covered the events
of previous days of the trial.*

*Editor's Note: An Ixquick search for Mikhail Kryzhanovsky, who is
mentioned extensively below, yields two results, both of which link to
completely unrelated material. However, another search yields a related
post which has not been vetted.*

SHARON: How did yesterday's testimony go?

*MIKI: It went very well. I was the first on the stand, and I showed the
birth certificates that I had from Kapi'olani Hospital. Then Rev. Manning
read a letter from a KGB/CIA operative who has fallen out of grace with
the agencies and has been pretty much pushed out to fend for himself so
he has nothing to lose.*

SHARON: Did he work for the KGB or CIA, or both?

*MIKI: He was a double agent. From what I understand, this letter
was also put out there on the Internet, but I haven't seen it. His name is
Mikhail Kryzhanovsky. He was involved in a program called "Millennium
Hilton Conspiracy." He claims that Obama was a CIA operative in
Pakistan and Afghanistan and traveled freely through the area. The
consensus is that Obama's passport was Kenyan, and the reason is that
the investigative reporter, Al Landry, who testified by Skype earlier in the
week, was explaining that the roster that is maintained of people*

traveling into the country lists the names, country of origin, and the country issuing the passport. That would make sense to me, having traveled internationally. They keep a record of where you're from.

Kryzhanovsky reported that Obama was supplying money, guns and resources to the Mujahideen to fight the Russian invasion of Afghanistan, which we know happened. So you're going to have to ask yourself, "Well, who were the people who were supplying the money to perhaps even the Taliban?" That's why you have to ask the question, and the answer would be people just like Obama who, according to his book (and there's a big question on whether or not he even wrote that; Bill Ayers might have had a big role in it), was essentially a loner. The only friends he had, according to what he has said, were Muslims or foreigners. If you read the names of his friends, they weren't black Americans.

SHARON: In his book, he said he "sought out the foreign students."

MIKI: Absolutely. So that's who he is. His tendency was to hang out with Islamic students. Neither Obama nor the roommate he mentions in the book as having transferred with him to Columbia are found at Columbia, and yet, the president of Columbia at that time has not denied that Obama graduated from there, and he is actually aiding and abetting and perpetrating fraud to the American people. So it's pretty-much proven that Obama is a liar. He didn't attend Columbia. So where was he, then? It makes a lot of sense that he was working for the CIA. In that case, he was doing a duty to the American government.

SHARON: There apparently wasn't anything wrong with working for the CIA, if he did?

MIKI: No, but all of this was perpetrated on lies, so he should have been vetted to run for president. There is just absolutely no excuse. Congress, the government, and the DNC are complicit for allowing this to happen, and then you multiply that by all of the voter fraud that went on, which will be proven by the studies, research and lawsuits which are all over the country. Multiply that with the funds for his campaign coming from foreign countries: that's going to be proven.

SHARON: Is anyone looking into that?

MIKI: Yes, and I can't say specifically who right now, but I know that's happening. With all of this information that has come out of the trial, these people who are involved in this are shaking in their boots. At the trial, Rev. Manning said that the CIA had a "hit" on him, but the person who was given the order refused to do it.

SHARON: I read that last night.

MIKI: So there's a break within the CIA. The crack has happened, and Columbia is the giant crack, and we're going to keep pounding on these things. Now that the trial has found them guilty on all of these charges, the American Grand Jury will be serving not presentments, but indictments. It's going to take a couple of weeks to get this done, but the American people are going to be serving these indictments on governors, sheriffs in every single county where we can, elected officials, attorneys general, and district attorneys. There are so many people coming on board, and the news is traveling like wildfire throughout the United States. We're going to have so many numbers of people who have been waiting, asking, "What can we do?" This gives them something specifically to do, because Barack Obama and the president of Columbia University were found guilty of the fourteen or so charges brought.

At any rate, Columbia cracked the thing right open, because there's the blatant lie, and the big mistake that the CIA didn't take care of. They neglected to put evidence there to make Columbia look as if it were legitimate.

SHARON: They're not usually sloppy, are they?

MIKI: No, they're not, but they made huge mistakes, too, when they tried to go "fix" a problem that happened in the passport office, and then somebody ended up getting killed.

SHARON: Yes, that was horrible.

MIKI: So it is two years later, and they still haven't solved that case, and it's in the hands of the local police, not the FBI or the CIA. The local police are trying to solve the case of Lt. Quarles Harris, so it's cracking open.

Getting back to the letter from the CIA agent, he has very specific questions which the prosecutor, Rev. Manning, was reading. It was a little too fast for me to write all of it down, but Obama's assignment was from 1981 to 1985. I have the name here of Patrick Fitzgerald.

SHARON: The D.A. in the Chicago area?

MIKI: They're all complicit in the whole thing about Blagojevich, Valerie Jarrett; they're all in on this. Remember Biden said about Obama that he was "clean"? That's because he has no record; there's nothing. You can't find a traffic ticket or anything like that. This man has no past.

There was supposed to be an indictment in December by the federal prosecutor, Patrick Fitzgerald, in Chicago that never happened. That was one of the questions that Kryzhanovsky asked, "Why it didn't happen?" Another thing he said was that the whole Obama administration is a carryover from the Clinton administration. The Clinton administration wanted to stay in power no matter what, and so they had a system that was called "the professional system," and it's a KGB-type of plan which uses the authority of the government. It's a plan to overthrow and suppress the opposition party. So they had targeted a number of Republicans who, at any cost, they had to keep them from getting elected. That included assassination, although I don't know that any of that happened. But the plan calls for that.

SHARON: Is this plan written anywhere?

MIKI: Yes, this is in Kryzhanovsky's letter which Rev. Manning was reading. As far as the plan goes, Rev. Manning said that Columbia aided and abetted, part and parcel, obstructing facts and not cooperating. That was one of the charges against Columbia.

Kryzhanovsky's letter stated something to the effect of "nothing to lose" to participate, and basically, he ended up on the street in Russia with no money and no job because the promises they made to him to bring him and his family to the United States, they reneged on.

SHARON: Who was it who made these promises?

MIKI: The U.S. government — the CIA. They're all in this together. He kept talking about somebody named Deutch, who was the ringleader of this conspiracy, and it includes Clinton, Panetta, Rahm Emanuel . . .

SHARON: Could this explain why a lot of ex-Clinton administration people have ended up serving under Obama?

MIKI: Absolutely. It became just a carryover with a new person in the presidential spot.

SHARON: So the KBG/CIA agent submitted a letter of things that he claims he had seen?

MIKI: Bob Campbell from American Grand Jury said that he saw it online.

SHARON: Oh, OK.

MIKI: So they did everything in their power, including voter fraud, etc., to get the Democrats back in power so it would just be a carryover with the forced-down healthcare bill that Hillary wasn't able to get. Among other things, you take over the transportation, healthcare, and so forth . . . and the plan is to turn the United States into a socialist nation. That's the main plan. As they were conspiring to do all of this, somebody said that this young man who worked for them in the CIA would be perfect to be president. So then all of the work went to getting him on the ballot.

SHARON: And obfuscating his past?

MIKI: Yes. They had to do that to get him on the ballot. A lot of the story we know from there. Nancy Pelosi has committed fraud on the letters of nomination that she signed. We have to ask that question, "Why were there two, and why was that clause taken off?" We have to nail her on that, and it's coming. American Grand Jury is working on that.

I mentioned "Victoria" in Virginia to you before; she's part of the Richmond Patriots. I joined the group, and they have a lot of members; I don't even know how many. It's kind of like a Facebook thing. I'm really enjoying being in that group.

SHARON: What are they involved in?

MIKI: They're doing research, and the State of Virginia is going to be really good friend to us because of the Attorney General, Ken Cuccinelli, and the governor are going to work together. We're going to get the information about Nancy Pelosi signing the two different forms to them, and they're going to carry it forward; at least it sounds as if they will.

SHARON: I know AG Cuccinelli was the first one to sue over the healthcare mandate. Is Victoria or are both of you saying that he has given an indication that he will now go forward in prosecuting Obama for ineligibility?

MIKI: Not yet, no. He hasn't done that. The only thing he's done is what you just said about the healthcare bill.

SHARON: I know people have written to him and asked him, instead of a very expensive lawsuit on behalf of the Commonwealth of Virginia on the healthcare mandate, which is questionably unconstitutional, why not go after Obama for not being eligible to sign it?

MIKI: As far as I know, he hasn't committed to that, but personally, I know he's aware, and personally I know that he has shown an interest in getting all the information about the two different DNC nomination forms.

SHARON: Was there any thought on the part of the former KGB/CIA agent as to why Obama was chosen?

MIKI: Because they knew him, and they said he had done good work for them on the Millennium Hotel project, which was the Pakistan deal. It included the bank where his mother worked, Asia Development Bank. So that's all tied in: the money and the arms, the bank, Obama's Social Security numbers for the money laundering, getting the money through Pakistan into Afghanistan to fight the Russians.

SHARON: How much influence did the KGB agent think foreign countries had in getting Obama into office?

MIKI: He didn't really go into that, but my conjecture is that another Columbia connection is the professor, Rashid al-Khalidi, is a personal friend of Obama's, and in Obama's book, it says that the professor and his wife spent "many a late night over the kitchen table." So he had to be instrumental in making the recommendation for Obama to get into Harvard with the Columbia credentials, probably made-up stuff, to get into Harvard. Somewhere in my notes, there's the name of a person who made the recommendation and then later retracted it. So there's another Columbia connection in there.

With that connection and the Arab connection influencing American elections, we don't know and can't prove it, but everyone was talking about the fact that Obama raised close to one billion dollars to fund his campaign, and again, he lied. He said he was going to take the public money, which was limited, and John McCain pledged to do that, and then he ends up with almost one billion dollars. Can we go to the FEC website and look at who his donors were the way you can for me?

So where did that money come from? And even if it wasn't put into his campaign account, where else could all of this money go from a foreign country? There's no telling. But when you look at how many dirty dealings during his campaign, the donations from Mickey Mouse and the basketball team and other phony names, plus picking up homeless people and giving them cigarettes through ACORN... we know all of this happened. The facts that we do know came out in the trial, all of these things tie in so neatly that you have to ask yourself, "How could it be anything else" This all just makes such perfect sense for anyone who has any common sense at all.

SHARON: Who else testified besides the KGB agent and you yesterday?

MIKI: No one, just closing arguments from Rev. Manning.

SHARON: Did the jury vote after that?

MIKI: Yes, they were in deliberation for three hours. The double agent's account kept posing questions.

SHARON: So he himself wants answers to things?

MIKI: He is saying that we can prove these things if you ask them these specific questions. He suggested asking them, "Did you do this?" and if they answered, "Yes," then your follow-up question should be, "Then you will step down" or "When will you step down?" or "We want *your resignation if you did this." There's a suggested question: "Did John Deutch recruit KGB Filament?" Filament was the code name for somebody, and I think that's referring to Obama. So we have to get that word out there — "Filament" — because that's going to scare the pants off the CIA.*

SHARON: Does anyone know if he fulfilled the four-year commitment from 1981 to 1985?

MIKI: Yes, that was his term of service.

SHARON: And did he perform well?

MIKI: Yes. They knew he was effective, and he never blew his cover. They knew that they could trust him with the job they gave him. The first question posed out there was, "Did you recruit KGB Filament?" I don't know if "Filament" was the group or the mission; it might have been a mission. And then, "If yes, explain the purpose of 'Filament.' "

SHARON: Of whom will these questions now be asked?

MIKI: We have to find out who John Deutch is, because it could be "Did John Deutch recruit somebody as a KGB Filament," and, if yes, "Explain the purpose." And then another question was, "Did you teach Democrats to use this plan to socialize the American people?"

I just found in my notes that John Deutch was with the CIA, and we can check this: "Did Clinton pardon Deutch?"

SHARON: I will research that name.

MIKI: They also were getting their hands into immigration and sanctioning of Republican senators, meaning making trouble for them. Another question was about the "professional system." Clinton, the CIA and the staff were all involved in this, and we were urged to ask Clinton why he pardoned Deutch. Also, ask Rahm Emanuel, White House chief of staff, about why he continued destabilization of the American people through the "KGB plan" socialism program, keeping us all riled up, basically. I have to say we are destabilized, and this is all part of the "professional program."

SHARON: When you say "destabilized," do you mean economically?

MIKI: Yes, absolutely. As a whole, the healthcare crammed down, and the deficit, and all of these things, it's all part of it. Every bit of it is the plan. I like to use the term which I've used in sales all of my life: you plan your work and then you work your plan. And this is exactly what they're doing. Panetta really needs to be put on the stand; we need to ask him, "What did you know about 'Filament?' And why now is the CIA not concerned about Russia, but they're concerned about the American people?" They're concerned about us. Basically, we're enemies: Rev. Manning, and investigations he's doing; the Tea Party people are to be watched; we're pushing back and we're asking the questions, and they're just pulling their same Alinsky tactics: isolate us, freeze us, whatever.

SHARON: Is Hillary Clinton as much a part of this conspiracy as Obama?

MIKI: Yes, she is. She had brought up a lot of questions about his past; she was the one who was putting the word out there about his background, and what about this and what about that? Then she just shut up totally.

SHARON: Why would she have fallen silent?

MIKI: I think that she really wanted to be the person who became president, but her husband and the powers that be who were working on this didn't want her; they wanted Obama because he was black so he could get the black vote. Also, part of their plan is elevating the Muslim people, and that is quite evident in that transition team report, the one where Nidal Hasan was one of the task force members. All of these things tie in, because whomever they were grooming for Homeland Security (not so much Napolitano, who's there now); somebody else was instrumental in setting that up the way that it was set up and had a big, big influence in that presidential transition team.

This is speculation on my part, but I think they picked Janet Napolitano only because she runs with that pack, but I don't think that she was part of setting up all of this; they just gave her a role, and she's fulfilling the role. Because she runs with that pack, she is looking at us like the enemy . . . the returning vets . . . we're the ones to be concerned about because we're supposedly the radicals and be the next McVeigh. That's what they're doing to us. So that's why I believe that she was just installed after the decisions were already made.

SHARON: I know you said that testimony is over, the jury has voted, so everything is over. What is the next step?

MIKI: In about two weeks, the American Grand Jury is going to have the indictments prepared, and people are going to be able to go to the website and become a member and sign up as a jury member. There are going to be a lot of people who want to get involved by doing that. Then there will be people who want to take it a step further and will take the indictments to an elected official and serve it to them. A number of people are going to have different roles in doing this, but we're going to set a goal of 1,000,000 to get involved and become members. When we have that many people out there and serving, we're going to try to serve in every single county across the United States to serve these indictments to elected officials: county sheriffs, governors, attorneys general, and they were talking about judges, but we may not do that because we'd rather keep it simple. We want to make sure that we're going to get it to the officials who are going to take it to the next step and do something about it.

SHARON: I know American Grand Jury has been involved in doing that for over a year. What could be done differently to get a better response from elected officials?

MIKI: The difference is that what was done before were the presentments including Walter Fitzpatrick's criminal complaint. There are a number of cases, perhaps 100, that are sitting in various courthouses because they don't know what to do with it. They're scared. There are so many of these counties that don't know what to do with something like this. So they're waiting to see someone else do it or what's going to happen, or maybe they're Democrats who love Obama and love the situation of being on the dole who don't want anything like this to move forward. But we're finding out that there are a lot of people who do want answers, so what will be different is that it's not the presentment of Fitzpatrick that has been out there; this is different because it's indictments on charges that Obama, Columbia, and the president of Columbia were found guilty. So these are the charges on which they were found guilty.

SHARON: So it has nothing to do with where Obama was born or his eligibility, then?

MIKI: That's correct. It's about dishonesty, and a cover-up and perhaps a plot to undermine our form of government.

SHARON: What will happen if the officials who receive the indictments refuse to act?

MIKI: Another thing we're doing is calling our representatives in Congress and demanding that they open an investigation into the alleged cover-up, because really, they're the only ones who can investigate the CIA.

Another note I have is that "Filament" is involved in 2012, so something is coming up about that. So it's ongoing, and I think now they're a little bit leery. Because this information is becoming public, they have to be careful about doing specific things. They didn't care when they were planning how it was going to be carried out. I think one of the glaring examples of allowing only certain congressmen to get in and trying to suppress the Republicans whom they didn't want in there was that whole fiasco with Al Franken and Coleman. That is the perfect example. They made it work; no matter what, he was in there. Just like the healthcare bill; no matter what, it got done. And no matter what, if he says that they're going to have immigration reform, or amnesty — if they set their mind to it, it's going to get done because the way that they're doing it is so hard to prove that there's any wrongdoing. We know it's wrongdoing, but how do we stop it? Just as we couldn't stop them getting the healthcare bill done.

SHARON: Because the Congress is voting on it, and they're the elected representatives of the people.

MIKI: Yes. And the only recourse we have is the states filing suit and exercising their Tenth Amendment rights.

SHARON: Is there any evidence that there are other elected officials who are aware of what this double agent has been saying or that they're doing something about it?

MIKI: I don't know if Cuccinelli knows about any of this. They're working on the healthcare bill and suing the government, but I don't think he knows any of this yet. But he seems to be on our side over the fraud that Nancy Pelosi and the DNC perpetrated, so he's aware of that and is interested in looking into it. But I'll tell you who would be interested in this, and if he doesn't know, I know he's going to pick up on it pretty quickly: Gino DiSimone. We already know that he's on our side and will do anything he can to expose this government and help take our country back. There are a lot of elected officials out there who are giving lip service to the Constitution and upholding their oath, but they haven't demonstrated that. So that's why Tea Parties and all of the freedom groups are looking at the people who have a record of doing the right thing, and we're going to be careful about who we put into Congress.

I can't specifically tell you who the true patriots are because there haven't been any demonstrating that they are. However, there are a number that the Tea Parties are finding and helping to get elected who are saying all of the right things. Even in my case in Oklahoma, there are four Republicans that I'm running against, and all of us are newbies. We've never been involved in politics before, but we've learned enough over the past two years, seeing the criminal actions of this government, and we're fighting back. As for myself, anybody can look for my name and go and look at my record for the past two years and see how I *founded a Tea Party, have been involved with FairTax, have been involved with the GOOOH program and fighting for the past two years. I have records that people can see that I don't just talk the talk; I do the right thing as far as loving this country and doing as much as I can to get our country back and put the criminals in government behind bars.*

The Post & Email.

After returning home from the trial in New York City, I had a clearer picture of what I needed to do with my future. For one, I would drop out of my bid for the U.S. House of Representatives. More and more, my heart wasn't in it. Even in the beginning, I never really relished the idea of working in the cesspool of the federal government, especially in Congress. I loved my life in Oklahoma finally free of stress and worry as I entered my "sunset" years. But I had really believed I could win the vote of the Constitutional Conservatives in Oklahoma and knew I could never be compromised in my dedication to the intent of our founding fathers when I went to Washington. Being called the "birther candidate" by political blogger Jeremy Vaught didn't bother me because I knew I had a large following of Article II, Section I natural-born citizen constitutionalists as we were also called. It did bother me that he was a Tea Party leader and had the ear of a lot of people. Personal attacks never came from any of my opponents, and I had great respect for all of them. Before going to the trial, I had the opportunity to debate the other candidates and came away believing that Charles Thompson had the best shot at beating Dan Boren.

I had to decide if I wanted to be on the ballot for the Republican primary on July 27. If so, the deadline to file was June 7 to 9 and would require a $750 filing fee. My campaign was broke, and Fred's and my personal savings and investments were pretty much broke too. The donations that once poured in after my appearance at the Tea Party convention had dried up. There were lots of reasons I would not and could not continue, but the most important reason for dropping out was that I wanted to put my full support behind Charles Thompson.

Thompson was facing huge obstacles to running against Boren. In addition to Boren's $1.3 million war chest, he had the family name. His father, David Boren, was once Oklahoma governor and U.S. Congress-man, and the younger Boren was following in his father's footsteps. The fact that the elder Boren was a member of the Council on Foreign Relations (CFR) wasn't lost on me. The same machine that put Obama in power would do the same for their Oklahoma son. The party would make sure Boren was reelected no matter what. Just like making Rahm Emanuel mayor of Chicago. No matter what needed to happen to put people into the positions they wanted and needed to have, they would make it happen, no matter what, even if it meant lying, cheating, scheming, and even killing. Just ask L. Quarles Harris and the three homosexual members of Obama's former church, Trinity United. But they can't answer — they're dead.

I called Thompson and pledged my full support and then went about the business of notifying everyone by e-mailing, blogging, writing letters to the editor, and distributing a press release by ghostwriter "Cinnamon Fowler":

FOR IMMEDIATE RELEASE
CONTACT: Cinnamon Fowler
Email:route66teaparty@yahoo.com

Boren Challenger Favored by Tea Parties
Retired Army Maj. and Veterinarian Charles Thompson to Speak at 9.12 Rally,

Miami, OK, September 10, 2010 - Since Dan Boren, (D) was elected to the U.S. House of Representatives in 2004 from Oklahoma's 2nd Congressional District, his political career has run mostly unchallenged. With the Boren family name, NRA endorsements, big oil money and favored by Speaker of the House Nancy Pelosi, to serve on prestigious committees, he could breeze into a fourth term.

But Tea Party leader and former challenger, Miki Booth (I), is quick to point out that Boren's constituents are tired of the politics as usual, and the form letters generated by his office in response to serious inquiries regarding national issues are "disappointing" and "insulting."

She further claims that requests for debates and meetings by herself and other candidates have been ignored. "Mr. Boren is very well liked in our district. Everyone will tell you that he's a 'nice guy' and that he's going to be 'really tough to beat,' but the conservative and Tea Party movement is huge in Oklahoma and Charles Thompson is getting phenomenal support because he's a true Constitutional Conservative."

Thompson, a retired Army Major and veterinarian, who looks very much the part of a leader with his officer carriage and booming speaking voice, is in great demand to appear at rallies and county fairs. "Even in a big crowd you feel like he's talking directly to you," said Jay Calan, local rancher and small-business owner.

Thompson won the Republican nomination in the primary held July 27. "He became the front-runner the moment he appeared on the scene," Catherine White of the Ada, Oklahoma, Tea Party remembers. "He's not in our district so we can't vote for him, but we can sure support him a lot of other ways. He's our best bet to replace the last remaining Democrat Oklahoma has in Washington." White refers to the fact that four of the five congressional house seats are currently held by Republicans as well the Senate seats held by Sen. Jim Inhofe and Dr. Tom Coburn.

The number of registered Democrats far exceeds Republicans and Independents, but they vote conservatively, as evidenced by the state Legislature. "We have the opportunity in November to replace our liberal governor, Brad Henry, with conservative Mary Fallin, but it's kind of frightening to realize so many people are oblivious to what's happening in state and national politics and the dire straits our country is in," says Tad Snyder, who recently moved to the area from Alaska. "I see a lot of Jeri Askins (D) for Governor signs around, and it would be disastrous if people just voted for her because she has the most signs."

A similar concern is voiced by Cris Kurtz, founder of Tulsa's USA Patriots (District 1 OK), who feels that unseating Obama supporter Dan Boren is important and a very worthwhile endeavor. "We see Charles Thompson as a strong contender against the incumbent. Our group of patriots likes his qualifications: formal military, formal education, and business owner. To beat a system that selects the winner by who has the most money or the most signs will take as much grassroots involvement as we can all rally up," Kurtz is quoted as saying.

"We will make history in November," says Miki Booth. "We expect English as Oklahoma's official language, and banning Sharia law from ever being used in Oklahoma's courts to pass with flying colors, and those colors are red, white, and blue." Booth added, "If the voices of the Tea Parties are as strong in District 2 Oklahoma as they are across the nation, I'm sure we're going to see Charles Thompson in the roster of the 112th Congress."

There was growing support for Thompson in Ottawa County, centered in the small town of Miami. We put together a gathering of supporters, and everyone met at my house to plan the agenda. Each person accepted an action item or would speak at the rally planned to coincide with 9.12 rallies being held all over the county. We needed flyers and handouts. Others would look for a sound system, and everyone would distribute flyers and send e-mails. Thompson would be the main speaker.

We handed out more than 800 flyers around town, but only 100 people showed up. We thought for sure we would get around 200 but found out later about the college kids who had sabotaged our event. Carfuls of students positioned themselves at the entrance to the park where the rally was scheduled and told people the event had been cancelled. It's unknown how many people were turned away. It was the very next day that Google disabled my e-mail account. George Soros's Tea Party Trackers had effectively shut me down at least for the time being.

Charles Thompson didn't win, but we were proud to report that three of the twenty-five counties in District 2 carried him. Although the three counties, Rogers, Delaware, and Ottawa, had more registered Democrats than Republicans, they had the most active Tea Party and conservative groups and turned out for Thompson. I asked him what his thoughts were on losing Muskogee County when Jeremy Vaught and the Muskogee Tea Party were such a huge and active conservative entity there. I wasn't surprised to learn that although Vaught pledged his support to Charles after his favored candidate was defeated, he did nothing to help. Neither did candidate Dan Edmonds. Immediately after the primary, Howard Houchen and Dan Arnett rallied and pledged their support to Charles. Edmonds would not.

Chapter 33

Prisoner No. 89996

I'd heard of the term "kangaroo court" but never really knew what it meant. So I looked it up on Wikipedia and copied it here:

Kangaroo court
From Wikipedia, the free encyclopedia
A kangaroo court or kangaroo trial is a colloquial term for a sham legal proceeding or court. The outcome of a trial by kangaroo court is essentially determined in advance, usually for the purpose of ensuring conviction, either by going through the motions of manipulated procedure or by allowing no defense at all.

A kangaroo court's proceedings deny due process rights in the name of expediency. Such rights include the right to summon witnesses, the right of cross-examination, the right not to incriminate oneself, the right not to be tried on secret evidence, the right to control one's own defense, the right to exclude evidence that is improperly obtained, irrelevant or inherently inadmissible, e.g., hearsay, the right to exclude judges or jurors on the grounds of partiality or conflict of interest, and the right of appeal.

After the kangaroo court martial of Terry Lakin, he was taken into custody, handcuffed and shackled, to begin the punishment handed down by the kangaroo court. I wasn't able to attend. I just didn't have the funds to go to Ft. Meade, Maryland, to show my support for Terry Lakin, but those that did attend were shocked to the core with what they witnessed.

Dr. Kate, well-known conservative political activist and host of the Revolution Radio Show, and I met for the first time in Phoenix on April 16th for a meeting arranged by Jeff Lichter of Arizona to compile evidence that would be given to Michael D. Cohen, executive vice president and special counsel to Donald Trump. At a little known meeting weeks earlier in New York City, Jeff, Arizona State Rep. Carl Seel, and Kelly Townsend, organizer of the Greater Phoenix Tea Party, met with Trump for a brief 30 minutes discussing the Arizona eligibility bill which Trump fully supports and pledged to go to Arizona in June. Wrapping up the meeting when the topic changed to the birth certificate and "natural-born citizen," Trump's time had run out, but he gave a "homework assignment" to Jeff by saying, "I want to know everything about 'natural-born citizen,' and I want to know about these reports from Kenya when members of the Kenyan Parliament had talked about Obama having been born there."

My name had been circulating as the "go to" person for everything one wanted to know about Hawai'ian birth certificates, and I ended up on a list of experts of Obama's frauds, forgeries and other criminal activity. Jeff and a few others located in Arizona put together an impromptu meeting to discuss ideas on how the evidence would be presented. Lyle Rapaki, whom I met at Pastor Manning's trial transcript meeting was going to be there, and I'd just met another Arizona friend of Pastor Manning I wanted to visit so I went to the Arizona meeting, and that's when I met Dr. Kate.

I was late to the meeting, having gotten lost between the airport and Glendale. Dr. Kate was even later, and I didn't know she was even going to be there, but there she was — one of my greatest heroes. I was flabbergasted that she even knew who I was. She even told me I was one of her heroes. Who'd have thought it! After the others left Dr. Kate and I talked for hours. I felt that I'd known her forever. She had gone to Terry Lakin's trial and talking about it didn't come easy for her. She couldn't explain the feeling that came over her when she witnessed Terry's appointed military defense lawyer attack Terry with accusations. Over and over, with "didn't you . . . ? didn't you . . . ?" Dr. Kate's couldn't wrap her mind around what she was hearing and seeing. The man was Terry's defense lawyer, but he was acting every bit the prosecutor.

"Miki, they broke him." Tears filled Kate's eyes, just as they did every time she thought about it. Terry, by then, had been in prison for four months. I asked Kate to tell me more about the trial. I knew that Pastor Manning had been there and was detained for about three hours along with his driver. They were removed from the courtroom by military police, held against their will, and interrogated like common criminals. Pastor Manning was there to bear witness to the travesty but the military machine, bought and paid for by Obama and the Democrat Socialist Party, denied him his constitutional and God-given right to do so.

The Army Treats a Murderer like a Prince but Vilifies Lakin
"INNOCENT UNTIL PROVEN GUILTY" UNLESS YOU'RE QUESTIONING THE USURPER'S ELIGIBILITY
by Miki Booth

(December 18, 2010) — We all know the hell that the Army put LTC Terrence Lakin, Army flight surgeon, through. Makes one wonder what's going on with another Army officer, psychiatrist Nidal Hasan. Surely he's getting special attention. After all, he served on Obama's task force to recommend policy and procedures for Obama's presidency regarding homeland security. The summation of recommendations was implemented to tilt heavily in favor of Muslims and treating anything Islam with political correctness. It stands to reason a different set of rules will apply to Hasan and, in fact, were considered the instant he began killing people on a military base.

Last we checked Hasan has unlimited access to family and friends and more legal advice than he can shake a stick at. Every cohort who knows how to game the system is lined up at Hasan's feet. Will he ever face justice? Will Eric Holder ever weigh in on the prosecution of a Muslim who murdered thirteen people? It's doubtful. He only believes in prosecuting white America. Besides, it's up to the Army, right?

Nidal Hasan is a Muslim terrorist and the U.S. Army knew he was out of control when he made anti-American statements over and over, and they chose to ignore it because of political correctness. Conversely, they persecuted and prosecuted LTC Lakin for questioning Obama's eligibility to be commander in chief. Lakin was denied discovery. Military Judge Col. Denise Lind ruled she would not allow her courtroom to be used to embarrass Obama. After three days of court martial trial at Ft. Meade, Maryland, and a guilty verdict for disobeying orders, the jury deliberated Lakin's punishment. If upheld, he will spend six months in Leavenworth Prison, forfeit his pay, and be dismissed from the service.

Will Lakin have unlimited access to his family in Leavenworth as Hasan has? Upon conviction, Lakin's military pay is cut off, but Hasan continues to receive pay until when, or if, he's convicted of murder and that can be strung out forever. In the meantime, Hasan enjoys the art of using the Constitution against America and We the People, something we've taught Islam how to do very well.

Editor's Note: Why does the military leadership traitorously continue to cover for Obama? Is it that they don't want to give up their pensions, pay, benefits, and prestige? What do they think they will have once Obama has completely destroyed the U.S. government, which is the source of their income? Once there is no more money to pay them and they are left with nothing, as Lt. Col. Lakin is, perhaps they will wish they had spoken out against a foreign national who seized the U.S. presidency by dissembling and deceit.

There is still a treason complaint against Obama that has never been answered. How do Col. Denise Lind and her cohorts respond to that? If Obama can be accused of treason, so can they, for pretending that Obama is legitimate when they know he isn't.

The Post & Email.

Miki Booth: The Constitution Matters to Me
BUT NOT TO OBAMA, WHO HAS OBSCURED EVERYTHING ABOUT HIMSELF
December 22, 2010

Dear Editor:

The following letter was sent to Maj. Gen. Matthew Kemkes, the designee to receive all communications regarding Lt. Col. Terrence Lakin, who was sentenced last week to six months at Ft. Leavenworth Prison without the opportunity to present a defense or obtain discovery relating to Barack Hussein Obama's eligibility to serve as commander in chief of the U.S. military.

Dear Maj. Matthew Kemkes,

I wish I had died before this travesty befell this honorable and patriotic officer, Terrence Lakin, and never had to witness this. There are millions of us who believe Barack Hussein Obama was never eligible to

*serve as commander in chief of our country's military. Terry Lakin spoke
for us as we want proof that Obama has met qualifications to be in the
White House and orders originating from him are legitimate.*

*Terry is a hero and one day he will be recognized as the bravest
American of our time. He was right to ask for proof that his orders were
legal. Obama hides behind millions of dollars of legal protection. Six out
of ten Americans now believe Obama is not qualified to hold the office of
president. Why don't you ask and have answers to the question, "What is
he hiding?" No one will investigate. No one cares. Well, the Constitution
matters to me. The truth matters to me.*

*I challenge you to take on one, just one, piece of suspicious
information no one will answer. Why is Obama's Social Security number
issued out of Connecticut when he never lived or worked there? His Social
Security number 042-68-4425 is linked to his Selective Service record.
This can be seen at https://www.sss.gov/RegVer/wfVerification.aspx.
Enter last name, Social Security number and date of birth 08/04/1961. Do
this soon; they are already talking about changing the way Social
Security numbers are issued, another act to cloud the issue.*

*Why are all his records sealed — not just court sealed but executive
order sealed and CIA sealed. What is he hiding? And why do you protect
him when he could have just showed Terry his long-form birth certificate
from Kapi'olani if he has one? No, he wants Terry incarcerated and his
secrets safe.*

*Maybe I'm just wasting my time once again. Anyone that questions
Obama gets silenced. Terry is the latest proof of that. The buck is being
passed again, Maj. Kemke. We're now directed to address this issue to
you.*

*I'm sure Judge Lind wants Terry to stay in the darkest confines of Ft.
Leavenworth and hopes this issue will just go away. If you haven't
followed Terry's case, know this, Lind denied discovery for Terry saying
she would not allow her courtroom to be used to embarrass Obama. Oh,
really? What does she know? Again, I ask does anyone care? Do you?*

Sincerely,
Miki Booth

---

*Editor's Note: Ms. Booth's husband and son were both born in Hawaii,
and their original birth certificates can be seen online at
www.wnd.com/index.php?fa=PAGE.view&pageId=124656. Obama has*

never produced such a document, and Hawaii has routinely issued "certifications of live birth" to people not born there but who have a relative who can prove one year of residency. It is widely known and was reported before Obama entered the Oval Office that no hospital in Hawaii has claimed that it is Obama's birthplace.

The Post & Email

Chapter 34

Is the GOP a Party of Morons?

The Constitution of the United States was written in 1787 and ratified in 1789. While it was being written, John Jay, founding father and the first chief justice of the United States (1789-1795), wrote a letter to George Washington dated July 25, 1787, and said, in part:

"Permit me to hint, whether it would not be wise & seasonable to provide a strong check to the admission of Foreigners into the administration of our national Government, and to declare expressly that the Command in chief of the American army shall not be given to, nor devolved on, any but a natural born Citizen."

Obviously the founders were concerned that a traitor, someone with allegiance to a foreign country, would not faithfully execute the office of president and would not preserve, protect and defend the Constitution of the United States even if they solemnly swore to do so. Such is the nature of a traitor.

A natural born citizen is a citizen whose parents are themselves citizens but the left has made a mess of the issue, and it is intentional. I pray people will wake up and understand that "WE HAVE A TRAITOR IN THE WHITE HOUSE!" And it's not just the left. Republicans contribute greatly to the mess because they are easily fooled, easily manipulated, getting "the wool pulled over their eyes," which is a phrase or idiom especially germane to politics in 1789 and today. It means "to blind to the facts and deceive," which is what happened when Congress was prepped to dismiss "birthers."

For over a year representatives and senators were replying to their constituents saying Obama's eligibility to be president was a "non issue" or that Obama had met the criterion by posting his birth certificate on the Internet. They were satisfied that Obama was a legitimately sitting president. Their letters to us were their final word on the subject. We were suspicious early on since comparing letters from across districts throughout the country found the letters to be similarly worded. Our proof came when we got hold of a memo issued by the Congressional Research Service (CRS) entitled "Qualifications of Barack Obama to Be president of the United States."

The memo was authored by Jerry W. Mansfield, an information research specialist in the Knowledge Services Group, (tasked with providing legal and true information to members of Congress), and dated June 5, 2009. When "birthers" got hold of it, it became known as "The Mansfield Memo" and went viral on the Internet. We had the proof that our "so-called" representatives had been "prepped" and told what to say to negative questions about Obama, "natural born citizen," and the fake certification of live birth. What was given to Congress is propaganda, a word every American should have in their vocabulary and understand what it means if they are to get "their heads around" what has happened.

Dr. Jerome Corsi, writing for WorldNetDaily, explains the fourteen page memo best:

"Attached to the memo was an attack piece published by FactCheck.org to dismiss claims that Obama's short-form certification of live birth, or certification of live birth, originally published during the 2008 presidential campaign by DailyKos.com, was a forgery.

The memo was addressed to Rep. Brian Bilbray, R-California, and sent to Jeffrey Post, a staff member in the congressman's office. Attached to the memo were copies of four articles from the Internet aimed at debunking and dismissing arguments questioning Obama's eligibility.

Mansfield told WND that he had written the memo to provide responses Bilbray could give to constituents who were peppering his congressional office for a response to eligibility challenges.

WND has reported that Bilbray is on the record saying there is no need for the president to have been born in the United States — or to have two parents who are U.S. citizens — to be a "natural born citizen" and be eligible for the Oval Office.

The controversy over Bilbray's comments developed when a YouTube video was posted. In the video of a television interview on MSNBC's "The Ed Show," Bilbray said, "It's just like people thinking that you gotta be born in the United States to be president. You don't have to be. That's a legend. We got to clarify that."

Mansfield said he "did not conduct any investigation."

"I merely responded to a request from a congressional office to answer a constituent," he said.

Asked why he did not balance his memo with published articles questioning Obama's eligibility, Mansfield responded, "I reported what Hawaii Department of Health officials said because they were official statements made by government employees. There has been nothing official said by any official of government, so far as I know, supporting questions raised about Obama's eligibility. So, there is no issue here."

When WND asked Mansfield if it was his job, in writing the memo, to draw a conclusion for Bilbray, he objected. "The attachments were articles in print," he said. "I was simply trying to pass on what is in the press."

Mansfield was reluctant to talk to the press, and he ended the call abruptly saying, "I am getting contacted by irate people over this memo. It was meant as an advisory to a member of Congress. It was never meant to be released to the public."

The attachment from FactCheck.org was a posting on August 21, 2008 entitled: "The truth about Obama's birth certificate."

The first paragraph makes clear the piece was aimed at refuting the claim that the certification of live birth was "fake."

To refute the claim, FactCheck.org cited a statement by Hawaii Department of Health official Chiyome Fukino asserting she and the registrar of vital statistics, Alvin Onaka, had verified that the health department holds "Obama's original birth certificate."

What Fukino said was that she had "personally seen and verified that the Hawaii State Department of Health has Sen. Obama's original birth certificate on record in accordance with state policies and procedures."

The key phrase was the qualification "in accordance with state policies and procedures." Fukino did not explicitly say she had seen Obama's original birth certificate or his long-form hospital-generated birth certificate.

WND has reported that the Hawaii Department of Health in 1961 would issue a certification of live birth on the basis of family testimony, without any additional proof the child was actually born in Hawaii.

WND has also reported that the Hawaii Department of Health has refused to substantiate the claim made by FactCheck.org and other Obama supporters that the short-form certification of live birth is an authentic document issued by the Hawaii DOH.

The FactCheck.org article, updated Novevember 1, 2008, included a mention of Fukino's carefully worded statement issued October 31, 2008, claiming the statement "confirmed . . . Obama was born in Honolulu," even though Fukino made no such direct claim.

Nor did Mansfield point out in his CRS memo to Bilbray that the Annenberg Public Policy Center that finances FactCheck.org also financed Barack Obama who served as the chairman of the Chicago Annenberg Challenge in 1995. At that time the CAC made a $482,662 grant to a workshop project headed by Mike Klonsky, a former top communist activist who is an associate of former Weather Underground terrorist leader William Ayers, as documented by WND reporter Aaron Klein.

The three other Internet pieces Mansfield attached to his CRS memo to Bilbray were:

A story from the Honolulu Star-Bulletin November 1, 2008, entitled "Officials verify birth certificate of Obama," reporting on Fukino's October 31, 2008, press release.

An editorial published in the McClatchy-Tribune Business News December 9, 2008, entitled "Obama birth certificate gets a pass from the Supreme Court," in which the litigation brought by Leo Donofrio in the case Donofrio v. Wells was described by the newspaper as "wacky" and "specious";

A story by Tim Jones published in the McClatchy-Tribune Business News December 8, 2008, entitled "Internet drives Barack Obama birth-certificate battle: Web allows opinions to 'live forever,' expert says," in which WND was characterized as "a popular, political right-leaning site" that has chronicled "the campaign challenging the legitimacy of Obama's 1961 birth certificate or the legality of his taking office."

Mansfield attached to his CRS memo to Bilbray no articles published on the Internet by WND or any other source examining critically the Obama eligibility issue.

As WND reported a CRS memorandum authored by Jack Maskell, the legislative attorney in the American Law Division, April 3, 2008, admits openly that no one — not Congress, not the states and not election officials — ever bothered to check Obama's eligibility to be president.

But WND has reported statements from members of Congress that are based on arguments presented in the material provided by CRS.

Among the statements from members of Congress that have appeared:

Sen. Jon Kyl, R-AZ: "Thank you for your recent e-mail. Senator Obama meets the constitutional requirements for presidential office. Rumors pertaining to his citizenship status have been circulating on the Internet, and this information has been debunked by Snopes.com, which investigates the truth behind Internet rumors."

Sen. Mel Martinez, R-FL: "Presidential candidates are vetted by voters at least twice — first in the primary elections and again in the general election. President-elect Obama won the Democratic Party's nomination after one of the most fiercely contested presidential primaries in American history. And, he has now been duly elected by the majority of voters in the United States. Throughout both the primary and general election, concerns about Mr. Obama's birthplace were raised. The voters have made clear their view that Mr. Obama meets the qualifications to hold the office of president."

Sen. Sherrod Brown, D-Ohio: "President Obama has provided several news organizations with a copy of his birth certificate, showing he was born in Honolulu, Hawaii on August 4, 1961. Hawaii became a state in 1959, and all individuals born in Hawaii after its admission are considered natural-born United States citizens. In addition, the Hawaii State Health Department recently issued a public statement verifying the authenticity of President Obama's birth certificate."

U.S. Rep. Ginny Brown-Waite, R-FL: "The claim that Barack Obama is not a citizen of the U.S. is false. This rumor is simply election year politics." She referred questioners to Snopes for documentation.

Sen. Charles Schumer, D-NY: "The courts have held that President Obama is a natural-born American citizen. Moreover, in December 2008, the Supreme Court declined to hear a lawsuit challenging Mr. Obama's eligibility to serve as president, concurring with three other federal courts in Pennsylvania, Ohio, and Washington. The courts have confirmed the determination of state officials in Hawaii that health department records prove that Barack Obama was born a U.S. citizen in Honolulu."

Sen. Saxby Chambilss, R-GA: "President Obama demonstrated his citizenship during his campaign by circulating copies of his birth certificate, which showed he was born in Hawaii on August 4, 1961."

Sen. Robert Casey, D-PA: "I am confident that Mr. Obama meets all the constitutional requirements to be our 44th president. Mr. Obama has posted a copy of his birth certificate on his campaign website and submitted an additional copy to the independent website FactCheck.org. The birth certificate demonstrates that he was born in Honolulu, Hawaii in 1961, thereby making him a natural-born citizen eligible to be president."

U.S. Rep. Wally Herger, R-CA: "As you know, some questions were raised about whether President Obama is a natural-born citizen. There was a recent lawsuit arguing that he is not eligible for the presidency for this reason. I understand that the Supreme Court considered hearing this lawsuit, but it ultimately turned down the request to have the case considered before the full court. I further understand that the director of Hawaii's Department of Health recently confirmed that President Obama was born in Honolulu and has personally verified that her agency has his original birth certificate on record. As you know, the U.S. Congress certified his election on January 8, and he was sworn into office on January 20, 2009. While I may disagree with President Obama on a multitude of issues, he has been elected as president of the United States through a fair process and has shown sufficient documentation, via a state birth certificate, that has been verified as being authentic. In short, therefore, I do not believe sufficient evidence was brought to light to conclude that President Obama was ineligible for the office."

U.S. Rep. Paul Hodes, D-NH: "President Obama publicly posted his birth certificate on his campaign website which confirms that he was born in Hawaii in 1961. This birth certificate confirms that President Obama is a natural born citizen of the United States, above the age of 35, and is, therefore, qualified to be president of the United States of America. If you would like to view President Obama's birth certificate, I encourage you to go to the fightthesmears.com website ."

Sen. Mike Crapo, R-ID: "The Constitution and federal law require that, among other things, only native-born U.S. citizens (or those born *abroad, but only to parents who were both American citizens) may be president of the United States. In President Obama's case, some individuals have filed lawsuits in state and federal courts alleging that he has not proven that he is an American citizen, but each of those lawsuits have been dismissed. This includes a recent decision by the United States Supreme Court to not review an "application for emergency stay" filed by a New Jersey resident claiming that the president is not a natural-born citizen because his father was born in Kenya. Furthermore, both the director of Hawaii's Department of Health and the state's registrar of vital statistics recently confirmed that Mr. Obama was born in Honolulu, Hawaii on August 4, 1961 and, as such, meets the constitutional citizenship requirements for the presidency. If contrary documentation is produced and verified, this matter will necessarily be resolved by the judicial branch of our government under the Constitution."*

Sen. Arlen Specter, D-PA: "On June 13, 2008, the Obama campaign released a copy of his birth certificate after numerous claims were made about his eligibility to hold the office of president. The released copy created additional questions, because it contained a blacked out department file number and was apparently missing a seal, and it was impossible to detect raised text, a common characteristic of official documents. There were satisfactory answers to such questions, however: the department file number had been blacked out to prevent hackers from breaking into the Health Department's system, and the state places the seal on the back of the certificate. The website Factcheck.org investigated the matter and provided high-resolution photos taken at multiple angles that revealed the raised text and the seal on the back of the document... Accordingly, it has been concluded that President Obama has met the constitutional qualifications to be president of the United States."

U.S. Rep. Vic Snyder, D-AR: "According to State of Hawai'i officials, the Hawai'i State Department of Health has President-elect Obama's original birth certificate on record in accordance with that state's policies and procedures.

Here in Oklahoma, letters received from Senators Inhofe and Coburn were very similar to Rep. Wally Herger, R-California, above.

They were condescending and wrong, of course, and following a Republican exemplar.

I received an e-mail message from long time supporter and fellow activist Dick Irish of Oklahoma City tipping me off to a bill co-sponsored by Sen. James Inhofe. I could hardly believe what I saw. Inhofe tried to pass a bill defining "natural-born citizen" as any person born inside or outside of the United States as long as one parent is a citizen. I went ballistic. Yes, really, but after I calmed down I wrote him a letter which Sharon Rondeau, editor of The Post & Email, also posted:

Why Did Sen. James Inhofe Propose an End-Run Around the Constitutional Eligibility Requirement for President?
WHAT WERE HE AND OTHERS THINKING?
Dear Editor,
The following letter was sent to Sen. James Inhofe this morning.

January 15, 2011
Sen. James Inhofe
453 Russell Senate Office Building
Washington, D.C. 20510-3603

Dear Sen. Inhofe,
I am aware of the position you and many members of the legislature have taken on Obama's "question of eligibility" in that Gov. Lingle said he was born in Hawaii and that's good enough for you. Well, it's not good enough for me. Whether he was born on U.S. soil or not is irrelevant. Basic civics teaches that the "natural-born citizen" requirement means born on American soil to two U.S. citizen parents. That both parents be citizens mostly ensures there would be loyalty and allegiance to America alone. Natural born is not "native" born.

I'm convinced that you know the difference, but for the life of me I cannot understand why you along with Mary Landrieu and former Oklahoma Senator Don Nickles would presume to interpret the Constitution (which is a violation of the Constitution itself) and proffer a bill (108th Congress, 2nd Session S2128.IS) reducing to a minimum the qualifications for eligibility for the office of president as any person born in or out of the United States as long as one parent is a citizen.

Thank God and the profound wisdom of our founding fathers your bill was not passed. It does compel me to question why two Oklahoma senators and one Louisiana senator would attempt to pass such a bill that invites and allows foreigners in the very sense of the word with loyalty and allegiance to another country, culture or ideology to attain the highest office in our great nation.

I was shocked, saddened and outraged when I learned about this bill. Ten days earlier I sent you a letter thanking you and telling you how very proud I was of you for refusing to ride your horse in the Tulsa Christmas parade because they dropped the word "Christmas" from the event. I thought you were a champion of Christian America and the values and principles that make us the greatest nation the world has ever known. Now I feel betrayed.

As your constituent in Oklahoma I'm going to insist on an explanation as to why you did this. The number of Americans now questioning Obama's eligibility is in the millions, and I dare say his continuation as putative president has become a constitutional crisis and cries out for attention. What conversations did you have with Nickles and Landrieu in the time frame leading up to February 2004? Was Bobby Jindal discussed? Was Obama discussed? It seems to me this bill was tailor-made to clear the way for Obama, and Jindal too, for that matter, to run for president. Had your bill passed, Obama would have met the criteria he is being challenged on today. That it didn't, proves he did not and never did meet the "natural-born citizen" status as required in Article II, Section 1, Clause 5 of the Constitution of the United States.

Anxiously awaiting your response I remain, sincerely,
Miki Booth

ATTACHMENT: BILLS-108s2128is
DISTRIBUTION:
Gov. Mary Fallin
Letters to Editors
e-mail Lists
The Post & Email.

Not only did I not receive an answer I was barred from meeting with Inhofe's state director and field representative. Shortly after alerting everyone about the Inhofe bill, Shireen Boddy, a friend and close ally since meeting at the "Clouds Over America" event in

Oklahoma City, was able to get an appointment with Brian Hackler, the young field representative in Inhofe's office. I was prepared to drive the three and half hours to Oklahoma City to accompany her to the meeting with my evidence of fraud in the form of actual birth certificates from Hawai'i to compare against Obama's forged short form (Shireen also had copies of the certificates), but as I was getting ready for the long trip Shireen called to say they wouldn't let me in. She'd just gotten a phone call advising her that only she would be allowed to meet with them. And instead of meeting with Brian she would be meeting with John Collison, Inhofe's state director.

Constituent's Meeting with Senatorial Staff Leaves Much to be Desired
"SENATOR INHOFE HAS MADE HIMSELF UNAVAILABLE TO HIS CONSTITUENTS"
by Shireen Boddy

(February 3, 2011) — I had a meeting with Senator James Inhofe's state director, John Collison, and Brian Hackler, field representative, regarding the corruption in our federal government on Monday, January 31, 2011. It was a very interesting meeting, and very eye-opening. Now there is no confusion as to how important the constituents' opinions are to the Senator.

I am saddened that I was not allowed to bring with me a few others to voice their concerns. John Collison read my e-mail and said they could not allow more than one person at a time to meet with them. He said that it would be non-productive. I told him that a few of my associates wanted to come with me to this meeting. He said that anyone could make an appointment to meet on a one-by-one basis.

I am offended at how this was handled by our senator's office. Senator Inhofe has made himself unavailable to his constituents. He does not hold town hall meetings and does not answer our letters or e-mails on the below listed issues. I was told to watch what he is doing in the Congress and that would be how I would know that he is in touch with us! I explained that the average person is so busy trying to work and keep the lights on that they do not know what is going on and do not have the time to watch the bills being passed. I also told them that we wanted them to pass bills that would make them live by the same rules and laws that they pass for us to live under. We are tired of the legislators being exempt from the laws they pass.

I was laughed at when I asked for an investigation and the desire to know if the standing commander in chief was a natural-born citizen and was truly eligible to hold the office of the president. Brian tried to tell me about the U.S. Constitution and how there was issue with interpretation. I was very insulted at these comments, as I have read the Constitution and am in the process of completing my second constitutional study course. I explained that the Constitution is very clear on this subject of eligibility. I gave them copies of two lawsuit cases from an attorney and copies of the certificate of live birth for Frederick Newton Booth and a copy of the certification of live birth for Barack Hussein Obama II. I asked if they could tell me the difference between the two Hawai'i birth certificates. John Collison could not tell me the difference, and Brian made no comment. I explained that the difference was that one was proof that a child was born in Hawai'i, and the other was to certify that there was a live baby. I informed them of the history of how both types of birth records were provided. I also gave them copies of other documents regarding this issue and was told very succinctly that this was a non-issue and that there is not one senator or congressman that was going to investigate the eligibility issue of the president. John said, "The people have spoken and Obama would complete his term as president."

I would like to know the following; this was not brought up in the meeting:

Who is Barry Soetoro and who is Soebarkah — the names used in 1969 passport and school registration in Indonesia? I would like to know why Obama is using a Social Security number issued from Connecticut, SSN 042-68-4425, a state in which he never resided. But I digress!

How do you feel about this issue?

I, for one, stand for the Constitution and consider this to be a very serious issue. (We are in a constitutional crisis — We have massive corruption at all levels of our Federal Government. I made this statement very clearly in our meeting). Senator Inhofe, Mary Landrieu, and Don Nickles tried to get a bill into committee on February 25, 2004 to change the requirements for citizenship. See S.2128. I was told that Inhofe loves people so much that he wanted to make it easier for more people to become citizens of the United States. This was only driven by his love for people. What do you think?

I also asked for the Federal Reserve to be audited and done away with. Again I was laughed at and told that we would never return to a gold standard and that we are now a GLOBAL ECONOMY!!!! I am outraged!!! Right back to George Soros and his control!

I also made a complaint that the bankruptcy laws, tax burdens were too difficult to bear for the average American citizen. The tax burden for the average Oklahoma wage earner in 2009 was 65 cents out of every dollar. That means that we are able to keep 35 cents of that dollar. I also asked about helping Terry Lakin to be released from Ft. Leavenworth. John did write down my request and told me he would check into the situation and that he would let me know.

I also asked that they investigate Agenda 21 which John Collison knew nothing about. Brian said that he knew the people who had put Agenda 21 in place in Edmond, OK, and that this had a lot of really good things in it. I told him to investigate this further and that it had to do with controlling private property rights, a very scary agenda right out of the United Nations! I also gave them copies of documents and asked if he would sign that he received these documents. John Collison said he wasn't going to sign anything, but that he would take the copies. He kept saying that we agreed on 99 percent of everything we discussed, but that the eligibility issue was a non-issue, and that we could agree to disagree about this. He also stated that the people had spoken and that the majority of people in this nation are satisfied with the eligibility issue. I disagreed with that take. I asked how many signatures would it take for me to give to them, a hundred, a thousand, a hundred thousand? This question was ignored.

I also asked about the TSA illegal searches. I said that these are illegal searches. John asked me if I would be opposed to having a background check done in order to fly? I said that it did not bother me, but in retrospect, I also disagree with a background check also. That too would be unconstitutional, as it infringes on my right to travel freely within the United States. WE NEED TO SEND A PETITION TO THE HOUSE AND SENATE TO ADDRESS THE ISSUE OF ELIGIBILITY!

The Post & Email.

Constituent to Sen. Inhofe's Staffer: "You Made a Fool of Yourself"
OKLAHOMA SENATOR'S STAFF SAYS IT'S A "NON-ISSUE"
February 18, 2011

The following letter was sent in response to the letter posted at The Post & Email submitted by Shireen Boddy about the treatment she received from Sen. James Inhofe's staffer, John Collison, during a face-to-face meeting earlier this month.

To: John_Collison@Inhofe.Senate.gov*February 18, 2011*
Mr. Collison,

I'm a retired Oklahoma state trooper, 25-year veteran, shot four times in the line of duty, two-time cancer survivor, cattle rancher, conservative voter, and Vietnam Veteran.

I heard what you told Ms. Shireen Boddy about her concerns over this issue with Obama hiding his original true birth records, and hiding the first 30 years of his life. You stated that it was a non-issue, that 90 percent of the country believes he was born here, and I'm told you laughed at her. I'm also told you have not responded to other requests as you promised to do.

Well, you made a fool of yourself, of your office, and of Senator Inhofe. I have always supported Jim, but if he doesn't get out of his office and correct this mistake, I will never vote for him again. And, I will tell EVERYONE I meet just how arrogant your office has become.

I'm not saying this man wasn't born here, not saying he was. But, YOU DON'T KNOW. Well, that isn't good enough for us. Rather, I am appalled that the senator does not have the courage to DEMAND that Obama cough up his records due to your constituents' overwhelming concerns and demands that the truth come out. The senator's avoidance of merely ASKING Obama to provide that "most open & transparent administration" that he so boldly promised, is a disgrace and an embarrassment. You men now appear to be either gutless or bought off.

All I know is that if you TRULY believe that it is a small fringe group in this country that is seriously concerned over Obama's effort to hide what is evidently some sort of huge fraud, then you are not capable of staying in touch with your people, and I must inform you that those people are your base! Everywhere I go, this is all people are talking about.

Please relay to the senator how disappointed and disgusted I am with him and you for circling the wagons around a communist/Marxist-centered man that has lied his a** off to the American people. You chose to support him over that of a Constitution-protecting Oklahoma constituent. It amazes me that Jim would cow down to this arrogant re-distributor of wealth as he has so obviously done.

Signed: Proud to be an Okie, but Ashamed to be your constituent,
Jack Horath (Oklahoma State Trooper #196, Retired)
The Post & Email.

Sharon Rife, a very good friend of mine in the nearby town of Grove, remembered statements made by Inhofe during the Freedom Summit in September, 2009. She found the video and transcript and sent it to me:

Inhofe: It's Not Worth Suing Obama for His Birth Certificate Because It Would Take Ten Years to Get a Decision

By David Weigel | 09.10.09 | 5:08 pm

This morning, at the "Feedom Summit" that kicked off three days of small government Tea Party protests, I broke from a conversation I'd been having with some attendees when one of them approached Sen. James Inhofe (R-OK) and asked about the feasibility of suing the government over unconstitutional legislation. Inhofe, seemingly out of nowhere, brought up the example of President Obama's citizenship.

Inhofe: You, as a citizen, can say, "This is unconstitutional." File the lawsuit; go through the whole thing. Now, on the whole idea of the birth certificate for Obama, for example, you can do that. By the time you got a decision, it'd be ten years from now. And then the damage is already done.

There were many great constitutional scholars and lawyers on our side and I even got to know some of them personally but, like me, they got shut down at every turn, betrayed by every branch of government clear up to the Supreme Court because we were branded, "birther!" Justice Clarence Thomas told a House subcommittee that when it comes to determining whether a person born outside the 50 states can serve as U.S. president, the high court is "evading" the issue:

("Oh really?" asked Serrano [Rep. José E. Serrano, D, NY-16. Born Puerto Rico 10/24/43] "So you haven't answered the one about whether I can serve as president, but you answer this one?"

"We're evading that one," answered Thomas, referring to questions of presidential eligibility and prompting laughter in the chamber. "We're giving you another option.")

The following e-mail was written by my very good friend David F. LaRocque. He patiently and thoroughly tries to educate a typical conservative commentator who has the ear of the people but woefully ignorant of facts.

I thoroughly read David's e-mail. I didn't have to follow the links to attorneys Mario Apuzzo and Leo Donofrio, watch the video of Dr. Herbert W. Titus, or read Dr. Corsi's new book because I'd followed them all along and did my best to get the information to everyone I knew. So much had gotten lost from my memory, though. I often joke about reaching the age where, "Whenever I learn something new, it goes into the front of my brain but displaces existing brain cells and something falls out the back." But, "Here it is," I said to myself, "absolutely everything to be said about 'natural-born citizen' and it's right here in less than four pages."

I quickly e-mailed David to ask if I could use it in my book. His reply was immediate:

"You don't even have to ask."

Hi Chris,

I enjoy listening to you on-line from Carlsbad, CA. I admire your intelligent conservative analysis of the craziness of the times as well as your sardonic sense of humor.

This morning you had Brian Darling filling in for you. A caller asked about the eligibility of Bobby Jindal to serve as president under the "natural born citizen" clause of Article II of the U.S. Constitution. Brian incorrectly stated to the caller that Bobby Jindal is unquestionably qualified to serve as president by virtue of having been born in the United States.

This is a classical example of the error being made by numerous commentators on the subject in which the terms "native born citizen" and "natural born citizen" are conflated. These terms are not synony-

mous. The two categories of citizens are each a sub-set of the class "U.S. citizen," along with naturalized citizens, but they are not the same.

There is strong evidence that this conflation of native born and natural born citizen was carefully designed by conspirators in the Democratic Party as a critical part of an intentional plan to subvert the Constitution in order to carry out the fraudulent election of an ineligible candidate for president of the Unites States.

Dr. Jerry Corsi discusses this matter extensively in his new book "Where's the Birth Certificate?"

A number of constitutional experts have conducted extensive research on the meaning of the NBC clause, all concluding that it means "born in the country of parents who are citizens" as defined by the political philosopher Emerich de Vattel, whose treatise "The Law of Nations" was a primary reference work for the participants in the Constitutional Convention in 1787.

Dr. Herbert W. Titus, founding dean of the Regent University School of Law, explains the definition of "natural born citizen" in a YouTube video.

Attorney Mario Apuzzo, another expert on this pivotal clause in the United States Constitution, has written extensively on the subject of the definition of natural born citizen:

Article II of our Constitution has a lot to say about how a would-be president is born. "Natural born Citizen" status requires not only birth on U.S. soil but also birth to parents who are both U.S. citizens by birth or naturalization. This unity of jus soli (soil) and jus sanguinis (descent) in the child at the time of birth assures that the child is born with sole allegiance (obligation of fidelity and obedience to government in consideration for protection that government gives (U.S. v. Kuhn, 49 F.Supp.407, 414 [D.C.N.Y]) and loyalty to the United States and that no other nation can lay any claim to the child's (later an adult) allegiance and loyalty. Indeed, under such birth circumstances, no other nation can legally or morally demand any military or political obligations from that person.

Our Constitution requires unity of U.S. citizenship and allegiance from birth only for the office of president and commander in chief of the military, given the unique nature of the position, a position that empowers one person to decide whether our national survival requires the destruction of or a nuclear attack on or some less military measure against another nation or group. It is required of the president because such a status gives the American people the best constitutional chance that a would-be president will not have any foreign influences which because of conflict of conscience can most certainly taint his/her critical decisions made when leading the nation. Hence, the special status is a constitutional eligibility requirement to be president and thereby to be vested with the sole power to decide the fate and survival of the American people.

The first thing that we have to understand about what Vattel wrote is that he made a distinction between a "citizen" and a "natural-born citizen." A citizen is simply a member of the civil society who is bound to the society by certain duties and subject to its authority. "Citizens" also participate equally in all the advantages the society has to offer. On the other hand, a "natural-born citizen" means much more than just "citizen." Vattel required that for a child to be a "natural born citizen," or what he called in French in his 1758 first edition of The Law of Nations or Principles of Natural Law, les naturels, ou indigenes (the "natives or indigines"- The Venus, 12 U.S. [8 Cranch] 253 [1814]), the child must be born in the country to both parents who are also citizens of the same country.

Attorney Leo Donofrio, who uncovered the previously unknown fact of the ineligibility of Chester Arthur as a result of his father's British citizenship at the time of Chester Arthur's birth, has also conducted extensive research on the origin of the NBC clause in the Constitution and its meaning. Leo has posted a new article this morning in which he states: "Article 2 Section 1 of the U.S. Constitution lists the requirements for president: No person except a natural-born citizen, or a Citizen of the United States, at the time of the Adoption of this Constitution, shall be eligible to the Office of president; neither shall any Person be eligible to that Office who shall not have attained to the Age of thirty-five Years, and been fourteen Years a Resident within the United States."

The key phrase here is "born" Either — at the time of your birth — you were born as a U.S. citizen, and you are eligible, or you are not. It can't be cured at a later stage. The word "born" is unequivocal. You must be a U.S. citizen at the time of your birth...the moment you enter the world determines eligibility. Obama fully admits that his birth "status" was governed by the United Kingdom.

I have always wondered how it is possible a person whose birth status was governed by the United Kingdom can be considered a natural born citizen of the United States. I feel that is a very rational question to ask. The contradiction is self evident. Obama eligibility supporters seek to redefine the constitutional requirement listed in Article 2 Section 1 - "natural born" to mean "native born." And Obama supporters would argue that all native born are natural born. "No exceptions."

Their argument rests on a very simple claim: If, at the time of your birth, you are born on U.S. soil, then you are a U.S. citizen at the time of your birth, and, therefore, you are eligible to be president.

But President Obama does not agree with that simple definition.

Donofrio goes on to discuss Obama's strange ideas regarding the status of aborted fetuses which leads to anomalous conclusions regarding the citizenship status of children born prematurely.

Chris, I find it extremely disturbing that a responsible conservative radio host would make such an obviously incorrect statement on a matter of such critical importance to our nation in this time of serial attacks on the Constitution by the Obama administration.

In his response to the caller, Brian referred to a recent article on WND discussing the application of the NBC requirement to Bobby Jindal and Marco Rubio, both of whom were born to at least one parent who was not a U.S. citizen at the time of the child's birth. The article concluded that both Jindal and Rubio fail to meet the constitutional requirements to serve in the office of president. Mr. Darling summarily dismissed the conclusions of this article without explanation.

I urge you to look into this matter, to correct the error in Mr. Darling's thinking, and to issue a public correction of this egregious misstatement of the meaning of Article II of the Constitution.

The fact that we have a usurper in the White House who may not even be a U.S. citizen constitutes a serious national security crisis. This is no time to be misrepresenting the constitutional provisions regarding presidential eligibility on a public radio broadcast. David F. LaRocque CDR USNR (ret) Captain TWA (ret) Carlsbad, CA

Why Doesn't Obama Have an Original Birth Certificate?
FORMER CONGRESSIONAL CANDIDATE EXPLAINS THE DIFFERENCE BETWEEN "CERTIFICATION" AND "CERTIFICATE" TO SENATOR JAMES INHOFE'S STAFFER, WHO APPEARS CLUELESS
February 19, 2011

The following was sent to Mr. John Collison, state director for Sen. James Inhofe (R-OK) in response to the letter written by constituent Shireen Boddy.

Mr. Collison,

My name is Miki Booth from Wyandotte, OK.

Shireen Boddy gave you my husband and son's birth certificates from Kapi'olani Hospital in Hawaii. I had intended to bring them in person planning to accompany Shireen to the scheduled meeting, but at the last minute I was notified I was barred from attending.

Shireen, myself, and many others in Oklahoma and throughout our great nation are still waiting for a response from your office addressing answers to questions we've posed on a number of issues. Since I'm an expert on the birth certificate controversy and you have had time to study the official Hawaii State certificate of live birth documents, I would expect you have your own questions as to why Barack Hussein Obama would have a "certification" of live birth instead of a "certificate" and why the difference in the two. Allow me to explain.

Look at my husband's certificate and note in 1949 Hawaii was a territory and in 1981 as a state the certificates list the same information: hospital, doctor, doctor's address, doctor's signature and date, names and addresses of both parents, their age at the time, address at the time and race, and raised seals and stamps, and signatures of the registrars, and more. Obama's document, the certification of live birth, has none of the irrefutable documentation that proves my son, Alan, and my husband, Fred, are who they say they are.

In 1959 Hawaii became the fiftieth state. For generations immigrants from China, Japan, Philippines, Portugal, India, Spain/Mexico, Korea, etc. came to Hawaii to work in the cane and pineapple fields. Many brought their families and relatives from their native countries. Those that were not born in Hawaii needed documentation to go to school, get shots, etc., and the new State of Hawaii Department of Health issued certifications of live birth to those with none or didn't want to use the ones they might have had coming from their native country. (In fact, *people that were not of Hawai'ian blood, merely said they were so their children could go to private Kamehameha schools reserved for Hawai'ians only.)*

Obama was born two years after statehood to the very month. Statehood was August 21, 1959 and Obama was born on August 4, 1961. The new Department of Health had a form to fill out to request a certification. Note on Obama's certification of live birth the disclaimers: "This copy serves as prima facie evidence of the fact of birth in any court proceeding" and "Any alterations invalidate this certificate." (Obama's copy was altered.)

It's a fact of birth that a baby was born and all the information on Obama's certification of live birth is data taken from the application. Who filled out the application? Who attested to the facts shown? Where is the original application?

This is a prime example of "garbage in — garbage out." Without the long form certificate there is no proof the information on his certification of live birth is accurate or even truthful. Looking at his certification of live birth, Obama could very well have been born in Hawaii, perhaps at home, perhaps in a marijuana patch, but it does not prove he was born in Kapi'olani like my husband and son were. Obama wrote a letter to Kapi'olani Medical Center when they celebrated 100 years of operation. Obama claimed it was the hospital where he was born. The letter was typed on official White House stationery and signed by him. When conservative news giant WorldNetDaily reported the fraud, the letter disappeared from the Internet and White House Press Secretary Gibbs would not comment on it or acknowledge that it ever existed. A copy of the letter can probably be found on WND.com. To date neither Kapi'olani nor Queens Hospital will claim Obama was born there, neither has Tripler, Kaiser, Kuakini, St. Francis, or any hospital in Hawai'i for that matter.

I will be more than happy to travel to Oklahoma City and meet with you in person to discuss this issue. However, it would be much easier if you would ask Sen. Inhofe to request of Obama that he come clean about the facts of his birth by showing his long form birth certificate if it exists and stop the nonsense of creating and perpetuating the crisis we find ourselves in. While you're at it ask why he hasn't released any of his historical documents.

"The only people who don't want to disclose the truth are people with something to hide." — Barack Obama in his weekly televised address to the nation.

Further, Sen. Inhofe has not responded to my letter where I asked him to explain why he tried to pass bill S.2128. I wrote: "I cannot understand why you, along with Mary Landrieu and former OK Senator Don Nickles, would presume to interpret the Constitution (which is a violation of the Constitution itself) and proffer a bill (108th Congress, 2nd Session S.2128.IS) reducing to a minimum the qualifications for eligibility for the office of president as any person born in or out of the United States as long as one parent is a citizen."

The real question no one wants us asking regarding Obama's eligibility is how did Americans vote for a man who is obviously not a "natural-born citizen" according to Article II, Section 1, clause 5 of the Constitution of the United States when the candidate is clearly a British/Kenyan subject at birth where citizenship passed from his father.

Sincerely,
Miki Booth
The Post & Email.

Chapter 35

Hawai'i Department of Health On the Ropes

Exposing the Birth Certificate Lies Used to Cover for Obama
ABERCROMBIE "OPENED THE CAN OF WORMS"
by Miki Booth

(April 7, 2011) — On February 6, 2010, I stood before a large Tea Party crowd and held up my husband's and son's birth certificates for all the world to see. It was a sensational moment and caught on C-SPAN at the National Tea Party Convention in Nashville, Tennessee. People clamored to see what real Hawai'i long-form birth certificates looked like. I was interviewed and allowed reporters to take photographs of the documents. There were no redactions on the copies — we had nothing to hide.

I was a minor celebrity for a while. There hadn't been much progress breaking into the mainstream with proof of fraud since Obama was elected. The Democrat party and national press had successfully tamped down any negative news about Obama that might have surfaced. Even among Tea Party leaders I was scorned and ridiculed. The proof was right before their eyes, and they still didn't believe it. Such had been my plight for nearly three years.

However, there has been a growing number of people who have asked, "Where's the birth certificate?" and now that Donald Trump has asked the question, we've finally broken into the mainstream.

One has to remember that most attempts to obfuscate the issue are a direct result of intentional misinformation, outright lies, and propaganda perpetrated by Obama's machine. Others unwittingly perpetuate lies and information because they just don't know, don't understand, and don't want to think about the ramifications of a constitutional crisis brought on by an illegal president.

The birth certificates I showed at the convention belong to my husband, Fred, and our son, Alan. Both were born in Kapi'olani Hospital *over thirty years apart. Fred was born in 1949 and Alan in 1981. Fred's is the black copy with white type (microfilm) which they still used in 1961, Obama's alleged year of birth. Alan's is the newer green version. If Obama was born in Hawai'i in Kapi'olani, as he has claims, it would be the black version. The title at the top of Fred's and Alan's documents is CERTIFICATE OF LIVE BIRTH.*

The document posted on the web alleged to be and wrongly referred to as Obama's birth certificate is titled CERTIFICATION OF LIVE BIRTH, and only certifies a baby was born. The purpose of the certification is to provide documentation for those babies and children who do not have a real birth certificate because they were born at home or outside the country without benefit of a hospital or doctor. When there is no proof of hospital or doctor it proves nothing, just the information attested to by the person filling out the application for a certified document. This is one of the biggest lies promulgated by people ignorant of the facts such as Bill O'Reilly and Megyn Kelly of FOX who continue to claim that what is posted on the Internet is the real deal.

O'Reilly continues to mislead Americans by saying the announcements in the two newspapers are proof enough for him. He appears ignorant of how those announcements are generated. When Alan was born, Fred and I filled out a form with information that would go on the official birth certificate. We were asked whether we wanted to announce the birth in the newspaper (births, deaths, marriages statistics), and we chose to have the birth listed. "Mr. and Mrs. Frederic N. Booth II, 1512 Glen Ave., Wahiawa, a son, November 24." It should be noted that the address of the Obama listing is the Dunhams' address — the grandparents. (Note: There is overwhelming evidence of an Obama birth in Kenya. If indeed he was born there and returned to Hawai'i as an infant, the only form of birth documentation he would be given by the State of Hawai'i would be the certification of live birth and that would generate a listing in the "stats" column. It may be supposition, but what kind of citizenship would a parent or grandparent want for their child if given a choice — American or Kenyan?

The State of Hawai'i has gone out of its way to cover for Obama's narrative. There has been deliberate misinformation to obfuscate the truth and their attempts to change legislation to fit new policy have become apparent and telling. The Post & Email has uncovered extensive incidents of mischief and stonewalling among the Hawai'i Department of Health (DOH) leadership. Former Governor Linda Lingle sealed Obama's records and instructed the DOH to make sure no one got access to the original document *"under any circumstances."* This executive action was done days prior to the 2008 election. A year and a half after Obama was elected, she publicly stated, *"The president was, in fact, born at Kapi'olani Hospital in Honolulu, Hawai'i,"* but she had not seen any proof to make such a statement. She was relying on statements of Dr. Chiyome Fukino, director of the Hawai'i State Department of Health, who never said that Obama was born in Kapi'olani. But she did say, *"I, Dr. Chiyome Fukino, director of the Hawaii State Department of Health, have seen the original vital records maintained on file by the Hawaii State Department of Health verifying Barack Hussein Obama was born in Hawaii and is a natural-born American."* What did she see? The same thing, the only thing that Gov. Abercrombie found? An entry in the birth index data book? The only listing in the index that has an anomaly? Was she qualified to state that he's a *"natural-born American?"* What does that even mean, and why did she say it? If born on American soil, Obama may be a native-born American, but he is not and can never be an Article II, Section 1 constitutional *"natural-born citizen"* when his father was a foreign national. The intent of the framers of the Constitution was to eliminate all possibility of divided allegiance to the United States of America.

The media, including FOX, never investigated any of this, but worse, they vilified and marginalized anyone who brought up the subject of Obama's birth certificate and made the leap that we were crazy for believing that Obama was born in Kenya. They never realized that there are millions of Americans who wanted to see the proof. Why doesn't he just show it and why has he spent close to $2,000,000 to keep it and all his historical documents sealed? Why would he let an 18-year decorated Army flight surgeon go to prison for asking to see the birth certificate? Obama could have prevented the court-martial of LTC Terry Lakin before he was dismissed from the Army with all pay and benefits forfeited and six months in Leavenworth prison where he currently resides. There are a million questions we have for Obama, but he looks down his nose at us, laughs or calls us names, and he's gotten away with not having to show the birth certificate he claims to have. But now we have a champion in Donald Trump and the truth may be told finally.

I have some fine friends in Hawai'i who share my fears for our country and my fierce desire to expose the lies that shield Obama. They have helped shed new light on the Hawai'i issues, and this newest long-form birth certificate dispels the rumor that one can no longer obtain a long-form birth certificate. The Post & Email reported last year that one can indeed get a long-form birth certificate, but it wasn't until a few weeks ago that a friend sent me this one. The friend whose daughter was born at Tripler Army Hospital reported it took seven days and cost $10.00. A short-form certificate would have taken a lot less time and perhaps been available the same day. Here is the proof also that there is not and never was a box for religion. Note that the father's race is listed as "Black," not "African," about which there have been considerable debate and speculation. No proof has been found to date with regard to a set statute for classification of races. I believe either are used according to the petitioner. Hawai'i is so unique with the blend of many races that we take pride in the fact that we are endowed with a multitude of cultures. Note the many races on this birth certificate: of course, English and German would be Caucasian as well as Portuguese. Chinese and Korean could be listed as Asian, but the people of Hawai'i would not want our races and cultures to be lumped together in a category for our posterity. We are unique.

It is not easy for my friends in Hawai'i to step forward with what they know. Recently I received a report from a contact who walked all the public areas of Kapi'olani Hospital and could not find one shred of memorabilia indicating that Obama was born there. There were restricted areas where he could not go, but none of the floors, lobby, hallways and areas not restricted to visitors contain a shred of evidence that Obama has any connection to the hospital.

Hawai'i is a liberal state ruled by Democrats and unions. It is unfortunate that a known drug addict is now governor of Hawai'i, but I have to give him credit for taking on the issue of Obama's birth certificate. Unwittingly he opened the can of worms that will be Obama's undoing when the truth is revealed at last.

Editor's Note: Miki Booth made this additional comment in regard to her son's certificate of live birth pictured above: There are persistent rumors that Hawai'i DOH changed the short-form birth certificate to certifications and that was all one can get. Well, we've proven that long-form certificates are available upon request and $10 and to dispel the rumor that only certifications are given out. Please note the recent short-form son, Alan, received in March, 2010. Alan's is a certificate and what Obama has is still "a piece of junk."

The Post & Email.

∞∞∞

Hawaii Official and Ex-Official Lie to Cover Their Tracks
DISINFORMATION CAMPAIGN RAMPS UP IN RESPONSE TO DONALD TRUMP'S ASSERTIONS THAT OBAMA HAS NOT SHOWN A REAL BIRTH CERTIFICATE
by Miki Booth

(April 10, 2011) — Donald Trump is really turning the heat up on Obama's missing birth certificate, and far-left zealots have found it necessary to drag ex-Hawai'i official, Dr. Chiyome Fukino, former director of Hawaii's Department of Health, back to the podium to recite her tale of viewing the elusive document. This time, unlike her first obtuse and lawyered-up comments, Fukino has gotten bolder since Abercrombie slipped his Obama "born in Hawaii" sentence into the 50th anniversary commemorative bill.

But the latest attempt to put out the flames has backfired and exposed some naughty children huddled in a back room playing with matches. Michael Isikoff, MSNBC's "so-called" national investigative correspondent, was caught with Joshua Wisch, former chairman of Howard Dean's presidential campaign in Hawaii, now spokesman for the Hawaii attorney general's office, Wisch apparently colluded with Fukino to validate Obama's alleged "certification of live birth."

"What he got, everybody got," said Fukino. "He put out exactly what everybody gets when they ask for a birth certificate."

Not true, Dr. Fukino. When my son, Alan, requested a copy of his birth certificate he got just that — a "certificate of live birth," not the same as Obama's. Different titles and different information. Obama's is sorely lacking information required for obtaining a passport — mother's state/country of birth and father's state/country of birth.

It appears specific people are lining up to take a bullet for Obama. Conspiracy to defraud the American people is a serious crime and MSNBC has become the epitome of yellow journalism, brashly covering-up for Obama and the entire anti-American agenda of the socialist left. This latest cover-up attempt is laughable and speaks volumes to the desperation of the Democratic Party.

Michael Isikoff writes, "But Wisch, the spokesman for the attorney general's office, said state law does not, in fact, permit the release of "vital records," including an original "record of live birth" — even to the individual whose birth it records.

"It's a Department of Health record, and it can't be released to anybody," he said. Nor do state laws have any provision that authorized such records to be photocopied, Wisch said. If Obama wanted to personally visit the state health department, he would be permitted to inspect his birth record, Wisch said.

But if he or anybody else wanted a copy of their birth records, they would be told to fill out the appropriate state form and receive back the same computer-generated "certification of live birth" form that everybody else gets — which is exactly what Obama did four years ago.

Not true, Mr. Wisch. A friend of mine filled out the appropriate state form and received back a "certificate of live birth" as shown below:

(Photo caption: Long-form certificate of live birth from the state of Hawaii received in March 2011 by the requester)

Enough with the lies already. You will be held accountable.

As long as the debate over Obama's birth records drag on, we will have that much more time to inform Americans that the birth certificate doesn't even matter. We don't care whether he has one or not; Obama is clearly illegally occupying the office of U.S. president since he is not by any stretch of the imagination an Article II, Section I, clause 5 "natural-born citizen" born of two citizen parents in the country of which they are citizens. It becomes more evident every day that his allegiance is not to the United States of America.

Truth will out.

Editor's Note: The Post & Email will be calling Mr. Wisch tomorrow to confront him with his false statements about obtaining vital records in Hawaii. We will also be contacting for the third time the health department, Governor Neil Abercrombie, and Lt. Gov. Brian Schatz, all of whom have spokespersons who have failed to return our calls or answer our letters regarding the many contradictions evident in Obama's birth story and documentation, or lack thereof. The health department registrar,

Dr. Alvin Onaka, whose stamp appears on the long-form document above, is apparently squeamish about picking up the telephone and answering our questions.

How many people will be going to jail over this massive cover-up? And what else, other than Obama's "records," are they hiding? Perhaps 50 years of defrauding the federal government?

The Post & Email.

Shireen Boddy tenaciously hammered away at Inhofe and he, just as committed, kept himself unavailable. Shireen then got involved in state politics and took on the local legislators. Lunchtime, free time, after work, whenever she could, she'd go to the Capitol to follow the progress of the Oklahoma presidential constitutional eligibility vetting bill SB-91. She lobbied, she spoke to anyone who would listen about the importance of passing the bill. She got into arguments with Democrats who couldn't see beyond Obama's skin color as the reason for the bill. She never lost her temper or raised her voice, but her opposers spewed hateful rhetoric in her face.

She persevered and immediately upon leaving the House chamber after the vote, called me to report, "It passed, 77-13 and 11 not voting."

Great news, right? Now Fallin signs it, and it becomes law in five days, right? Not so fast. The bill went to a "process" for "clean up," corrections, amendments, that sort of thing. Shireen kept everyone updated until we learned, "the bill is stalled in committee."

Sharon Rondeau and I hammered away at Hawai'i's Department of Health. It was a game to them. They knew we had them dead to rights on their stonewalling, obfuscation and outright lies but they were used to getting away with everything. They were accountable to no one and operated under the auspices of corrupt government leadership.

Update: Breaking from Hawaii: No More Long-Form Birth Certificates!
HAWAII DEPARTMENT OF HEALTH MAKES UP THE RULES AS IT GOES ALONG . . . TO PRISON?
by Sharon Rondeau

What is the Hawaii Department of Health hiding? Have they told so many lies that they are now cornered?

(April 12, 2011) — Miki Booth has just reported via telephone to The Post & Email that a man born and currently residing in Hawaii went to the Department of Health this morning and requested a copy of his long-form birth certificate. He was refused, told that it was no longer available and that all he could obtain is the short-form document.

The man had obtained his short-form "certificate of live birth" several weeks ago and reported to Miki that the request form had had two different boxes which could be checked: one indicating that the short-form was being requested and the other that the long-form was desired.

Today, the man reported that the form has been changed such that that choice is no longer available.

The Hawaii Department of Health's request form for a birth certificate is online.

The Department of Hawaiian Home Lands appears to be lying when it announced that it began "accepting" a "certification of live birth" as proof of genealogy in 2009. It claimed that, "When a request is made for a copy of a birth certificate, the DOH issues a certification of live birth." However, the documents which both the man and another requester in Hawaii have obtained this year, after the Department of Hawaiian Home Lands changed its policy, bear the label "certificate of live birth."

Directly preceding the claim that the "certification" is the document now issued, the Department of Hawaiian Home Lands stated that "original birth certificates are preferred for their greater detail." How can a person provide the "preferred" document when the department claimed that it no longer issued them? It has been proven that the Hawaii Department of Health did issue long-form certificates of live birth until Dr. Fukino made her statement to MSNBC.

The short-form document which the man received was labeled "certificate of live birth," unlike Obama's purported form which is a "certification of live birth." Likewise, Miki Booth's son, Alan, had received a short-form birth certificate last year which is entitled "certificate of live birth." The man who obtained his short-form document said that it does not contain the fields for "father's place of birth" and "mother's place of birth" as Alan Booth's does.

Could that be because Obama's certification of live birth image does not contain those fields, and the Hawaii Department of Health is attempting to legitimize it?

Therefore, when Dr. Chiyome Fukino spoke with MSNBC on Monday morning, she apparently was not lying when she said that long-form birth certificates are no longer available.

But why was that change made? Who ordered the change in policy? Was it made because Donald Trump has demanded that Obama release his original, detailed birth certificate to support his claim of a Hawaii birth?

The witness who accompanied the gentleman has a daughter who obtained a copy of her long-form birth certificate last month. The document was provided to Miki Booth, who supplied it to The Post & Email. Booth has reported that the woman has Fed-Ex-ed the original of the document to her.

On April 11, 2011, Dr. Chiyome Fukino, former director of the Hawaii Department of Health, told MSNBC that long-form birth certificates were no longer available. But when did that become policy? Who ordered this change in policy since at least one such form was issued to a requester last month and posted here?

2:47 p.m. EDT: The Post & Email has left a message with Dr. Alvin Onaka, registrar of vital statistics at the Hawaii Department of Health, requesting the documentation making long-form birth certificates unavailable to those born in the state. We also contacted Gov. Neil Abercrombie's office and asked the secretary why suddenly Hawaii residents can no longer have access to their original birth record. She asked this writer my name and where I was calling from, which I gave her. She then interrupted me and transferred me to the governor's spokesperson, Ms. Donalyn Delacruz, with whom we left a voice message with our phone number and e-mail address.

While Dr. Fukino claimed in her interview with MSNBC that she has seen Obama's original vital record, Gov. Abercrombie has stated that one does not exist. Why was Fukino inspecting Obama's alleged record if it is against the law, and the document doesn't exist? Or did it exist when she *was Health Department Director, and now it has disappeared since Abercrombie took office?*

Last night, Donald Trump was interviewed by Greta Van Susteren and said, "If he (Obama) had a birth certificate, I think he'd produce it."

Obama adviser David Plouffe called Trump's questioning of the existence of Obama's birth certificate "a sideshow."

What are the Hawaii officials hiding, why, and how many will pay a price? What is Obama hiding?

3:24 p.m. EDT: The following e-mail was sent to Donalyn Delacruz, to whom this writer was referred after reaching Gov. Abercrombie's secretary:

From: Sharon RondeauSent: Tue 4/12/11 3:23 PM
To: donalyn.delacruz@hawaii.gov
RE: CHANGE OF POLICY AT THE HAWAII DEPARTMENT OF HEALTH

Aloha, I operate an online newspaper, The Post & Email, and we have been investigating corruption in your state and all over the country for the last 20 months.

A resident of Hawaii went to the Health Department this morning and filled out the request form for a copy of his long-form birth certificate. The man was told he can no longer obtain one.

When did this policy change, and where is the documentation? Why would someone be refused a copy of his original vital record? I have one of mine.

I left a message with your office last week which was not answered, before Dr. Chiyome Fukino told MSNBC yesterday that long-form birth certificates are no longer available.

Your governor has stated that Obama has no long-form birth certificate, although the previous governor said that he did. In fact, Dr. Fukino said she had seen it twice, in violation of state law. Also discussing what was in the birth record is a violation of your law.

Can you tell me what is going on? Has the policy been changed to protect Obama? Why did Governor Lingle say that Obama had an original vital record but Governor Abercrombie says he doesn't? Was it made to disappear, or, as former Elections Clerk Tim Adams has stated, did one never exist?

What are officials in Hawaii hiding from the American people, and why?

Thank you.
Sharon Rondeau, Editor
The Post & Email, Inc.
www.thepostemail.comeditor@theposte-mail.com

An excerpt from a report given to us by a researcher who traveled to Hawaii last summer, funded in part by The Post & Email's Legal Fund, states:

MRS. RONDEAU: There have been reports and affidavits signed by licensed investigators that Obama is using a Social Security number that had been previously assigned to someone, and the Social Security Administration has been quoted as having said that numbers are never reassigned. And now your research raises the question as to whether or not his certificate number could have previously been assigned.

RESEARCHER: Yes, we're trying to ascertain to whom it may have been actually assigned and explore the possibility of obtaining a certified copy of the long-form birth certificate which, contrary to what has been reported, the DOH still issues. I don't know where I've seen the statement supporting the Department of Health's contention that it now issues only a certificate of live birth, but it's not true. When I was at the Department of Health, I observed a woman who was directly in front of me in line order a copy of her long-form birth certificate. She was told that it would take about a week to obtain. She made arrangements to pick it up at the DOH office in lieu of having it mailed to her since she worked across the street.

The Hawaii Department of Health's website has an online application form to request "certified copies" of vital records.

The Post & Email has reported previously that the Hawaii Department of Health has lied about birth index data and verbally changed the rules as events unfolded in regard to Obama. No one from the department has ever refuted our claims, and they will not return our calls.

11:20 p.m. EDT: None of our calls to Hawaii has been returned.

Long-Form Birth Certificates Were Available Until Trump "Trumped" Obama
COPIES OF ORIGINALS NOW DENIED TO THE PUBLIC IN VIOLATION OF STATE LAW
by Sharon Rondeau

(April 14, 2011) — On April 12, 2011, The Post & Email reported that a Hawaiian-born resident was denied a copy of his original, long-form birth certificate after visiting the Department of Health and submitting a formal request for it.

Since March 23, 2011, real estate developer, television show host and entrepreneur Donald Trump has been calling for Obama to release his original birth certificate to prove that he was born in the United States. On April 12, former Alaska Governor Sarah Palin evidently joined him.

Miki Booth, a former resident of Hawaii whose husband and son were born there, furnished the following information earlier today regarding someone's visit to the Hawaii Department of Health:

The following is from one of my contacts I received today:

I went to the DOH to see if the detailed birth certificate can still be attained and here's what I found out:

The year 1921 thru present, everyone will receive a computer generated form.

Any birth certificates 1909-1920 will have a photo copy of the detailed type of birth certificate like [her daughters] and here's why. The birth certificates before 1921 were never entered into the computer and, therefore, they must go into archives, pull the books with the information, photo copy onto the green certificate, and process with seal and stamp. The gentleman actually showed me what one of the books look like and proceeded to explain the photo copy process etc.

In [daughter's] case because her name has a kahako in it, the line that goes above the "O" in her Hawaiian name, would need to be photo copied because the computer program they have does not recognize the kahako and, therefore, would not place it on the name. The name has to read exact as entered on the birth certificate. The gentleman assured me that this would be the only reasons that anyone would get a detailed birth certificate before 1921 or Kahako in a Hawaiian name.

It was stated to me that the computer generated forms have been used for several years now and that the reason for that process was so people would not have to wait so long. At one point you did have an option to get a detailed one if you chose to wait and didn't need one right away. Then they just totally switched over to the computer generated birth certificates all together. When that occurred is not clear.

This is what I learned after my question and answer session with the gentleman at DOH. He was very helpful and patient in answering all my questions. I chose to go early in the morning and that helped out because no one else was in line. — J

Oh before I forget, I did ask if I really wanted a detailed birth certificate and would be willing to wait for it, could I get one then and he said no, because of the budget cuts that the state has been going through over the years, they simply don't have the manpower to do so.

However, Booth has told The Post & Email that the cost to obtain either the long-form or short-form birth certificate in Hawaii was the same: $10.00, at least until now.

The Department of Health states about "vital records" that, "Certified copies of these records may be issued to authorized individuals and used for such diverse purposes as school entry, passports, Social Security participation, driver's licenses, employment, sports participation, survivor's benefits, proof of property rights, and other needs."

A "certified copy" is a duplicate of the original record, not a composite such as the "certificate of live birth" which is a different form lacking the level of detail of the long-form.

Today Booth provided the following additional information:

In 1961 there were several hospitals in HI that had maternity/obstetrics departments not just the two that Obama and his family were confused about (Kapi'olani and Queens — Queens, however, did not have a maternity dept in 1961).

Wahiawa General had a maternity ward as did Kuakini (which closed their obstetrics in 1964.)

Kahuku Hospital had a maternity ward in 1961 but is now a medical center. Kaiser Permanente delivered babies as well, and, of course, the Army hospital Tripler Army Medical Center.

The Earthfrisk blog reported in late 2008 that no hospital in Hawaii had any records on Obama's birth or his mother ever having been there.

The Hawaii Office of Information Practices states that anyone denied access to a government record under the state's UIPA, or open records law, can file a complaint with the OIP, and, if unsatisfied with the decision rendered, may file an appeal in circuit court. The Post & Email *was denied access to records maintained by the Hawaii Elections Office and filed a complaint with the OIP last fall. When the OIP was unsuccessful in compelling the Elections Office to release the records, which were already in the public domain, we informed the OIP that we would file a lawsuit. The following day, the documents were released via e-mail.*

Why would a person be denied access to his original birth certificate by the health department in violation of the UIPA law? Over the last two weeks, The Post & Email has contacted the offices of Ms Loretta Fuddy, acting director; Dr. Alvin Onaka, registrar; Lt. Gov. Brian Schatz; and Governor Neil Abercrombie. None of them have responded by phone or e-mail. Our petition letter sent on March 17 has also been ignored even though we know they have been received.

Ms. Booth supplied the following scans of Hawaiian birth certificates:

Photo: Document which Miki Booth stated was obtained from the Hawaii Department of Health on March 15, 2011

Photo: This is the "document" which former White House Press Secretary Robert Gibbs said is Obama's birth certificate:

Why does this computer image lack the details of the birth certificates pictured above? Where is the raised seal indicating that it is an official copy from the health department?

Despite editorials masquerading as news reports which contend that Donald Trump has been "spouting all sorts of Four-Pinocchio innuendo that had long ago been debunked by my colleagues at PolitiFact and FactCheck.org" and that Obama's document has a raised seal, there has been no document shown in its entirety with such a seal. Requests for more information from Factcheck regarding the document have gone unanswered.

Miki Booth's son, Alan, obtained his short-form birth certificate last year entitled "certificate of live birth" as opposed to Obama's "certification of live birth." Booth's also bears an embossed seal, which Obama's does not:

Miki Booth recently explained to one of her senators the differences between a certificate of live birth and a certification of live birth. The variations between Alan Booth's certificate of live birth and Obama's certification of live birth were reported here.

If Factcheck.org and the officials in Hawaii have knowingly assisted in perpetrating a hoax on the American people, what should be the penalty?

Why are long-form birth certificates suddenly not available? Is it because Donald Trump has challenged Obama to show his, and it doesn't exist?

The Post & Email.

Is There One Honest Politician in Hawaii?
IT'S POSSIBLE!
by Sharon Rondeau

Hawaii State Senator Sam Slom is the only Republican senator in the Hawaii legislature. He represents Hawaii's Eighth District.

(April 16, 2011) — Last week The Post & Email made several calls to Hawaii officials at the Department of Health, Governor Neil Abercrombie, and Lt. Governor Brian Schatz regarding the health department's recent refusal to grant Hawaiian-born citizens a copy of their original birth record. We had also sent an e-mail to Ms. Donalyn Delacruz, Abercrombie's media contact, which went unanswered.

However, one Hawaii elected official returned our call last evening: Hawaii State Senator Sam Slom. We had left him a message on Wednesday, April 13, stating that the health department had suddenly denied access to a man who had requested a copy of his long-form birth certificate following a statement to that effect from former health department director Dr. Chiyome Fukino. We asked Senator Slom if he would be willing to interview with The Post & Email about this apparently unconstitutional development, and his phone message confirmed that he would:

"This is a message for Sharon. This is State Senator Sam Slom from Honolulu. I'm returning your call. I'll be glad to talk to you; when you get the message, you can give me a call back at 808-349-5438. Aloha."

We missed his call because of the time difference but will be returning his call on Monday, April 18. Coincidentally, shortly thereafter, we received a message from Miki Booth, who said she had just gotten off the phone with Senator Slom. She indicated that Slom "is well aware of the shenanigans going on at the Department of Health, and that he *found out just today or yesterday that somebody received a long-form copy. He said that they're just "messing around" and are being very selective. He's a good person to know."*

Booth stated that she now has Slom's personal e-mail address and will be sending him some information which Slom "doesn't know about yet" but which has been presented at The Post & Email and has been in the public domain for some time.

Slom's biography can be found online. He is a self-described entrepreneur and former economist with the Bank of Hawaii, where it is reported that Obama's grandmother, Madelyn Payne Dunham, was employed.

On February 25, 2011, Slom criticized Gov. Abercrombie's dismissal of his original nominee for health department director, Dr. Neal Palafox, who eventually withdrew his name from consideration. Ms. Loretta Fuddy is acting director now, but to date her office has failed to answer The Post & Email's inquiry about her receipt of the Hawaii Petition letter with petitioners.

The Post & Email.

Chapter 36

Wise Up O'Reilly

Update: O'Reilly Boycott Begins Today
STOP WATCHING "THE SPIN STOPS HERE!"
by Miki Booth

(April 14, 2011) — Bill O'Reilly was given one last chance to respond honestly to letters/questions relating to his April 12 FOX News show but, once again, he was caught bald-faced lying and spreading disinformation supporting Obama's manufactured lies, the biggest of which is Obama's use of Connecticut-issued Social Security number, 042-68-4425, which ties directly to his Selective Service registration record.

Private investigator Susan Daniels has debunked Bill O'Reilly's deliberate deception. O'Reilly, in response to an e-mail comment about Obama having a Social Security number from Connecticut, falsely stated that Obama's father lived for several years in Connecticut and "probably" obtained it for Obama, Jr. O'Reilly showed no documentation to support his supposition.

Not true, O'Reilly. Obama's father returned to Kenya long before the issuance of the Social Security number from Connecticut, believed to be in 1977. At that time, according to Obama's life story, he was residing in Hawaii and attending the Punahou School. A foreign national living overseas would hardly have been able to request a Social Security number for his son living in the U.S.

Harvard University is located in Cambridge, MA, near Boston, which is not particularly close to Connecticut. And if Obama had been in Hawaii when his Social Security number was issued it would have started with 575 or 576.

Barack Hussein Obama, Jr. allegedly worked at Baskin Robbins, 1633 King Street in Honolulu, as a teenager. Did he use a Connecticut Social Security number when he applied for that job? It is evident his Hawaii issued Social Security number, if he had one, was scrubbed along with his passport and other records. Then all records were sealed. Not just court-sealed, but executive order-sealed, and CIA-sealed. To further obfuscate the facts of his fraudulent Social Security number, the Social Security Administration is preparing to begin re-issuing numbers and changing the thus-far criteria of identification by state.

Is O'Reilly afraid that the facts will reveal that Obama is guilty of fraud? Perhaps, though, he really is doing his homework and getting the "facts" from FactCheck; you know, the Annenbergs, Obama, and William Ayers' buddies. Nice job, O'Reilly; you have spun yourself out of business. Today begins a national boycott of your show.

Editor's Note: Obama Release Your Records online blog is reporting that FOX News had eliminated the "Mailbag" portion of Bill O'Reilly's broadcast of April 13 in which he discussed Obama's Social Security number from Connecticut. Peter Boyle of KHOW in Denver converses with Dr. Jerome Corsi about the issue on YouTube.

Dr. James David Manning, who held a citizens' jury trial of Obama and Columbia University last May, contends that Bill O'Reilly's statements about Obama actually classify him as a "birther."

The Post & Email

Chapter 37

Death Threats

As far as I know there haven't been any death threats against me, but I have had a few troublemakers attempting to ridicule and criticize me over the past few years, but at least one came off like an admirer, calling me "Wild Woman of Wyandotte" for my obvious love of firearms. He called me a "homely" version of Sarah Palin and added this verse from Irving Berlin's musical, "Annie Get Your Gun" a fictionalized version of the life of Annie Oakley, or in my case, "Annie Okole."

"I'm quick on the trigger with targets not much bigger
Than a pen point I'm number one.
But my score with a feller is lower than a cellar —
Oh you cain't get a man with a gun."

I forwarded it to some friends who came to the same conclusion that I did, which is that it's more complimentary than not. I enjoyed being likened to Sarah Palin. I even appreciated being called "Wild Woman of Wyandotte," but I especially liked being recognized as a "good shot," according to the lyrics of the "Annie Get Your Gun!" musical.

"He must be a fan," we all concluded.

But there are far more hateful bloggers, even some "so-called" conservatives excoriated us for keeping the issue of presidential eligibility alive and in the forefront. To them we were "a distraction" or made them "look bad," but over time their voices faded into the background, and many joined our ranks if only as observers.

"Do you know what a slinky and a B/C questioner have in common?
Both are absolutely useless,
yet both will put a smile on your face,
when pushed down a flight of stairs."

After Sharon posted my April 10, 2011 editorial, "Hawaii Official and Ex-Official Lie to Cover Their Tracks," a left-wing blogger, "Bill," in one of his frequent and regular attacks on Sharon Rondeau, included me in his hateful rant:

"Is The Post & Email editor a moron, or just a liar? (Updated) April 10, 2011 by Bill

(Update: In an article published April 10, written by failed Congressional candidate and overall lying POS Miki Booth, Sharon Rondeau makes the . . . "

Dr. Kate is another conservative woman activist frequently a target of hateful rhetoric and threats:

"Dr. Kate I promise you this — I know what you look like from your picture on fogbow — if I ever see you in public I swear to god I WILL citizens arrest you for sedition for your calls for armed insurrection. I will have armed back up so it will be a very bloody mistake for you to resist arrest. Mark my words, you are going DOWN, you traitorous scum."

Another blogger refers to her as KKKHate. All high-profile conservative women have liberal attack dogs on their trail. Like Sarah Palin, the more popular the woman the more attacks. But unlike Sarah Palin, Sharon Rondeau who fearlessly questions Obama's eligibility gets no protection or assurances from the FBI in response to death threats made to her. Why? The explanation is simple. Sharon's been labeled a "birther" and, therefore, not worthy of any kind of government protection. Nor are the death threats newsworthy to any of the George Soros media, which is now nearly all and aptly named the "Fourth Branch of Government" state-run media.

Obama's machine is armed with tactics from Alinsky's Rules for Radicals and all anyone has to do to stop conversation of Obama's past is to breath the word "birther." If that doesn't work "racist" does well. And, of course, if that still doesn't work, name-calling and accusations of any kind are fine and acceptable because no one will hold you accountable. And when Alinksy tactics fail make death threats.

Death Threats from Obots Become More Strident
IF OBAMA IS ELIGIBLE, WHY ARE THEY SO UPSET?
by Sharon Rondeau

(May 29, 2011) — The following message was sent to the FBI through a secure connection established to investigate death threats against the editor of The Post & Email and others associated with the publication:

New death threat this morning:
Obama's Brother
obamasbro@yahoo.com
166.196.46.111Submitted on 2011/05/28 at 11:28 PM
God damn you Sharon, I swear to GOD you will die before this year is over. I've had enough of your ugly a**. You need to be punished for eternity for your sins.

Sharon: Are you looking into these threats? I believe as the target, I have a right to know. I would like to hear from one of you in the near future.

You should also be investigating Obama's use of a Connecticut Social Security number and possible multiple Social Security numbers; the forged images he has presented to the public as "proof" of a birth in Hawaii which did not occur; and his closed college records which most likely would reveal that he attended school as a foreign student with foreign student aid.

If these things were investigated, then the death threats against me and others would stop, as the proof of our case would be made. How much longer is the country to be hijacked by a constitutionally ineligible de facto president, a criminal Congress, complicit judiciary, and an FBI which won't do anything? Will you not uphold your oath to protect and defend the U.S. Constitution? I am risking my life to do so.

If anything happens, my family will hold the FBI responsible for having failed to act.

Sharon RondeauEditorThe Post & Email, Inc.

A second, more detailed threat was also made:

Obama's Brobrobamasbro@yahoo.com166.196.46.111
Submitted on 2011/05/28 at 11:27 PM

Someone needs to rise up and SHOOT people like Sharon Rondeau in the head ... I swear to god I'm going to do it myself if she keeps posting illegal calls for military coups. She needs to bleed to death on the

353

floor of her house IMMEDIATELY . . . The time is now!! Shoot this putrid bitch from hell!!!!!!!!!!!!!!!!!!!!!!!!!!!!!!!!!
obamasbro@yahoo.com
Obama's Brother

Sharon: If Obama's supporters are so peace-loving, why are they threatening violence? Is it because their ineligible usurper now wears no clothes? Where is the sin in exposing the truth?

They never use their real names, but hide behind fake names and e-mail addresses. They change their IP numbers constantly.

Why aren't they angry with Obama for deceiving them, and why do they protect a foreign-born domestic enemy?

How many traitors are there supporting this man who has lied about everything to the American people and changed our form of government to something we don't even recognize?

The Post & Email.

Chapter 38

Dr. David A. Sinclair

It was April 27, 2011, a typical Wednesday morning, and I was feeding the chickens when the first call came in. It was from Victoria, my friend at Richmond Patriots. She left me a phone message since I was outside and didn't hear the phone ring.

"Turn on the news — they've released a long-form birth certificate," she said, and hung up.

I turned on the TV, watched for awhile and went to the computer to look at the image posted on the White House website. I immediately looked to see who the doctor was because that could shed a lot of light on other questions we were asking. I was astonished to see the signature of Dr. David A. Sinclair. So sure was I that it would say Rodney T. West that I was taken aback. Over the years liberal bloggers were using Dr. West as proof that Obama was born in Kapi'olani since he was connected to the women and children's hospital. But now the signature of my doctor, my ob/gyn who delivered Alan was staring me in the face. I even recognized the signature to be authentic because I'd seen it so many times on Alan's long-form certificate of live birth.

The next several calls I received asked for my opinion of the electronic image. I told them that at a glance it looked okay except for the "over placement" of a sheet of security paper — I hadn't seen that done before, and that I was reserving any definitive comment because there were some things I wanted to check out. The first thing I did was to get Alan's long form and compare Dr. Sinclair's signatures. I actually thought it was possible that a forger took the signature from Alan's copy that had been posted un-redacted on the Internet since February 2010. It looked just like Dr. Sinclair's signature, but it wasn't a match, and I wasn't the only person that had the suspicion. Others called me later wondering the same thing.

I knew in my gut that it wasn't real because there was nothing on it that could be construed as embarrassing or a shocking new revelation so why would they work so hard, pay so much money and involve people in a campaign to force feed the American people to accept Obama's short form certification.

The next thing I looked at closely was Alvin Onaka's stamp because if he certified it and it wasn't real then he would be in a world of hurt. And that's when a cold chill ran over me. There was a misspelling in the stamp. Either Onaka for some reason used a defective stamp or he didn't, then he was either part of the fraud, or a forger had a defective stamp and used it. Or did the forger digitally alter the stamp to protect Onaka? The whole thing gave me the creeps. But nothing was more shocking and left me with such a feeling of disgust than the blatant, obnoxiously taunting "signature" of the forger — a "happy face" drawn into the "A" of Alvin T. Onaka's signature. I knew the Hawai'i Department of Health was engaging in a cover-up, but it wasn't until that very moment that I realized just how dangerous and committed Obama's enablers were and how far they would go to protect him. Worse, they felt untouchable and flaunted it in our faces.

Obama Supporter Unknowingly Confirms birth certificate Forgery
OBAMA'S HIGH SCHOOL TEACHER CLAIMS DIFFERENT DOCTOR
by Miki Booth

(April 27, 2011, Tulsa, OK) — The putative president and his enablers have really gone over the line today, Wednesday April, 27, 2011. It just goes to show there is a culture of fear and desperation in the house at 1600 Pennsylvania Avenue. First off today, WorldNetDaily published a scathing expose of Hawai'i Department of Health and their "helter-skelter" handling of requests for long-form birth certificates. They have been doing incredible documentary acrobatics changing policy and procedure to fit Obama's claims. And if that wasn't bad enough, Oklahoma votes today on SB 91, the presidential certification bill, which is expected to pass by a large margin and signed into law by Gov. Mary Fallin. The bill will then automatically become law within 5 days.

The Obama Public Relations machine decided today was the crucial day to release the recently cooked up certificate of live birth betting its unveiling will influence enough members of the Oklahoma House to have second thoughts about the necessity of such a bill.

The scramble was on when minions tasked to look for negative reporting on the Internet discovered the WND story by Bob Unruh. More scrambling. Call the players to the war room, things are unraveling. But Trump has moved on. He's not even talking about the birth certificate anymore, he's bringing up the school records. What does he know about Occidental? Does he know about Columbia too? Has he talked to Tea Party leaders about all the violations of the Constitution? With the release today of the newly "cooked" copy of his birth record Obama has brought the wrath of every red-blooded American down on his head. His father was a British subject, therefore, Obama is not an Article II, Section I constitutionally eligible "natural born citizen." He has illegally taken our government and surrounded himself with enemies of the Constitution, and those cronies decided today was the day to release this particular red herring.

Why now? Why not last year when he could have kept an 18-year decorated Army flight surgeon from going to federal prison for asking to see the document that Obama now flaunts with seeming impunity. Terry Lakin is nearing completion of a 6-month prison term, leaving Leavenworth stripped of his 18-year career, dismissed from the army and loss of all benefits. The most disgusting aspect of this travesty is the heartless punishment of putting him in prison three days before Christmas, away from his wife and three children — a clear message to anyone that would challenge Obama's legitimacy.

The unraveling has begun. Today there are big changes in the intelligence community, new players and musical chairs in the CIA. Create clutter, create confusion, backlog inquiries, and shake everything up to avoid evidence getting shook out.

Bernanke and Geithner are suspect financial manipulators who have done nothing but damage to the U.S. financial system and jealously guard what is actually in the Federal Reserve. Like Obama and his cronies they are unaccountable to the American people. Something big is coming down.

The birth certificate Obama is flaunting is an obvious fake to any of the millions of people who are on to the treacherous actions of Obama's push to socialism.

It is indeed convenient that Dr. David A. Sinclair has passed, therefore, he cannot attest to the fact of Obama's birth. The forgery looks good on the surface but is fraught with problems. It appears to be manufactured using the Nordyke twins' samples, and they cannot get *away with the higher chronological number belying an alleged earlier birth.*

Coincidentally, my husband, Fred, was delivered in Kapi'olani by the same doctor that delivered the Nordyke twins. It might have been too much fudging to claim the Nordyke's doctor on the certificate revealed today, but it doesn't really matter since neither doctor delivered Obama according to supporter Barbara Nelson, Obama's English teacher at Punahou High School and perhaps "the only person left who specifically remembers his birth."

Nelson stated for The Buffalo News on Tuesday, February 17, 2009, "I may be the only person left who specifically remembers his birth. His parents are gone, his grandmother is gone, the obstetrician who delivered him is gone," said Nelson, referring to Dr. Rodney T. West, who died in February at the age of 98. Here's the story: Nelson was having dinner at the Outrigger Canoe Club on Waikiki Beach with Dr. West, the father of her college friend, Jo-Anne. Making conversation, Nelson turned to Dr. West and said: "So, tell me something interesting that happened this week," she recalls.

His response: "Well, today, Stanley had a baby. Now that's something to write home about."

The new mother was Stanley (later referred to by her middle name of Ann) Dunham, and the baby was Barack Hussein Obama.

The Post & Email.

In February, 1981, Fred and I had been married for three months when I went looking for a "female" doctor, you know, the kind of doctor that takes care of women's issues? We were living in my little apartment near Ala Moana Shopping Center just off Kapi'olani Blvd. on the mauka side of the mall. There was a low-rise building on the Ewa (west) side of the Ala Moana building where several medical professionals had their offices including Dr. David A. Sinclair, a doctor of obstetrics and gynecology. It was within walking distance of our apartment and as luck would have it, Dr. Sinclair was accepting new patients.

I liked Dr. Sinclair immediately. He had a kindly and patient manner. I'd been through the awful experience of test-driving some horrible ob/gyn's in the past, and a first run with a new doctor was always an interesting adventure to say the least, but my first visit with Dr. Sinclair wasn't bad at all. The difficult part was over quickly, and I got dressed and waited for Dr. Sinclair to return and tell me what I'd heard after every regular gynecological check up in the last four decades or so. "You're fine!" they always said.

Dr. Sinclair came into the examination room holding my chart and flashing me a big smile. "You're fine!" But that wasn't what he said. He really said, "You're pregnant!"

I was stunned, and it took a while to recover, but I finally said what I was thinking: "There's got to be a mistake. Are you sure I'm not mixed up with another patient?"

He looked at the chart and then looked back at me. His smile faded into sadness, as he assured me it was no mistake. "Is this not good news?" he asked me.

I wasn't sure. "I just got married," I said. "This is so unexpected. I don't know what my husband will think."

A million thoughts ran through my head. I wasn't ready for this. I used over-the-counter prevention and had for years. I was a DINK. I never thought of being a mother. I'd never been faced with such a predicament. I was panicked inside and started to sob. I never even had a hint that I was pregnant. There were no bouts of morning sickness. Hell, I hadn't even missed a period.

Dr. Sinclair put his arm around me and assured me that things would work out.

"Talk to your husband," he said, "And come back next week. We'll go from there."

I took his words to mean that he would support whatever decision I made. I had no idea what that decision would be. I was thankful that Dr. Sinclair was such a nice man. He seemed to genuinely care about me.

Back at our apartment I fidgeted and fussed until Fred got off duty from his shift patrolling the North Shore. When he finally walked in I asked him to sit down, and then I told him exactly what happened at the doctor's office. Fred's reaction surprised me almost as much as Dr. Sinclair's diagnosis. Fred had a loving smile and tears in his eyes.

The next week I was in Dr. Sinclair's office.

"You look like you have good news to tell me," he said smiling.

"Yes," I answered, "very good news."

Not long after finding out we were pregnant Fred was promoted to Honolulu P.D.'s traffic division "Solo-Bike" unit. He went through a rigorous training period along with several other trainees before earning his own Harley-Davidson with which he would enforce Hawai'i traffic laws. We moved from the little apartment in Honolulu to a three-bedroom rental house in Wahiawa near Fred's parents. I commuted to my job in Honolulu until I went on maternity leave. Our new neighborhood was quiet, and I could hear Fred's Harley approaching from a block away as he came home from his shift.

One day when I was in my eighth month Fred wasn't home on time. I listened for the sound of his Harley, nicknamed "Boot Boot" and stenciled on the white police saddlebags. All the guys had nicknames, and those names were on their bikes too. But Boot Boot was nowhere to be heard. It got later and later and I grew more worried. Finally the phone rang. It was Fred.

"I'm okay," he said. "I couldn't call you sooner because there was an incident, but I'll be home soon and tell you all about it. Okay?"

"Okay." I was relieved.

The reason Fred couldn't call me before he did was because he was being debriefed. He was "shooting radar" on a highway near the Haleiwa "Sea Spree" festival on the north shore and stopped a speeder who got very upset when Fred wrote him a ticket. He sped off and returned with a rifle holding Fred at gunpoint and threatening to kill him. Fred was able to talk the gunman down by agreeing to meet with a third party — a cop that lived nearby.

But when the gunman saw that Fred drove off in a different direction he turned his truck around and gave chase. Fred's radio calls were not being answered by dispatch so he pulled into a service station to call for backup by phone. He was on the phone with dispatch when the gunman's truck swung into the parking lot. Fred pulled his gun and a stand-off ensued. He took cover behind a Coke machine while the gunman was hiding behind the door of his truck all the while taking aim at Fred and swearing to kill him. Police backup arrived and while Fred was keeping the gunman's attention focused on himself, an officer took the gunman down from behind.

Since then Fred has told the story countless times. People always want to know what went through his mind when he had a gun aimed at him. He remembers thinking, "Please don't kill me. I want to go home to my pregnant wife and have Ding-Dongs (snack cakes) with milk."

One evening, a few weeks after his encounter with terror, Fred had his snack of Ding-Dongs and milk and we went to bed. We'd had spaghetti, salad and garlic bread for dinner, and it wasn't agreeing with my stomach. It wasn't indigestion. I just didn't feel right. I tossed and turned and grew more and more uncomfortable.

Is this baby related? I wondered.

My due date was only a few days away, but there had been nothing "textbook" about my pregnancy. I never experienced morning sickness or ailments common to most women. It was pretty much a breeze so far, but something was definitely going on.

We were prepared. Fred had accompanied me to every Lamaze session at nearby Wahiawa Hospital. He was always the class clown joking and making everyone laugh. He was chosen to demonstrate the pain focusing technique on me: "tense right leg, tense left arm, release right leg, release left arm, tense left leg, release bladder ..." He was a hoot.

A bag was already packed. "Fred, wake up! I think this is it."

Timed cycles of pain and discomfort were starting to occur regularly, and Fred timed them and called Dr. Sinclair and woke him up. He instructed us to go to Kapi'olani Hospital, and he would meet us there to deliver our baby who we knew was a boy.

Glossing over all the dreadful, undignified and painful prepping for childbirth, we find ourselves in the shiny stainless steel world of the delivery room. I'm propped up on a gurney lost in a world of pain with Fred at my shoulder cooing encouragement and smoothing my sweaty hair plastered on my forehead. Finally Dr. Sinclair arrives. He got a good night's sleep knowing it would be hours before I was ready to deliver. Fred and I on the other hand hadn't gotten any sleep, and here it was the next day already.

There was a huge round mirror that Fred and I could look into to watch our baby being born, but I couldn't bear to watch. I was too absorbed in extreme pain. Fred tried to help me to remember to breath like they taught in Lamaze.

"I'm going to throw up!" I pleaded with Fred to get me something to vomit in, and I heard the nurse behind me say, "She's not going to throw up, it just feels that way."

I got angry. "Fred, tell her! You know I'm going to throw up!"

"She's going to throw up," I heard Fred say.

Fred knew that I would throw up because I told him that I always throw up from severe pain. I threw up when I broke my leg. I threw up when I hit my thumb with a hammer and split the tip of the bone. I threw up when the lid of a steel horse feed bin fell on my fingers, and I threw up when I fell on a pile of boards and drove a nail through the palm of my hand. Those things hurt but not near as bad as labor pains. I leaned over the rail of the gurney and the entire undigested spaghetti dinner from the night before ended up on the delivery room floor. A split second later Fred stuck a waste basket in my face.

"See I told you I was gonna throw up!" I admonished the nurse.

"See, she told you she was gonna throw up!" Fred admonished the nurse.

While I struggled through labor I saw a reflection in the mirror of two men standing behind me, and I demanded to know, "What are they doing here? They don't belong here!"

"This is a teaching hospital," said the nurse; the implication being that she invited them in.

"I don't give a rat's ass. I want them OUT!" I shouted.

Dr. Sinclair asked them to leave. "You're upsetting my patient, and she's working extremely hard here." He told the nurse to close the door and not allow anyone else in. He seemed not pleased with her.

And then Alan was born. Dr. Sinclair handed him to his attendant who cleaned him up, took some measurements and handed him to Fred. Then Fred turned to me and showed me our son who looked at me with large dark eyes. Fred had tears in his.

Dr. Sinclair proclaimed Alan a "Perfect 10" which he explained is the highest score a baby can receive for being born healthy with no defects or imperfections. I think Dr. Sinclair had a lot to do with that.

I was sad to learn Dr. Sinclair had passed away. When his name appeared on Obama's forged document, reporters interviewed his family. But they were surprised to hear that their husband and father delivered the "first black president" in American history. No, he never mentioned delivering a black or mulatto baby, as unusual as that would be in 1961 Hawai'i. But Dr. Sinclair's family was quite pleased to learn about it especially since they're Democrats.

Chapter 39

Felony Forgery

Introducing Hawaii's Star Bad Actors
*ARE THEY GOING ALONG TO SAVE THEIR BACON, OR IS IT
SOMETHING ELSE?*
by Miki Booth

Photo: Image released yesterday by the White House after which
Obama held a short press conference without the paper document in
hand.

(April 28, 2011) — Who are the suspect people in Hawai'i who would
go to great lengths to produce such a blatant forgery and conspire to
defraud the American people? Let's look at the players in Hawai'i and
consider the stakes:

Alvin T. Onaka, PhD, state registrar and chief of the Office of Health
Status Monitoring of the Hawaii Department of Health, president of
NAPHSIS (National Association for Public Health Statistics and
Information Systems) working with Canada, Mexico, the United Nations,
and the U.S. Government to re-engineer the national and international
vital and health statistics systems to be prepared against threats of
international terrorism, identity fraud, and the electronic registration of
birth and death vital events. May 15, 2001 stopped issuance of copies of
long-form birth certificates.

Chiyome Fukino, former director for the Hawaii Department of
Health. The only person to claim she saw Obama's actual birth certificate in a bound book in a vault at the DOH. She continued to embellish
her story as time went on, ramping up to the eventual release of the
forgery.

Joshua Wisch, spokesman for the Hawaii attorney general's office,
former chair of Howard Dean presidential campaign in Hawai'i.

Howard Dean, failed secretary of Health & Human Services and surgeon general appointee to Obama's cabinet, former chairman of the DNC.

Brian E. Schatz, former chairman of the Hawai'i DNC; now lieutenant governor. While chair of the DNC, he changed the wording of 2008 Hawai'i OCON which required a hasty trip for Obama to Hawaii to meet with Schatz in time for the filing deadline. The trip was marketed as a visit to his dying grandmother.

Neil Abercrombie, former U.S. Representative from Hawaii, left his post early to campaign in Hawaii for governor. The well-known socialist and friend of Obama Sr. was supported by unions and organized crime in Hawai'i and is now governor. It is my opinion that Abercrombie truly believed Obama was born in Hawaii because he did know Obama as a young boy. However, he is on record that when he visited Obama Sr. in Kenya, he was surprised that Sr. never brought up his alleged wife and child in Hawaii. Abercrombie is also on record saying he could not find a birth certificate for Obama as he promised to do upon becoming governor. It is from personal knowledge that I charge Abercrombie as a drug user and cut from the same cloth as Obama, who has admitted to drug use.

Bobby Titcomb was recently arrested for soliciting a prostitute in Honolulu. Titcomb is Obama's inseparable Punahou classmate buddy and parties at his Waialua beach house whenever in Hawaii.

Editor's Note: The Post & Email will have a story coming out shortly about the friendship between Obama and Bobby Titcomb.

The Post & Email

Donald Trump turned out to be a huge disappointment. When he came out demanding Obama's long form birth certificate his ratings shot through the roof. But like so many others he got lambasted by Obama's machine and after the release of the elusive document, Trump declared victory and skulked off with his tail between his legs. Or did he? What was that all about anyway? He asked us to give him everything we had on "natural-born citizen." We did that. We gave him evidence of criminal activity, irrefutable evidence. We did like we were told and gave everything to his executive vice president and lawyer, Michael Cohen, although he never confirmed to us that he got anything at all — just nothing. We watched and waited and prayed that any day Donald Trump would come out swinging again, but it never happened. Instead we learned some awful truths. Mr. Cohen is a Democrat, and Donald Trump played us like a fine violin.

The release of the latest forgery, the long form document, was timed as a preemptive strike against Jerome Corsi's book, Where's the Birth Certificate, and Trump was in on the deal. He called Corsi daily and pumped him for information until Corsi got wise to him. Trump told Corsi that he knew the birth certificate was a forgery because his golf course designer opened the document using Adobe Illustrator and saw the multiple layers others were screaming about. But then Trump denied saying that he knew the document was a forgery. That's the same as calling Corsi a liar.

Trump did help to get a dialog going again about Obama's non-eligibility to be president. For that we can be grateful, I suppose. Conservative talk-show hosts hid behind Trump's trousers going so far as to ask why he didn't just produce it. But they didn't have the guts to say Obama is an illegal president, so scared were they of the "b" word and the "r" word. Hannity was one such coward. It became well known that his screeners would block any callers mentioning the birth certificate or eligibility. You could talk about Obama's policies but not about his birth story and his crimes.

Trump was all anyone was talking about and that included Obama's birth certificate. During that time I was on several conserva-tive talk radio shows double-billed with Jerome Corsi. It was always an honor to be a guest on The Manning Report and Terry Lakin Action Fund radio. Pastor Manning and I didn't get to visit very frequently but when we did, he always asked after Fred and Alan and our animals as did his wife, Elizabeth. Pastor Manning introduced me like I was a regular guest on his show. I felt like part of the family although half a continent away. Marco Ciavolino, host of the Terry Lakin Action Fund, TLAF Radio Hour had me on his show again, too. Terry had been given a release date from Leavenworth, and Marco and I talked about the plan for Terry's homecoming at BWI Airport in Baltimore and shared the details with listeners.

John Clark of America Betrayed invited me on his show again, too. John billed my return guest spot as a "re-match" with Sonny Turner, former lead singer of the Platters, whose rebuttal to me on the show was simply, "I don't believe any of that."

John Clark left a message on my home phone the day a killer tornado hit central Oklahoma. Knowing we were also close to the Joplin tornado that hit us two days earlier, he expressed concerned for our well-being. His message was a complete surprise. Here was a well-known radio show host calling to check on us. Fred and I were very touched. There were so many people that cared for us and appreciated what we were doing.

On May 3, it was "Birther night" on The Andrea Shea King Radio Show and the intro read: "This will be a full-on birther extravaganza. If this subject is too much for you to handle in normal portions, tonight's show will be a heapin' helpin' of birther craziness. For health reasons alone, I urge you not to tune in. It takes boldness to take on this type of show. You've been warned. Leading off, Attorney Gary Kreep will give us the latest on the oral arguments he gave yesterday before the Ninth Circuit. Batting clean-up, Cmdr. Charles Kerchner and attorney Mario Apuzzo will educate those listeners who were able to weather the onslaught of birtherism presented by the previous guest. Not everyone will be able to make it this far in the show, so pace yourselves."

By the introduction I figured Andrea believed Obama's story was legitimate and expected haughty criticism of the "birthers." I'd never listened to her show before and was pleased to be wrong. Whether or not she was convinced before or after discussing the eligibility issue with her guests, she has a keen intellect and open mind, and I became a fan and listener because she was one of us, daring to take on the issue. Mario Apuzzo and Cmdr. Charles Kerchner recommended me to Andrea Shea King and Peter Boyles of KHOW in Denver. As a result I was Andrea's guest on May 12 talking about Terry's homecoming scheduled for the 14th and Obama's fraudulent birth record released two weeks earlier. I was on Peter Boyles' show the day after Corsi was cancelled from Hannity. Peter Boyles said I came highly recommended, and I followed Corsi on the show.

On Friday the 13th of May, Terry was released from Leavenworth, and I flew to Baltimore so I could be there to welcome him when he arrived at the BWI airport the following day. Marco and others had organized a homecoming at the Southwest baggage claim where we hoped to have at least 200 people. While we were waiting a flight arrived carrying World War II veterans courtesy of the free Honor Flight Network. As the veterans arrived in the baggage claim area we gave them a rousing welcome. There were about fifty of us at the time and so the welcome was quite loud. It was an unexpected patriotic and heart-warming moment for us all.

By the time Terry's flight arrived we had a pretty large group. Pili, Terry's wife, was there with their children, and we had a chance to meet them and pledge our continued support. When Terry came into view a loud shout went up and cheering, applause and chanting. "Te-rry! Te-rry!" continued nonstop while he hugged his wife and children. It was a day we so looked forward to. Terry was home. He was in the arms of his family. Our prayers had been answered.

Jerome Corsi's book, Where's the Birth Certificate made it to number one on Amazon.com and stayed there. Obama had to be panicked, we believed. The book hadn't even hit the bookstore shelves yet. Advance copies were sent out. I got mine, so did Trump. Hannity would have the first book interview. It was a tradition. Corsi introduced his two No. 1 New York Time bestsellers, The Obama Nation and Unfit for Command on Hannity's show and by all indication Where's the Birth Certificate would be a blockbuster eclipsing his previous works, and I marked the date of Corsi's first interview post-release with Hannity.

It was very exciting. "Dr. Corsi will be on Hannity's radio show May 17th, Mark your calendars," I wrote, I blogged and I posted on Facebook. I wasn't going to miss it for the world. Corsi was lining up interviews back to back on radio shows. I checked his Facebook blog several times a day and "shared" the information with my friends there and copied the blogs to e-mail and asked my contacts to make them go "viral."

Tuesday, May 17th arrived, and I checked Facebook. I could hardly believe what Dr. Corsi had written, "Hannity cancelled me."

I read on. Corsi was given no explanation. Hannity would have a guest discussing Arnold Schwarzenegger's love child instead of Where's The Birth Certificate. Corsi was angry and so were the hundreds, thousands, perhaps hundreds of thousands of us that felt that "punch in the gut" of betrayal from the one person in media we held out hope on to tell the truth about Obama. We were betrayed by Hannity, and we weren't going to go away quietly. We spread the word, and Hannity's call-in number 800-941-7326, went viral. Some people actually got through during the radio show, like Gordon Smith, who told me the woman screener was in "attack mode," first demanding, "Who told you that?!" And when told it was Corsi himself her answers became, "We don't have to give you a reason why." She grew nastier as the calls came in. Eventually she just hung-up when Corsi or his book was mentioned.

The next blow, another "pre-emptive strike" by the Obama media, came from Hearst Corporation-owned Esquire on-line magazine. Mark Warren "reported" that WorldNetDaily editor and CEO, Joseph Farah, announced plans to recall and pulp the entire 200,000 first printing of Where's the Birth Certificate.

The news was too outrageous to be believed and drove people like me to Corsi's Facebook page where we learned immediately that it was a lie, a deliberate sabotaging of Corsi's book. Less than two hours later Warren would add a disclaimer calling the report, "satire." However damage was done and WorldNetDaily would take legal steps to hold Esquire and Hearst Corporation accountable.

"Who is this Mark Warren?" I wondered, "and why would he do something that is completely illegal?" And then I remembered that anyone can do or say anything against "those crazy birthers," and they won't be held accountable. Warren even followed the guidelines, or rather, rules for radicals tactics by Alinsky, numbers 3, 5, 6, 8, 11, and 13. No doubt his attack on birthers was to curry favor with his superiors and perhaps get noticed by Obama. We may even see Warren in the White House Press Corps soon.

Immediately after Obama released the long form forgery and announced "We provided additional information today about the site of my birth," Jerome Corsi left to Hawai'i to gather more evidence and interview witnesses. Obama's usage of the pronoun "we" implied his personal involvement in what was released. Obama now absolutely owns the forgery that was posted on the White House website. I received a message to contact Dr. Corsi, which I did, and provided names of people in Hawai'i that had evidence to share with him. More people were stepping forward. Obama's long form birth certificate was so obviously manufactured, and badly at that, that people could hardly contain their anger.

Many of us just knew, absolutely knew, that it was the end of the line for Obama. Here was proof that Obama lied all along. There was no refuting the blatant "in your face" forgery. It was only a matter of time and Obama would be doing the "perp-walk" out of the White House. His crime was a felony, a class B felony in Hawai'i, and multiple violations under U.S. Code section Title 18, Part 1, Chapter 47, Sec. 1028, and, therefore, an impeachable offense. However, most Americans cognizant of Obama's illegal takeover of the office decried impeachment because that would imply legitimacy. Obama was a common criminal and every day more evidence of a crooked past bubbled up to the surface, but no one would listen, least of all those that could do something about it.

Four days after the release of the long form forgery, the Obama machine created the Bin Laden diversion. It was so huge it knocked the "birther movement" back on its heels. There was no one more affected than me. Evidence of forgery was coming in fast and furious, and I was doing my best to stay on top of it sending e-mails and posting on Facebook. The process was time consuming, and I was also trying to wrap up my book by the deadline I had set for myself.

May 1, 2011, the day Obama made the great announcement that Bin Laden had been killed, Fred asked me if I noticed that Ping was sick. I had noticed. He was lethargic and spent hours sleeping in the same spot. His eyes didn't look right either. I told Fred we'd give it another day before I called our vet. The following day Ping wasn't any better. I read a missive from Ulsterman that explained the weird actions in the war room of the White House the day before. It kept me busy all morning and I hardly gave Ping a thought.

According to Ulsterman's White House insider, Obama was reluctant to take out terrorist Osama Bin Laden and was ultimately overridden by senior military and intelligence officials. There was a significant push to take Bin Laden out months earlier, but senior White House staff resisted and caused much strain between Hillary Clinton and Valerie Jarrett. Clinton and Leon Panetta, CIA director, were in constant communication over the matter and attempted to persuade the administration to act. But Jarrett and Obama were afraid of failure that would result in a negative effect on Obama. Intel was disgusted over politics trumping national security. The insider suggested checking the timeline to corroborate staff resignations and departures. Intel had leaked to media facts surrounding how the information was obtained, namely from enhanced interrogation efforts via GITMO prisoners. Obama and his administration was put in a corner by this and a split occurred among reporters where some would close ranks protecting Obama while others chose to investigate further. There was a clear divide between military and the White House. Valerie Jarrett was completely marginalized on the decision to take out Osama Bin

Laden and she played no part. The point of determination was made for Obama not by Obama.

The insider stressed an important specific: When the 48-hour "go order" was issued, the commander in chief (CoC) was told, not requested. At that point "administration scrambled to abort," but that order was overruled. This order did not originate from CoC. He complied, but did not originate. Independent military contacts have confirmed this, and their accounts corroborate one another.

Ulsterman's insider concludes his report by writing, "This is legit," and "The killing of Osama Bin Laden was, in fact, a coup within Obama White House."

I was really wrapped up watching news accounts and reading blogs about the killing of Bin Laden but finally remembered to take Ping to the vet since he wasn't any better, but he didn't seem any worse either. It had been a long time since we used the pet carrier to transport a pet for any reason, and the chickens had been using it to lay eggs in. I went to get it, but there was a chicken nesting in it so I put Ping on the passenger seat of the van, and he calmly curled up and went to sleep on the seat next to me. Ping loved sleeping in the van and a few times he accidentally got closed in, but when he turned up missing we'd hunt for him and usually find him in the van.

The vet didn't know what was wrong with Ping, but there had been several cases of a blood virus spread by bobcats through their urine. Ping was running a fever, and if he had the virus the prognosis was not good. I left Ping at the veterinary hospital and went home to continue watching the news. I was sick. I knew Obama would get a jump in the polls, and those of us pushing for an investigation into his criminal activities would be further marginalized.

On Tuesday, May 3, I checked my e-mail in the early morning and noticed a Yahoo! news story about Obama's golf shoes being a clue to the Bin Laden raid. I read with growing interest. It lined up perfectly with Ulsterman's insider's account of what went down. Reporters noticed that Obama's Sunday golf outing ended unusually early, and he made a bee-line for the Situation Room, the "war room" in the West Wing of the White House — you know, the room that used to be reserved for national security meetings in past administrations but now is used by the Obama administration for strategizing Obama's campaign and photo-ops for rappers like Jay-Z.

Obama did not know the raid was going down and certainly did not order it. He was summoned off the golf course and looking at the photograph showing Obama in a light golf jacket and shrunken into himself, it's evident he's just along for the ride. He is not the driver of the Bin Laden raid.

The Associated Press and major media spun the story into Obama carrying around a momentous secret for 72 hours while maintaining "his poker face throughout the weekend." On Saturday, the day before the raid, Obama attended the White House Correspondents Association annual dinner poking fun at Donald Trump — paybacks for Trump's unrelenting requests for Obama to show his real birth certificate. Within the stings and barbs of ridicule lobbed at Trump came certain truths. The Obama White House was confident that the document released three days earlier would be accepted as the real thing, and Trump would be marginalized and looked the fool. Intel of Bin Laden's whereabouts was shared with Seth Meyers. There is no other explanation to his astonishingly prescient joke about Bin Laden hiding out.

Later that morning I remembered to check on Ping but went to check my e-mail messages first. Then the phone rang. It was the vet. Ping died.

Chapter 40

Finding Kaluakauka

In early 1995 our plans to move to Oklahoma were falling into place, and the realization that it might be a long time before we came back to Hawai'i left us feeling sad. We even had second thoughts, but looking into a future for us in Hawai'i left little doubt that life would only get more difficult and complicated, not easier.

The Big Island that had been our home for most of Alan's life might have been a great place to realize our dream of having acreage and horses. But even though Hawai'i was the largest and least populated of the eight major islands in the chain, land was expensive, and we were living from paycheck to paycheck. If Fred had inherited his parent's house he probably would have sold it to purchase a place on the Big Island, at least that was our dream.

We had a piece of unfinished business that we kept intending to do. One of those things that you keep saying, "Yeah, we gotta do that," but never get around to doing. For us it was to resume the quest for Kaluakauka, the doctor's pit. Now that we were leaving it was now or never, or at least not for a very long time.

We loaded up my truck with a cooler full of sodas, fruit and cheeses, sandwiches and chips. Alan and Tesi got into the cab with us, and we headed for Hilo. This time we would take Saddle Road all the way to where Mana Road, the dirt road, begins or ends depending on which way you're trekking.

It was a beautiful day and we drove along with the windows down. Fred was playing Hawai'ian music tapes with the volume cranked up so we could hear it over the wind rushing in the windows. The sliding glass rear window was open, and Tesi would jump through it to ride in the bed of the pickup and jump back into the cab when she decided she liked inside better. Sometimes Fred would get irritated and yell, "In or out!" Alan would close the window with Tesi usually inside the cab.

We stopped briefly at our Hilo house, which was up for sale, and everything looked fine so we continued up Alahelenui Street which becomes Saddle Road that runs between the two big volcanoes, Mauna Kea and Mauna Loa, one dormant one not. Saddle Road leads to the gravel road that ultimately takes you to the summit of Mauna Kea where the world's largest observatory and telescopes that are owned by countries from around the globe are located. We'd been to the summit many times, especially during the winter when there's lots of snow, and we would bring boogie boards to slide around on. At the summit almost 14,000 feet the air is thin and strenuous activity leaves you struggling to catch your breath. Tesi never seemed to be out of breath, though, maybe because she usually got to be the one riding down the slope on the boogie board. She loved that!

We weren't going up to the top that day, we were on a quest to find Kaluakaua, and at the point where the road to the summit becomes steep we saw tracks in the dirt going off to the right.

"This has to be road," Fred said. "I don't know of any other road between Saddle and the visitors' center."

Fred was referring to the Ellison Onizuka Center located at an elevation of 9,300 feet. Visitors going to the summit are encouraged to stop at the center to acclimate themselves before heading to the top of Mauna Kea. People that work at the observatories live in accommodations near the center at the lower elevation. The road leading to the barracks was once a trail used by wild sheep.

There were no signs indicating we were on Mana Road, but we followed the trail which was little more than tire tracks in the dirt. We didn't remember going thru any gates, but apparently we traveled over a cattle guard grate because suddenly we were surrounded by cows and there was lots and lots of cow piles on the road. The cowpiles on the road became imaginary bombs and when Fred ran over one with the truck, Alan would make explosion sounds, and we would rock the truck.

We made some stops to photograph spectacular views of the ocean and breathtaking scenery. As we continued our trek, the climate went from arid pasture and scrub brush to outcroppings of ohelu berries and koa trees where the air was cooler. Ever present were the ugly ohia trees with their beautiful red lehua blossoms.

Finally, we reached a gate and just beyond were a few houses. We wondered how many gates we would come across before reaching

Kaluakauka. We saw a man walking our way and he motioned for us to stop. Fred and the man talked story for a while and found out they knew many of the same people. We learned there would be no more gates before reaching the doctor's pit. The man told us we didn't have much further to go, and that it was ranch land all the way.

We kept thinking that the doctor's pit would be around every "next" corner, but around every bend was "nothing." We drove and drove and then, there it was — a sign and it pointed off to the right. And there was another sign. It was dilapidated and covered in lichens but still readable: Kaluakauka.

We parked the truck on the side of the road and followed the path through tall lush grass in the direction the sign pointed. There was a clearing and a large fallen tree but not much else. We made it, though, and it was a lot closer than approaching it from Waimea. We sat on the trunk of the fallen tree and ate our lunch deciding not to carry the cooler and sacks of food too far away from the truck. There was no telling how far away the marker was that indicated the place where Dr. David Douglas died or which direction to go. There was no clear path anywhere. No one had been there for a long time. Few people even knew about it.

Beyond the clearing was a jungle of tropical growth. It was kind of eerie. There was no wind or human activity for miles. It was so quiet you could hear your own heartbeat. And then we heard the sound of a bird, a sound we'd never heard before. What are they? We wondered. We stopped moving and stayed quiet and soon we heard more birds, and then we saw one. It was a honeycreeper, an endangered red i'iwi bird. Or was it the equally rare and elusive apapane? As long as we remained quiet the birds called out and sang to one another. Eventually they got used to our being there, and we continued our quest to find the doctor's pit. Fred went in one direction with the video camera, Alan went another, and I chose yet another direction looking for a path through the dense jungle.

"I found it!" Fred yelled. But he was pointing at the sky. It made no sense.

"What are you looking at?" I shouted back.

"Look!" He kept pointing up, "Douglas fir!"

Sure enough, there were Douglas fir trees towering above the jungle growth, every bit of fifty feet high. While Alan and I were looking for some kind of a trail, Fred was videoing, and when he zoomed in for a close-up of the tree-line he saw the familiar looking needles of a Christmas tree.

Now we knew where the marker would be, and we made our way through the thick growth of vines and tropical forest. We entered a clearing that was carpeted with Douglas fir needles and the giant trees created a canopy for the simple nine-foot tall stone cairn that stood before us. A bronze plaque on the front of the monument had a simple message, "In Memory of Dr. David Douglas, killed near this spot in a wild bullock pit. July 12, 1834 A.D."

The question of whether Douglas was killed by a wild bullock or murdered by Ned Gurney has gone unanswered for over a century and a half, but there are some who will always remember him. The Perthshire Royal Horticultural Society built an impressive 23-foot-tall stone cairn in the Scone Churchyard in Scotland with donations they received from around the world.

On the 100th anniversary of Dr. Douglas's death, July 12, 1934, seven men from Hilo, some of Scottish descent, hauled cement on horseback up the Mauna Kea slope to build a monument out of lava rock. They also planted 200 Douglas fir seedlings nearby. Today only a fraction of the trees survive, but they are mighty and stand in silent tribute to a remarkable man. On the back side of the cairn is another plaque. It bears the names of the seven men who honored Douglas with their labor of love. One of the names is Wilson, a distant relative of Fred's and another was Ross, grandfather of Sean Ross, Fred's friend and employer at Goodenow Private Investigations.

Chapter 41

Crimes Have Been Committed

Document Analyst Files Criminal Complaint with the FBI on Obama Long-Form Birth Certificate
"THIS IS TREASON"
by Sharon Rondeau

Why was this image created and supplied as a certified copy of Obama's original birth certificate? Why is the Kenyan government investigating Obama's possible birth there?

(June 2, 2011) — Mr. Douglas Vogt is the author of several books which focus on science and religion as well as owner of Vector Associates, a book publishing company. He has also worked as an accountant and owned a typesetting company for 11 years. Regarding the image purported to be Obama's birth certificate released to the public on April 27, 2011, Vogt states:

I have a unique background for analyzing this document. I owned a typesetting company for 11 years so I know type and form design very well. I currently own Archive Index Systems since 1993, which sells all types of document scanners worldwide and also developed document imaging software (The Repository). I know how the scanners work. I have also sold other document imaging programs, such as Laser Fiche, Liberty and Alchemy. I have sold and installed document imaging systems in city and county governments, so I know their procedures with imaging systems and everything about the design of such programs. This will be important in understanding what has happened with Obama's certificate of live birth.

On May 12, Vogt submitted an affidavit which was included in a Motion to Intervene filed by Atty. Orly Taitz with the United States District Court in the Eastern District of Louisiana in regard to the case of Horbeck v. Salazar. The affidavit consisted of a sworn statement and detailed report stating Vogt's conclusion that the image a purported long-form birth certificate bearing the name of Barack Hussein Obama II is a forgery.

Vogt told The Post & Email that he had written the report for his own purposes prior to its inclusion in Taitz's Motion to Intervene.

On May 22, 2011, Vogt updated the report, which declares that forgery of a government document would be a felony under U.S. Code, Title 18, and included it in a criminal complaint filed with the FBI.

The Post & Email asked Mr. Vogt how he arrived at his conclusions, and his answers are presented here in great detail. He referred to the May 22 updated analysis by the number of each subtitled section. The graphics are referred to as "Figures."

MR. VOGT: I have no financial interest in this whatsoever. But here is what happened: I heard the presidential announcement on the 27th, and a friend of mine contacted me and said that there were layers in the image. He sent me a link to the White House blog. I logged on on the 28th and got another version. It explains in Subsection 8 of the long (updated) report that people were reporting nine layers. I decided I was going to write a report of what I found, and it was written independently of Orly's case.

This is a blatant, obvious forgery. The thing I had in my mind as I was discovering it was, "Why did the forger go to such trouble to do these things which were seemingly unnecessary and blatant?" the last one being the stamped signature on the lower right-hand side, supposedly done on the 25th of the month. Where the words are, "THE" is deliberately misspelled as "TXE." If you scroll down to page 11, you can see it. That's not an "H." The graphic artist who did this thing literally built that "X" by clicking pixels. It wasn't an "H." Also, the "F" in "OF" has also been doctored or came from someplace else because it's closed off on the right-hand side. It's not like the stamp that was done about a month before on the bottom of page 10; that stamp is perfectly fine, not crooked.

Those two things gave it away as a fraud: the "X" in "THE" and what they did to the word "OF." But also, the stamp is too straight. This is hand stamp that someone takes with his hand and slaps it down. It's called "skewing." It's skewed, but this one is off only two pixels over three inches over the length of the thing, which is unusually straight, which I don't think they could do. That's 1/150th of an inch off, and that's really somebody placing it on the background image of the security paper.

The other thing is that on the "A" for "Alvin," there's a script "e" embedded on it, and if you look at the bottom of the previous one, it's not *really there. The "A" is smudged because of the rubber stamp, and they must have hit from the right-hand side of the stamp, as it's darker there. But the point is that somebody has put something there.*

Now the question is, "Was the 'e' originally there on the original paper, and they didn't erase it before they put this thing down, or is the forger basically screaming at us that this thing is a forgery?" And I'm beginning to think that the forger may actually be the hero here because some of this stuff is so blatant, figuring that when he or she sent the PDF to the White House or to Hawaii and then Hawaii sent the PDF to the White House, they would have just printed it out on a color printer and scanned that in and presented it to the public.

I know the state of Hawaii has to have it. Besides, when I saw the image that Obama produced, I knew they had scanned this thing from one of the postbinder books, which is what #1 is, where I describe it. That's one of the first things that gave it away: The typewriter lines were straight, but there was a paralax for the form itself, and I said, "OK, it's been overlaid. That's impossible."

MRS. RONDEAU: Could you explain the term "parallax?" What does that mean?

MR. VOGT: It's an optic term. It's a distortion of the image. That's all it means. It's because when you put the paper down on the flatbed scanner, which is what they did, where the binder is (known as a gutter), was higher off the glass than the rest of it. So it looks as if it's stanched down to the left. That's an optical distortion, because they never took the pages out of the postbinder. These are all originally single pages, and the pages were actually printed most likely on letter-press, hot-metal letter-press, which was developed in the '50s and '60s.

The county would print up the birth certificate forms and send them to the hospital, and from the birth certificate, the hospital would type up and fill in the long form that the county gives them. Then the doctor would sign it, the mother would sign it, and they would mail it to the county.

I tried to explain the whole procedure so that people understood that this is what actually happened in all counties. This is how the procedure goes. In the old days, the county would microfilm it like the examples we had there that had been recorded before — the Nordyke twins.

The stamp that the state of Hawaii has is two and one-quarter inches; that's larger than normal. Usually they're less than two inches. You'll notice the stamp on the Nordyke twins' birth certificates are very close to the edge of the paper, and there is another one that was printed and stamped on the right-hand edge near the top. You can clearly see the embossing of the county seal. That's Figure 18 on the latest report. I know the machine they used; they used an electronic machine, and it's pretty obvious that the one that Obama presented was a second- or third-generation image of what was originally on the background color that the artist used.

I gave examples where, even on the Nordyke twins' birth certificates, which is really an inverse of the microfilm copy, you can clearly see the imprint of the embossment seal. You can't see it at all on Obama's, and his is brand new. Those electronic stampers produce a lot of force. They'll emboss three or four pieces of paper at once which can be seen very clearly. But this thing was just an artifact on the background image, so it's just a joke. From that, I know that the whole story is not plausible.

If you open up the file in Wordpad or Notepad, then you'll actually see the hexadecimal code and the commands within the document. I put the one I have on that page on Vectorpub.com, and that basically showed clearly that objects 13-21 were the parameters, in pixels — it tells you horizontally and vertically — where these images are. So there's no argument, and they can't prove it wrong. I have it from within the document from the White House that the thing is a multi-layered document. It had XML code on the very bottom of the file. If you open it yourself, you'll see it. It gave a creation date and a modification date.

MRS. RONDEAU: What were those dates?

MR. VOGT: Well, the one I had had a creation date of April 27, 2011 at 12:09 p.m.; modification date of April 28 at 9:58 a.m. That's the one I had pulled out. Dr. Corsi had sent me two more, but his were dated May 9 and 12, and one them didn't have the XML data.

MRS. RONDEAU: Where did he find those?

MR. VOGT: People sent it to him thinking that was the first one, and it wasn't.

MRS. RONDEAU: So you did an analysis and found that they were created on yet different dates from the first two?

MR. VOGT: That's correct. I have one from at least the second day, but it really doesn't matter at this point; I have the evidence from the White House.

MRS. RONDEAU: Do you have any thoughts on the short-form certificate which former White House Press Secretary Robert Gibbs claimed he "put out on the Internet?"

MR. VOGT: I don't know. I've seen it, but they blocked out the serial number on the upper right-hand corner because they probably didn't have one. It's unknown right now.

Let's go through the eight so that you understand what they are.

We already talked about the distorted image that's covered in #1. If you scroll down just above Subheading #2, you'll see that the letters "N," "s," "H," and "al" are grayscale, and the rest are binary, black and white. Even below it, the "d" in "residence" is grayscale. The document is just loaded with that kind of stuff, where you have letters that are grayscale and the rest are binary, black and white. At first I asked, "Well, why did he or she do that?" and I realized that the form is such that he or she needed to establish the baseline of the original form. That's why it was done. Some of the letters were still there from a previous form, in grayscale, because he had to establish the baseline of the type, because if he got that wrong, it would have been really obvious that it was a forgery because the baseline would have been different from what is normally on any of the forms in points or picas.

That gave it away: the type, the name of the hospital, and the graphic above, "Male," which didn't bend down, but everything on the paper did bend down. So the typewriter stuff was another layer imposed on top of the form.

Subheading #2 is about the haloing around all the type. I gave examples of what it's supposed to look like, both in grayscale, binary or even in color. With a background security paper, the type is supposed to show through, and his doesn't at all. It's due to a couple of different things. I didn't go into it totally because it might be too technical, but basically, if the person was scanning in on grayscale or color, and then did that to the black and white but he had thresholding, what would happen is the boxes around real 100 percent black would still have a value in it; 256 is totally black, and zero (0) is white. But if he mistakenly didn't have the thresholding correct, what would happen is that the boxes around the type would still have a value in it. It might be 20, 30 or 10; it would still look like white, but it really isn't. So when he overlaid it on the color background and he said, "Type forward," that it should be above the layer of the security paper, it would then block out the image of the security paper behind it because there was still a value in those little pixels. That's the reason for the haloing effect around all the type.

MRS. RONDEAU: So that haloing should not be present on any copy of an original document?

MR. VOGT: That's correct. That's why I gave examples on page 3 and at the top of page 4. You can clearly see on Figure 6 or 7 that there is no haloing whatsoever, and you see the security paper behind it, both the green or the grayscale one. Figure 5 is a haloing effect; it should not be there: period, end of subject. It just can't be there.

At the top of the next page, Figure 9, is a blowup of what grayscale letters look like. What happened when they went to binary, they made a mistake on the thresholding, so those little boxes that look like a faint gray when the program would convert it to a black and white image as with Figure 8, it still had a value around those letters. The value might have been 10, 20 or 30, but it still looked like white. But when they overlaid it, it really was a color, so it blacks out the background color, the background layer. That's technically how it would happen, but if I did go into it, it would really be over everyone's head.

MRS. RONDEAU: Is there a way to create a forged document which no one can detect?

MR. VOGT: It depends on the type of document. With this one, the unusual part is the parallax, or the curved image from the book. If it's a flat image, it's a lot easier. The curved one makes it much tougher. It's really tough. The ones who are the experts at doing things like that is the CIA, and I can tell you right now that the CIA did not do this or any other intelligence agency. They would stay so far away from something like this; they never would have touched it. In fact, it would be the biggest red light to all of them; they'd investigate who is this guy in the White House now? They wouldn't tolerate this; they just wouldn't tolerate it at all.

Figure 10 is an inverted image of the black and white microfilm copy of Susan Nordyke's birth certificate, and you can clearly see what it looks like and what the inverted image looks like.

Subsection #3: Obama's document is loaded with both binary and grayscale. The person did it because they needed to establish the baseline of the type. Sometimes he didn't do such a hot job. I'm saying "he," but it could be a "she." That's the reason why they left these letters in there; they needed points by which to register the baseline of the forgery.

If you scroll down to Figure 13, which is on page 7, it's his name: "Barack," and the "r" is grayscale, visibly, and the rest is binary. They did that for registration reasons; they had to register the type. They figured no one would ever see it.

MRS. RONDEAU: What does "registering the type" mean?

MR. VOGT: The baseline. The baseline is where the type sits, the bottom of the type; that's called a baseline, or baseline rule, in the typesetting business. That's why my unique experience in typesetting told me immediately that this was a fraud. I recognize things that other people would not have.

Figure 14 is a separate offense. Do you see the "1⬚ where the number is in #14? That's grayscale. Its baseline is different from the rest of it.

MRS. RONDEAU: So it will always look different if it's grayscale?

MR. VOGT: Yes, that's it, because it's not a white dot or a black dot, which is binary; it's rather 256 levels of gray to black. That's the whole point. So it's easy to spot like that. That told me immediately that we really don't know what number he is or if he even has a number. He probably doesn't at all. The interesting thing is this: the way the federal law is written, this is a separate offense that gives you five years in prison: that alone.

MRS. RONDEAU: Why would someone create something that is such an obvious forgery? I haven't heard of one analyst who has vouched for the document except for one on FOX News, but even he didn't declare it authentic.

MR. VOGT: Yes, you'll read it on the bottom; I answered him. He knows nothing. I'm going to send my material off to FOX News, but in my humble opinion, the guy is an idiot for even saying it.

Anyway, let's go on. The sequential number is a fraud; that's #4, and it goes through the law section a little bit and also the fact that even though his was submitted three days earlier than the Nordyke twins', who have a lower number, he has a higher number, and it's just impossible. In counties, when any document comes in, regardless of department, they open up the mail and they stamp it because that's the legal requirement. They wouldn't have forgotten that; it's a legal requirement, and they're forced to do it. So it is impossible for him to have a number higher than someone's who was mailed or OK'd three days earlier, just impossible. It's an immediate red flag.

MRS. RONDEAU: From the paragraph which begins "The facts I have shown you in #3 and #4," it looks as if you have heard the story of baby Virginia. Some researchers believe that Obama could have been given her number because she was born on August 4 and died the next day. It's possible that they assigned the death certificate before the birth certificate, which might account for the higher number.

MR. VOGT: *If you read that paragraph, you'll see that there are two possibilities. She was born in one hospital. They're the ones who are legally supposed to submit the birth certificate. They would have mailed it, and they would have assigned a number to her. Then she was transferred to the other hospital, Kapio'lani, where she died the next day. They would have been legally responsible to file the death certificate, which would have been mailed that next week. So the point is that she would have had a birth certificate and a death certificate. The law that the federal government passed in December 2004 said that you had to link the two together; they both had to be in the database. So they had access to who had died, so it was very convenient. But it also means, as I have in the third or fourth sentence, that we really don't know if Obama's birthday was really the fourth. We can't assume anything at all. Maybe a long lie has been out there for all these years, but it doesn't mean it's true. You have to prove it. That's the whole point. And I don't think he has; it's just a joke, the whole thing.*

But the security hole is that the Kenyans say that his birth certificate was stolen or destroyed, which means that it probably wasn't destroyed, but whomever is blackmailing him has the original. They have the original. So that's the problem.

Number 5 is two different colors. This was really weird. Actually, it was in three places. I mention all three. There are two things here with the rubber stamp; it's not just one curiosity. It's on page 8 and 9, having to do with boxes 22 and 20. When the document comes into the registrar's office, it's the same rubber stamp; they stamp it on the left-hand side; they stamp it on the right-hand side, and the guy signs it off. The guy's name in this case is U.K.L. Lee.

MRS. RONDEAU: *A lot of people have questioned if that was a real person.*

MR. VOGT: *The other part that I was suspicious about, even though I've seen his name on a 1962 certificate of live birth, he was supposed to legally have signed his whole name; no initials. That's the law: it's supposed to be his whole name. But he didn't do that.*

MRS. RONDEAU: *Do you think that was a law in 1961?*

MR. VOGT: *You could see that for the Nordyke twins; the registrar signed his whole name without middle initials. His whole name was there. So the person who signed that one knew that he had to sign his whole name with no initials. So that's suspicious.*

Now, look at #22 and then #20. This should never have been, because there's a color value to date "A" — August (Aug) and then the sixth, and that can't be. This thing is supposed to have been scanned in grayscale or binary. We can't have a color here, but we do. It is a dark green. I gave the color value on the bottom of page 8. Then we have box #20 at Figure 16, and we have a rubber stamp. This can't be. They used the same rubber stamp the same day: the guy has a rubber stamp in his hand with the date, and he stamps left and right, and then he signs it. This can't be. So it's not only just the color, but it's also the fact that it was two different rubber stamps with two different sizes. That's can't be.

Also, he grabbed the word "Date" in "A" because the "August" touched those letters, so he was stuck having to grab the top part as well as the date part. When you read the whole report, it is so obvious that this thing is a Frankenstein form.

That's not the only place. In the third place it shows up, it's mentioned just above Figure 16, that in box 17a, it displays the word "None," but "Non" is in dark green, but not the "e." It's crazy stuff! That's why I'm saying that the forger either was paid a lot of money but didn't like what he was doing or hated what he was doing and was being forced to do it by his boss, and he was going to put enough things in there that a professional who knew this stuff could wind up spotting and say, "This thing is a forgery." So in essence, the forger may actually be the hero.

Why did he insert a color in it? There are two different color values here. It's not the same color.

Subsection #6 is about the seals. If you scroll down, Figure 19 is really an image under a color filter of the one that Obama submitted through the PDF. It's only faintly there. If you scroll down to the next page, page 10, it's actually invisible. In Figure 20, it's almost not noticeable; it's really a distortion in the background image. His first short-form is Figure 17, and you can clearly see that this thing was at least three inches from the bottom of the paper. I know the machine which embossed it; it was an electronic machine, not a hand stamp. It does a good job. You can clearly see it through their photographs.

Figure 18 is the positive — the inverted image from the microfilm copy of the Nordyke twins — and even if it was a microfilm, you can clearly see the embossment. It's practically at the edge of the paper because the throat on those hand stamps won't allow for very much distance between the edge of the paper and the edge of a two-and-one-quarter-inch seal. You can see it even on a microfilm copy. But we do not see it on his. That told me immediately that that was a second- or third-generation image from something else.

MRS. RONDEAU: Is there any stamp at all on the April 27 release?

MR. VOGT: No. There isn't any, which means it's not legal. Figure 21 was interesting: that was on a hand stamp, again, near the edge of the paper, less than an inch away from the edge, and you can clearly see the embossment. That's an original, and it was from 1962.

Subsection #7 is the rubber stamp, which is skewed. That is normal; it's a hand stamp, and nobody is trying to place the thing down by the pixel, but the one we have on Obama's certificate of April 27 is about as straight as you can get with an eyeball. It's only two pixels off over three inches. That's been electronically leveled.

In Figure 23, the script on the capital "A" on "Alvin" in the signature, and the "X" in the word "TXE" were literally done by hitting pixels. They hit pixels to make something that looked like an "X," but it's not. When you blow it up, you can see it's not an "X." It's something else. Again, it's someone screaming at us, "This thing is a fraud!" That may be the most logical answer here.

Subsection #8 deals with the layers. This is embedded from within the PDF that the White House put up. It clearly shows from object 13-21 is the nine layers. It tells you the horizontal and vertical pixels of each one of the layers. Under each one of these headings, there's a bunch of hexadecimal codes. This is where I pulled them all out and I sorted them, putting them in sequence. You have to actually open the file up in Wordpad, and you'll see exactly what I mean: just search for "style type/image" or something like that, and you're going to find each one of the layers. There's a bunch of layers in there, more than just these. Each one of the layers means something else. I could recognize it and know how to read some of the stuff. I could actually pull out one of these layers from the PDF and save it again, and that layer would disappear. You have to know how to do it, but it does tell you where the object starts and where the object ends. It's something like an HTML, but it's a different kind of code.

I put the links for videos that were on YouTube which explain the layers pretty well. I wanted to give these people credit; they deserve it. In Figure 25, I displayed the layer that has most of the type on it. As prima facie evidence, this thing is toast.

MRS. RONDEAU: What about the analyst from Canada whom FOX News featured who said that the image could be authentic?

Editor's Note: The "leading expert" which FOX News quoted as having said, "You should not be so suspicious about this," Jean-Claude Tremblay, states that his professional background includes more than 20 years in teaching Adobe products, Quark, and technical editing. It is this writer's opinion that the title of the FOX News article, "Expert: No Doubt Obama's Birth Certificate Is Legit," is not an accurate reflection of Tremblay's analysis of the birth certificate image, but rather, conjecture on the writer's part.

It appears that Tremblay's is the only analysis which FOX News has presented, despite the many reports and allegations that the image is a forgery.

MR. VOGT: On page 13, I wrote a rebuttal to discovery of the multi-layers found in the PDF. You'll see in the last paragraph what my qualifications are for OCR. This guy knows nothing; he plainly does not know anything about it. You know something? Considering he wound up defending it on the 29th, the day after somebody found the layers, he would be my first suspect. If you looked at his qualifications, certified on a bunch of Adobe's products, I would say he would be the first candidate I'd have for the one who put the thing together.

Somebody looked it up and said he was a supporter of Obama. Also, if they found a graphic artist who was sympathetic and was not from the country, there is less chance of his being subpoenaed to give testimony to Congress. They're actually wrong about the investigation part; the reason is that there is a security treaty between the United States and Canada concerning national security, which this definitely does, and that means that the Royal Canadian Mounted Police will be investigating this guy to find out. He can be extradited to the United States to testify. He is not exempt from prosecution.

MRS. RONDEAU: Why do you think no one from the FBI has gone out to Hawaii to investigate the forgery?

MR. VOGT: If you go to the next section, page 13, I say in the Conclusion section that it is a "Frankenstein certificate." Some guy actually drew a picture of Obama looking like Frankenstein. They're selling T-shirts like that; they got the idea from me.

But here's the answer to your question: Orly said she has reported things to the FBI and they haven't done anything with it. This is the way a law enforcement agency works: First, the FBI is part of the Justice Department, and the Justice Department is controlled by a guy who is an Obama handmaiden. Unless a policing agency is notified that a crime *has been committed, they're not going to bother with it. It's nothing. No matter how many YouTube things are out there or things on the web, unless somebody formally notifies a policing agency like the FBI, nothing is going to be done, because they weren't told a crime has been committed.*

For instance, if a bank is robbed, the banker will call the police department, which will in turn call the FBI, because it's their purview. The banks are insured by the FDIC; therefore, they robbed the federal government, and the FBI investigates. They collect the data, hopefully catch the criminal, and then they give it to a federal attorney who prosecutes. But again, they have to be told that a crime has been committed. That's the key thing; no one has ever done it.

I did. I sent it off to the director of the FBI and also to the field agent in charge in Hawaii. I sent it off twice to each one in different ways, all by mail. Hawaii will probably get it earlier because of the mail screening that occurs in Washington, DC. However, the crime was committed both in Hawaii and in Washington, DC. It's very possible, since I see that the form was modified on the day of its presentation and the day after, that somebody in the White House was modifying it.

MRS. RONDEAU: So they might not have created it, but now they have it and are modifying it.

MR. VOGT: Correct, so the crime has been committed in both places. When you read the law at the bottom of the report, and I included the sections in red that I want people to understand, you realize that it's a very, very serious crime. This comes under the heading of defrauding the United States. Everybody in the White House who knows this thing, as well as in the Department of Health in Hawaii, is in huge trouble. They have no idea that just on the face of the document itself, and the security number, is 20 years in prison. Considering they flagrantly flaunted their arrogance and knew what they were doing was wrong for somebody to become president of the United States who wasn't even a citizen is treasonous. If the prosecution goes to the level of treason, which it should be, these people go to prison for the rest of their lives.

Some of those people are going to be talking their heads off not to go to prison for the rest of their lives. What I've done is make it irrelevant where the guy was born. It's no longer a case of trying to prove he was born in Kenya, Timbuctu, Manchuria or New York City; it's now a simple, provable case of forgery in the first degree.

Without question, this is the greatest scandal in American history. Everybody agrees: nothing comes even remotely close; not the scandals in

the Grant administration; in Harding's Teapot Dome; in Watergate; Clinton was nothing . . . this tops everything.
   The Post & Email.

————&&&————

While performing legal, financial and criminal database searches, skip tracer Al Hendershot, Jr., discovered several discrepancies and anomalies in records tied to Barack and Michele Obama's Chicago mansion including multiple Social Security numbers for Barack. Further investigation found that Barack Hussein Obama, II and one Harrison J. Bounel share the exact same Social Security number, home address, family and more.

So who is Harrison J. Bounel? Hendershot's investigations unravelled a tangled mess of crimes including real estate fraud, identity theft, cover-up and more. When details were made public on the Internet and shared among conservative networkers, Obama's alias quickly began to vanish from the web as "damage control" went to work. But evidence was plentiful and enough was saved before any "scrubbing" took place to prove that the Social Security number Obama is using was stolen from Harrison J. Bounel. But perhaps "stolen" isn't the right word to use in this case, maybe more like "borrowed" since it belonged to someone close to Michelle's Connecticut relatives, and the poor fellow is dead so no one thought he would mind.

Bounel lived in a Connecticut rooming house owned by the Robinson family and late in life applied for a Social Security number most likely for the purpose of obtaining government assistance and medical care. U.S. Census records list Harrison J. Bounel as a "roomer" under the listed members of the Robinson family living in the house at the time.

————&&&————

On September 26, 2011, I received an e-mail from a Linda Jordan that read: "Here is the introductory letter that will go out with a mass e-mail to D.C. about my e-verify results and follow up letter to Obama. You can share it if you want. Linda"

I didn't know who Linda Jordan was but her contact information was on a list of hundreds of people connected in one way or another to

BirtherSummit.org, and therefore, I had embraced her immediately and set to work getting her information out to the masses with my first stops on Facebook. I was gratified to see her letters quickly going viral on Facebook and among our partner electronic media and bloggers.

September 25, 2011
To whom it may concern:

For years we have had credible evidence that Barack Obama is a fraud, a fake and a forger.

And there wasn't one single person with the legal responsibility and authority to protect our nation from this usurper, who was willing to do their job. Not one "Catch Me if You Can" FBI agent? No one in the CIA, the military? Not one judge or attorney general? No one? No one in the Senate or Congress. No one in the Social Security Administration? No one in the Hawaii Department of Heath? No one in the Department of Elections? Nobody. Nobody cared for our republic.

My head reeling from the full realization of what this meant I finally stopped fretting about it and asked myself, "Well, what are you going to do?"

I decided I was one of the employers of the POTUS, and I registered with the government run E-Verify System. Employers are required by law to check if their employees are eligible to work in the United States.

On August 17th, 2011, I ran Barack Obama's name, birth date, citizenship status, and the Social Security number he has been using since 1980 and on last years tax return, a number issued out of Connecticut when he was a teenager in Hawaii, through an E-Verify check. I got back a "Notice of Mismatch with Social Security Administration records: SSA record does not verify, other reason." In a nutshell Obama's SSN had been flagged with a Special Indicator Code primarily reserved for cases of fraud. (See the full story and documentation at WorldNetDaily article by Jerome Corsi, 9/12/11.)

Today I sent a letter to Obama, as I am required to do by law, informing him of the Notice of Mismatch and asking him to confirm or correct the data I entered in to the E-Verify System. (Attached) I will pursue this until I get the truth.

Obama may not be a natural born citizen, but he is a natural born liar. Why would anyone let him get away with the crime of the century?
Linda Jordan

Chapter 42

Come Talk Story

"Eh, try come. Wassup wit dat Obama guy? How come he makin' dis country all hemojang? Geddeen moah pilau every day, brah. Uncle doonah and Antie Malia had fo' go close da stoah, da won stay up Kalihi-side. Nobody get kala for buy na-ting. Auntie, you lucky you go mainland. Da braddahs all scared da union goin' strike again. Fak up no toilet pepah no rice, gotta stock up da kine befoah go run out. Everybody stay warry dey goin' be lay-off. Moah werse dey goin' lose deah healt insurance. We no need warry about da kine Obamacaah Hawai'i get da kine exemp but if lose job den wat?"

Interpretation of sorts:

"Pardon me. Would you come over here? I'd like to have a conversation with you and ask a few questions. Could you explain to me what this president is up to? His policies are destroying our country, and it's getting worse every day. Recently Uncle Junior and Aunt Mary were forced to close their place of business. You might be familiar with the location, the one in Kalihi. Wholesale prices have skyrocketed and passing the cost increase on their customers is something they just can't do anymore. Besides, their volume of customers dropped off dramatically. People just don't have the money to spend.

Miki, you were smart to move to the mainland. Everyone is worried that there will be another shipping strike. Every time they strike we run out of toilet paper and rice. So whenever there's a threat of a strike there's a run on those necessities, completely emptying the store shelves. Unfortunately we all have to stock up and hoard supplies. It would be disastrous to run out of those two items, and there's no telling how long a strike would last.

People are worried of losing their jobs or being laid off. Companies have scaled back their operations and cutting employee hours. We're really concerned about losing our health insurance. Even though Hawai'i was exempt from the Obamacare bill for having a good system through employment, if we lose our jobs we lose our coverage as well. What happens then?"

I hear from friends and family regularly, and they voice their concerns about what they see happening in Hawai'i. Most are too scared to speak publicly about what they know because Obama is still very popular in the islands, and they don't want to become a "social pariah," a term I've heard more than once, but there is a growing underground of dissent just like on the mainland. Because Hawai'i is a union and welfare state, many people don't see what cram-down government regulation is doing to their state. They are the proverbial "frog in the pot," but unfortunately, even if they know, they don't care.

On July 13, 2011, I got the disappointing news from William Temple that the Freedom Jamboree had to be canceled due to low participation of individual Tea Party groups. I read through William's letter so I would understand the reasons for the cancellation, and then my first course of action was to notify everyone on my list of contacts and post the notice on Facebook.

I knew many people that had planned to attend and were in the process of arranging transportation and lodging. Fred and I had an RV reserved and paid for parking it on-site. We also booked and paid for four booths reserved in the name, "Booth's (birther) Booths," which would be staffed with key champions for the Constitution, specifically Article II, Section I, clause 5, the framers' iron-clad requirement for the president to be a natural-born citizen, one devoid of allegiance and loyalty to any country other than the United States of America.

I was to host the event "Night of the Generals" where I would introduce retired Maj. Gen. Paul Vallely, chairman of Stand Up America.com to Jamboree attendees as well as Gen. William Boykin, both retired. At least two more retired generals were tentatively scheduled to appear.

After notifying everyone I could about the cancellation, I called William to ask him if I could include in my book the portion of his letter explaining the reason for the cancellation. Of course, he didn't mind. He knew how invested personally I was in the event.

Our committee has speculated for the last month why registrations from the Tea Parties have been so low, with some e-mails and phone calls suggesting that the poor economy, national debt, high fuel prices, unemployment, double-dip recession, fear about the future (all the usual suspects), as well as political frustration with elected officials in both parties, and political burnout as principle reasons. Others have said that many groups just don't want to do anything outside of their own states this year, and are in disagreement with other groups about what and who the Tea Party movement should support and represent. There is some disarray in the movement right now as to its next move. The fact is, the spirit intrinsic in 2009 has diminished nationwide and some lethargy and weariness persists.

These factors combined with the failure of the national Tea Party umbrella groups, other than "Tea Party Nation," to support or promote Freedom Jamboree was also sadly evident, especially after each group was individually invited to attend and work toward a unified movement going into the 2012 election season. The preoccupation with prospering their own organizations at the expense of the "grassroots" movement as a whole was also apparent; with one group even going so far recently as to place their own "convention" on the same days as Freedom Jamboree, inviting all the national candidates to a "straw poll" in the middle of the country, to speak on Saturday, October 1 (the same day as our event), while paying some of the same speakers that had already been invited to Freedom Jamboree. And yes, their event is a paid event for those participating. This is the kind of cynical, self-serving, and dis-unifying behavior that had already frustrated many in the movement by the end of 2010, and caused others to quit participating altogether.

Freedom Jamboree could have been the Tea Party movement's "Yorktown," where big-government autocrats in both parties and the national media are concerned. Our committee started with the idea that it was essential to our movement that the Tea Parties show up and put on a defiant national face this year, and get behind Tea Party candidates *(those who have supported our cause), whoever that turned out to be. Whether that can happen in 2012 now is debatable.*

The national debt continues to grow, despite the rise of the Tea Party movement in 2009 and the takeover of the House in 2010. If anyone in the movement has a plan or direction that can unite the movement again, and reverse the nation's headlong march toward the economic abyss, please take the reins! It appears the Tea Party horse is riderless, and riding off in all directions at once!

To all of you on the committee who worked so hard, held your place in the ranks, and gave your all for the cause, it was a pleasure to march with you! Though we did not realize the fruits of our labors, we did all we could with what we had for this "grassroots" effort. Unfortunately, it wasn't to be! God's will!

We must, however, continue to do whatever we can to return the nation to its constitutional principals.

May God bless you, and "Up the Revolution!"

William Temple

Chairman, Freedom Jamboree

William sums up perfectly the Tea Party story of today. Everyone has their own idea of what the movement is or isn't or what it should or shouldn't be. Both major parties make up stuff to suit them and, of course, Obama and company lie about us and everything else, for that matter, with impunity.

"Who specifically were you referring to in your letter?" I asked William. "Who was it that booked a Straw Poll event on the same day as ours?"

"Well they denied that they were the ones that did it," William replied, "but Tea Party Patriots' logo is all over the website."

That would be Jenny Beth Martin, spokesperson for Tea Party Patriots. Martin and Amy Kremer, of the other national Tea Party "umbrella" group, Tea Party Express, were both invited to participate in Freedom Jamboree but chose not to, opting instead to advance their own agendas. Martin and Kremer have exchanged petty jealousies as the two groups attained commercial status and lobbed lawsuits against one another as grassroots patriots and small tea parties drifted away. Heck, these women won't even appear together on TV. Like leaders of so many groups, they didn't want anyone "stealing their thunder."

I got a call from Carma Neta Morris, my roommate in D.C. when we attended the first 9.12 March in 2009. She called to ask if I was interested in joining the Texans for Palin bus tour to the Tea Party of America rally for Sarah Palin. I jumped at the invitation. Of all the politicians being touted as a possible presidential candidate, Sarah was the only one I trusted. Even though she made some mistakes and disappointed me in her "kingmaker" role endorsing establishment Republicans over Constitutional Conservatives, she believed she was doing the right thing at the time. After hearing her speak at the Iowa rally, I knew she had changed her position when she spoke out against "crony capitalism" — the entrenched politicians.

While we waited for Sarah to arrive, a rainstorm drenched us, but most of us came prepared and brought out the rain ponchos and umbrellas. Carma Neta, me, and our bus companions had arrived early and procured some of the best seats to be close to Sarah and were rewarded with handshakes and photographs with whom we believed would be the first woman president. At the end of the rally and after Sarah had shaken hundreds, perhaps a thousand or more hands and autographed programs, T-shirts, hats, books, and the occasional arm or two, Carma Neta and I gathered up our folding chairs and headed for the bus. We were approached by two reporters: one from Politico and the other from NBC, and I gave an interview to both. Although Politico did not quote me, the NBC reporter ran a favorable account in MSNBC's First Read of Sarah's appearance and asked me the "big question that remained on the minds of those who sat through periods of torrential downpours in the Hawkeye State following the almost 40-minute speech — Will she herself be a contender in the 2012 race?"

"I've admired her ever since she came on the scene," attendee Miki Booth of Wyandotte, Oklahoma, said. "This country is in bad shape, and I'd really like to see us go back to the principles of the founding fathers, and I think Sarah Palin can lead us back to those ideals."

That evening, we met up with other state chapters of Palin4President at the Machine Shed, a farm-themed restaurant, in Indianola, Iowa, and listened to Tammy Bruce, conservative talk radio host and regular on FOX news, as she gave an "insider' scoop that Sarah had given what sounded an awful lot like a campaign speech, and we might look to her announcing a presidential bid very soon. We were elated.

On the bus ride home the following morning I was invited to talk about my soon-to-be-released book and share the contents of the black 3-ring binder I carried with me everywhere I went. By showing the different birth certificates from Hawai'i and comparing them to Obama's forged documents, I quickly established myself as an authority on the subject. My companions on the Texans4Palin bus understood immediately they were hearing the real deal. I answered their questions about the Connecticut Social Security number and told the story of Harrison J. Bounel.

With each page in my binder laying out overwhelming evidence of fraud, my friends, my fellow Palinistas, shook their heads in disbelief that the American public could be so completed defrauded.

Once home I was barely rested when I geared up to head to Honolulu to meet up with Dean Haskins, executive director of the Birther Summit. We, and others, had planned to go to the federal courthouse in Honolulu to support Orly's court case against Loretta Fuddy, who was ordered to appear on September 14, 2011 and show cause why she did not comply with the subpoena compelling her to produce Obama's birth certificate.

In a series of legal maneuvers the case before the federal district court was moved to November 12, 2011 and then rescheduled again to November 30th. Since Dean and I already had our travel arrangement confirmed we met up in Honolulu and the following report by Dean describes "Our Most Excellent Hawai'ian Government Adventures."

What Are You Hiding, Honolulu?
The Birther Summit
By Dean Haskins

Last year, Barack Obama made what must be the most dubiously ironic statement in history: "The only people who don't want to disclose the truth are people with something to hide." This, from a person whose entire life seems to be purposely hidden from even the most assiduous scrutiny; and, it appears to have been kept that way at great expense and vast assistance. At the heart of this clandestine artifice are two institutions in Honolulu that are purportedly part of the Obama nativity narrative; however, they both appear either unwilling or unable to corroborate the veracity of their inclusion in that story to any degree of comfortable certainty. A recent visit to both the Kapiolani Medical

Center and the Department of Health in Honolulu revealed little more than the furtive mystery that has been characteristic of all things Obama.

In the middle of September, Miki Booth, George Peabody, and I visited both of those establishments hoping to glean any bit of information we could to provide answers for the myriad Americans who have sought the truth, but so far, have found little to none. Our first visit was to Kapiolani Medical Center, one of the two hospitals for which there have been claims made of being the birthplace of baby Barry (Queens Medical Center being the other). Our intention was to capture the visit on video, but we were informed that we could not do so inside the building.

We first visited the records office, where Miki completed and filed a form requesting the hospital records for her son's birth. While there, an extemporaneous conversation occurred, simply because a clerk happened to question a co-worker about the "race" field on a document. The conversation is recounted in a report on the Birther Summit website. After I had released that report, there were the expected comments from the truthaphobes, otherwise known as Obots, dissecting and doubting everything in it but the punctuation. There were subsequent statements made by Miki and George attesting to the facts presented, but facts are not the strong suit of those aforementioned creatures.

Allow me to digress for a moment. I recently witnessed Dr. Corsi, having obviously grown weary with the debased online comments made by a small group of Fogbow wannabes, uncharacteristically assail them verbally, and I must say, those brief diatribes were some of the most enjoyable comments I can remember ever reading. There is a Steven, a Cindy, and a couple Patricks who appear to do nothing else in life but sit at their computers and deride those of us with whom they disagree. As pitiful an existence as that must be, it can still be somewhat of an irritant to those of us who are daily targets of their mendacious manure. Nobody enjoys lies being told about them. One of the Patricks enjoys reading his deluded words so much that he copies and pastes many of his own comments to multiple websites, I suppose in a vainglorious attempt to receive some sort of praise for them. I'm no psychotherapist, but there appears to be some possible mommy issues involved.

Anyway, this Cindy critter reported that she had called someone at the Kapiolani Medical Center who first told her that, in that particular office, there would have only been one person working — a receptionist.

Since that was a blatant lie, I reported the layout of the office, recounting the multiple desks and employees who work in that office. Then, supposedly, the hospital official told her, "We have no comment on this topic, except to say it is not true." Now, the official didn't clarify what part of the "topic" she believed not to be true; was it that the conversation itself didn't happen, or was it the content of the conversation?

I guess we'll never know, for immediately prior to leaving the hotel in Honolulu to go to the airport, I called the hospital in an attempt to verify that the "official" did tell this lie. In the first call I made, I merely started to explain the comment that had been made, and the individual to whom I was speaking abruptly stated, "We have no comment on this," and then hung up on me. I called back five times, and each time (there were at least three different people who answered), I would barely start to speak before the hospital employee would just hang up on me. That is certainly not indicative of forthrightness and honesty. I attest to the veracity of that report, and note that the purported hospital "official" was not even present in the room, so she couldn't possibly report what was or was not said.

But wait, there was a second meeting at Kapiolani that day! Because the person to whom we spoke in that second meeting was so cordial and accommodating, and because we really do not desire to cause the individual any grief, I will not disclose a name or position (even though I can already imagine the vast Obot scrutiny not doing so will likely cause). That meeting lasted nearly an hour, and during the meeting, Miki asked about a purported letter from the White House to Kapiolani, and asked if the letter existed, if it was in a vault somewhere in the hospital, and if we could see it. The person to whom we spoke denied knowing anything about the letter, but said that the answer to Miki's questions would be researched, and sent to her via e-mail.

Having heard nothing for several days, Miki sent this e-mail:
Aloha XXXXX,
I tried calling a couple of times but was unable to reach you.
Thank you for your graciousness and patience hearing out our concerns.
If you were able to find an answer to the question whether a letter from the White House exists, I would appreciate hearing what you found out if anything.
Thanks again,
Miki

To which Miki received this response:

Good Afternoon Miki,

It was a pleasure meeting all of you last week. With regards to your inquiry of if I was able to find an answer to the question whether a letter from the White House exists please know that we have politely declined these inquiries.

I hope that your trip home was a safe one and my e-mail finds you doing well.
Mahalo,
XXXXX

Hmmmm. Wouldn't one expect a hospital in which a president was born to take every possible opportunity to exploit that fact for PR purposes? Wouldn't one expect there to be some indication of it somewhere on their grounds? We saw none, and now, we get an e-mail informing us that they won't even talk about it? What could be the possible reasoning in this? I'm sure it wouldn't have anything to do with receiving government money for a hospital expansion.

The next day, we ventured over to the Department of Health, where we were met with further shrouding and deceptive doublespeak. Since much of the conversation was recounted in a report posted on the Birther Summit website I won't repeat it now; however, one must wonder about these elements of the dialog:

When asked about the apparent misspelling of the word "THE" in Alvin T. Onaka's stamp, why would the clerk first say that one of the "three sealers" they have might have a misspelling in the stamp, and then later state that they have "five sealers?"

Why would the clerk inform us that the only way one can obtain a copy of one's original long-form birth certificate would be to get a court order, and then tell us that Obama got a court order to get his? In the official White House narrative, there is no mention of any court order, only that Loretta Fuddy approved Obama's attorney's request for a waiver. The last time I checked, Fuddy is not a judge. What does this lie accomplish, other than a continued clouding of the facts?

Why would the DOH institute recent policies limiting access to long-form birth certificates, and concealing parental information on birth certificates issued before 1976, forcing those people who need that information for passport purposes to go to the DOH and get their birth certificate information updated to include it?

Aside from the obvious motivations of loyal liberal operatives, and Hawaii's interest in someone who claims to have been born there being president of the United States, what other reasons could Alvin T. Onaka have for conveniently altering these policies? Could it be that his globalist agenda lines up perfectly with Obama's, so he has an extra incentive to manipulate policies to further obfuscate the truth about Obama?

Why must these (and many other) questions even have to be asked about someone who claimed his would be the "most transparent" presidency in history? Why does Honolulu continue to be either tight-lipped or downright deceptive about its purported "native-born son?" Are they planning to build the first underground presidential library that will be accessible by only a select few (who can keep a secret)?

Barack Obama's history continues to be nothing but a question mark, but it is unmistakeable that there are those who are, willingly or otherwise, aiding and abetting the secrecy. The Birther Summit participants will continue pursuing the truth in these matters until the American people get factual answers to all these questions — including what Honolulu is hiding.

The rebirth of the Tea Party has begun! It's all Big Government and the main stream media can talk about as the 2012 election cycle gets under way. Democrats despise us. Republicans are wary. Both parties are rethinking their strategies. Obama hit the road in a bus motorcade Tea Party Express and Sarah Palin style. Two days on the road and his Canadian-built busses have backfired big time. The hypocrisy of visiting small town America to talk about jobs while cruising around in foreign-built vehicles paid for with American tax dollars will surely wake up the remaining diehard Obama supporters. Surely they can see now that the emperor wears no clothes.

Obama was confronted by a Tea Party leader, and he had no answers to the questions asked him except to deny or shift blame. Earlier he stood alone with a microphone and spoke to a compliant group of supporters. He promised a plan for jobs was in the works. His feeble attempt to emulate a Tea Party strategy fell flat. He looked small on the makeshift platform with a barn as the backdrop. He looked uncomfortable. He didn't fit. He looked, well, pathetic.

Not all "birthers" are Tea Partiers, but Tea Partiers are joining the ranks of "birthers" in hoards. Scott Rasmussen on Sean Hannity's radio program August 16, 2011, put "birthers" and tea parties together as political groups supporting Texas governor Rick Perry and by doing so acknowledged that we are a force to be reckoned with. Hannity, Rasmussen and guest John Zogby, political pollster, concurred: Obama was "not vetted." But that is as far as they will go, even though we know for a fact Hannity is well aware of the April 27th forgery. His superiors have warned him and others to stay away from the birth certificate, the eligibility controversy.

As Obama's power base in Chicago grew, there were no less than eight attempts between June 11, 2003 and February 28, 2008, to remove the Constitution's requirement that a president be a natural-born citizen. Rep. Vic Snyder, D-Ark. tried in 2003 as did Rep. John Conyers, D-Mich. Sen. Don Nickles, R-OK tried in 2004 (Sen. James Inhofe, R-OK & Sen. Mary Landrieu, D-LA co-sponsors). Rep. Dana Rohrbacher, R-CA tried in 2004. Rep. John Conyers tried again in 2005. Rep. Dana Rohrbacher tried again in 2005. Rep. Vic Snyder tried again in 2005. Sen. Claire McCaskill, D-Mo. tried in 2008 (Senators Hillary Clinton, D-NY, Robert Menendez, D-NJ, Tom Coburn, R-OK, and Barack Obama, D-IL co-sponsored the bill). Thankfully, none of these passed.

What does the future hold for our United States? It's a frightening proposition that the socialists, Marxists and communists in and out of government will create or take advantage of diversionary tactics to forestall or prevent the 2012 election. We live with that fear.

Who are we, really, and why does Obama and his administration fear us so?

"Overwhelmingly we believe we are accountable to a sovereign God who grants us unalienable rights to life, liberty, and the pursuit of happiness. Overwhelmingly we believe the Constitution strictly limits the power of the federal government and uniquely recognizes and protects those unalienable rights." — Joseph Farah, The Tea Party Manifesto

I'm frequently asked where the funds come from for me to do what I do. Who pays for me to fly and drive around the country and stay at hotels in costly cities? The answer is easy: Fred.

Oh, I have an allowance every two weeks, but when that's depleted, funds come out of Fred's income since he's the only one that's gainfully employed. I have the support of dear friends who allow me to stay in their homes and who chauffeur me around and those that press a $20 or $100 bill into my hand, but most importantly they pray for me. And that is how I keep doing what I'm doing.

If you've read this far you know I'm not an outwardly devout Christian. I have my personal relationship with God. I know our prayers for this great country are being answered. I see Obama's evil regime fraying around the edges as more Americans start pushing for answers. It's only a matter of time before the unravelling explodes. Our prayers can complete the job.

Fred has been asking anxiously when this book project will be finished and we can get back to some semblance of a normal life. This morning I told him I'd be finished with it today, and he gave me a huge smile and asked, "Are you going to take a break now?"

"Sure," I answered, "right after the Veterans Day rally in November and the Birther Summit in March and Pastor Manning's forgery trial in May and after we see Obama in handcuffs doing the "perp- walk" out of the White House and after we take our country back and...."

[Pau]

Epilogue

―――∞∞∞―――

Three years ago when I first heard of Barack Obama, I was pleased to know that a fellow Hawai'ian Islander was running for president. However, the more I learned about his radical connections the more I began to distrust him, and soon I was outright afraid of him. But stronger than fear was my outrage at a system that would allow our Constitution, our rule of law to be trashed and put an anti-American, dual citizen of dubious background into the highest office of our country.

There were a lot of forces at play, and we will never know the names of all the traitors responsible for the biggest political hoax in American history, but I know who Obama really is, and my gut feelings are rarely wrong.

His roots are not of the Aloha Spirit that is Hawai'i. At his core is a mixture of Islam, atheism, communism, socialism, Marxism and every anti-American ideology that feeds his drive to destroy the greatest country in the world. To many Christians he is evil personified.

He's a dope-smoking slacker that through his family contacts left Hawai'i for Occidental College to hook up with Marxist punks. He was recruited, along with other Muslim misfits, by CIA operatives under the auspices of Zbigniew Brzezinski, national security advisor to President Jimmy Carter, to go to Pakistan. His task was to facilitate the arming and funding of the mujahideen in Afghanistan to push back the Soviet invasion.

When Obama's assignment in Pakistan concluded, Brzezinski continued to mold and nurture Obama for greater roles in the socialization and Islamization of the United States for the ultimate goal of communism for America.

Whether Obama was given a new identity before, during, or after his stint in Pakistan is anybody's guess, but at some point he did acquire a new Social Security number starting with 042, the prefix for Connecticut.

The number he might have had when, or if, he worked at Baskin Robbins on King Street in Honolulu, HI, which had to have had the prefix 575 or 576, (numbers reserved for Hawai'i residents) was then scrubbed from the Social Security databanks.

Through private investigators and skip-tracers associated with birthersummit.com, we learned that Obama's Kenyan family members' Social Security numbers were issued around the same time as his. When Obama's long-lost "Uncle Omar" was arrested for drunk driving, he was exposed as an illegal alien but has a valid Social Security number. Digging deeper they found it was assigned in the late 1970's as was a Social Security number for Obama's half-aunt, Zeituni Onyango, who had also been issued a deportation order but was allowed to stay when she surfaced in government-subsidized housing collecting welfare in Boston, MA. Zeituni's Social Security number begins with a prefix reserved for residents of Indiana, but there is no evidence she ever lived in or even visited the state.

Orly Taitz has brought many of the major lawsuits charging Obama's ineligibility to serve as president since he does not meet the U.S. Constitution's requirement of a "natural-born citizen." In the most recent case Federal Judge Royce Lamberth ruled against her latest attempt to get to the truth about Obama's Connecticut Social Security number in the lawsuit Taitz vs. Astrue (Commissioner of the Social Security Administration, Michael Astrue.) "Today is not her lucky day," wrote Lamberth. He concluded that there's no real interest in determining whether the Obama Social Security number is genuine or fraudulent, arguing that the need for privacy for the president trumps all else.

The news was devastating. Obama was above the law. I was horribly depressed and easily brought to tears. There would be no court case in Hawai'i for Loretta Fuddy, director, Hawai'i Department of Health, to produce Obama's birth certificate or show cause why she did not.

"Obama's privacy trumps all else," wrote Lamberth. I mulled over those words. "There's no real interest in determining whether the Obama Social Security number is genuine or fraudulent."

How could he say, "No real interest?" I kept asking myself. That just boggled my mind. By now the number of Americans aware of Obama's questionable Social Security number had grown exponentially in recent months.

On September 20, 2011, WND.com broke the story that G. Gordon Liddy, Talk-radio host and former Nixon White House operative, reported that one of his trusted informants in Hawai'i reported to him that while the document was forged recently, there may have been tampering with official Obama birth records as far back as 1978.

I knew, of course, from Dr. Jerome Corsi that his Hawai'i informants reported tampering in the Department of Health records weeks before April 27 as the forger(s) ramped up for the presentation of the fraudulent document. It was also an obvious preemptive strike against Dr. Corsi's book, Where's the Birth Certificate, but it was the date Liddy brought into focus that intrigued me, 1978 — the same period that Obama's Kenyan relatives were issued their Social Security numbers and brought to the United States, albeit illegally.

Who can do this? It's been clear to those of us who attended the CIA Columbia trial. In Dr. James David Manning's ATLAH church courtroom in Harlem in May 2010, that it was the CIA who "packaged" Obama, making him a U.S. citizen and "scrubbing" all mention of Barry Soetoro, Indonesian citizen, and all mention of his Kenyan birthplace.

The CIA "packaged" Obama with college credentials from Columbia and padded a résumé for him with his job at Business International Corporation, (described as "the left wing of the ruling class" according to Wikipedia), and both institutions serve as CIA cover.

The ruling class is well aware of Obama's true identity, and every high ranking government and military official needs to keep the public from ever finding out the truth about them because they are all complicit in the cover-up, and the truth would destroy the Democrat Party and severely damage the establishment Republican Party.

For too long there have been those who accepted "slush fund" money to keep their mouths shut, and to expose their misdeeds now would ruin their elitist lifestyles and, of less importance to them, their reputations.

It is telling that when a secret meeting was held with Supreme Court justices and Obama and Biden before the election, they did not invite Justice Samuel Anthony Alito. Perhaps we should take that to mean Alito is the only justice of the Supreme Court of the United States that cannot be bought. And what was the meeting about? Could they have been conspiring to make sure that the eligibility issue does not come before them and continue to ensure that the challenge is struck down in every lower court?

Well, we're talking CIA and a matter of national security.